"Truth Behind Bars"

Reflections on the Fate of
the Russian Revolution

"TRUTH BEHIND BARS"

PAUL
KELLOGG

◈ AU PRESS

Copyright © 2021 Paul Kellogg
Published by AU Press, Athabasca University
1200, 10011 – 109 Street, Edmonton, AB T5J 3S8

https://doi.org/10.15215/aupress/9781771992459.01

Cover image: Village in Siberia, Adwo / Alamy Stock Photo, F23D4K
Cover design by Marvin Harder
Interior design by Sergiy Kozakov
Printed and bound in Canada

Library and Archives Canada Cataloguing in Publication

Title: "Truth behind bars" : reflections on the fate of the Russian Revolution /
    Paul Kellogg.
Names: Kellogg, Paul, 1955– author.
Description: Includes bibliographical references and index.
Identifiers: Canadiana (print) 20190182768 | Canadiana (ebook) 20190182814
    | ISBN 9781771992459 (softcover) | ISBN 9781771992466 (PDF) |
    ISBN 9781771992473 (EPUB) | ISBN 9781771992480 (Kindle)
Subjects: LCSH: Martov, L., 1873–1923. | LCSH: Lenin, Vladimir Il'ich,
    1870–1924. | LCSH: Vorkuta (Komi, Russia: Concentration camp)—
    History. | LCSH: Glavnoe upravlenie ispravitel'no-trudovykh lagereĭ
    OGPU—History. | LCSH: Forced labor—Soviet Union. | LCSH: Soviet
    Union—History—Revolution, 1917–1921.
Classification: LCC DK265 .K45 2021 | DDC 947.084/1—dc23

This book has been published with the help of a grant from the Federation
for the Humanities and Social Sciences, through the Awards to Scholarly
Publications Program, using funds provided by the Social Sciences and
Humanities Research Council of Canada.

We acknowledge the financial support of the Government of Canada through
the Canada Book Fund (CBF) for our publishing activities and the assistance
provided by the Government of Alberta through the Alberta Media Fund.

Canadä   Alberta
                    Government

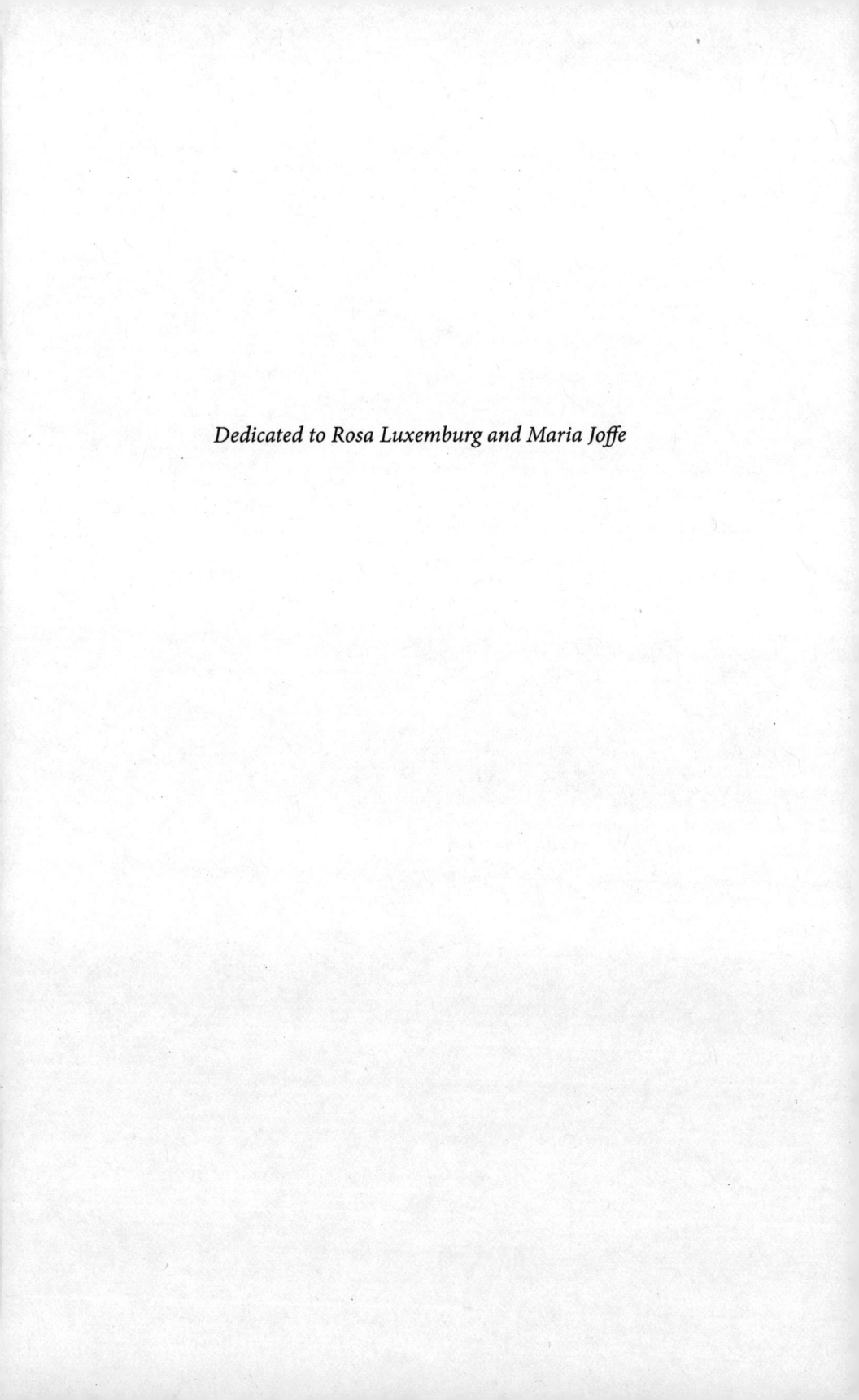

Dedicated to Rosa Luxemburg and Maria Joffe

Contents

Preface

On Forgetting to Read Solzhenitsyn

It was in 1974 that I first picked up a copy of *The Gulag Archipelago*. I didn't finish reading it until this century. It is a very long book—seven books to be precise, published in three volumes that together run to roughly two thousand pages in English translation. But it shouldn't take forty years to read a book, even a very long one. Why it took me four decades to finish reading Aleksandr Solzhenitsyn's crowning achievement requires a little backstory and can serve as an entry point into the present book.

Solzhenitsyn's epic work documents one of the great crimes of the modern era, the Gulag—the network of prison camps in the former Soviet Union, which more than any other institution came to symbolize Stalinism—the authoritarian political system derived from the name of the Soviet Union's long-time ruler, Joseph Stalin. *Gulag* is an abbreviated form of "*Glavnoe upravlenie ispravitel'no-trudovykh lagerei*," or the "Chief Administration for Corrective Labour Camps." But the term has come to signify much more than this. It refers, as Anne Applebaum notes, to an entire array of "labor camps, punishment camps, criminal and political camps, women's camps, children's camps, transit camps."[1] It was not just a prison system, but a system of forced labour.

An *archipelago* is, of course, a chain of islands. In Solzhenitsyn's view, the series of prison camps extending across the Soviet Union formed "that amazing country of *Gulag* which, though scattered in an Archipelago geographically, was, in the psychological sense, fused into a continent—an almost invisible, almost imperceptible country inhabited by the zek people"[2]— *zek* being camp slang for "prisoners."[3] This archipelago, Solzhenitsyn continues, "crisscrossed and patterned that other country within which it was located, like a giant patchwork, cutting into its cities, hovering over its streets. Yet there were many who did not even guess at its presence."[4] The Arctic city of Vorkuta was a principal site in the Gulag archipelago. Michael Allen traces Vorkuta's origins to the summer of 1932, when a secret-police supervised "geological survey group, primarily made up of prisoners" arrived in the area. The city that grew from these small beginnings was constructed entirely by forced labourers.[5] According to Alan Barenberg, the two labour camps associated with the city, "*Vorkutinskii lager*' ('Vorkuta camp,' better known as Vorkutlag) and its twin, *Rechnoi lager*' ('river camp,' better known as Rechlag) saw approximately half a million prisoners pass through their gates by the middle of the 1950s."[6]

Barenberg suggests that, in employing the archipelago metaphor, Solzhenitsyn was exaggerating the extent to which the Gulag was an "almost invisible, almost imperceptible"[7] world of its own—that, in fact, the borders between the Gulag and the rest of the Soviet Union were more porous than Solzhenitsyn implies. Pointing to the constant churn of prisoners entering and leaving the system, at a rate far more rapid than was previously recognized, he joins historian Lynne Viola in insisting that our understanding of the Gulag system must be extended to include what Viola calls "the other archipelago"—the massive resettlement of former "kulaks"[8] (a controversial term about which much will be said in the following pages). This approach brings the Gulag system into focus not as one of exception but rather as an extreme point on a continuum of unfree labour and "follows the conclusions of historians Sheila Fitzpatrick and Donald Filtzer, who separately argued that 'free' labor could hardly have existed under Stalin, particularly from 1940 until 1953"[9]—that is, from the 26 June 1940 introduction of a law making it a criminal offense for a worker to leave their job without the employer's permission, to the 5 March 1953 death of Stalin.

One aspect of this approach is both necessary and important, bringing into focus the massive, forced resettlement of millions of peasants. The resulting exile colonies need very much to be understood as part of the Gulag.[10] However another aspect—the notion of placing the Gulag experience on a continuum of "unfree" labour—while compelling on an abstract level, in the concrete can have the effect of obscuring the unique and terrible experiences of those condemned to the Gulag prison camps *per se*. Besides the appalling death rates, there were the hidden injuries of broken relationships and damaged lives.

Suzanne Rosenberg was one of the hundreds of thousands who were labelled "enemies of the people" and unjustly incarcerated in the forced labour camps of the Gulag. She did survive and was eventually released, but she returned home to a cold reception—including from her own young daughter, who at one point "tore to shreds a photograph" of her mother. "Longing to disassociate themselves from their arrested parents," writes Rosenberg, "such children all the more eagerly proclaimed their loyalty to the socialist regime."[11] Over several years, Rosenberg repaired relations with her daughter, but her story helps bring into sharp relief the different life experiences of those within and those without the Gulag prison camps. Even if the category of "free" labourer did not exist in Stalinist Russia, Solzhenitsyn and others are absolutely right to emphasize the extreme circumstances faced by "residents" of the Gulag prison camps. The experiences of those confined within these prisons merit separate treatment from the experiences of those who managed to remain in regular society.

Estimating the total number of people who, at some point in their lives, experienced the forced labour regime of this archipelago is not a straightforward exercise. Applebaum, in the appendix ("How Many?") to her monumental *Gulag: A History*, calculates that between 1929 and 1953, some eighteen million Soviet citizens were incarcerated in the camps of the Gulag. If we add to this figure the four million (mostly German) prisoners of war interned during World War II; the approximately seven hundred thousand former Russian prisoners of war who, once released from German camps, were sent to the Gulag; and the six million "special exiles" (including "kulaks deported during collectivization, Poles, Balts and others deported after 1939, and Caucasians, Tartars, Volga Germans, and others deported during the war"), then "the total number of forced laborers in the USSR comes to 28.7 million."[12] We don't know how many died. A very conservative estimate is close to three million.[13] Many of the millions who were sent to the Gulag were political prisoners. According to Solzhenitsyn, of these political prisoners "on whom the thunderbolt of arrest at one time or another fell . . . I doubt whether a fifth, I should like to think that an eighth lived to experience this 'release.'"[14]

Pages of *The Gulag Archipelago*. Photograph by Adam Jones, 25 July 2017, Wikimedia Commons.

The Gulag Archipelago was, in the words of Solzhenitsyn, an "experiment in literary investigation." It was an experiment conducted in the laboratory of the author's own bitter experiences. A captain in the Red Army taking part in the war with Germany in 1945, Solzhenitsyn was arrested, as he puts it, "because of my correspondence with a school friend," in which the two "indulged in fairly outspoken expressions of our political outrage and in derogatory comments about the Wisest of the Wise," i.e., Stalin.[15] This correspondence was, according to Solzhenitsyn, an example of "childish stupidity."[16] According to the authorities, it was counter-revolutionary and he was sent to the Gulag, where he survived eight years in the camp system before being released into exile just in time to learn, from the radio, of the death of Stalin. It was "the moment for which every zek in Gulag (except the orthodox Communists) had prayed! He's dead . . . ! The villain has curled up and died!"[17]

It was an experiment conducted in almost impossible circumstances. "I had to conceal the project itself," he explains, "my letters, my materials, to disperse them, to do everything in the deepest secrecy. I even had to camouflage the time I spent working on the book with what looked like work on other things." He hid various portions of the book in different apartments and offices of friends and supporters, so that "*never once* did this whole book, in all its parts, lie on the same desk at the same time!"[18]

Despite these constraints, Solzhenitsyn accumulated the "reports, memoirs, and letters" of 227 individuals who had experienced the horror of the camps.[19] Their names were to have been listed when the book was published, but because of the repressive conditions in the Soviet Union in the 1960s and 1970s, they had to remain anonymous. Solzhenitsyn persevered in overcoming all these obstacles and produced a work that will no doubt continue to be read for generations to come.

In 1974, when the paperback version of the English translation of the first volume became available, I was a teenager from small-town Ontario, Canada—newly arrived in Toronto. Before my move to the big city, an interest in Russian literature and history had taken me to Tolstoy's *War and Peace*. During my first summer in Toronto, I added Leon Trotsky's *History of the Russian Revolution* to my reading list, among other long and compelling literary products of Russian culture. So, when the paperback edition of *Gulag Archipelago*, volume 1, appeared, it was quite natural to add it to the reading list. In October 1974, I bought a copy for $1.95 and began reading and carefully underlining portions that I, an impressionable small-town teenager just discovering politics and history, found relevant.

———◆———

October 1974 marked not only my introduction to Solzhenitsyn, but also my introduction to student and Left politics in Toronto. At the end of one student council meeting, a Leading Member of the Toronto Left suggested that he and I have coffee. We did, and we talked about revolution,

Russia, the Cold War, and other things political. That I had read Tolstoy did not impress. That I was studying Russian impressed a bit. That I was reading Trotsky—along with Lenin, the most well-known figure from 1917 and, in the years since, the most well-known of Stalin's opponents—impressed greatly. But when the subject of Solzhenitsyn came up, the Leading Member frowned.

"*Gulag* is not a good book. Solzhenitsyn is not reliable. His views of events are distorted."

I felt myself blushing with shame. The Leading Member was an important person. Everyone knew him. I didn't want to be reading a bad book. I asked the Leading Member what exactly made it a bad book.

"Well," he said, "Solzhenitsyn is very colourful and impassioned about the Gulag. And it was a horrible thing, the Gulag. But he's made himself a member of a Cold War chorus which insists that the Gulag is not just about Stalin. They say it's about Lenin as well. Solzhenitsyn says the Gulag begins with Lenin. He says that Lenin led to Stalin. He's an anti-communist."

I was mortified. The book I was annotating, the book that had me hooked, was a bad book. It had a bad line on Lenin. It was anti-communist. I felt terrible. The early 1970s were profoundly shaped by the long Cold War between the United States and the Soviet Union. Those on the Left who were opposed to the crimes of the United States in, for instance, Indochina experienced tremendous pressure to be suspicious about any criticism of the Soviet Union, since such criticism might open the door to anti-communism. Solzhenitsyn's book went on the shelf and stayed there for almost four decades.

Flash forward to 2013. In addition to returning to the study of the Russian language, I was picking up threads of old research and acquiring material on the Mezhraionka, the Inter-District Committee, a four-thousand-strong organization of radical, mostly young workers that in July 1917, along with Trotsky, joined Vladimir Lenin and the Bolsheviks—the left-wing party that, along with its counterpart and rival the Mensheviks, originated as a faction in the Russian Social Democratic Labour Party (*Rossiiskaia sotsial-demokraticheskaia rabochaia partiia*, or RSDRP).[20] I was also writing conference papers on three generations of class struggle in the Arctic coal-mining town of Vorkuta (pronounced with the stress on the last syllable), research that forms the basis of part 1 of this book. Vorkuta, a town surrounded by multiple prison camps, was one of the principal "islands" comprising the Gulag Archipelago. From 1936 to 1938, Vorkuta's prison camps were the site of the last stand of anti-Stalinist socialists, many of them Trotskyists (followers of Trotsky), who waged a heroic hunger strike and, against all odds, won their demands, only to be taken into the Arctic tundra and massacred *en masse*. In the period from 1947 to 1953, Vorkuta became one of the principal sites of the strike wave that sounded the death knell for the Stalinist forced labour system. And, in the years from 1989 to 1991, coal miners in Vorkuta—many of them descendants of the former camp inmates, including the murdered Trotskyists—stood up, organized independent trade unions, and struck again and again and again, until Stalinism was swept into the dustbin of history. I wanted to know everything I could about this town called Vorkuta.

I knew that Solzhenitsyn had mentioned something about the first generation of resistance—the 1936–37 hunger strike (and subsequent massacre) of the Russian Trotskyists. I also encountered in his work references to the second generation of resistance, the 1953 camp rebellions. But the bits I managed to gather together weren't systematic; they were more a series of elliptical remarks in one of his most famous novels, *The First Circle*.[21] Furthermore, Solzhenitsyn was a novelist, not a historian. It didn't occur to me to look at *The Gulag Archipelago*. Truth be told, I had almost forgotten that it existed. I had also forgotten that it wasn't a novel but a historical document of the first order.

However, in the course of my research, *The Gulag Archipelago* kept appearing in this or that footnote. When I tried to follow up on the references, I realized something else I had forgotten—that it was a three-volume work. All I had was the first volume. So, I went out and bought used copies of the two missing volumes. Especially valuable for my research was volume 3, in the 1978 English translation. What I encountered in those pages was one of the twentieth century's greatest chronicles of heroic mass workers' resistance.

And let's be clear, this is a *workers'* story. Many years ago, the great W. E. B. Du Bois persuasively argued that chattel slaves toiling on the plantations of pre–Civil War United States—their exclusion from the wage system notwithstanding—absolutely had to be included in the category "working class," and their long history of collective rebellions included in the category of "class struggle."[22] The analysis developed in these pages accepts this framework. The twenty-eight million forced labourers who were chewed up in the Gulag system constituted a forced labour proletariat, grinding out under compulsion the goods and services deemed necessary by the Stalinist ruling class to creating a modern, industrialized society. The Stalinist ruling class was wrong. The industrialization created through this coerced labour proved to be a mirage, melting away into irrelevance upon the disintegration of the Stalinist system in 1991. The Lada could not compete with the Corolla. The Zenit B could not compete with the Nikomat. Like the Confederate slave-holding rulers before them, the Stalinist rulers demonstrated at some cost (to others) that coerced labour does not work well as a method by which to modernize.

But coerced or not, the *zeks* were *workers*. Any book that tells the life stories of these workers, and even more, any book that documents their struggles and forms of organization, is a chronicle of the movement of workers and the oppressed seeking liberation. Anyone who is a partisan of the workers' movement needs to take such a chronicle seriously.

The second wave of rebellion, culminating in the year 1953, saw a series of strikes sweep through the Gulag. I had learned something of these strikes through memoirs and accounts that came out in print in the years that followed, particularly the key strikes that occurred at Vorkuta.[23] But I had yet to read Solzhenitsyn's account. When I finally had in my hands the third volume of his *Gulag*, I knew from the chapter headings that I was holding something exceptional—"The First Whiff of a Revolution," "Chains, Chains . . . ," "Poetry Under a Tombstone, Truth Under a Stone," "Tearing at the Chains," and "Behind the Wire the Ground Is Burning." These chapters form the bulk of part 5 of *The Gulag Archipelago*, which comprises most of the first three hundred pages of the third volume. What Solzhenitsyn has written here is a beautiful, moving chronicle of workers' resistance against exploitation, resistance in horrendous conditions and against impossible odds. Here is a sample.

In early August 1953, "eleven truckloads of soldiers drove up" to Vorkuta's struck pit No. 29.[24] "The prisoners were called out onto the parade ground, toward the gate. On the other side of the gate was a serried mass of soldiers. 'Report for work, or we shall take harsh measures!'" At the sight of the soldiers, some of the strikers melted away into the background. "But there were others, who forced a path through the ranks—to stand in the front row, link arms, and form a barrier against the strikebreakers." Bullets ended the stand-off. "There were three volleys—with machine-gun fire in between. Sixty-six men were killed." Not all the soldiers could stomach the murdering of unarmed striking workers in cold blood. "A number of thin wood patches appeared on the roofs of huts at pit No. 29, covering the bullet holes made by soldiers firing over the heads of the crowd. Unknown soldiers who refused to become murderers."[25]

The Vorkuta prisoners would not have known it, but one week earlier, eerily similar events had taken place in far away Noril'sk. A clandestine "self-help group" in which Danylo Shumuk was a key activist helped organize a strike that for several weeks stopped production in the Noril'sk-area mines. But 4 August 1953, the strike—like the one at Vorkuta—was violently broken. Massed soldiers appeared at the camp gates. In response, hundreds of unarmed prisoners "took up their positions, empty-handed, opposite the companies." When after a brief stand-off, the soldiers opened fire, 79 prisoners were killed and 280 were injured.[26]

At Solzhenitsyn's own camp, located at Ekibastuz, in the Karaganda region of Kazakhstan, resistance had already taken the form of a three-day hunger strike in January 1952:

> None of those who took part will ever forget those three days in our lives. We could not see our comrades in other huts, nor the corpses lying there unburied. Nonetheless, the bonds which united us, at opposite ends of the deserted camp, were of steel. . . .
> This was a hunger strike called by men schooled for decades in the law of the jungle: "You die first and I'll die later." Now they were reborn, they struggled out of their stinking swamp, they consented to die today, all of them together, rather than to go on living in the same way tomorrow.[27]

In the near term, many of these individual strike actions failed, drowned in bloody repression. Yet, in the longer term, the strike movement as a whole was victorious. The strikes were crucial in forging a new class consciousness, a commitment to solidarity that, as it grew, made the forced labour system more and more untenable. The mass resistance by the united *zeks* ultimately helped to force the rulers of the Soviet Union to dismantle the camp system, ending the practice of forced labour, at least on a systematic mass scale.

Some "mainstream" historians are uninterested in the deep stories of the workers' movements, fixated instead on developments "at the top" of society. When workers struck *en masse* against the communist state, the official communist historiographers adopted a mainstream attitude: they wanted nothing to do with it. "Like all embarrassing events in our history . . . these mutinies have been neatly cut out, and the gap hidden with an invisible join," writes Solzhenitsyn. "Those who took part in them have been destroyed, and even remote witnesses frightened into silence; the reports of those who suppressed them have been burned or hidden in safes within safes within safes—so that the risings have already become a myth."[28] We need to rise above both mainstream indifference and Stalinist opprobrium and read Solzhenitsyn's master work.

There is much to learn from Solznehnitsyn's three volumes. There is also much with which to disagree. If the third volume of *The Gulag Archipelago* reveals a hidden story of workers' resistance, the second displays a deeply problematic, latent, and not-so-hidden antisemitism. One of the most powerful memoirs to emerge from the Gulag, that of Mikhail Baitalsky, critiques Solzhenitsyn's second volume on precisely this point.[29] Solzhenitsyn clearly documents the sexual violence against women that existed in the camps. To illustrate his point, however, Solzhenitsyn focuses in on and names just one perpetrator: "the fat, dirty old stock clerk, Isaak Bershader . . . nauseating in appearance."[30] Baitalsky challenges Solzhenitsyn's choice:

> This is the only rapist named in the entire chapter. There is not another hint as to the nationality of the men who bought women's bodies. Meanwhile, Solzhenitsyn knows as well as I do . . . that the entire practice of buying women originated with the camp criminals; that it was the camp criminals who played cards for women; and that in the criminal world there were very few Jews. . . .
>
> He named Isaac; he named a Jew. It does not matter that for every Isaac there were many thousands of non-Isaacs. He was specific about the nationality of only one. This is a half truth.[31]

Solzhenitsyn's approach is reprehensible. However, this does not mean we should leave his book on the shelf unread. Baitalsky himself, his biting critique notwithstanding, takes Solzhenitsyn seriously as an indispensable source for our understanding of the Gulag.

I doubt that the Leading Member whom I encountered more than forty years ago intended to adopt the restricted horizons of Stalinist and mainstream historians. However, discouraging a young enthusiast from reading a magnificent chronicle of workers' resistance simply because one disagrees with one aspect of the story—linking the Gulag not only to Stalin but also to Lenin—was, at the very least, bad mentoring. Solzhenitsyn's *The Gulag Archipelago*—in particular, its third volume—helps bring to light a hidden story of workers' resistance. It is a book that should be an acknowledged part of the literature for all who study the great story of the collective resistance of workers and the oppressed, the resistance that is at the core of all human progress.

———◆———

In the years following my encounter with the Leading Member, my political activism and that of my friends followed a trajectory that will be familiar to some others of my generation. We took our inspiration from the Russian revolutions of 1905 and 1917. We saw at the heart of those revolutions—both the "dress rehearsal" of 1905 and the monumental events of 1917—the great hope of freedom for the workers in the form of soviets (workers' councils) and for the peasants in the form of access to land. We saw the great hope of life for the planet in the end of the slaughter of the so-called Great War. We saw as central to the story of the Russian revolutions the singular individual figure of Vladimir Lenin and the singular collective figure of the Bolshevik Party.

We were also anti-Stalinist. We detested Leonid Brezhnev, head of the Russian state from 1964 to 1982. We breathed the hope created by Poland's magnificent Solidarność union. We shed no tears when the Berlin Wall fell. During the Tiananmen Square protests, we were with the young man and against the tanks he faced. And we insisted, with Trotsky, that there was "between Bolshevism and Stalinism not simply a bloody line but a whole river of blood"—which is, in fact, historically undeniable.[32]

But what of Solzhenitsyn's insistent question: Where did it begin? This book will not pretend to answer this question. It will ask something more modest: What can we learn? For me, this learning has happened over many years and in at least three phases. The first phase, which dates back to the years following the encounter with the Leading Member, was organized around a simple epistemology that denied *any* connection between the Lenin moment of revolution and the Stalin moment of counter-revolution. Some of us were even uncomfortable with the thoughtful position of Victor Serge.

> It is often said that "the germ of all Stalinism was in Bolshevism
> at its beginning." Well, I have no objection. Only, Bolshevism also
> contained many other germs, a mass of other germs and those who
> lived through the enthusiasm of the first years of the first victorious
> socialist revolution ought not to forget it. To judge the living man by
> the death germs which the autopsy reveals in a corpse—and which
> he may have carried in him since his birth—is that very sensible?[33]

The second phase evolved in the context of the new radicalizations of this century, which emerged in opposition to the effects of globalization, to imperialist war, and to the stubborn persistence of settler colonialism. As in any such moment of radicalization, a new generation of young people was looking to examples from the past for inspiration—and some were drawn to the figure of Lenin in the context of the Russian Revolution. But, problematically, some of the material from which they were learning their Lenin was rehabilitating not only Lenin but also Stalin.[34]

In a 2009 article, "Leninism: It's Not What You Think," I tried to draw out the democratic and self-emancipatory side of the Leninist moment. Following Marcel Liebman in *Leninism Under Lenin*, I pointed out how democratic centralism did not emerge as a concept in Lenin's 1903 argument for greater *centralism*, but rather in his 1906 argument for greater *democracy*. Following Liebman again, I insisted on seeing the overly centralist and sometimes sectarian aspects of Lenin's theory and practice as determined by the repressive and authoritarian conditions of tsarist Russia ("tsarist" being derived from the name for the ruling monarch of the Russian empire, "tsar"). I argued that when this veil of repression momentarily lifted—during the revolutionary upheavals in 1905 and 1917, for instance—Lenin strove to overcome that sectarianism and authoritarianism. In the same article, I reminded readers of one of Lenin's last public appearances in November 1922, his closing remarks to the Fourth Congress of the Communist International (Comintern). Lenin referenced a resolution, adopted at the previous congress, regarding "the organisational structure of Communist Parties" and "the methods and content of their activities"—a resolution he described as "almost entirely Russian," in that it reflected the conditions prevailing in Russia. While praising the resolution itself, Lenin warned the gathered delegates, "we have not learnt how to present our Russian experience to foreigners." He went on to argue that

> our most important task today is to study and to study hard. Our foreign comrades, too, must study. . . . Among other things they must learn to understand what we have written about the organisational structure of the Communist Parties, and what the foreign comrades have signed without reading and understanding. This must be their first task. . . . The resolution is too Russian, it reflects Russian experience. That is why it is quite unintelligible to foreigners, and they cannot be content with hanging it in a corner like an icon and praying to it. Nothing will be achieved that way.[35]

In other words, one cannot simply cut and paste Leninist methods into the context of the very different conditions prevailing in, for instance, western Europe.

The book you are reading represents the third phase in this evolving epistemology—and could very well have been titled "Leninism: It's Not What I Thought." The theme of self-emancipation versus substitutionism runs like a thread throughout the chapters in the book. The concept of self-emancipation has at its core the idea that liberation from oppression can be achieved only by the self-activity of the oppressed, who must become the agents of their own emancipation. By contrast, substitutionism refers to attempts to substitute the actions of others for the agency of the oppressed. A serious, unfiltered study of the Russian Revolution reveals that, while there was a profound self-emancipatory current at its heart, that current can only sometimes be located within the section of the Left that we retrospectively call Leninist. Certain aspects of the Leninist epistemology, which emerge at certain moments in Leninist history, are completely substitutionist, run completely counter to an emancipatory politics, and must be rejected.

To get at this concept of self-activity, this book is framed by an introductory chapter sketching both the hope and the horror associated with the Russian Revolution and its aftermath and a conclusion linking self-emancipation and substitutionism to ethics and the relationship between ends and means. The intervening chapters relate a narrative divided into three parts.

Part 1, "Vorkuta: Anvil of the Twentieth Century," provides a three-chapter historical pivot for the book, telling the story of the three generations of class struggle mentioned above—three moments of mass resistance to Stalinism centred in the Arctic settlement of Vorkuta, concluding with the 1989–91 wave of strikes "that heralded the collapse of the Soviet Union."[36] "The vengeance of history," said Leon Trotsky in his last book, "is far more terrible than the vengeance of the most powerful General Secretary."[37] The story of Vorkuta certainly makes real these prescient words. It also provides an indispensable foundation for our understanding of the arc of history from 1917 until today. No theory in the social sciences can be more than an approximation of the lessons of experience. All such theories require a concrete grounding in knowledge of the collective resistance of workers and the oppressed. In these chapters, I attempt to create that grounding by sketching three remarkable moments of workers' struggle and self-organization.

Part 2, "Self-Emancipation Versus Substitutionism," provides a four-chapter conceptual pivot for the book. Chapter 4 centres on the forgotten insights of Iulii Martov and Raphael Abramovitch, both of whom theorized the central importance to the Russian Revolution of the mass actions of a temporary new class: peasants-in-uniform. The role of this temporary new class, and in particular the way in which the Bolsheviks leaned on these peasants-in-uniform, represented substitutionism—peasant-soldiers for workers—on a truly grand scale. Chapter 5 provides some clarity on the political economy of the agrarian question—the complex political and economic problem of the relationship of the peasants to the land on which they worked and to control over the products of their labour. Such clarity is indispensable to evaluating the competing claims as to the role of peasants, in uniform or otherwise. The chapter also outlines a conceptual confusion in the use of the category "petit-bourgeois," a confusion in theory that was to have tragic consequences in practice. Chapters 6 and 7 outline case studies in substitutionism—the former focussing on the 1920 invasion of Poland and the 1921 invasion of Georgia, the latter on the 1921 German "March Action" and the 1919 Hungarian "revolution"—and the politics surrounding each that dominated the early congresses of the Communist International.[38] The German and Hungarian events bring to light the forgotten insights of another key political theorist, Rosa Luxemburg's close ally Paul Levi.

Part 3, "The Rear-View Mirror," is comprised of four chapters organized around two twenty-first-century contributions to our understanding of the Russian Revolution and its legacy. Marshall McLuhan made famous a tragic and pessimistic view of how we use historical knowledge. "The past went that-a-way," he wrote. "When faced with a totally new situation, we tend always to attach ourselves to the objects, to the flavour of the most recent past. We look at the present through a rearview mirror. We march backwards into the future."[39] A similarly tragic, but somewhat more optimistic approach comes from Greek mythology, where knowledge and understanding are symbolized by the owl of Minerva, famously referenced by the German philosopher Hegel: "The owl of Minerva takes its flight only when the shades of night are gathering"[40]—tragic because, as with the rear-view mirror analogy, it asserts that knowledge and understanding are always clearest retrospectively; optimistic because at least understanding is possible, even if only in hindsight. Looking into the rear-view mirror, chapters 8 and 9 develop themes broached in Leon Trotsky's path-breaking political biography of Joseph Stalin, written in 1940 but only published in full in 2016. Chapters 10 and 11 examine themes introduced by Tamás Krausz in his ambitious political biography of Lenin, published in 2015, but based on forty years of research.

The conclusion explores ends and means, a binary as stark as the "hope and horror" duality that begins this book. Many readers will recognize the issues raised in this text as real and problematic. Some will nonetheless ask: Didn't it turn out all right in the end? Didn't the ends justify the means? Any serious confrontation with Vorkuta—and the reactionary reality of which it was a fragment—can lead to only one conclusion: it did *not* turn out all right. The ends were shaped by the means deployed.

The conclusion takes its last subheading from a phrase famously coined by Rosa Luxemburg in her 1918 pamphlet "The Russian Revolution": "Freedom is always and exclusively freedom for the one who thinks differently."[41] Here again, we are drawn back to Martov. He and his co-thinkers were among those who dared to "think differently." Their much maligned, ethically based, and creative class analyses of the events of 1917 need to be pulled out from under a century of opprobrium and taken very seriously. The conclusion does *not* try to answer the tired question: Did Lenin lead to Stalin? The utility of such a question in the twenty-first century is not clear. There was a revolution. Lenin's party played a key role in that revolution. What can we learn from that experience? There was a counter-revolution. Stalin's party played a decisive role in that counter-revolution. What can we learn from that experience? That learning will only happen with our eyes wide open. Not forgetting to read Solzhenitsyn (and Martov, and Abramovitch, and Levi) are steps in that learning process.

◆

Let us return to the Trotskyists at Vorkuta in the terrible years of 1937 and 1938—the years of the Great Terror. Even when denied books, paper, and pens, they fought, to the end, with their minds. One anonymous "thin man," who was one of the only survivors of the infamous Vorkuta-area prison known as the Brickworks (described in more detail in chapter 1), recounts how—in the face of death at what was to be the site of mass executions—the prisoners found ways to resist even under appalling conditions:

> We had a verbal newspaper, *Truth Behind Bars*, we had little groups—circles, there were a lot of clever, knowledgeable people. Sometimes we issued a satirical leaflet, *The Underdog*. Vilka, our barrack representative, was editor and the illustrations were formed by people against a wall background. Quite a lot of laughing, too, mostly young ones there. When everything suddenly came to an end, the part of the Brickworks for those sentenced to death was closed down.[42]

The word for "truth" in Russian is *pravda*—the iconic name associated with newspapers of the Soviet regime. So, the name of their newspaper, *Pravda za reshetkoi*, or *Truth Behind Bars*, had a bitter, ironic meaning for the anti-Stalinist socialists imprisoned in the Gulag. It seems appropriate, as a tribute to those defenders of truth from behind bars, to borrow their newspaper's title for this book.

Incarceration was a weapon frequently deployed against opponents of tyranny in the era of the Great War and the Russian Revolution. A minority of those imprisoned were women: in 1942, in the Gulag, for instance, women accounted for just 13 percent of those interned.[43] Minority or not, women prisoners experienced extreme suffering. Those classified as "political" lived with the constant threat of sexual violence from, in particular, male prisoners classified as "criminal." Edward Buca provides graphic detail of the fate of one woman political prisoner, a university student, who successfully fought off the advances of one predator only to be brutally gang-raped by him and his friends.[44] Some members of that gendered, oppressed minority put pen to paper, among them Aleksandra Chumakova, Brigitte Gerland, Maria Joffe, Nadezhda Joffe, Elinor Lipper, and Suzanne Rosenberg, all from the camps of the Gulag, as well as Rosa Luxemburg, writing from a German prison cell. They provided analyses and memoirs indispensable to our understanding of this era. It is not coincidental that many of these were Jewish women. The Jewish community experienced extreme oppression under kaiserism, tsarism, and Stalinism, the opposition to which led thousands toward political activism.

Most readers will recognize the name Rosa Luxemburg. While the events of 1917 were unfolding, she was in prison because of her antiwar agitation, and by January 1919, she was dead, brutally murdered by military thugs acting with the complicity of the social democratic government of the day. Her insights into the dynamics of the Russian experience were necessarily preliminary, given her brutal murder when that revolution was not yet two years old. Preliminary or not, her analysis—on which this book relies heavily—remains central to any attempt at evaluating those fateful years.

Some readers will recognize the surname Joffe. The 1927 suicide note that Adolph Joffe penned to his close friend and comrade, Leon Trotsky, is a fitting epitaph to the tragic close of the first decade of the revolutionary epoch.[45] Few people today know the name of Joffe's second wife, Maria. Her memoir documenting her time in the Vorkuta camps, captured in the riveting *One Long Night*, has been central to my understanding of the essence of incarceration and the forced labour experience.

It seems appropriate, as a tribute to all those who spoke truth from behind bars, to dedicate this manuscript to Rosa Luxemburg and Maria Joffe.

Mackenzie Paul Kellogg

July 2021

Acknowledgements

Some important preliminary research for this book was carried out in 2011 using the collection at Joseph S. Stauffer Library, while on annual research leave and visiting my alma mater, Queen's University in Kingston, Ontario. The bulk of the research was completed while I was on sabbatical from Athabasca University in 2016. An appointment as associate professor (status only) with the Ontario Institute for Studies in Education (OISE) allowed me access to the unparalleled resources at the University of Toronto. Much of the writing was done in the quiet setting of the United Jewish Peoples' Order's Camp Naivelt, on the banks of Ontario's Credit River. It was at one of the camp's regular summer Sunday bagel brunches where I was first introduced to the writings of Isaac Babel, writings that helped clarify key issues about the Soviet Union in the 1920s. My interest in things Russian goes back to the 1970s. The Russian language professors at York University then and my instructors at Hansa Canada and the University of Toronto in recent years were and have been helpful and patient. The anonymous manuscript reviewers made insightful and helpful comments, many of which I incorporated. The diligent Russian–English translation work of Mariya Melentyeva and Russian language copy editing of Elizabeth Adams from World Communications were indispensable in helping me navigate Russian-language source material. As always, Angela Pietrobon has been indispensable in making a "final pass" over the manuscript. The index was expertly prepared by Michel Pharand. Thanks to Abbie Bakan, who pointed out to me in 2016 that my research into the Russian Revolution was, in fact, the preparation of a book manuscript. As always, every idea in this book emerged in long discussions with Abbie, with whom I have travelled a parallel political and intellectual journey for many years. Responsibility for the final product is, of course, mine alone.

Adam, Rachel, and Michael are members of a younger generation that provides the motivation for all meaningful intellectual labour. And as I was going over initial copy editing in July 2019, Gabriel—the youngest of the next generation—was born. Welcome.

A Note on Translations and Transliterations

For the most part, I have chosen to quote from and cite standard English translations of sources originally in Russian, as these translations are readily available to English-speaking readers. For writings by Lenin, those are found primarily in the English translation of the fourth edition of his *Collected Works* (*Lenin: Collected Works*, or *LCW*). Where no such translations exist, or where the published translations seemed in some way deficient, I have provided my own translations—for Lenin, translating primarily from the Russian fifth edition of his *Collected Works* (*Polnoe sobranie sochinenii*, or *PSS*). The excerpts from *World Bolshevism* were translated jointly by myself and Mariya Melentyeva. Otherwise, all translations are my responsibility alone.

Several systems exist for the transliteration of the Cyrillic alphabet. To facilitate library searches for the sources cited, I have opted to follow the system used by the American Library Association (ALA) and the Library of Congress (LC), although without recourse to diacritics. There are some exceptions. When a name has acquired a standard English spelling (such as Gorky, Lunacharsky, Preobrazhensky, and Trotsky), I have adopted that. For some, we have competing standards. The last name of the author of *The Soviet Revolution: 1917-1939* has been transliterated in two ways—Abramovich and Ambrovitch. I have opted for the latter, as it was the transliteration that he himself approved when *The Soviet Revolution* was published in English in 1962. For the first name of his mentor and co-thinker Martov, we similarly have two standards—Julius and Iulii. I have opted for the latter as it more accurately reflects the Russian pronunciation. For the same reason, I would have preferred to spell the surname "Joffe" as "Ioffe," but I have retained "Joffe" for all three Joffes, Adolph, Maria, and Nadezhda, in accord with what has become standard practice.

Translation of Russian language titles has respected the practice in that language of using minimal capitalization. As a result, normally, just the first word of the translated title has been capitalized, or the first word following a colon. However, there are no articles in the Russian language, and thus where the first word of a translated title in English is preceded by an article (or the first word following a colon), I have capitalized both the article and the noun that it modifies. The German language texts used have the opposite issue—in German, all nouns are capitalized, and my translations of German-language titles respect that practice.

Access to the works of different authors is affected by geopolitics and history. For the majority of the authors quoted, we have, for the most part, "traditional" sources—published books and journal articles. For individuals such as Martov—who became *persona non grata* in the decades following the revolution—there is a dearth of these even in Russian let alone in English translation, despite the fact that he was a prolific author. For Lenin, by contrast, we have access to far more. Massive quantities of his writings have been carefully, almost reverentially, preserved for posterity. Some were originally published as books, journal articles, or pamphlets (that is, essays, often quite lengthy, issued as independent publications). Some were letters to individuals that were never intended for publication. Some were unpublished drafts. Some were consciously withheld from publication. A great many were short, often polemical, newspaper articles commenting on issues of the day.

Why does this matter? The type of publication in which an argument appears has a strong impact on the manner in which that argument is developed. Articles written for a book or journal are composed over months and years with the anticipation of acquiring an audience. Necessarily, they involve considerable reflection and editing. Articles written in haste for a daily or weekly newspaper tend to use sharper and more extreme formulations and to be pitched in a higher emotional register than what would typically be found in a 300-page book or a 15,000-word journal article. Knowing the kind of publication, then, can be helpful in assessing the merits of a particular piece of writing. Consequently, as I was conducting my research, I found it useful to be very specific, identifying exactly what "type" of publication I had before me when I cited Lenin in particular, and I think this might, where appropriate, be similarly useful for readers of the book. For many authors in this book—particularly the "scholar activists" (Abramovitch, Lenin, Luxemburg, Martov, Marx, Serge, and others)—it is helpful to know when a work was written, and this is not always evident from the bibliographic entry (such as when it is part of a collected works project, a compilation, or a reprint). So, on many occasions, I have found it helpful to indicate (within square brackets) in the bibliography, as well as at the first use of each of the appropriate sources, the year in which such works were first published (or first written, in the case of works that remained unpublished for some time).

All works directly cited are listed in the bibliography. A complete reference for works by Lenin that are taken from *LCW* or *PSS* can be found in the first reference. For items not taken from *LCW* or *PSS*, publication information is listed in the bibliography.

Finally, a text that plays a central role in part 3 of this book—Leon Trotsky's last (and unfinished) manuscript, his biography of Joseph Stalin—exists in English translation in two versions, both titled *Stalin: An Appraisal of the Man and His Influence*. One is an abridged edition, translated by Charles Malamuth and published in 1941, and the other is a complete edition, prepared by Alan Woods, that was published in 2016. The earlier translation has been charged, on occasion, with being misleading, a charge with which I do not agree. However, to address any concerns on this issue, whenever I quote from a passage that appears in both versions, I have cited the appropriate page numbers for each.

"TRUTH BEHIND BARS"

Introduction

Hope and Horror

This book represents one attempt to reflect on and rethink the arc of the Russian Revolution of 1917 and its aftermath. It confronts both the great hope unleashed at its birth and the despair that ensued with its Stalinist denouement. It attempts to precisely identify class agency in this process, by rediscovering the key role of peasant-soldiers in the revolution that took place in the cities and by considering the forced labourers in the Gulag as part of a new proletariat in the making. Woven through the book is an interrogation of the contradiction between self-emancipation and substitutionism. The essence of self-emancipation was captured by Karl Marx in October 1864, in his draft of the inaugural rules for the International Working Men's Association (often referred to as the First International). Its very first line was unequivocal: "the emancipation of the working classes must be conquered by the working classes themselves."[1] The essence of substitutionism was captured forty years later by the young Leon Trotsky, when—in a devastating critique of Lenin and the Bolsheviks—he contrasted "two opposing methods of work. . . . In the one case we have a party which *thinks for* the proletariat, which *substitutes itself* politically for it, and in the other we have a party which politically *educates* and *mobilises* the proletariat to exercise rational pressure on the will of all political groups and parties."[2] His thesis—that there can be no substitute for the workers' own mass activity as a pathway to emancipation—is a core premise of this book.

That there was a revolution in Russia in 1917 is undeniable. A magnificent mass movement erupted on 23 February (8 March) 1917—that is, on Women's Day—today known as *International* Women's Day.[3] Orlando Figes captures the mood perfectly:

> Towards noon huge crowds of women began to march towards the city centre to protest for equal rights. . . . Photographs show the women were in good humour as they marched along the Nevsky Prospekt.
>
> But in the afternoon the mood began to change. Women textile workers from the Vyborg district had come out on strike that morning in protest against the shortages of bread. Joined by their menfolk from the neighbouring metal works, they had marched towards the city centre, drawing in workers from other factories on the way, and in some cases forcing them out, with shouts of "Bread!" and "Down with the Tsar!" By the end of the afternoon, some 100,000 workers had come out on strike.[4]

The movement mushroomed over the next two days, and the tsar's future rested on the loyalty of the armed forces, in particular the cavalry known as the Cossacks, who had a deserved reputation for brutality and violence. The afternoon of 25 February (10 March) proved decisive.

> Part of the crowd was brought to a halt by a squadron of Cossacks blocking their way near the Kazan Cathedral. . . . A young girl appeared from the ranks of the demonstrators and walked slowly toward the Cossacks. Everyone watched her in nervous silence: surely the Cossacks would not fire at her? From under her cloak the girl brought out a bouquet of red roses and held it out towards the officer. There was a pause. The bouquet was a symbol of both peace and revolution. And then, leaning down from his horse, the officer smiled and took the flowers. With as much relief as jubilation, the crowd burst into a thunderous "Oorah!" From this moment the people started to speak of the "comrade Cossacks."[5]

A working-class-centred movement, now growing into a general strike and increasingly operating in sync with the peasant-based armed forces, was a movement before which none could stand. There would still be violent clashes and many casualties. Figes says that from the urban crowd's perspective, the soldiers were "ours," whereas "the police were 'theirs'—hated agents of the regime. The people called them 'pharaohs' (much as some today might call the police 'pigs') and they had no doubts that the police would fight to the end."[6] But despite vicious police violence against the movement, the workers and peasant soldiers swept away the oppressive tsar and re-established the extraordinary 1905 institution of workers' councils (soviets), which, for the next few months, would coexist uneasily alongside a provisional government hastily improvised through negotiations among the political parties.

Demonstration of Putilov factory workers on the first day of the February Revolution of 1917. Wikimedia Commons.

October Song

In his evocative poem "October Song," Dan Georgakas described the way in which the October Revolution inspired millions: "The lights went on all over Europe. / Nothing / can ever be the same."[7] The revolution pulled into public political life millions who were striving to find a way out of the morass of war, famine, and despair to which they had been condemned by the old regime. It was a revolution underpinned by enormous mass movements of people, most of these unplanned, uncoordinated, and

Funeral on the Marsovo Pole (the Field of Mars), in Petrograd, where close
to two hundred of those who died fighting in the February Revolution
were buried on 23 March 1917. Photographer unknown, Russian State
Photographic Archive, Wikimedia Commons.

spontaneous.[8] These movements provided the immediate background to the seizure of power by the Bolsheviks in November, an event that has gone down in history as the October Revolution (based on the Julian calendar).

Isaac Steinberg, who had for a few months served as the People's Commissar of Justice in the post-October regime, by 1919 would find himself in Moscow's Butyrka prison, following his arrest by his former Bolshevik allies. He was to become one of the harshest and most eloquent critics of the regime. Nonetheless, in a book published in 1953, only a few years before his death, he clearly identified the emancipatory feel of the momentous events of 1917:

> The October Revolution brought tremendous exaltation to vast sections of the Russian people. After eight months of frustrated expectations, there was now a profound sense of relief. . . . The deepest sensation which October aroused in the people was joy. In city, village and Army people rejoiced in the fullness of their liberation, in the limitless freedom that now summoned their creative efforts.[9]

Iulii Martov (born Iulii Osipovich Tsederbaum), another harsh critic of the regime, according to P. Iu. Savel'ev and S. V. Tiutiukin, believed that "Russia after 25 October 1917 was in many ways reminiscent of France under the Jacobin dictatorship, with Lenin playing the role of Robespierre and with its red terror and bold experiments in social leveling."[10] Martov was a principal leader of the Mensheviks and vociferously opposed many Bolshevik policies, including the resort to executions and mass terror, suppression of elections in the soviets, and deployment of armed soldiers to the countryside to forcibly seize grain from the peasants. However, this "did not detract from his high opinion of the imperishable democratic gains of October: the liberation of the country from the Entente's [the wartime alliance of Great Britain, France, and Russia] imperialist influence, the overthrow of the propertied classes, and the radical elimination of all remnants of serfdom. . . . These, in Martov's eyes, were the progressive features of the Russian events of October 1917, their historical justification, and their everlasting significance."[11]

Significantly, however, Martov and his co-thinkers did not call the events of October a revolution. According to Leopold Haimson, they "insisted on calling October an 'overturn' (*perevorot*)."[12] This word has an ambiguous (and evolving) meaning. In 1917, it was often used interchangeably with revolution (*revoliutsiia*) and uprising (*vosstanie*) to describe both the events of February/March and October/November. However, by the mid-1920s, the term *revoliutsiia* (revolution) had become, in effect, the officially sanctioned term for what would later in English become some version of "The Great October Revolution." But for Martov and the Mensheviks, the October/November events were never a revolution, but rather a *perevorot*—an overturn. In modern usage, the term *perevorot* can in fact, be translated as "coup" or "putsch," words with much sharper, more negative connotations.[13] But Haimson's stress on translating it as "overturn" does accurately coincide with Martov's political analysis of the October events, an analysis developed in detail through many publications in the years that followed. Martov's use of the term began in the very heat of the long, chaotic 1917 night when the Second Congress of the Soviets was in session. As the Bolshevik-directed military operation unfolded, Martov read out a joint declaration from his Menshevik-Internationalists and the Jewish Socialist Labour Party (*Paole-Tsion*), which read: "The overturn which gave power in Petrograd into the hands of the Military Revolutionary Committee the day before the opening of the Congress, was perpetrated by the Bolshevik Party alone by means of a purely military conspiracy."[14] "Overturn" (*perevorot*) was used by Martov again in his 1919 book *World Bolshevism*, a book to which we will return on many occasions throughout this text.[15]

Where did the October Revolution (or overturn) come from? Just before the outbreak of war in 1914, Russia had a population of more than 170 million.[16] It was a multinational and overwhelmingly peasant-based empire, with the minority of wage-earning workers and the educated middle class largely concentrated in a small number of cities—most notably, Petrograd (known before 1914 as St. Petersburg) and Moscow. The rural population was caught in a hellish netherworld, formally freed from feudalism and serfdom in the 1860s, but in fact trapped in extreme poverty, "producing food crops primarily for its own consumption and for the satisfaction of its immediate obligations to some superior authority."[17]

Chained by debt to local usurers and village strong men, peasants were condemned to exist within the illiterate, patriarchal, and oppressive structure of the so-called commune, or *mir*. In that small world, petty power was in the hands of the male heads of households, whose ruling weapon of choice was the cudgel, wielded equally against "their" women and "their" children.[18] In 1922, Maxim Gorky wrote that "women are nowhere beaten as mercilessly and terribly as in the Russian village" and that "children, too, are assiduously beaten." These beatings were justified through folklore. "Probably in no other country do proverbs offer such advice. 'Hit your wife with the butt of the axe, get down and see whether she is breathing. If she is and shamming, she wants more.'" According to Gorky, "hundreds of such aphorisms, embodying the people's wisdom accumulated over centuries, circulate in the countryside."[19] Figes tells the story set in 1908 of Grigorii Maliutin, a male peasant who had for years been the chief elder of his village. He "was a heavy-built and heavy drinking septuagenarian. . . . Vain and jealous of his power, he was a strict disciplinarian, a village despot of the old school, who still beat his elderly wife and, as the elder of the village, flogged any peasant found guilty of a crime. Most of the villagers lived in fear of him."[20]

In 1914, this patriarchal violence of the village was joined by the mass violence of the trenches. With the outbreak of World War I, a huge number of peasant boys were removed from the fields and placed into uniform. Of the sixteen million mobilized in total, at least twelve million were peasant males.[21] Roger Pethybridge estimates that "by 1916, 36 per cent of the male population of working age was under arms."[22] For peasant males, that percentage was certainly higher: fully 66 percent of the roughly eighteen million peasant males between the ages of fifteen and forty-nine were called up.[23] An extraordinary proportion of the able-bodied young peasant men (and many of the not so able-bodied older men) were pulled into the trenches and subjected to unimaginable suffering. By 1917, writes Boris Souvarine, "the dead already numbered two million and a half; there were three million wounded and prisoners. Hospitals and ambulance stations were overflowing with the sick."[24]

The repercussions from this mass mobilization and mass slaughter were enormous. The creation of a mass army of peasant male soldiers created a critical labour shortage in the countryside, "which the employment of prisoners of war and refugees from the combat zone only partly alleviat-ed."[25] As a result, the number of acres of land sown with wheat fell steadily, from 270 million acres in 1913, the year before the war, to just 138 million in 1916, two years into the conflict.[26] In the country, says Richard Pipes, "landlords, for lack of farm labor, were unable to fulfill their traditional role as suppliers of food to the cities."[27] Furthermore, the sixteen million young men pulled into the army were not merely lost as labourers but were added to the rolls of consumers dependent on surplus grain from the countryside. The main thread connecting the countryside to the urban areas had always been the trade in grain, on which the cities relied to feed their growing populations. That thread was now broken. By 1917, the cities were haunted by hunger. It was no accident that the Women's Day demonstration in Petrograd, which sparked the revolution, was a plea by women for bread. As Marcel Liebman describes it: "Procession after procession passed through the street to cries of 'Bread,' 'Our children are starving,' 'We have nothing to eat!'"[28]

The uprising in the cities, sparked by hunger and fatigue with the war, was like an electric shock in the already seething trenches. Soldiers were restive even before the revolution: in January 1917, the inspector general of artillery estimated that "one million or more soldiers had shed their uniforms and returned home."[29] The new provisional government, which assumed power in the vacuum created by the abdication of the tsar on 2 March (15 March) 1917, promised an elected Constituent Assembly where the agrarian question would be discussed and settled. For the peasant sol-diers at the front, settling the agrarian question meant one thing—seizing and redistributing land that was outside the control of the commune. In part, this meant land controlled by the rich landowners, but it also meant the land of family farmers, a class newly created through a package of radical policy changes introduced in late 1906, often called the "Stolypin reform" after their chief architect, Petr Stolypin, the minister of the Inter-ior, appointed prime minister by the tsar in July 1906. Stolypin's reforms aimed to increase agricultural productivity by enabling peasants to choose to leave the *mir* and set up on their own piece of land as independent family farmers. By 1915, as a consequence of these reforms, approximately 2.5 million households had opted out of the traditional commune and established family-run farms.[30] The land of this new class of family farmers was coveted by those peasants still engaged in communal farming.

The provisional government—an unstable coalition of liberal democrats and non-Bolshevik socialists in which the latter soon became dominant—could not navigate these waters. Over the roughly eight months of its existence, it tried to bridge the demands of the workers and peasants for bread, peace, and land and the demands of the business class and the general staff of the army, whose shared agenda was military victory and a free rein for a liberal, capitalist society along West European lines and who feared and distrusted the peasants and workers. It was a bridge too far.

We can add Isaac Steinberg to the list outlined in the preface of writers who produced truth from behind bars. Imprisoned in 1919 as part of the suppression of all left-wing challenges to the Bolsheviks, he wrote what is perhaps the best survey of the immense forces that led from the February Revolution, through the stalemated months of the provisional government, to the October Revolution—a survey where one key chapter was written "on tiny scraps of paper, which were smuggled out to his wife from the Butyrka prison in Moscow,"[31] and on which the narrative that follows relies heavily.

The provisional government, while opposed to the old tsarist regime, nonetheless refused to pull Russia out of the tsar's murderous war. On 18 June (1 July) 1917, Alexander Kerensky, associated with the peasant-based Social-Revolutionary Party then serving as the provisional government's minister of war (and soon to become its official leader), pushed the peasant-soldier mass into one last futile offensive—an offensive that ended in defeat, death, destruction, and a chaotic retreat. The very launch of the offensive was the tipping point, resulting in what Steinberg describes as "deep moral and psychological disturbances within the Army. Soldiers considered themselves betrayed by their democratic and socialist leaders."[32] This sense of betrayal led directly to what has come to be known as the "July days."

In the first week of July, Steinberg writes, "tens of thousands of workers, Petrograd soldiers and Kronstadt sailors poured into the streets to demand a radical change. The Bolshevik Party, still weak at that time . . . attached itself to this mass movement and furnished it with a slogan: 'All Power to the Soviets!'"[33] These demonstrations, associated with considerable violence, had only just ended when "military catastrophe at the front broke. The mass retreat of the Russian Army began. . . . Nothing was left of the offensive."[34] Kerensky and the other government socialists lost their legitimacy and, unable to rely on popular support, increasingly turned to the general staff of the army as their only ally. This alliance with reactionary militarism saw them sanction what had once been unthinkable—"the *death penalty* was reintroduced at the front for soldiers who refused to enter battle. . . . In restoring the death penalty, the revolution tumbled from its moral height and delivered to the military clique a weapon that would later be used against the revolution itself."[35]

For a few weeks, military reaction carried the day. The government socialists and the army general staff were able, for a while, to pin the blame on the far Left for the defeat on the battlefield, accusing them of having "sabotaged" the armed forces. These charges were, in particular, levelled against the Bolsheviks and the Left Social-Revolutionaries—the radical wing of the peasant-based Social-Revolutionaries (SRs) that, as the revolution unfolded, emerged as an independent party. "Together with the Bolsheviks Trotsky and Lunacharsky, the Left Social-Revolutionaries Proshyan and Ustinov were arrested," Steinberg notes, and their organizations were pushed underground.[36]

Again, it was developments at the front that transformed the situation. On 21 August (3 September), the German armies broke through and began moving toward Petrograd. This time, the situation could not be blamed on the now underground far Left. As Steinberg tells it, people began to ask whether this military debacle resulted from "some evil plan on the part of the military reactionaries." These sentiments crystallized on 26 August (8 September), when "General Kornilov and his headquarters began an open rebellion against the Government." But his attempted coup quickly disintegrated: "The counter-revolution had miscalculated."

> The entire country—from the capital to the last forgotten village—rose as one. . . . As on a signal, workers, soldiers, railway men, postal officials armed themselves, occupied all danger points, cut off the military headquarters from the rest of the country and forced them to complete capitulation. Tremendous strength was thus uncovered in the soviets when Kerensky, in despair, turned to them for help. But the masses who defeated the rebellions, clearly conscious of

the political issues involved, were not out to save Kerensky's Government, but their own independence which, they now realized, dwelled in the power of the Soviets. The road to the October Revolution, from that moment, lay open.[37]

Travelling on that road to revolution were millions of deserting soldiers. Roger Pethybridge notes that, on 25 October 1917, more than 9.3 million men in total were stationed at the front and the rear, but, by spring 1918, "most of them had literally melted away."[38] Throughout 1917 and into 1918, millions of young peasant men and boys, arms in hand, turned toward home. "Fearing a division of land in their absence," Souvarine reports, they "returned *en masse* to the villages without permission" and "began to pillage the great estates, and to seize cattle."[39] But their pillage was not restricted to the great estates. According to Richard Pipes, "the communal peasants, at first cautiously and then with increasing boldness, raided landed property, first and foremost that belonging to fellow peasants who had withdrawn from the commune and taken title to private land."[40] This was, indeed, a revolution, but with ominous contours. For peasants to take land from the great estates was both just and progressive, but for the patriarchal commune to assert ownership over small family farms was neither. In economic terms, it was a serious retreat, since the two areas that had traditionally been able to produce a grain surplus— the large estates and the family farms—were now swallowed up by the unproductive commune, whose members were always just on the edge of subsistence production, unable to develop the productivity of labour necessary for bringing large surpluses to market. Finding a solution to the agrarian question had begun, but it was by no means finished.

These mass movements of peasant-soldiers, urban women, and factory workers—movements that took the form of mutiny and desertion in the army, the forcible appropriation of land by peasants in the countryside, and bread riots, strikes, and the formation of soviets in the cities—were the background to the November 1917 seizure of power by the Bolshevik Party. It was a seizure of power done in the name of the soviets under the slogans "Bread, peace, and land!" and "All power to the Soviets!" and with the promise of convening an all-Russian Constituent Assembly.

The End of an Era

How did the hopes of 1917 metamorphose into the horrors of Stalinism? Leon Trotsky and Boris Souvarine—whose pathbreaking studies of Stalinism will anchor chapters 8 and 9 of this book—differ in their interpretations of what has come to be known as the October Revolution. Neither would have entertained Martov's much more nuanced approach in seeing the October events as an "overturn"—the imposition of a new governmental authority (*vlast*) through the armed actions of a minority, within a still-intact, but damaged, revolutionary process. For Trotsky, it was a proletarian uprising, calling into existence the first workers' state since the Paris Commune of 1871, a workers' state representing, in the minds of many in his generation, a higher form of democracy than a parliamentary state. For Souvarine, October 1917 was a *coup d'état* by the Bolshevik Party in alliance with radicalized soldiers and sailors, a largely military undertaking with the urban workers *per se* playing a very small role. The resulting state was only nominally proletarian, the real power resting in the hands of the Bolshevik Party machine—that machine resting not on the self-active urban workers organized in workers' councils, but rather on the mobilized masses of pro-Bolshevik peasant-soldiers and sailors. Trotsky saw the January 1918 dispersal of the Constituent Assembly to be inevitable and just, since a higher form of democracy now existed through the soviets. Souvarine regarded soviet democracy as being more formal than real and saw the dispersal of the Constituent Assembly as a tragedy, making inevitable a civil war between the Bolsheviks in the cities and the peasant masses in the countryside.[41]

Differences aside, Trotsky and Souvarine agree on many of the key contours of the counter-revolution that followed. Both understood the underpinnings of the counter-revolution to be the harsh conditions in which the original revolution unfolded—world war, civil wars, foreign intervention, famine, social dislocation, mass unemployment, and population dispersal. The pressures from these conditions came to a head in early 1921, with strike waves sweeping the major cities and peasant rebellions sweeping the countryside in reaction to the period of what has come to be known as "war communism," from 1918 to 1921, during which Lenin's Bolshevik government dispatched urban squads to seize grain from the peasants while simultaneously outlawing free trade in grain. The unrest culminated in the Kronstadt rebellion, an uprising against Bolshevik rule carried out by the sailors who had, just a few years before, been the military bulwark of the regime. In 1921, the Bolsheviks, at the cost of thousands of lives, crushed the Kronstadt rebellion, and in the immediate aftermath, the revenge of the security forces was fierce. Isaac Steinberg describes the terrible consequences of Kronstadt: "Every night groups of imprisoned sailors were taken from the Petrograd jails and shot. Great numbers were sent to the prisons and concentration camps of Archangel and Turkestan."[42] The former, Archangel, was the extreme northerly district in which, in the summer of 1923, the notorious Solovki camp was established, the first post-revolutionary hard labour concentration camp. Socialist prisoners interred there encountered those survivors of Kronstadt, who had been promised an amnesty in 1922. Tragically, however "a good half" of these Kronstadt sailors "(and their number was in the four figures) did not live long enough to enjoy the amnesty."[43] Steinberg concludes that "Kronstadt marked the end of an era. After Kronstadt the Russian people no longer had the strength to stand up in such a manner for their rights and honor."[44]

Lenin and the Bolsheviks did, however, accede to the Kronstadt sailors' principal economic demand—the end of war communism and a return to distribution of grain through the market. As a result, the regime was able to achieve some degree of stabilization. But many of the most politically active workers, on whom all hopes rested for a workers' revolution, had been killed in the civil wars, dispersed to the countryside, or pulled into the burgeoning state and party apparatus that controlled both political and economic life in what became in 1922 the Soviet Union. Although an important and politicized workforce still existed in the cities, it operated under conditions of surveillance, repression, and fear. Souvarine calls the resulting years of political backsliding a "counter-revolution." Trotsky stops short of this, preferring the term "Thermidorian reaction."

Thermidor was the month in the French revolutionary calendar of 1794 when Maximilien Robespierre was overthrown and executed by others in the French revolutionary elite. Trotsky used the term consciously, suggesting an internal fight within an "intact" revolutionary process, but he stretched the definition beyond politics. In the Russian case, he writes, "the substance of the Thermidor was, is and could not fail to be social in character. It stood for the crystallization of a new privileged stratum, the creation of a new substratum for the economically dominant class."[45] He thus pushes the notion of a Thermidorian reaction very close to the broader notion of a "counter-revolution." This is not surprising. Trotsky, as we will see in chapter 8, was immersed in a milieu that found it difficult to stick with the restrictive category of Thermidor and then apply the adjective "progressive" to a regime associated with artificially induced famines, forced labour camps, purges, and mass executions—actions that destroyed the lives of millions.

Catastrophe in the Countryside

Whether labelled "Thermidorian reaction" or "counter-revolution," the consolidation of Stalin's rule brought catastrophe to the countryside. In 1928, the Stalinist regime declared its intention to "liquidate the *kulaks* as a class."[46] This was, in fact, a declaration of war against the entire peasantry. According to Lynne Viola, "During the collectivization of Soviet agriculture, almost anyone could be labeled a kulak." Although, in theory, the term was applied to "rich" peasants—rural capitalists, symbolic of the emergence of class stratification in village settings—Viola observes that "as the state entered into what would be a protracted war with the peasantry, the kulak came to serve as a political metaphor and pejorative for the entire peasantry."[47] As Donald Treadgold suggests, in deciding whether to label someone a kulak, the Soviets probably most often used a criterion "openly voiced by Tito in 1949, namely, that the test of being a *kulak* was not the size of a man's holding, but whether he was for 'socialism' or against it"—a criterion by which, Treadgold comments, "the number of *kulaks* in Russia must be reckoned as very large indeed."[48]

The essence of the war on the kulaks was the forced move of millions of peasants onto "collective farms" (*kolkhozy*), which might better be described as agricultural forced labour camps. Peasant resistance was intense, and even before the forced collectivization drive was over, millions died. The worst moment was the winter of 1932–33, when millions starved to death in what Souvarine rightly calls an "artificially organized" famine.[49] Souvarine cites a correspondent for the *Socialist Courier* who reported in May 1934 that the 1932–33 famine had claimed five million lives—an astonishing figure that was actually less than that reported by an American socialist, Harry Lang. According to Souvarine, Lang had returned "utterly dismayed" from a stay in the Soviet Union, where he had learned from a senior government official that "at least six million starving people perished in the Ukraine at that period"—information that Lang subsequently published in the New York paper the *Forward*. Lang further reported that "40 per cent of the population disappeared in certain districts of the Ukraine and White Russia."[50]

While readers today may not be familiar with either the *Socialist Courier* or the *Forward*, in the 1930s they were essential reading for any concerned with developments in the Soviet Union. The *Forward* was a Yiddish-language daily newspaper, founded in 1897, that by the early 1930s had a daily circulation in excess of 275,000.[51] The *Socialist Courier* (*Sotsialisticheskii vestnik*) was a Russian-language periodical launched in 1921 by the Menshevik Delegation Abroad, at the time consisting of just three members—Raphael Abramovitch, Iulii Martov, and Eva Broido.[52] Produced by the Mensheviks in exile, it was smuggled into Russia and eagerly read by thousands. The editorial offices of the *Socialist Courier* followed the Mensheviks as they went from place of exile to place of exile—in Abramovitch's case, from the Soviet Union to Berlin in the 1920s, to Paris in 1933 after Hitler came to power, and finally to New York in 1940 after the Nazi invasion of France. More than seven hundred issues of the journal appeared, until, with the passing of the last of the veterans of 1917, it ceased publication in the early 1960s. Sidney Hook was not alone in his opinion that the *Socialist Courier* was "the most knowledgeable journal on Soviet affairs published anywhere."[53]

These eye-witness accounts notwithstanding, the existence of the famine—particularly as it concerned the *Holodomor* (murder by hunger) centred in Ukraine—was disputed by many on the Left then, as it often is to this day. Late in March 1933, at the height of the famine, the *New York Evening Post* reported that "official quarters" in the Soviet Union "declared flatly that actual famine did not exist" and "vigorously denied . . . reports published abroad that the nation is suffering from famine. A statement that thousands were dying of starvation was branded as 'nonsensical.'"[54] This version of events was repeated by supporters of the Soviet Union in the West, including the editors of *Weekly People*, one of North America's most established left-wing papers, whose editors wrote in early April:

"Every now and again scare stories originate to the effect that the Russian mass is seething in counter-revolt or is starving by the millions."[55] Writings such as these echoed the words and relied on the research of award-winning journalist Walter Duranty, accurately labelled a "bourgeois admirer" of Stalin by Jay Lovestone.[56] At the end of March, Duranty spoke derisively of "a big scare story in the American press about famine in the Soviet Union with 'thousands already dead and millions menaced by death from starvation.'"[57] The evidence of catastrophe was so strong, however, that even Duranty had to make some concessions. "There is no actual starvation or deaths from starvation," he wrote, just "a serious food shortage throughout the country" and "widespread mortality from diseases due to malnutrition."[58]

Victims of hunger, Kharkiv district, Ukraine, 1933. Photograph by Alexander Wienerberger, Wikimedia Commons.

Those dying from lack of food would have been uninterested in the subtle distinction between "mortality from diseases due to malnutrition" and "starvation." Duranty's sophistry was an attempt to challenge the path-breaking journalism of Gareth Jones, "Foreign Affairs secretary to former Prime Minister David Lloyd George of Great Britain," who was "the

first foreigner to visit the Russian countryside since the Moscow authorities forbade foreign correspondents to leave the city."[59] As Jones recounted
to an American journalist,

> I walked along through villages and twelve collective farms. Every-
> where was the cry, "There is no bread. We are dying." This cry came
> from every part of Russia, from the Volga, Siberia, White Russia, the
> North Caucasus, Central Asia. I tramped through the black earth
> region because that was once the richest farm land in Russia and
> because the correspondents have been forbidden to go there to see
> for themselves what is happening.[60]

During his walking tour in 1933, Jones had managed to evade government officials and enter the hunger-stricken areas, where he interviewed
hundreds of peasants.

> I stayed overnight in a village where there used to be 200 oxen and
> where there now are six. The peasants were eating the cattle fodder
> and had only a month's supply left. . . . "We are waiting for death"
> was my welcome, but "See, we still have our cattle fodder. Go farther
> south. There they have nothing. Many houses are empty of people
> already dead," they cried.[61]

Malcolm Muggeridge, another eyewitness, described his visit to the North
Caucasus and the Ukraine:

> I saw something of the battle that is going on between the Govern-
> ment and the peasants. The battlefield was as desolate as in any war,
> and stretches wider; stretches over a large part of Russia. On the
> one side, millions of peasants, starving, often their bodies swollen
> with lack of food; on the other, soldiers. . . . They had gone over the
> country like a swarm of locusts and taken away everything edible;
> they had shot and exiled thousands of peasants, sometimes whole
> villages; they had reduced some of the most fertile land in the world
> to a melancholy desert.[62]

Famine Denial

So overwhelming was the suffering experienced in 1932 and 1933 that today the fact of a mass famine cannot be denied. However, the goal posts have been moved. The denial of famine has been replaced by emotional denials of this famine having resulted from a genocidal plan directed by Stalin against the people of Ukraine. A Canadian author, Douglas Tottle, played a role in perpetuating this denial with his *Fraud, Famine and Fascism: The Ukrainian Genocide Myth from Hitler to Harvard*, which one critic dismissed as "an unabashed, book-length argumentum ad hominem."[63] More scholarly is the work of Mark Tauger, who argues that the "low harvest" in 1932 was "the result of a failure of economic policy, of the 'revolution from above,' rather than of a 'successful' nationality policy against Ukrainians or other ethnic groups."[64]

But is the central task really to discern Stalin's genocidal intentions? First, in the absence of evidence, how will we ever know? Second, it deflects attention from what we *do* know. The famine was clearly rooted in the catastrophic policy of forced collectivization. "We peasants are all hungry," a Russian peasant told journalist Gareth Jones, after eating Jones's discarded orange peel. "The Communists took away our grain. They robbed us of our land. They came to our village and left only a few potatoes for us to live through the winter. There's bread in the big cities, but there is no bread in the villages in the homes of the people who grow the wheat."[65] Third, is it legitimate to blame the peasants' starvation on nature? When Jones asked the peasants "Why is there famine?" they replied:

> "It is not the fault of nature. It is the fault of the Communists.
> "They took away our land. Why should we work if we have not our own land?
> "They took away our cows. . . .
> "They took away our wheat. . . .
> "The Communists have turned us into slaves and we shall not be happy until we have our own land, our own cows and our own wheat again."[66]

Jones had no doubt that the crisis was man-made. "The famine now killing hundreds in the Soviet Union cannot be attributed to the weather," he wrote, "for in the last few years climatic conditions have—with the exception of drought in some areas in 1931—blessed the Soviet Government." He went on to blame the disaster on the "Soviet policy of abolishing the private farm and replacing it by large collective farms, where the land and cattle were owned in common. . . . When the Government attempted force to make them [the peasants] yield their cows they retaliated by massacring their cattle and eating them."[67]

Contemporary research firmly backs up these 1933-era accounts. According to R. J. Rummel, "The weight of evidence suggests that the attempt to collectivize the peasant, even the nomad, and liquidate the kulak as a class, massively disrupted the agricultural system and brought about the famine."[68] N. M. Dronin and E. G. Bellinger blame the government's "race to achieve the unrealistic plan figures for grain delivery" for the famine in 1931. They go on to explain why the crisis deepened, despite the weather being conducive to farming:

> In the next years, 1932 and 1933, which were years of good weather, the excessive procurement of grain from devastated collective farms was the single cause of mass famine in the Ukraine and other productive regions. The authorities seemed to do everything possible to aggravate the situation. They prevented starving peasants from leaving the affected regions, even though such migration had saved millions of lives in previous bad years.

Dronin and Bellinger point out that despite an extremely severe drought in 1936, "the recurrence of mass famine was avoided due to a few elementary measures such as the radical reduction of the grain procurement plan (by 60 percent) and the halting of grain exports."[69]

This contemporary research is compelling. But in fact, impeccable research demonstrating these truths has been sitting on our bookshelves for decades. One of the classics of 1970s scholarly writing on the Russian Revolution is *Bukharin and the Bolshevik Revolution*, Stephen Cohen's study of Nikolai Bukharin, a leading figure in the Russian movement. Cohen's scholarship provides overwhelming evidence regarding not only the reality of the devastating famine of 1932–33 but also the roots of this famine in the forced collectivization policies of the Stalin regime.

In 1928, after a few years of relatively "normal" economic urban–rural relations, the Soviet regime was faced with a fall in grain deliveries from the countryside to the cities. Under Stalin's initiative, the regime reverted to the methods of war communism, sending thousands of party activists, backed by the armed force of the state, to seize grain "surpluses" from the peasants, seizures that shifted the burden of hunger from the cities to the countryside. The policy proved catastrophic. Cohen, quoting Bukharin, notes that "as a result of Stalin's 'extraordinary measures,' . . . peasant agriculture was 'regressing' because 'the basic peasant masses have lost any stimulus to produce.'"[70] A "new wave of peasant unrest" swept the country in the summer and autumn of 1929 as "state agents—their methods increasingly coercive—swarmed the countryside procuring grain."[71] This was the prelude to the catastrophic "great assault that was to come in December," an assault whose aim was to shift twenty-five million peasant families off their individual plots and into collective farms.[72] It was, in effect, the launch of a one-sided civil war—the armed forces of the state against the pitchforks and bodies of the peasants.

We can pick up the story from another classic author, Alec Nove, whose books have also been available for decades. The forced collectivization of peasants began in the dead of winter, in late December 1929. Nove indicates that "it was announced by 20 February 1930 . . . that 50 per cent of the peasants had joined collective farms." The usually detached Nove resorts to the use of an exclamation mark, to emphasize that this represented "half of the peasant population in seven weeks!"[73] Tens of millions had been ripped from their small plots and deposited in their new collective farms. The resulting chaos was intensified at the beginning of March 1930, when Stalin called a temporary halt to the process in his "dizzy with success" article.[74] "Within weeks," Nove writes, "the proportion of the peasantry collectivized fell from 55 per cent (1 March) to 23 per cent (1 June)."[75] In other words, there was, once again, a mass movement of tens of millions, this time reversing the flow, with peasants leaving the collective farms and returning to their old small plots—all in the middle of winter. It is impossible to convey "the fantastic ups-and-downs in the lives of the large majority of the population of the Soviet Union within a few short months."[76]

Those ups and downs were about to intensify. Among the immediate consequences of this war of the Soviet state against most of its population—the vast masses of the rural peasantry—was the destruction of much of the productive capacity of the countryside. Cohen provides some stark statistics: "Figures published in 1934 revealed that more than half of the country's 33 million horses, 70 million cattle, 26 million pigs, and two-thirds of its 146 million sheep and goats had perished," most during the catastrophic months of January and February, 1930. "Twenty-five years later, livestock herds were still smaller than in 1928."[77]

From within the Soviet Union, this appalling destruction of livestock was blamed on the kulaks. From 10 February until 22 March 1934, the Bolsheviks, since 1918 officially called the Russian Communist Party (Bolsheviks) or RCP(B), gathered at their 17th Party Congress. Central Committee member Ianis Rudzutak, delivering a CC report to that congress, said: "Of course a lot of damage has been done to agriculture by the kulaks who campaigned to wipe out the herd."[78] This explanation has no credibility. The very scale of slaughter would have entailed a level of organization and coordination far beyond the resources of any in the countryside.

The livestock and the farmers died for the same reason—the seizure of their grain by the Soviet state. The whole point of forcing peasants off their land and onto collective farms was to make systematic the seizure of their grain. In the first year of collectivization, the scale of the pending catastrophe was not yet apparent. As Nove puts it: "The heavens chose to smile. The weather was excellent, somehow most of the sowing did get done, and the 1930 harvest was better than that of 1929," increasing by about 15 percent.[79] But if the heavens chose to smile, the authorities did not. An increase in grain production simply meant intensified state pressure to procure even more grain. And just to be clear, procurement meant the violent seizure of grain from the peasants by armed agents of the state. In 1931, Nove writes, these seizures "left many peasants and their animals with too little to eat. Ukraine and North Caucasus suffered particularly severely."[80] By 1932, "all forces were directed to procurements," which included the use of the death penalty for any who "refused to deliver grain for procurements."[81]

As was inevitable in these circumstances, millions of animals and humans died. All relied on grain—feed grain for the livestock, grain to make the bread for the peasantry. When party policy led to extremes such as in the North Caucasus, where, according to Stalin's close ally Lazar

Kaganovich, "all grain without exception was removed, including seed and fodder,"[82] the animals had to be slaughtered immediately: not only could they not be fed but their meat provided an emergency (but temporary) food source for the starving peasants. The seizure of grain "surpluses," especially when grain production was declining, forced the peasants to abandon bread and turn to meat, slaughtering their animals to stave off hunger. But that solution could happen only once. By the winter of 1932–33, grain was still being forcibly seized, but the animals were gone. The result was a famine of catastrophic proportions. Nove has no doubt that these policies were the direct cause of the famine, which he describes as "part and consequence of the struggles described above."[83]

The events of these disastrous years, sometimes called a "revolution from above," but in reality, more resembling a counter-revolution, did lead to industrialization. The cities received both bread and the labouring bodies of ex-peasants, who were starving, homeless, and desperate for work. But the price for this industrialization was paid with the lives of millions of small farmers and by "those inseparable partners of peasant destiny, their livestock."[84]

The latter quotation is taken from Stanisław Swianiewicz in his path-breaking exploration of the economics of forced labour in the Soviet Union. Swianiewicz draws a direct parallel between the experience in the Soviet Union and that of Great Britain some centuries before, where "the policy of enclosures provided a cheap labour force for industry by squeezing the peasant out of the countryside."[85] In both cases, the rural population suffered displacement and impoverishment. But the compression of the time frame meant that this suffering was felt far more acutely in the Soviet Union. "For three centuries," Swianiewicz writes, the enclosures "provided English industry with a cheap labour force by compelling the peasants to move to the towns. The Communist Government carried out the same task in a few years."[86] Forced collectivization—like Great Britain's enclosure movements—could be accomplished only by depriving peasants of the means of subsistence. Both policies in effect expropriated land formerly worked in common and created a mass proletariat available for exploitation. Both measured their success in broken bodies and broken communities.

The story of forced collectivization is an appalling one. Horrendous suffering swept whole areas of the Soviet Union, suffering that resulted directly from the war on the peasantry launched by Stalin in the context of what was grotesquely labelled a five-year plan. Yet, there had been generations of goal posts being moved—first, denying that the famine existed, and then, when the reality of that famine was too obvious to deny, arguing, without reflection, that the issue in dispute was whether policy was motivated by anti-Ukrainian chauvinism, all the while leaving hanging the main issue: the destruction of agricultural productivity caused by the imposition of so-called collectivization. In reality, it was a return to policies of the era of war communism, doing the work of the British enclosure movement, but in a matter of years, not a matter of generations.

In 2003, without conceding that what happened was genocide, the Russian Federation added its signature to a UN resolution that said, in part: "The Great Famine of 1932–1933 in Ukraine (Holodomor), which took 7 to 10 millions of innocent lives, became a national tragedy for the Ukrainian people. . . . We also commemorate the memory of millions of Russians, Kazaks and representatives of other nationalities who died of starvation . . . as a result of civil war and forced collectivization."[87] This retroactively confirms the research of Cohen in the 1970s, of Nove in the 1960s, and of Souvarine in the 1930s, as well as the eyewitness accounts of Gareth Jones and Malcolm Muggeridge, both of whom managed to evade government authorities and actually visit the devastated areas in 1933.[88]

Catastrophe in the Cities

Whether labelled a "Thermidorian reaction" or "counter-revolution," the consolidation of Stalin's rule brought devastation to the countryside. It also brought catastrophe to the urban areas. Solomon Schwarz has meticulously documented the steady decline in workers' living standards during the first five-year plan (1928–33). "Nominal wages . . . greatly exceeded Plan estimates," he notes, "but a much greater inflationary rise in living costs considerably depressed the level of real wages."[89] There was some improvement up to the summer of 1938, but then "the trend reversed itself, with nominal earnings lagging far behind the price level. By 1941, real wages had taken a new plunge, and on the eve of the Soviet Union's entry into the war they cannot have been much higher, by and large, than at the end of the First Five-Year Plan period."[90]

Decline in real wages was only one aspect of the misery for urban workers. Sergei Kirov, one of the regime's most popular figures, and a formidable potential rival to Stalin, was assassinated in confusing circumstances in December 1934. After his death, purges swept through the cities. Roy Medvedev writes that "every *oblast* [province], Leningrad especially, was swept by the first wave of mass arrests, which was later called the 'Kirov flood' in the camps."[91] Ante Ciliga says the Kirov flood sent 30,000 to 40,000 inhabitants of Leningrad into exile in Siberia.[92] Boris Souvarine writes that "some 100,000 innocent inhabitants of Leningrad" were deported.[93] And Solzhenitsyn states that "one-quarter of Leningrad was purged—*cleaned out*—in 1934–1935. Let this estimate be disproved by those who have the exact statistics and are willing to publish them."[94]

This was just a taste of what was to come. In 1937 and 1938, the counter-revolution reached a chilling climax in what would come to be called the Great Terror. These years are well-known as the years of the "trials" of Grigory Zinoviev, Lev Kamenev, and other leading figures of the party. With painstaking devotion to detail, Medvedev's classic account of these horrendous years tells the story and lists the names of seven hundred individual victims, "the best-known officials, military commanders, writers, artists and scholars."[95] These individuals were among thousands falsely accused and arrested from every key sector of politics and civil society, including:

- the central organs of the ruling Communist Party
- the party committees in the regions
- the trade unions
- the upper echelons of the Red Army
- the very security apparatus that was conducting the purges
- leading members of non-Russian communist parties living in exile in the Soviet Union
- the "technical intelligentsia" working in science and technology

- writers and cultural workers, including "every kind of creative person and organization . . . painters, actors, musicians, architects and film people."[96]

While we have Medvedev's seven hundred names, most who suffered in the Great Terror were anonymous. "Numerically" he says, "the chief victims were hundreds of thousands of rank-and-file Party members."[97] There were also thousands of non-party victims and those whom Suzanne Rosenberg calls "small fry." These latter, according to Rosenberg, "by the thousands and hundreds of thousands were also being caught in the net. . . . When you arrived at your job you never knew who would be missing next."[98] Souvarine writes that "mass arrests and wholesale executions made the population live again through the darkest hours of the Civil War. Groups of several dozen 'citizens' were shot each week, then each day, without formality, without the least guarantee of justice, or after secret trials, tantamount to pseudo-legal assassination."[99] Medvedev says that "there were days when up to a thousand people were shot in Moscow alone."[100] Nadezhda Joffe amplifies this, saying that in 1937–38, "about 28,000 people a month were annihilated."[101]

Medvedev's estimate for the total number of victims summarily shot, based on information available in the 1970s, was "at least four to five hundred thousand."[102] Contemporary research on those two terrible years, 1937 and 1938, puts the figure at 681,692.[103] In addition, the victims of famine, forced exile, and imprisonment in the Gulag numbered in the millions. Souvarine cites evidence from the suppressed census of 1937, which Stalin anticipated would show a population of 171 million, up from 147 million in 1926. The actual total, according to Souvarine, was just 145 million, meaning that more than 20 million people were "missing."[104] Nove makes the same point, but with different arithmetic, saying: "well over 10 million people had 'demographically' disappeared" between the two censuses.[105] Contemporary figures put the 1937 census figure at 162 million against an expectation of 170 million, a gap of "only" 8 million.[106] Whether we rely on Souvarine's 1930s figures, Nove's 1960s figures, or figures from contemporary research, it is clear that from the late 1920s to the mid- to late 1930s, something horrifying took place in the Soviet Union—hence, the suppression of the census and the demand by Stalin for a revised one in 1939. Whatever the actual figures, this really is the arithmetic of horror.

Whether focusing on the countryside or the city, the move from hope to horror must be the starting point for any assessment of the Russian Revolution. To focus only on the horror and blur the experience of hope in the revolution's early months is to deny the efficacy of mass action by the oppressed. To focus only on the hope and blur the experience of horror is to become an apologist for what was to become a grotesque totalitarian regime.

PART 1

Vorkuta: Anvil of the Working Class

Anvil—A heavy block on which metal can be hammered and shaped, typically of iron or (now) steel, having a flat top, concave sides, and (typically) a pointed or tapering projection at one end . . . in figurative contexts, esp. with reference to the use of an anvil as a block on which something is forged or shaped. (*Oxford English Dictionary*)

The Arctic settlement of Vorkuta was in every respect an anvil, a block on which was forged the emergent postrevolutionary working class. Letting fall into the background for a moment the received wisdom and theories about communism and the Russian Revolution and instead bringing to the fore issues of class formation and class struggle can assist mightily in understanding revolution and counter-revolution in the territories of the former Russian empire. In the chapters of part 1, I develop this class formation through an examination of three pivotal moments of class struggle in and around Vorkuta.

Chapter 1 examines Vorkuta in the 1930s, when the town was fast becoming one of the Soviet Union's most important sources of coal. In the years from 1936 to 1938, Vorkuta also became the final resting place of Stalin's political opponents—the same radicalized workers who had raised the Bolsheviks to power in 1917. Before their extermination, the political prisoners at Vorkuta—many being followers of Leon Trotsky, who had formerly constituted the Left Opposition within the Communist

Party—organized a mass hunger strike, which became the stuff of whispered legend in the following decades.

In chapter 2, we move to the 1950s, by which point, as was indicated earlier, the forced labour camps at Vorkuta had seen "approximately half a million prisoners pass through their gates." Vorkuta had grown to become a major mining centre and the principal supplier of coal to Leningrad, a city of well over three million people. In 1953, in the period following Stalin's death, thousands of Vorkuta's forced labourers organized a massive strike in protest against the Gulag labour system, demanding improvements to their living and working conditions. The strike, which ended in violent repression, nonetheless played a pivotal role in ending the forced labour system in the Soviet Union.

Chapter 3 focuses on the late 1980s and an even more massive strike. By then, the mines of Vorkuta were employing "free" wage labourers, some of them the grandchildren of those imprisoned at Vorkuta during the 1930s. In July 1989, the thousands labouring in Vorkuta's coal pits were central to the wave of strikes that were instrumental in the collapse of the Soviet Union. From its origins as a graveyard for revolutionaries, then, Vorkuta gave birth to the gravediggers, first, of the forced labour system and, eventually, of the Stalinist state system itself.

1   One Long Night, 1936–38

Above the Arctic Circle, in a lost corner of the world,
The earth is shrouded by coal-black eternal night.
The wind howls like a wolf and will not let us sleep.
Oh, for just a glimmer of dawn in this oppressive gloom!

A sinister presence floats in the shadows.
We are alone with our anguish and our sense of doom.
Above the Arctic Circle, there is no joy my friend.
A furious blizzard erases all our tracks.

Don't come for us, don't be tormented by us, save yourself.
But maybe, if you find a moment . . . remember me, my friend.[1]

An anonymous historian identifies the author of these haunting lines as Lyova Dranovsky, an old communist and prisoner in the Gulag who, some time prior to 1938, "began to write some very fine and moving poetry . . . sitting by the stove in the tent, by the bank of the Vorkuta River."[2] Truth be told, we cannot be sure of the exact name of the poet. From another account by Hryhory Kostiuk, one of the very few eyewitnesses who survived the events to be described here, we learn of another poet with a slightly different name—Comrade Granovsky. Kostiuk remembers prisoners reading, and even singing, Granovsky's poems.[3] Comparing that with our first eyewitness, who says that Dranovsky's "poems became the common property of the whole Vorkuta camp and were set to music, to sad and mournful tunes,"[4] it is likely that Lyova Dranovsky and Comrade Granovsky were the same person. Even if they were two different people, however, they met the same fate. Granovsky was "doomed to die in Stalin's camps."[5] Dranovsky "was shot at Syr-Yaga in 1938."[6]

Our knowledge of Comrade Granovsky comes from a standard peer-reviewed, scholarly source. Our knowledge of Lyova Dranovsky has a quite different pedigree. It derives from a remarkable memoir, circulated as part of the underground anti-Stalinist literature known as *samizdat*. The memoir was "written over a period of years and completed in the late sixties" and "became known to the world in 1970." Its anonymous author was one of the only survivors of the 1936–38 massacres visited upon anti-Stalinist socialists.[7] The Granovsky/Dranovsky poem was written on the banks of the Vorkuta River. Near the source of that river, two hundred kilometres from where it drains into the Pechora and more than one hundred kilometres north of the Arctic Circle, lies the town of Vorkuta, epicentre of the 1936–38 Great Terror.

The Arc of Repression

Located at the extreme northern tip of what is today the Komi Republic, roughly two hundred kilometres south of Baydaratskaya Bay on the Kara Sea, Vorkuta is further north than Great Bear Lake, Repulse Bay, or Bathurst Inlet in Canada.[8] As a settled area in the far reaches of the Arctic, Inuvik, on the Mackenzie River delta, might be offered as a point of comparison. But Inuvik remains an administrative centre, the population of which has rarely exceeded 3,500. In contrast, by 1993, Vorkuta had a population of 217,000, with most of its workers employed in the 13 coal mines that surrounded the city.[9] By 2013, the population of the town had plummeted to just 96,000, but this was still far greater than any comparable Arctic settlement in Canada.[10]

Vorkuta is a forbidding place. Some of its inhabitants in 1993 described the climate as "twelve months of winter, followed by summer." In the words of one resident, "after ten years here you stop being human because of the cold, depression, polar nights, tough work."[11] Joseph Scholmer—a German communist arrested in 1949 and sent to Vorkuta—recalled the "old hands" telling him: "You mustn't stay here too long. It's a murderous climate. Anyone who stays here too long gets the guts knocked out of him."[12] So grim are the environs that, when advisors to Tsar Nicholas I proposed that "he should make the territory around the rivers Petchora and Vorkuta into a colony for exiles, he sent for a report on conditions there and decided that it was 'too much to demand of any man that he should live there.'"[13]

Vorkuta first entered the pages of history as prison ground and massacre site for thousands of socialists who opposed the rise to power of Stalin and his bureaucracy. The introductory chapter laid out the horrendous statistics of repression for 1937 and 1938—681,692 "documentable" executions carried out by the Stalinist state in those terrible years.[14] Vorkuta was a principal site of that state-organized terror. In impossible conditions, anti-Stalinist socialists—many of them followers of Leon Trotsky—fought to uphold the ideals of the Russian Revolution. They fought with their bodies, launching a series of mass hunger strikes, some of which they actually won—at least in the near term.

In fact, their victories were the very definition of pyrrhic. Almost to a person, these anti-Stalinist socialists were executed, most in what came to be known as the "Kashketin executions," so called because they were overseen by Efim Iosifovich Kashketin, a senior staff member with the NKVD, or People's Commissariat of Internal Affairs.[15] Robert Conquest tells us that only children aged twelve and under escaped execution.[16] This is confirmed by the account of an extraordinary eyewitness to these awful events, Ivan Mitrofanovich Khoroshev, writing under one of his several pseudonyms "M.B." The real identity of M.B. was only discovered after Khoroshev's death in early 1991.[17] Born in 1904, he had been sentenced in 1936 to six years in the Gulag on charges of "counter-revolutionary Trotskyist activities." In October 1991, just months after his death, he was officially rehabilitated. Khoroshev writes: "At the time of execution of a male prisoner, his imprisoned wife was automatically liable to capital punishment; and when it was a question of well-known members of the Opposition, this applied equally to any of his children over the age of twelve."[18] Once Kashketin's work was done, he was in turn imprisoned and executed, a fate that befell many of those who were instruments of the terror. Mikhail Baitalsky captures the terrible irony, saying that several months after overseeing the slaughter in Vorkuta, Kashketin was heard shouting from a prison in the area: "Tell the people that I am Kashketin! I am the one who shot all the enemies of the people at Vorkuta! Tell the people!"[19]

The victims of this slaughter were part of a whole layer of Russian socialists who opposed the Stalin regime. Arriving at estimates for the size of this opposition is difficult, but the numbers clearly ran into the thousands. In October 1923, the "Declaration of the 46," one of the first opposition documents, was supported by half the party cells in Moscow, one-third of the cells in the army, and a majority of the students in the communist cells of Moscow's institutions of higher learning.[20] The years 1924 and 1925 were years of stalemate, when Trotsky's advice was "do nothing, don't reveal ourselves at all, maintain our connections, protect our cadres from 1923, let Zinoviev wear himself out."[21] According to Pierre Broué, during those years, the Trotskyist opposition in Leningrad might have numbered "just a few dozen," but "it was something else altogether" in Moscow, where the opposition claimed some "five hundred members, very well organized. There, the Bolshevik-Leninists [Trotskyists] knew that they had an absolute majority in the factory and army cells."[22] Roland Gaucher estimates that from 1926 to 1928, the United Opposition—now including Kamenev and Zinoviev, who had been pushed into opposition to Stalin—had some seven to eight thousand activists across the whole Soviet Union, much the same as the number of activists who formed the core of the Stalin-Bukharin bloc, which had replaced the earlier Zinoviev-Kamenev-Stalin troika.[23] There was, of course, one important difference: the Stalinist activists had the resources of the state and the party at their disposal, while the anti-Stalinist activists had only their own wits and initiative. In 1927, in the teeth of intensifying repression, the United Opposition platform received some four to five thousand signatures. At the beginning of 1929, the anti-Stalinist opposition estimated that "between 2,000 and 3,000 of its members were in captivity, but this approximate figure was later raised to 5,000."[24] Gus Fagan, in 1980, put the figure at between 6,000 and 8,000.[25]

This socialist, anti-Stalinist opposition found, from time to time, a hearing inside the mass of the working class. Michal Reiman argues that although many underestimate the importance of this opposition, "one can hardly agree with such views: they seem paradoxical indeed in light of the mountain of ammunition expended on the opposition by the party leadership in those years."[26] He goes on to argue that in 1926, "opposition activity was spreading like a river in flood":

The opposition organized mass meetings of industrial workers in Ivanovo-Voznesensk, Leningrad and Moscow; at a chemical plant in Moscow shouts were heard, "Down with Stalin's dictatorship, down with the Politburo!"

There were rumours of underground strike committees, in which the opposition were said to be participating, in the Urals, the Donbass, the Moscow textile region and Moscow proper—and of funds being raised for striking workers.[27]

Sergei Ivlev, a Left Oppositionist imprisoned with Khoroshev in the 1930s, told of an electric United Opposition meeting he helped organize in Moscow in the autumn of 1927. A former student of Moscow Higher Technical School, he obtained a key to the largest auditorium at the school, saying that he needed it for a geography club meeting.

> At seven o'clock in the evening, as soon as I opened the auditorium, crowds of students and worker-oppositionists began arriving from all over Moscow, having been notified in advance through their organisers. There were more than three thousand of them. The auditorium and the adjoining corridor were filled to capacity. Trotsky, Kamenev and Zinoviev attended the meeting. Unusual enthusiasm and unanimity prevailed at this meeting. The opposition leaders' fiery words landed on fertile soil.

When the authorities cut off the electricity, plunging the auditorium into darkness, the meeting organizers were prepared, handing out sterno candles collected in advance. "And when L. B. Kamenev, the chairman of the meeting, solemnly proclaimed: 'Let us dispel the Stalinist gloom with Leninist light!'—dozens of candles were lit in different parts of the audience to enthusiastic applause." The authorities escalated and rounded up "reliable men" to help them break up the meeting. But when the several thousand "ostensible Stalinist supporters" arrived, they stood around passively, "and some of them even joined the oppositionists. After finishing the meeting, the oppositionists left the auditorium singing, and lined up in two dense columns in the corridor and courtyard. Under their protection Trotsky, Kamenev and Zinoviev marched unhindered to their cars."[28]

Even in the early 1930s, when Stalinist repression was gathering steam and the bulk of Trotsky's Left Opposition had been driven into exile or sent to the Gulag, a workers' opposition continued, looking to the traditions of Lenin and Trotsky as a counter to Stalinist oppression. Aleksandra Chumakova provided an eyewitness account of one such episode. As a party worker in the Moscow Committee, she "was not in the Opposition," but "her husband was, and her fate was linked to his and to that of other Oppositionists close to them."[29] In 1932, she was sent to the Glukhovka textile mill, the oldest textile mill in Russia, to investigate complaints about working and living conditions. This was not an insignificant mill. It was in the Ivanovo district, not far from Moscow, and had a long tradition of working-class militancy, having played a critical role in the 1917 revolution. As Chumakova reports:

> When I arrived at the factory I was immediately struck by the horrifying unrelieved poverty of the workers. Gaunt from hunger, they were barely able to get to work and stand up at their machines for the allotted eight hours. Through the streets of the factory settlement wandered the starving, emaciated children of the workers. They gathered around the garbage cans of the factory dining hall and waited for something edible to be thrown out. The textile workers would call their children into the dining halls and share with them the one bowl of soup allowed each worker per day. . . .
>
> The Glukhovka workers had no respect for Stalin. During the 1932 May Day demonstration they had carried portraits of Lenin and Trotsky through the streets of the settlement and had shouted angry phrases against Stalin.[30]

This bitterness and anger moved from demonstrations to strikes, which were fiercely repressed.[31]

Precisely because the arguments of the Trotskyists had a hearing inside the working class, the repression against them was fierce. It was, in Maria Joffe's words, "one long night."[32] The darkest pit of that night was in the Gulag, in which were deposited millions of peasants who had defended their land and hundreds of thousands of communists who fought the rise of Stalin.

By 1936, the great majority of former Oppositionists had "capitulated," many of them in words only in order to preserve their lives and jobs. Joseph Berger describes the lifestyle of those Trotskyists who capitulated in the early 1930s and who were, temporarily, allowed to live and work in relative freedom:

> There was something wild about them in those days. At their famous parties, vodka flowed and an old gypsy song was sung with the refrain: "We'll booze away the lot, but we'll keep the concertina, and we'll make the bitches dance to our tune!" The concertina was their inner freedom, their integrity, their secret ideological "core." It was the justification of their hymns to Stalin, of their denial of the spirit of October, which they knew they were helping the "bitches" to bury. It was recklessly ignored that every tenth guest at the party was an agent who would be reporting what they said.[33]

Capitulation, however, would provide only a temporary reprieve. All would ultimately share the fate of the irreconcilables, the "hard core of uncompromising Trotskyists, most of them in prisons and camps."[34] According to Pierre Broué, Genrikh Yagoda, director of the NKVD, "proposed to Stalin the arrest of all the Trotskyists in exile and deporting them to the most distant camps of the Gulag, Vorkuta and Kolyma-Magadan."[35] Berger adds a third camp to the list, saying of the Trotskyists that in mid-1936, "they and their families had all been rounded up . . . and concentrated in three large camps—Kolyma, Vorkuta and Noril'sk."[36]

These three places of exile were grim indeed. Kolyma, the vast Siberian district in the far northeast of the Russian landmass, had a reputation for being home to the deadliest of the camps in the Gulag.[37] Travel some three thousand kilometres west from Kolyma, and you would encounter the camps centred around Noril'sk, roughly three hundred kilometres inside the Arctic Circle. Travel another eleven hundred kilometres west, and you would finally reach the camps at Vorkuta. A line connecting the three extermination centres would describe a vast arc stretching across some of the most forbidding land in the world—a vast arc of repression. Vorkuta was probably the most important of these three as a killing ground for the socialist, anti-Stalinist opposition, and it is the one from which the most eyewitness testimonies have emerged, allowing us to piece together a picture of what occurred. The most detailed report—that of Khoroshev—did not reach the West until 1961. "In the mid- and late 1930s," writes Khoroshev, "the Trotskyists in Vorkuta were a very patchwork group; some of them still called themselves Bolshevik-Leninists."[38] Khoroshev estimates that the "genuine Trotskyists" numbered "almost 500 at the mine, close to 1,000 at the camp of Ukhta-Pechora, and certainly several thousands altogether around the Pechora district."[39] Added to these, "there were in the camps of Vorkuta and elsewhere more than 100,000 prisoners who, members of the party and the youth, had adhered to the Trotskyist Opposition and then at different times and for diverse reasons . . . were forced to 'recant their errors' and withdraw from the Opposition."[40]

While "the Trotskyists formed the only group of political prisoners who openly criticized the Stalinist 'general line' and offered organized resistance to the jailers," Khoroshev tells us that organizing such resistance was difficult in the extreme.[41] The labour of the inmates at the time—in contrast to later years, when the Vorkuta area was transformed into a massive mining complex—had little economic importance to the regime. As the terror began to bite in late 1936, the Trotskyists at Vorkuta launched a hunger strike—the last resort in any collective struggle. While the tactic had been used by other prisoners, the 1936 strike was the largest we know of in the camp system. According to Khoroshev, its leaders were Sokrat Gevorkian, an Armenian researcher formerly affiliated with what Khoroshev calls "the Institute of Human Sciences"; the student Karl Petrovich Mel'nais, who had led a Left Opposition group at the University of Moscow before his arrest in 1927; Vladimir Ivanov, an Old Bolshevik and former member of the Central Committee who had supported an oppositional faction known as the Group of Democratic Centralism; V. V. Kossior, who had occupied a senior managerial post in the petroleum industry; and Igor' Poznanskii, formerly one of Trotsky's secretaries. The strike was launched on 27 October 1936 to protest the second frame-up trials being staged in Moscow (with Kamenev and Zinoviev as the star prisoners) and was to involve a thousand prisoners over an agonizing four months.[42] "Even the children persisted," writes Berger, "although the strike leaders begged the mothers to stop them because the sight was intolerable to the men."[43]

According to Solzhenitsyn, the strikers demanded, among other things, "separation of the politicals from the criminals; an eight-hour workday; the restoration of the special ration for politicals and the issuing of rations independently of work performance."[44] In his own account, Khoroshev's summary of the demands is similar, except for one concerning special rations. According to Khoroshev, the hunger strikers insisted only that "the food quota of the prisoners should not depend on their norm of output. A cash bonus, not the food ration, should be used as a productive incentive."[45] After 132 agonizing days, the strikers received a "radiogram from the headquarters of the NKVD, drawn up in these words: 'Inform the hunger strikers held in the Vorkuta mines that all their demands will be satisfied.'"[46]

This can only be considered a remarkable victory. Even more remarkably, it was not the first such victory. Solzhenitsyn reports that, before the Vorkuta strike, there was "a hundred-day strike somewhere in the Kolyma . . . : they demanded a free settlement instead of camps, and they *won*."[47] An anonymous survivor of Vorkuta mentions a 1934 hunger strike in the prison where he was before arriving at Vorkuta in which the strikers also won their principal demands.[48] Yet both of these victories were, again, pyrrhic. The strikers at Kolyma, writes Solzhenitsyn, were "scattered among various camps, where they were gradually annihilated."[49] Elinor Lipper, a German socialist who was a prisoner in the Kolyma system, has documented massacres of communists at this time in Kolyma. According to Lipper, in 1937 and 1938, "all who were still capable of independent thinking and independent decisions, all those who still knew what the word socialism meant, who still had some idealism, all those whose vision of freedom was not yet distorted, were to be robbed of their influence and liquidated."[50]

Lipper recalls that, in 1938, Stepan Nikolaivich Garanin visited the camps, "examining the list of counterrevolutionaries" and noting especially "those who were convicted of KRTD (counterrevolutionary Trotskyist activity)." Garanin had assumed control of the Kolyma camps in 1937 and presided over his own reign of terror. At night, he would have the prisoners "driven in a herd out of the gate" where they would be "shot en masse under his personal supervision." Many thousands of others, who escaped immediate execution, would be taken by truck to Serpantinka, which Lipper calls "one of the most ghastly institutions in the Soviet Union."[51] Its terrors were such that, even years later, survivors of this prison "were so gripped by the horror of it that they did not dare to tell their fellow prisoners of the inhumanity they had seen and experienced." According to

Lipper, "it was estimated that Garanin had the deaths of some twenty-six thousand persons on his conscience."[52]

At Vorkuta, the task of annihilating the Trotskyists fell to Kashketin. "He had been granted extraordinary powers," writes Vadim Rogovin, and he carried with him "order No. 00409. The significance of the order can be judged by the two zeroes, which were used only in cases when the order was undertaken on Stalin's personal initiative."[53] A special prison camp was established at an abandoned brickworks, about twenty kilometres south of Vorkuta. In the dead of winter, the surviving hunger strikers and all other hardline Trotskyists in the surrounding prison camp system were settled there in appalling conditions. Solzhenitsyn provides a chilling description:

> In the middle of the six-by-twenty-yard tent . . . stood one gasoline drum in place of a stove, for which one pail of coal per day was allotted, and in addition the zeks would throw their lice in to add a little to the heat. A thick layer of hoarfrost covered the inside of the canvas wall. There were not enough places on the bunks and the zeks took turns lying down and walking. They were given ten and a half ounces of bread a day and one bowl of gruel. Sometimes, though not every day, they were given a codfish. There was no water and they were given pieces of ice as part of the ration. It goes without saying, of course, that they were never able to wash themselves and that there was no bath. Patches of scurvy appeared on their bodies.[54]

These are the conditions in which the verbal newspaper *Truth Behind Bars*, described in the introductory chapter, was "published."

The intellectual life of the imprisoned Trotskyists is one of the most impressive aspects of their doomed struggle against Stalinism. Ante Ciliga was a leading Yugoslav communist who, with Victor Serge, was one of the last Oppositionists to escape from the Gulag just before the mass executions began. In 1933, he was imprisoned in the Verkhne-Uralsk isolator. "Isolator" was the shorthand for special political prisons, used from 1921 until 1937 as detention centres for political prisoners. Jacques Rossi says they were used for all the Bolsheviks' "former allies in the revolutionary struggle," who he describes as "the SRs, Mensheviks, anarchists and the like, followed by the members of their very own party."[55] The isolator at Verkne-Uralsk was one of the most notorious. In an account written in Paris in 1936 and 1937, Ciliga recalled encountering two prisoner-produced journals at Verkhne-Uralsk, each reflecting different political currents.[56]

> What a diversity of opinion there was, what freedom in every article! What passion and what candour, not only in the approach to theoretical and abstract questions, but even in matters of the greatest actuality. Was it still possible to reform the system by peaceful means, or was an armed rising, a new revolution required? Was Stalin a conscious or merely an unconscious traitor? Did his policy amount to reaction or to counter-revolution? Could he be eliminated by merely removing the directing personnel, or was a proper revolution necessary?[57]

The French-language version of Ciliga's book says these journals were titled *La verité en prison* and *Le Bolchevik militant* —rendered respectively in the English translation as *Pravda in Prison* (*Truth in Prison*) and *The Militant Bolshevik*. New issues were published every month or two, with each of the ten to twenty articles printed separately in booklet form. The booklets were then combined into a "packet," which "circulated from ward to ward." Ciliga recalls that "the papers appeared in three copies, one copy for each prison wing."[58]

Until very recently, it was believed that all trace of these underground prison publications had disappeared. However, in early 2018, while cell no. 312 was undergoing repairs at Verkne Uralsk, beneath the floorboards, a hidden cache was discovered, with 27 separate documents dating back to 1932 and 1933. They were in different states of preservation, some almost illegible.[59] One document—"The Fascist Coup in Germany" from *The Bolshevik-Leninist* No. 2 (12)—written in 1933 after Hitler's seizure of power in Germany, has been deciphered and republished—the unexpected return of a silenced voice from the distant past.[60]

Ciliga published a Russian-language article on a portion of his time at Verkne-Uralsk in the 1938 issue of *Sovremennyia zapiski* (Modern notes), a journal published by exiled Social-Revolutionaries living in Paris. In that article, we read that the name in Russian of *La verité en prison* ("truth in prison") was *Pravda za reshetkoi* (lit., "truth behind bars").[61] Some of the prisoners at the Brickworks were undoubtedly familiar with the printed *Pravda za reshetkoi* and adopted the same name for their oral "publication," *Truth Behind Bars*.

Although resistance was possible in the 1930s—including this kind of "literary resistance"—victories could only be temporary and, again, ultimately pyrrhic. For the vast majority of the imprisoned Trotskyists, their "convictions" were in fact death sentences. Under Kashketin's direction, the Vorkuta camps became the centre of extermination for the core of the Trotskyist opposition. At the end of March 1938, the first twenty-five prisoners were called up for transit. This "transit" was to the tundra, where they were shot and buried. According to Mikhail Baitalsky, "the first to be sentenced to death were all those who had taken part in the hunger strike."[62] Khoroshev gives a heart-rending description of "the executions in the tundra," both in his early 1960s article and in a longer, more detailed 1978 account. Every day or two, a few dozen prisoners were taken away, but "on one occasion about a hundred people were called out of their tents . . . Twenty-six people were taken from our tent alone." He goes on:

> Several people from our tent and other tents refused to come out. When the guards entered the tents and began to remove the desperately resisting people, outside, where the "convoy" was gathering, you could hear voices, at first scattered and discordant, but then increasingly stronger and stronger. They were singing the "Internationale". A minute later, almost simultaneously, the voices of our neighbouring tents joined in the chorus, and then, as if on command, our people joined in one mighty stream of menacing sounds. Huddled in the passage and standing on the upper bunks, they strained their voices as if their salvation depended upon it, singing furiously, menacingly and soulfully.[63]

The Brickworks's guards, Khoroshev says, were rewarded with six months of leave at full pay. "They were promised money and holiday documents in Ust-Usa. However, when they arrived in groups in Ust-Usa they were arrested and shot."[64]

"For thirty years now," writes Baitalsky in his brilliant memoir, "the memory of the Vorkuta executions has been like an open wound inside me. The sentence . . . was established in Moscow according to a list. How many there were on the list of victims remains a secret even now, buried in the archives. It was approximately 900—maybe more." This was Vorkuta's part in the complete destruction of the core of the Left from the Russian Revolution, and according to Baitalsky, the executions there "pale before those at Kolyma."[65] According to Berger, "the same system was followed in all three camps"—Vorkuta, Noril'sk, and Kolyma. Lipper's evidence from Kolyma, cited above, provides confirmation of that, at least for Kolyma. "By the end of 1937," writes Berger, "hardly a member of the Trotskyist cadres was left in the three camps."[66] Broué's account for Kolyma-Magadan is the most detailed for that camp. On 12 July, the Oppositionists in the camp launched a hunger strike that faced even more obstacles than the one in Vorkuta. Broué recounts that on 26 and 27 October and 4 November, a total of "87 hunger strikers . . . were condemned to death and executed." Broué says that this was not all—that there were, in fact, "many other executions."[67]

Shtrafnoi izoliator [penalty isolator or punishment cell] at the camp in Vorkuta, 1945. Russian Federation State Archive, Wikimedia Commons.

This extermination of the Trotskyists was the tip of the iceberg. By the end of the Great Terror in 1938, all the different sections of the party—from followers of Trotsky, to followers of Bukharin, to former loyal Stalinists— had been decimated by mass executions. According to Roy Medvedev, "the

NKVD arrested and killed, within two years, more Communists than had been lost in all the years of the underground struggle, the three revolutions, and the Civil War."[68]

Importantly, this was not the first round in the annihilation of the Left from 1917. I have already mentioned (and will document further below), the mass arrests and killings following the Kronstadt uprising of 1921, after which it was anathema to be considered an "anarchist." Through the course of the 1920s, thousands of members of the party with historically the most support in the countryside, the Social-Revolutionaries, were driven underground, into exile and forced labour, and the party itself was ultimately destroyed. In the same decade, thousands of members of the party with historically the most support among urban workers, the RSDRP-Menshevik, suffered the same fate.[69] Accompanying the destruction of the SRs was a disgraceful show trial in 1922, where to their shame, the Bolsheviks presided over staged mass demonstrations, demanding "death" for those on trial. Fortunately, one aspect of the 1930s show trials was not used. The accused were not tortured.[70] Nine years later, the fourteen defendants at the so-called "Menshevik Trial" were not so fortunate. One of these, Mikhail Iakubovich from the Commissariat of Domestic Commerce, survived into the 1970s. In 1969 and 1970, he published in the Samizdat underground his recollections of the trial and the methods used by the secret police to extract confessions. Vera Broido's summary of his report on the treatment of the defendants makes for difficult reading.

> They [the defendants] were beaten about the head and face and on the genitals, kicked to the ground and stamped upon with heavy boots; they were throttled. Or else they were kept standing, without sleep, for many days and nights, while they were interrogated by shifts of chekists (the so-called "conveyor belt"); they were put, half naked and barefoot, into icy punishment cells; they were threatened with execution.[71]

In spite of this horrendous treatment, only one actual Menshevik ended up among the fourteen defendants. The rest of the arrested Mensheviks—including Vera Broido's imprisoned mother, Eva Broido, then a woman in her early fifties—never appeared in the dock. In the words of Vera Broido: "Clearly only one of the real Mensheviks could be broken by torture."[72]

The full story of the 1920s repression of the non-Bolshevik Left requires its own full treatment at a later date. But in this book, the reality of what happened to the anarchists, the SRs, and the Mensheviks needs to be visible, at least to the extent of these few paragraphs.

"Who Will Prevail?"

Stalin's rise was opposed by many socialist workers and intellectuals, who found themselves grouped into various opposition categories, including followers of Leon Trotsky. The last acts of this opposition were the desperate hunger strikes in the far reaches of the Russian Arctic. The consolidation of Stalin's power involved the physical elimination of the core of his own party, including those who called themselves Old Bolsheviks—followers of Lenin from before 1917. Those who called themselves Trotskyists, or seen to be followers of Leon Trotsky, were killed almost to a person, many of them meeting their fate in the Brickworks at Vorkuta. In *The Time of Stalin*, Anton Antonov-Ovseyenko (whose father was a leading Bolshevik and a primary figure in the storming of the Winter Palace in 1917), describes the 1930s as a "historical epoch during which the vilest and bloodiest kind of evildoing flourished upon the earth."[73] Antonov-Ovseenko's *The Time of Stalin* uses a method similar to Solzhenitsyn's *Gulag*, organizing the story around oral testimony—a "wealth of personal testimonies . . . and oral accounts, by people who survived the Stalin era." However, unlike Solzhenitsyn's, Antonov-Ovseenko's circle included some very senior figures from that era.[74] One of these was Anastas Mikoyan—one of the few Old Bolsheviks to survive in Communist Party leadership from the revolutionary era into the postwar era, and the only member of the Politburo to support Khruschev at the Party's historic Twentieth Congress in 1956, when Khruschev began the process of exposing Stalin's crimes.[75] Drawing on oral accounts provided by Mikoyan, Antonov-Ovseyenko graphically illustrates the character of this counter-revolution. "The cells of the smaller prison at the Lubyanka were full to overflowing," he writes, going on to recount a dialogue among the prisoners lying on the floor. One of them, an Italian woman, described what was happening in Russia as a "fascist coup." She was executed in 1936.

That was the year the end came for Zinoviev and Kamenev too. Stalin was apparently afraid the death penalty might not actually be carried out against his two former allies. He sent Voroshilov to observe. This is what Voroshilov reported.

"They stood up in front of Stalin's executioner.

Zinoviev (shouting): This is a fascist coup!

Kamenev: Stop it, Grisha. Be quiet. Let's die with dignity.

Zinoviev: No. This is exactly what Mussolini did. He killed all his Socialist Party comrades when he seized power in Italy. Before my Death I must plainly state that what has happened in our country is a fascist coup!"[76]

If the events of 1917 to 1921 represented a partially successful attempt to install the rule of the working class, those of 1936 to 1938 represented the entirely successful attempt to consolidate the rule of the state bureaucrats grouped around Stalin. Trotsky struggled with the relationship between revolution and counter-revolution until his assassination by a Stalinist agent in 1940. To his death, he maintained that some remnants of workers' power remained in Russia. He argued that, although distorted by Stalinism, the Soviet Union remained a workers' state (if a degenerated one) because it remained in the control of the Communist Party. "If the party were excluded from the Soviet system, then the whole system would soon collapse," he wrote in 1930. "Freed from the control of the party, the trusts would immediately be converted into first, state capitalist, then, private capitalist enterprises."[77]

However, inside this party on which all depended, he said, "there are dispersed the elements of two parties."

From the official party there is emerging a party of the counter-revolution, whose elements exist at various stages of maturity. A symmetrical process is taking place at the opposite, at the proletarian pole of the party, above all, in the form of the Left Opposition. . . . The main question is: *who will prevail?* It will be *immediately* decided, not by the economic statistics of the socialist and capitalist economic tendencies, but by the relation of forces between the proletarian and Thermidorean flanks of the present so-called party.[78]

The events at Vorkuta, replicated in the even more remote camps of Noril'sk and Kolyma, made it absolutely clear who would prevail. The party of counter-revolution physically eliminated the Left Opposition—and every other organized leftist group then current in the Soviet Union. Following Trotsky's own logic, these hard facts would signify the final act in the destruction of any remnants of the attempt to construct a workers' state. Trotsky did not, and could not, know the scale of the destruction of the old Marxist cadres in the Soviet Union. Since most eyewitness reports of the extermination camps only reached the West in the 1950s, 1960s, and 1970s, an earlier generation, left with a paucity of information, had some illusions about what was transpiring in the Soviet Union. But we now know the extent of the destruction of the socialist, anti-Stalinist opposition. With this knowledge, it seems abundantly clear that the events of 1936 to 1938 completed the counter-revolution.

 **Striking Against the Gulag, 1947–53**

Scholars differ in their views of the origins of the Gulag system, of which Vorkuta was a part. According to one school of thought, the Gulag was a response to "the political imperatives of the Soviet regime's attempts to eliminate its perceived enemies . . . and not a response to the economic needs of industrialization."[1] Clearly, the elimination of the Trotskyists at Vorkuta fits this understanding. But can the Gulag's vast system of forced labour really be divorced from economics? The detailed research of Stanisław Swianiewicz tells a different story. This remarkable Polish author takes us into the complex geopolitics of the period between the two world wars of the twentieth century.

Swianiewicz, imprisoned by the Red Army after its invasion of Poland in 1939, was among the handful of Polish officers to survive what became known as the Katyn massacre of 1940. In September 1939, Stalin's armies invaded and occupied eastern Poland, the prize for their August signing of the Molotov–Ribbentrop Pact with Nazi Germany—usually referred to as the Hitler–Stalin Pact. In the process, the occupying Russian forces captured some 250,000 Polish soldiers, including 15,000 officers (army and police). The officers were interned in three "special camps"—Kozelsk (the camp in which Swianiewicz was held), Ostashkov, and Starobelsk.[2] On 5 March 1940, Stalin signed an order condemning to death more than 20,000 Polish prisoners, including all of the officer corps.[3] Among these thousands were "20 university professors; 300 physicians; several hundred lawyers, engineers, and teachers; and more than 100 writers and journalists."[4] Swianiewicz was one of just a few hundred to escaped execution and burial in a mass grave, the most notorious of which is in the Katyn forest.[5] By the end of the war, of the more than 20,000 put onto prison transports and taken to secret execution locations, he was one of the only, if not the only one, to survive.[6]

The Katyn massacre is intimately linked to the Polish–Soviet war of 1920 (to be examined in greater detail in chapter 6). As a young university student, Swianiewicz was part of a generation that volunteered for the armed forces to defend Polish independence in the post–World War I period. Many of the volunteers became noncommissioned officers— above the rank of private but below the established officer corps. These NCO-level patriotic intellectuals were an important counterbalance to the senior Polish officers, who Swianiewicz describes as having "come mostly from Imperial Austrian and Tsarist Russian Armies that had occupied Poland for more than 100 years." Although these senior officers were trained military professionals, their training was in the context of defending empire, not the Polish state. But when war with Russia broke out in 1920, it evolved into not a war for empire, but a war for Polish national survival. Unlike the senior officers, the mostly youthful NCO-level cadre were "imbued with the drive to build and defend an independent Polish state." As Swianiewicz observes, the success of the Polish army in halting the advance of the Red Army at the very gates of Warsaw was due "in a great degree to the psychological attitude that this 'corporal-academic' represented."[7]

Thousands of these "corporal-academics," patriotic volunteers who played a central role in successfully stopping Russian occupation of their country in 1920, were mobilized in 1939 as the war threat loomed. Many of them were among the thousands taken prisoner along with Swianiewicz. "In the forest of Katyn and in some other unknown place of torment," he writes, "there was the settling of scores by the Soviet Union with this 'corporal-academic.'"

> The Soviet *sledovatyels* [investigators] were very well informed about the fact that all the older first and second lieutenants of the reserve, who came to Kozelsk and Starobelsk, were the previous volunteers of 1920. I pondered over the fact that the high percentage of these volunteers might have had some influence on the fate of the Kozelsk camp.[8]

Swianiewicz was an accomplished scholar of economics. He was the author of several books including two in the Polish language published in the 1930s—*Lenin jako ekonomista* (Lenin as an economist) and *Polityka gospodarcza Niemiec hitlerowskich* (The economic policy of Hitler's Germany). In exile from 1942 on, he was appointed professor of economics at Saint Mary's University in Halifax in 1963, retiring ten years later as professor emeritus. In his view, however, his expertise in economics was not the main reason for the NKVD's interest in him. His life was spared because of his visits to Germany in 1936 and 1937: "Apparently, some high level echelons of the NKVD surmised that I possessed secrets of some of the behind the scenes political machinations."[9] After a year of interrogation, Swianiewicz was sentenced in 1940 to eight years of hard labour in the Gulag, and was released in August 1941, after Hitler's invasion of the Soviet Union, Stalin's move into an alliance with the Western powers, and the signing of a military pact with the Polish government in exile. After the war, he combined his expertise in economics with his first-hand experience with the Gulag to situate the Gulag system in the context of the economics of forced labour and the needs of industrialization, a path-breaking analysis on which this book relies heavily.

The Economics of Forced Labour

The key instrument directing political repression inside the Gulag system was the state security service, known by various names over the decades, among them the Cheka, OGPU, NKVD, and KGB.[10] According to Swianiewicz, "during the 1930's the NKVD became not only a security police with its own army . . . but also a huge industrial and constructional concern which organized production under its own administration." In addition, it played the role of a "contractor supplying labour force to enterprises." Central to these roles was the constant "search for new sources of manpower. The reign of terror which was a characteristic of the Stalinist period was to a certain extent a result of the atmosphere created by this extension of the NKVD's economic sector."[11]

> The profits from the camps covered a considerable amount of
> expenses connected with the increasing national expenditures,
> but most certainly, they covered almost completely the cost of

maintaining the huge NKVD apparatus, which in Stalin's time expanded to one of the largest, and one could even risk stating "the" largest enterprise in the world. It conducted huge construction projects, mostly in the far regions of the Soviet Union; it built railroads, roads, and canals; it exploited forests on the huge stretches between the Finnish border and the Pacific Ocean; it owned coal mines and farms, and it possessed its own research institutes in the same manner as great monopolistic industrial concerns. The aggregate amount of the work force, free and enslaved, employed in the NKVD enterprises during the period when I was there as a slave had to extend to more than 7 million people.[12]

This gigantic enterprise—centred in what Solzhenitsyn called his country's "sewage disposal system"—had an unending appetite for new labourers, the supply of which took the form of successive waves of mass repression and arrests. Solzhenitsyn identifies three such waves.[13] The first began as a small wave in the 1920s, but grew enormously in the years from 1928 to 1932 with the implementation of the first five-year plan—a wave that has been variously labelled as "liquidating the kulaks as a class," "dekulakization," the "great turning point," or, probably most accurately, the "war on the peasantry," the tragic consequences of which were touched on in the Introduction and to which we will return in chapter 5.[14] Solzhenitsyn reminds us that this first wave drove some fifteen million peasants "out into the taiga and the tundra," and that this massive displacement remained, for many decades, largely forgotten, not least because "peasants are a silent people, without a literary voice, nor do they write complaints or memoirs."[15] The second wave, the Great Terror of 1937–38, is somewhat better known, given that it "swept up and carried off to the Archipelago people of position," educated people, around whom were others who escaped incarceration and who, in Solzhenitsyn's time, were still "writing, speaking, remembering."[16] Then came the third wave, from 1944 to 1946, during which the Soviet regime "dumped whole *nations* down the sewer pipes," along with millions of individuals who had fought for Russia and become prisoners of war in Germany. This was the wave in which Solzhenitsyn was caught—a soldier who dared to make remarks critical of Stalin in letters to a friend.[17]

The harsh compulsion of economic necessity characterized the Russian Revolution from its inception. From 1921 to 1923, a horrific famine took place, centred on areas of what is today Ukraine. Roman Serbyn tells us that starvation and related epidemics claimed 1.5 million to 2 million lives.[18] Some food aid, in the form of grain shipments, arrived from the West to assist in feeding the starving millions. Nonetheless, in 1922, amidst much controversy, the Soviet government announced that it was resuming the export of grain to the West. While food was unloaded in the port of Odessa, coming in as aid to hungry Ukrainians, grain grown by Ukrainian peasants was simultaneously loaded to be shipped to Germany. Some rail workers who were ordered to transport grain out of the country went on strike. But the export went ahead, despite acts of sabotage against trains and elevators containing grain for export.[19] Roman Serbyn argues that this policy had economic roots. The five-year-old regime was seeking to industrialize, which required foreign exchange with which to purchase the technology and other inputs needed in modern industry. But because Western banks would not extend loans to the Soviet government, the only source of foreign exchange was trade, and one of the only commodities Russia could sell abroad for cash was wheat.[20]

In the 1930s, the decade in which the Gulag exploded in size, the catastrophe of forced collectivization so seriously damaged the agricultural sector that grain was no longer a candidate to be a commodity from which serious amounts of foreign currency could be acquired through external trade. Serbyn says that "timber was to a very great extent made to take the place of grain" and that to this end, "extensive exploitation of the forests became necessary in order to maintain a foreign balance. The forestry reserves were, however, mostly in the remote northern regions where there was no adequate supply of manpower." The first five-year plan projected a need for 900,000 workers in the forestry industry, but only about 50,000 became available through contracts with collective farms. Into the labour supply breach stepped the security services, leading to hundreds of thousands of prisoners engaged in forced labour in the "great timber industry run by what was then called the NKVD in the extreme north of European Russia."[21]

Another commodity was central to the Gulag: gold, the most precious commodity of all. Gold dug out of the ground at one of the most brutal camps, Kolyma, was "sold directly to the West, exchanged for desperately needed technology and machinery."[22] But it was a third commodity that dominated the lives of the prisoners in Vorkuta, an indispensable energy input for Soviet industrialization. The story of Vorkuta is the story of coal.

The Transition to Coal

The drive to industrialization accelerated in the 1930s, and with that acceleration came even greater compulsion. Industrialization depended on coal, which was extracted in large part from the forced labour camps in and around Vorkuta and which required thousands and thousands of coal miners—some forced and some "free." During World War II, after the loss of Ukraine and its vast coal supplies to the German invaders, the drive to extract coal from the mines in and around Vorkuta accelerated again.[23] By the early 1950s, the forced labour system, whether used for producing coal or some other product, with its millions of prison labourers, had become central to the Soviet economy. As Joseph Scholmer noted at that time: "Prisoners, who had been employed in the industrial ministries before their arrest, estimated that half of the entire coal production of the Soviet Union and eighty per cent of the wood supply is provided by forced labour."[24]

That this industrialization was based on forced labour was not atypical in the history of the world economy. As we saw in the introduction, Swianiewicz drew a direct parallel between forced collectivization in the Soviet Union and the enclosure movement in Great Britain. The Soviet forced labour system had similar historical parallels. Compulsion and unfree labour have often accompanied the early years of the development of a capitalist economy, particularly during the period of what Marx referred to as *ursprüngliche Akkumulation*—typically translated as "primitive accumulation" but which we should more accurately, and less offensively, translate as "primary" accumulation.[25] Robert Miles suggests that primary accumulation is "synonymous with the creation of a labour market and the commodification of labour power."[26] "Force or compulsion" writes Abigail Bakan, in a comment on Miles's analysis, "are employed as a precondition of moving from one mode of production to another, as it involves the physical separation of pre-capitalist laborers from the means of production and reproduction."[27]

Evgeny Preobrazhensky—a Soviet economist and Trotskyist who, in 1937, became a victim of Stalin's terror—tried to apply this notion of primary accumulation to the transition not only to capitalism but also to socialism. In 1926, he picked up a term originally coined by V.M. Smirnov—"primitive socialist accumulation" (or, as Preobrazhensky also called it, "preliminary socialist accumulation").[28] Preobrazhensky suggested that the concept should be understood as a necessary accompaniment to the development of a socialist economy. However, while related to capitalist primary accumulation, preliminary socialist accumulation could, in important ways, be distinguished from it, principally because the former is intimately connected with colonization. Preobrazhensky claimed that, with regard to "colonial plundering, a socialist state, carrying out a policy of equality between nationalities and voluntary entry by them into one kind or another of union of nations, repudiates on principle all the forcible methods of capital in this sphere. This source of primitive accumulation is closed to it from the very start and for ever."[29]

This claim rings hollow. In chapter 6, we will examine Russia's postrevolutionary approach to both Poland and Georgia, which is different in form but not in substance from the approach of capitalist great powers to states they wish to subordinate as part of their sphere of influence. Furthermore, if the economic essence of colonial primary accumulation was unequal exchange—the metropole extracting more surplus from its colonies than it returns to them—this is precisely the relationship that Preobrazhensky advocated in the relationship of what he called the "socialist" sector of the economy to the "petty," or presocialist, economy of the small peasants. In a nonindustrialized country such as Russia, *socialist accumulation* will *be obliged to rely on alienating part of the surplus product of pre-socialist forms of economy*—that is, from the peasantry.[30] From 1926 until early 1929, this idea was vociferously opposed by both Bukharin and Stalin. Suddenly, though, in the summer of 1929, Stalin did an about-face and adopted Preobrazhensky's approach almost without amendment.

Like Preobrazhensky, Stalin made the appropriate statement opposing colonialism. "In the capitalist countries industrialisation was usually effected, in the main, by robbing other countries, by robbing colonies or defeated countries," he argued, insisting that the Soviet Union "cannot and must not engage in colonial robbery, or the plundering of other countries."[31] What was the alternative to external colonialism? It was something that can only be called internal colonialism—the superexploitation of the Russian countryside by its cities. At first, this was to be enforced solely through a consciously distorted price and tax structure, to create what Preobrazhensky labelled "non-equivalent exchange" between the country and the city.[32] Stalin initially put this in bland economic terms: the peasantry, he said, "not only pays the state the usual taxes, direct and indirect; it also *overpays* in the relatively high prices for manufactured goods . . . and it is more or less *underpaid* in the prices for agricultural produce." In less bland terms, however, he characterized this as "in the nature of a 'tribute'"—and as we will outline in chapter 5, the extraction of this tribute went far beyond taxes and prices.[33] Stalin quickly moved to forcible seizure of grain stockpiles, pushing millions of peasants, at gunpoint, off their land and into collective farms. As with European colonialism, the extraction of a "tribute" cost the lives of millions. While in this "war on the kulaks," according to Alec Nove, "Stalin levied a tribute on the peasants on a scale greater than Preobrazhensky had ever conceived," it was in essence a policy completely consistent with Preobrahensky's theory.[34] And in fact Preobrazhensky, while upset at the pace of Stalin's forced collectivization, as were all in the Trotskyist opposition, did see such a link. Preobrazhensky's concept of "primitive socialist accumulation had been ruthlessly imposed by collectivization," writes Nove, and "industrialization was being made possible 'by exploiting the peasants, by concentrating the resources of the peasant economy in the hands of the state.'"[35]

It's all a bit esoteric. Without too much effort, we can demonstrate that the experience of Russia in the 1930s belongs in the category of industrialization and forced labour. But how can such horrific methods—which, as we have seen, cost millions of lives—result in something called socialism? Let's put aside the political rhetoric about "socialism" and examine the economics of forced labour in a bit more detail. There are two conditions in which many industrializing economies have resorted to compulsion and forced labour: when labour power is cheap and in plentiful supply, and when economically critical and labour-intensive tasks cannot be accomplished without coercion. Capitalism in the Americas, for instance, had an economically critical set of labour-intensive tasks to perform in its early years—the tasks involved in operating plantations to supply English textile mills with cotton and European dining room tables with sugar and coffee. However, the work on those plantations could not be performed by free labour, since, given a choice, the free labourers would, to a person, rather homestead on their own land (which was also in plentiful supply) than break their backs in the interests of international capital. But with a huge pool of cheap and available labour in Africa, that problem could be solved through a centuries-long forced labour system that was even more brutal, more exploitive, and longer-lasting than the forced labour system in Stalin's Gulag. In Russia, similar conditions laid the material foundations for the "high Stalinism" of the postwar period.[36] There was labour-intensive, economically necessary work throughout all of the Arctic, its treasure house of natural resources eagerly awaited by industry in the south. And there was a massive pool of millions of displaced peasants. Left to themselves, very few would have migrated to the far north to work and die in the coal and gold mines. But they were not left to themselves. Whole towns, whole nations, were interned in the vast camp system and forced to use their labour to accumulate wealth for Stalinist industrialization.

Vorkuta, in particular, became one of the most important areas to Soviet industrial development in the entire forced labour system. Joseph Scholmer described the situation in the early 1950s: "The coal from Vorkuta [that] supplies the whole of Leningrad and Leningrad is the heart of Soviet industry, with its factories making precision instruments, electrical equipment, optical lenses and engine parts."[37] In 1950, three of the coal mines in the Vorkuta complex won "first prize for coal production for the entire industry in the USSR," notes Edward Buca.[38]

The story of coal in Vorkuta—with forced labour as a unifying thread—links the area's first identity, as a place for the extermination of anti-Stalinist socialists, to its second, as one of Russia's largest coal producers. Barenberg narrates how the first seams of coal in the Vorkuta area were discovered by a young geologist, Georgii Aleksandrovich Chernov, during an expedition in the summer of 1930. A year later, Chernov returned with what he described as a group of thirty-nine "mining engineers of Ukhta," who began work on the first permanent settlement in the region. Chernov related this story in his memoirs, but, as Barenberg points out, he "failed to acknowledge the most important detail of the discovery of coal in Vorkuta. ... The thirty-nine 'mining engineers of Ukhta' who arrived in Vorkuta were in fact prisoners."[39] Once coal was discovered in the area, it was not long before the first mine began operating in 1934, although output remained limited until 1937, when electric power arrived.[40]

The centrality of forced labour to Vorkuta and coal is discernible even in usually dispassionate reports from academic congresses. Turn to the findings of the seventeenth session of the International Geological Congress, published in 1937. This dull, dry professional text, prepared under the direction of Mikhail Prigorovksy, carries the usual Stalinist verbiage about vast increases in production, breaking the limits imposed by the old tsarist system, and so on. It speaks of "the enormous growth of the socialist construction and exploitation of new regions," going on to list "the Tungus Basin, Lena field, Pechora and Bureya basins" as "prospective coal areas."[41] But the most significant sentence in the report is this: "Newly obtained data confirm the presence there of enormous . . . distributed coal reserves."[42]

This mention of "newly obtained data" was published in 1937, the year the mass killings of the Oppositionists began. Of the twenty-two specific locales on which the Prigorovsky volume reports, pride of place is given to the Pechora coal-bearing region in which Vorkuta is located, soon to become the killing ground of the Left Opposition. The Pechora district report is the first in the book, in spite of the fact that it is the district for which the authors have the least information, as its author (T. Ponomarev) admits: "The estimates of the reserves of the Pechora coals given in this article are but preliminary and most approximate ones, since most recent data concerning this question have not been received . . . in time for being included in the manuscripts prepared for print. For the same reason no figures of the actual and probable reserves of the region are given by us in this paper."[43]

Ponomarev's comment raises the question of where this "most recent data"—so recent that it could not be included—might have come from. As he notes, the presence of coal in the Pechora district was first "established by geological explorations carried on there in 1924–1930 by the Geological Service of the USSR. Nearly all the industrially important coal areas of the basin presently known to us have been detected in the result of these works."[44] This information clearly dovetails with Barenberg's account of

Chernov's discovery (with, however, no mention of the role of forced labour in this process). But again, 1930 does not qualify as "recent."

Ponomarev's report might seem like the end of the road—were it not for Maria Joffe's gripping account of her twenty-nine years in the Gulag. Central to her memoirs are the camps in the Vorkuta area, and the Brickworks several kilometres from Vorkuta where the mass executions took place. Joffe describes one of her fellow prisoners, a young geologist named Gleb Elizavetsky. Like Joffe, he was imprisoned for "Counter-revolutionary Trotskyist Activity" (KRTD). Elizavetsky was, in Joffe's words, a "non-party man."[45] But, like so many others, however, once painted with the KRTD brush, he had no hope of reprieve, and he would meet the same fate as if he had been an active member of the Left Opposition. Early in 1937, Elizavetsky announced to Joffe and others that "he had got a permit to go outside the zone to do geological research, outside working hours."[46] Describing his findings, he said: "There might be Devonian oil in one of the areas, but research would have to be carried out as to whether it's sufficient for industrial development. At the site of the precipice—there are slight traces of pelitsipods and this might mean coal." In a footnote, Joffe explains that pelitsipods (which should really be "pelecypods" in English translation) are "a kind of fossilised cockle-shell sometimes preceding coal seams."[47]

A doctor found Elizavetsky's report on coal lying in the camp warden's office. In an effort to save Elizavetsky's life, writes Joffe, "the doctor got the paper registered, packed up, sealed and speedily despatched with the rest of the mail." Joffe says that the "doctor had every confidence in the life-saving qualities of those 'pelitsipods.' Moscow was urging haste in the search for oil and coal." The discovery did not save Elizavetsky's life. In spite of his important findings, he was sent off to the death camps.[48]

If the coal of Vorkuta did not prove life-saving for Elizavetsky, it did prove to be life-sustaining for the people and factories of Petrograd. His early 1937 report on his findings could well be the "most recent data" to which Ponomarev refers, however we might never know with certainty. Perhaps buried somewhere in the old NKVD records are documents to prove that this "Trotskyist" geologist was in fact the person who discovered evidence of important new coal deposits in the Pechora coal basin, a basin that includes Vorkuta. Whatever the truth, Elizavetsky's story is emblematic of the overlap between Vorkuta's main role in the 1930s, as a death camp for Stalin's enemies, and its emergent role as a forced labour camp in the subsequent decades, a production centre of coal to feed Russian industrialization.

The Transition from Forced Labour

Industrialization in the USSR was conducted in the context of incredible repression against the Left, against the labour force inside industry, and against national minorities inside the Russian empire. All three of these "constituencies" found ways to organize against their jailers. That organization transformed into mass resistance when the various divisions inside the camps were bridged. And once again, this mass resistance, culminating in the great mineworkers' strike of 1953, made Vorkuta the focal point of a wave of anti-Stalinism, the second such wave since the triumph of Stalin in the 1920s.

Monument to the Estonians who died in Vorkuta in 1953, erected by former prisoners in 1956. Photograph by Oleg–2014, 6 April 2009, Wikimedia Commons.

The least studied of these three components of the anti-Stalinist resistance is the Left inside Russia itself. The contradiction between the words of the regime's rulers and the realities of life in a Stalinist society provided ideological conditions that nourished the re-creation of oppositional currents almost as soon as the old Opposition had been liquidated. German journalist Brigitte Gerland was arrested in Dresden in 1946 for reporting on conditions under Soviet occupation; after fifteen months in a German prison, she was transferred to Vorkuta.[49] Upon her release in 1953, she described a "program of resistance" developed by "small secret circles, meeting at night behind locked doors" inside the Soviet labour camps. One such movement "is said to have started from a discussion between five Moscow students on the long-banned poetry of Boris Pasternak." These students envisaged "a way of making room for spiritual freedom in a collectivist society by decentralization of state power, until the state could finally be replaced altogether by the workers and peasants 'syndicates.'" According to Gerland, this initial core of five "recruited hundreds of followers" until the group was infiltrated by police spies, arrested en masse in 1950, and sent to the labour camps.[50]

Elsewhere, Gerland tells a similar story with a more explicitly political focus. In 1948, a manifesto written by a dozen students began circulating in Moscow.[51] The students called their group *Istinny trud Lenina* (Lenin's True Work), and such a name needs to be taken with a grain of salt. It is certainly not a coincidence that its initials—ITL—are identical to those for Corrective Labour Camp (in Russian, *Ispravitel'no-trudovoi lager'*), the Stalinist euphemism for the *forced* labour camps that comprised the core of the Gulag. P.M. Tashtemkhanova is not alone in believing that in choosing precisely this name for their clandestine organization, "it was the Corrective Labour Camps (ITL) which were being referred to allegorically and sarcastically by the young interlocutors of B. Gerland."[52] It is probable that Gerland, in describing these students as "Leninist," is leaning too much on the literal meaning of ITL and paying too little heed to the deep sarcasm the choice of name expressed. Nonetheless, following Gerland, we can see a considerable amount in the analysis of the ITL that is reminiscent of the old Left Opposition—in spite of that Opposition's physical liquidation. The ITL argued that a political revolution was necessary against a bureaucracy that was strangling the original ideals of the 1917 revolution and that the foundation of a rebirth of real socialism would be a regeneration of work-ers' councils (soviets).[53] In this sense, they could be seen as reviving the classic framework developed by Leon Trotsky. Other oppositionists had revived the framework of the Group of Democratic Centralism, or Decists, who, in the 1920s, had called the USSR a "system of 'state capitalism'" that had "destroyed workers' democracy."[54] Echoing this analysis, some of the young members of the ITL referred to Russia as "state capitalist," argu-ing that no vestiges of the old revolution remained. Their manifesto was circulated underground, allowing the group to grow to an organization of several hundred, with links to universities in Leningrad, Kyiv (Kiev in Russian), and Odessa.[55]

In 1949, the group was broken by the Russian authorities. Accord-ing to Gerland, "in a single night, entirely unexpectedly, hundreds of its members were arrested and condemned to twenty-five-year terms at hard labor."[56] Scattered throughout the Gulag, these ITL students reconstituted an opposition, along with anarchist students and other oppositional cur-rents they encountered in the camps. Gerland was impressed by these student oppositionists: "Outstanding among them were the children of the generation of '37; their parents, once leading figures in party, army and government, had fallen victims to Stalin's great purge."[57] It was these ITL students, she says, who saw that the key to resistance lay in the collective action of workers:

> The idea of a mass strike of forced laborers was popularized in the
> camp by the Leninist students. . . . The Leninists knew that only a
> strike which embraced at least an entire forced-labor area that was
> important economically, such as Vorkuta, stood any chance of suc-
> cess. And so they undertook, systematically and patiently, to forge
> contacts between all the camps in the city of Vorkuta as well as in
> the Vorkuta district itself.[58]

For a strike to succeed, the divisions between the prisoners, which had been cultivated by the authorities, had to be overcome. There were two types of divisions that were the most intense—first, among the "criminal" population, between collaborators (*suki*) and irreconcilables (*blatnoy*), and second, among the entire prison population, between the Russians and the non-Russians.[59] Before the oppositional students arrived in the camps, however, the first remarkable steps at overcoming these divisions had already taken place.

Forty kilometres east of Vorkuta, four small prison camps, with about five thousand prisoners in total, contained the toughest of the "criminal" elements among the prison population. Added to these was a group of former Red Army officers, including three named Mikhtyiev, Nasarov, and Malmyga. In 1947, these three were at the centre of a conspiracy that resembled nothing if not the great Spartacus slave revolt in 71 BC inside the Roman Empire. They determined to kill their guards, seize their weapons, form an army from the prisoners in their camps, and march on the main camp system in Vorkuta proper. Once Vorkuta was conquered, "with an army of hundreds of thousands of prisoners, with food and weapons from the camp stores, they planned to march down the railway to the west. Their goal was nothing less than raising an army of the oppressed—prisoners, workers, peasants—to overthrow the system and the great leader [Stalin] himself."[60] Faced with the possibility of resistance, the *suki* stopped collaborating with the prison authorities and threw in their lot with the *blatnoy*. This was "the first time the *suki* and the *blatnoy* stopped fighting each other and allied themselves against the guards."[61]

The plan, of course, failed, but not before the rebels had killed all the guards in the four camps, formed an army of several thousand, and begun a march across the tundra to Vorkuta itself. There, the odds were stacked against them. Warned in advance, the Vorkuta authorities had airplanes and machine guns with which to greet the *zek* army, and they massacred these latter-day Spartacans by the hundreds. Few survived, but their example was to be key to the next round of struggle.

The surviving rebel *blatnoy* were imprisoned in one of the worst of Vorkuta's forced labour camps. There, one by one, they were ordered to perform tasks that would violate their code of solidarity. They each steadfastly refused, and, one by one, they were shot. Imprisoned in the same camp were a group of other "irreconcilables," who were there as punishment for being uncooperative and who bore witness to these events. One of them was Edward Buca, who later described the rebel *blatnoy* and their impact:

> Their solidarity was total. All to a man obeyed the *blatnoy* code,
> and refused to do anything connected with the oppression of other

prisoners. Their behaviour was an example to the rest of us. Naturally, only a few of us knew the details of what had taken place in the little zone [the four small prison camps east of Vorkuta], but most of us had an inkling—and this was enough. The seeds of revolt had been sown. More and more *suki* in the camp stopped persecuting the other prisoners, and eventually the *blatnoy* called a halt to their struggle against the *suki*.[62]

Six years later, Buca would be a key leader in the strikes that brought the forced labour system to its knees.

This was not the first such Spartacus-like rebellion, but it is the best documented. In his memoir *The Notebooks of Sologdin*, Dimitri Panin—on whom Solzhenitsyn based the character Sologdin in his epic novel about the camps, *The First Circle*—relates his eyewitness account of a similar revolt in 1942. A small camp in the Pechora district, south and west of Vorkuta and near Ust-Usa, was headed by a disgruntled "commandant" whose staff responsible for the work details were all former prisoners sentenced under Article 58. The commandant and these former Article 58 prisoners lured the camp's armed security guards into the bathhouse, stole their clothes and weapons, freed and armed the rest of the prisoners, and began marching on the central headquarters for the Pechora district, located in Ust-Usa. They liberated several camps on the way and amassed a small army. After weeks of fighting, the Soviet authorities finally suppressed this uprising. The insurgents were killed virtually to the last man. The handful of survivors committed suicide.[63]

In 1948, a group of war veterans (some perhaps belonging to or inspired by the underground veterans' organization, Democratic Movement of the North of Russia) seized their guards' weapons and tried to take a town in the Noril'sk labour-camp region, east of the Urals. "The effort failed," writes George Saunders, "and they fled toward the mountains—reportedly over 2,000 strong—but were annihilated by the Kremlin's airpower. A similar revolt apparently occurred in the eastern Siberian region of Kolyma."[64]

Through these uprisings—even though most ended in failure and death—the evidence was accumulating "that it was possible to wage an open struggle against the tyranny practiced in Stalin's camps."[65] The 1947 uprising, in particular, showed that the divisions between *suki* and *blatnoy* could be overcome if resistance against their common enemy, the prison authorities, was seen as possible. It also showed that the *blatnoy* were more than just hardened criminals—they could constitute themselves as a fighting force.

Significantly, resistance methods soon began to shift from the tactics of Spartacus to the tactics of the modern workers' movement. In 1949, the ITL students, in alliance with the *blatnoy*, attempted to organize a strike in one of Vorkuta's most important coal pits, but their efforts met little response from the miners.[66] In 1951, in the hard labour camp near Ekibas-tuz in the southwest of the USSR, a five-day work stoppage and hunger strike of three thousand prisoners ended in a victory.[67] These were the first rumblings of a storm that was to explode two years later.

Although collective rebellion could demonstrate the possibility of unity between *blatnoy* and *suki* (and the politicals), another equally profound division confronted these activists in the preparation of strike activity: the national divisions between Russians and non-Russians inside the camp. Edward Buca describes the situation well:

> One result of our desperate condition was increased hatred and strife between the different nationalities, with each group trying to blame another for our plight. The basic conflict was between Russians and Ukrainians. The Russians regarded the Ukrainian nationalists and separatists as the *real* guilty men. . . . enemies of the Soviet fatherland, aliens who didn't deserve to be fed; they should be worked until they dropped dead, and left to rot in the tundra. The Russian prisoners had picked up these ideas from the NKVD officers and guards. When the NKVD noticed this, they gladly encouraged it in order to keep the prisoners divided among themselves.[68]

These divisions resulted in a highly complex and conflictual situation. On the one hand was Russian chauvinism, a hatred of the Russian prisoners for the non-Russians, cultivated by the NKVD and captured perfectly by Buca. On the other was bitter anti-communism, particularly of the Ukrainian prisoners, whose experience of national oppression at the hands of the Stalinists made them hate all things Russian and all things communist, and who looked to the Western democracies for salvation. Among many of the non-Russians, this faith in the West made them distrustful of any camp conspiracies. Waiting on Stalin's death, which they were convinced would lead to war with the West and liberation from Stalinism, their main objective was to stay alive and stay out of trouble.

Activists within the largely Russian Left and among the non-Russian national minorities worked hard to break down these divisions. For the Left, it meant including demands for "national minority rights" in their political slogans. As Gerland reported, the ITL students "categorically condemned the Stalinist policy of nationalistic expansion" as well as "all the annexations by the Soviet Union perpetrated after the war, because these annexations run counter to the principle of national self-determination so passionately defended by Lenin."[69]

More concretely, activists organizing among the national minorities ensured that representatives from all of "the nations of Vorkuta" were on their underground committees. When the young Pole Edward Buca asked an old Ukrainian prisoner for advice on how to organize, he was told: "Before you act, you must do everything possible to organize all nationalities." Accordingly, in the initial work of pulling together clandestine groups, Buca recalled, "it was arranged that each national group would have its own leader; these latter would together select the supreme commanders."[70]

But it took outside events to force the pace and make mass resistance a possibility. The catalyst was the death of Joseph Stalin in March 1953, which had four important impacts. First, it raised expectations massively. "I'll always remember that morning," recalled Buca, a Polish national. "We were on our way to the mine when the announcement came over the loudspeaker. . . . We stopped in our tracks . . . Some prisoners were weeping, everyone was moved. This was like a great earthquake which could affect even our lives. It was certain that one era in history was over and who could know what the next would be like?"[71] Joseph Scholmer also remembered that moment:

When the actual announcement of his death came, bearded *moujiks* [peasants] with tears in their eyes went down on their knees and prayed. "I've been in this camp nineteen years now," said one of the Georgians. "But this is the best news I've ever heard." "God has saved the Jews," a Polish Zionist whispered to me. . . . "If he hadn't died, there would have been pogroms again as bad as anything at the time of the Black Hundred, or Petljura, or Hitler."[72]

Second, the death of Stalin temporarily paralyzed the camp authorities, who were unsure which faction in the Kremlin would gain control. This became even more pronounced after the fall of Lavrenti Beria, the long-time head of the Soviet secret police and, until overthrown in a palace coup in June 1953 and eventually executed, the presumed heir to Stalin's power.[73] An authoritarian regime needs iron discipline from top to bottom. When a split opens up at the top, when it is unclear who the final authority is, the entire system can become temporarily paralyzed. In the context of such paralysis and confusion, mass action that seemed unthinkable just days before can suddenly be on the agenda.

Third, among the non-Russian national minorities, Stalin's death set in motion a chain of events that led to massive disillusionment with the Western democracies. Scholmer recalled that "Churchill's statement that the new men in the Kremlin had to be given a chance to show their good-will and work out their policy in peace . . . caused the most profound dismay in the camps."[74] The national minorities had been reluctant to support resistance activities, banking everything on Western intervention. With the West having indicated its willingness to coexist with a post-Stalin Russia, thousands who had remained aloof from all talk of conspiracy and strike were now ready for action.

Fourth, and most importantly, the post-Stalin paralysis in the Soviet bureaucracy made possible the rise of a new workers' movement in Eastern Europe, culminating in the massive East Berlin workers' uprising, whose example electrified the millions of forced labourers in Russia's Arctic. Anne Applebaum describes the discontent building in the last years of Stalin's life, discontent that was not confined to East Germany. "The Soviet ambassador to Prague had written of 'near-total chaos' in Czech industry in December 1952," notes Applebaum. This chaos existed throughout Eastern Europe and expressed itself as mass marches in Czechoslovakia, strikes by tobacco workers in Bulgaria, and, perhaps most significantly, a huge population movement from East to West Germany. "More than 160,000 people had moved from East to West Germany in 1952, and a further 120,000 had left in the first four months of 1953."[75] Beria himself had a clear eye as to the reasons for this chaos, citing, among other causes, "the unwillingness of individual groups of peasants to join the agricultural production cooperatives" and "the severe difficulties that the

GDR [German Democratic Republic, official name of East Germany] is experiencing with the supply of food products and consumer goods."[76]

This crisis situation came to a head on 16 June 1953, when East Berlin "witnessed its first major mass strikes since the war," and the next day, when thousands of construction workers marched through the city carrying banners saying "Berliners, join us! We don't want to be slaves to our work!"[77] The movement became massive and, before it was put down by the brute force of Russian tanks, spread throughout the country. Applebaum describes the size of the uprising: "Demonstrations took place in all of the major cities and industrial centres . . . especially those with a strong communist or social democratic tradition: Rostock, Cottbus, Magdeburg, Dresden, Leipzig, Erfurt, and Halle. In total, about 500,000 people in 373 towns and cities went on strike in about 600 enterprises. Between a million and 1.5 million people took part in demonstrations of some kind."[78]

This magnificent upsurge in resistance to Stalinism galvanized the forced labourers in Vorkuta. As Scholmer recalled: "Although official news of the rising in Berlin and the Eastern Zone on June 17 only appeared late and in a garbled form in the camps, it wasn't difficult to form an objective picture of what had happened. . . . Even the ordinary prisoner felt instinctively that what had happened in Berlin and the Eastern Zone was a revolt against the police system which had arrested, sentenced and enslaved himself."[79] Strike committees soon formed in various sections of the camp. According to Gerland, even members of the non-Russian minorities, who had until then sought to avoid activism, began to join these committees.[80] She goes on to report that, on 21 July 1953, six thousand forced labourers at mine Pits no. 1 and no. 7, where ITL students and anarchists were particularly influential on the strike committees, refused to go to work. Feverishly working to spread the strike, prisoners "requisitioned all the available stocks of paper" and produced thousands of leaflets, which read:

> Fellow prisoners, you have nothing to lose but your chains!
> Don't expect to gain your freedom through anyone's efforts but your own. No one will help you; no one will save you; only you yourselves can change your lot.
> Down tools! The strike is our only weapon![81]

Scholmer, imprisoned in Camp 6, which he describes as "one of the relatively quiet camps," estimates that more than ten thousand workers eventually took part in the strike—although, even according to an official estimate, this figure is too low by half.[82] Gerland, whose information comes from Pits 1 and 7, where the key organizing took place, says that, by 23 July, some thirty thousand labourers were on strike, halting operations at ten of the mines. The strike continued to spread, and "within ten days, twenty big pits inside the city and its environs were shut down tight."[83]

Whatever the exact numbers, given the conditions, what the strike committees accomplished was remarkable. Even though the authorities had surrounded the striking sections of the camp with troops, thus effectively isolating them from one another, news spread like wildfire. "This was accomplished in the main," Gerland writes, "thanks to the aid of soldiers who sympathized with the strikers and therefore incurred the risk of maintaining the contacts which had been broken by the work stoppage."[84] As well as keeping lines of communication open, the strike committees had to ensure the day-to-day survival of the strikers. To this end, the committees assumed control over entire sections of the camps, putting the strikers in charge of routine operations. It was, in effect, a kind of workers' control.

Edward Buca, who was at one of the more isolated camps, oversaw a strike committee that arranged for maintaining the abandoned mine shafts so that gas would not build up and explode.[85] The strikers also provided staff for the bakery, "which made bread for both guards and prisoners," maintained a functioning hospital for the many sick and disabled camp inmates, and even ran a laundry, again for both the inmates and the guards.[86] Not only did this self-organization build the confidence of the strikers themselves, it also helped them gain the sympathy of the soldiers who surrounded the camp. Buca reports that, when the first batch of guards' laundry had been washed, "it was hung out in the sun to dry, and the guards, most of them simple peasant boys, were impressed. 'We'll never fire on you,' several of them said."[87]

But the strikers were vulnerable, especially if the prison authorities could find loyal troops.[88] By the end of July, such troops were in place, and the striking sections of the camp were surrounded. The relatively isolated camp, under the control of Edward Buca's multinational strike committee, was chosen to serve as an example to the rest. That example would take place "the first day of August, 1953," when the striking prisoners were given an ultimatum: surrender within the next forty minutes or face the consequences.[89] Buca describes what happened next:

> I asked those around me what they wanted to do. These were my closest collaborators, and their decision was unanimous: they would not leave the camp, even if it meant death.
>
> Then I went from group to group, asking for their decisions. It was the same everywhere: death rather than surrender.[90]

The prisoners massed at the camp gates, linking arms, to confront the troops. They were first attacked by a fire engine, "but before the hoses could be unwound," a wall of prisoners advanced, "turning the vehicle out of the gate as if it had been a toy."[91] Then the massacre began. Roman Rudenko, chief prosecutor of the Soviet Union, who had arrived to oversee negotiations with the strikers, pulled out a pistol and shot Ihnatowicz, one of the key strike leaders. "It must have been a signal," writes Buca:

> There was a salvo of shots from the guards, straight into the mass of prisoners. But we were standing with our arms linked, and at first no one fell, though many were dead and wounded.
>
> Only Ihnatowicz, a little in front of the line, was standing alone. He seemed to stand for a moment in astonishment, then turned round to face us. His lips moved, but no words came out. He stretched out an arm, then fell.
>
> As he fell, there came a second salvo, then a third, and a fourth. Then the heavy machine-guns opened fire. . . . Then the firing stopped. There was silence. After waiting a few moments, I gave orders to stand up. Hundreds lay dead. I gave orders to take the wounded to hospital as quickly as possible. Some refused to go and turned back with some notion of trying to stop the guards from entering the camp. Some tore off their ragged shirts and yelled at the guards, "Shoot, you red devils! Shoot!"
>
> But there were no more shots.[92]

We will never know how many died. Buca's friend Greczanik, who had been on the front line, said it was "hard to tell," but he thought there must have been "at least four hundred killed."[93] Scholmer quotes the surgeon

Blagodatov, who, after the massacre, was ordered to the camp and found about two hundred seriously wounded prisoners, "most of them hit in the chest and stomach. . . . Sixty-four prisoners had been killed on the spot." Many of the wounded died. "We operated for a whole week," said the surgeon. "We did what we could, but they were dying from their wounds all the time."[94]

This did not signal an immediate end to the strike. Even though news of the massacre at Buca's camp spread throughout the Vorkuta complex, other strikers held out for a while longer. Moscow made some concessions: allowing letters to be written home twice a month instead of twice a year, allowing yearly visits from family members, eliminating the hated identification numbers, and removing the iron bars from barracks windows. The strikers rejected these concessions out of hand as inadequate. Moscow responded with promises of better food, higher pay, and shorter work shifts. Still, the strikers held firm. General Derev'ianko, who had been one of those responsible for the massacre at Buca's camp, then "resorted to a ruse" in Gerland's words: "Members of the strike committee and of the central strike leadership were politely invited to an interview at the headquarters, an invitation they naturally accepted. They were cordially met at the camp gate by orderlies, who accompanied them to the city; but not a single one of them returned from this talk."[95]

Finally, strikers at Camp 7 were presented with an ultimatum to "march out and form up in the tundra or else the camp would be taken by storm."[96] The strike leaders decided to march into the tundra as ordered to avoid a massacre. Once there, the authorities arrested strikers who were in any way suspected of being among the leaders of the strike, four to five hundred in total. "This action in fact eliminated the entire strike committee though they were not known individually," writes Scholmer. "All the active elements in the camp were now missing. The masses were leaderless. The morale of the strikers had been broken. Work began in the pit again next day."[97] Some pits held out to November, for more than three months, but, as Gerland tells us, "they finally returned to work only because the supply of food and, what is even more vital in polar regions, the supplies of coal gave out."[98]

While it is the one for which we have the best eyewitness accounts, the strike in Vorkuta was not the only one that year—some of them preceding the dramatic events in East Berlin. Danylo Shumuk was a prison-labourer in the Noril'sk area camps, sent there along with thousands of others to exploit the copper and other non-ferrous metals in the surrounding hills. The conditions were brutal. In the summer of 1947 during a clandestine meeting of prisoners, in the first stages of organizing the "self-help group" referred to in the Preface, he reported to those assembled that "close to fourteen thousand prisoners sentenced to hard labour were brought to this camp. After only three years approximately eight thousand remain, many of whom have been partly or completely crippled; the other six thousand, broken by the cold, hunger, harsh work and constant brutality, are no longer with us."[99] In 1953, out of these appalling conditions, a strike movement broke out, parallel to that in the Vorkuta camps. According to Shumuk, "by the second half of May close to twenty thousand political prisoners were on strike in the Noril'sk area."[100]

At the core of Shumuk's account of the strike at his camp—the last to be engulfed by the strike wave—is a story of self-organization that parallels Buca's. The clandestine "self-help" group formed in 1947, by the end of 1949, had grown to include approximately "fifty of the most capable Ukrainians in the camp."[101] It saw its role as building the morale of the prisoners, and finding ways to push back against violence and excesses from the camp administration. It won considerable influence throughout the camp as a result.

The strike in Shumuk's camp began on 4 June 1953. Three days earlier, twenty political prisoners had been transferred to the camp, including Ivan Vorobev, "who had gained a legendary reputation because of his many escapes from the camps."[102] On 4 June, when it became clear that these new prisoners, Vorobev included, were being beaten mercilessly, a rebellion to save their lives began among the rest of the inmates. "The fourth of June 1953 was a memorable day" says Shumuk. "All the prisoners had left the barracks and were now in the street, waiting to see what would happen next."[103] What did happen was a remarkable two-month long strike.

Robert Conquest says that the prisoners "struck for comparatively mild demands—contact with their families, letters and parcels, regularisation of the ration system and so on."[104] While formally true, there was actually much more involved. Like the events in Vorkuta, it was an uprising of the very oppressed against absolutely appalling conditions. As in Vorkuta, the events ended with a massacre. "Many attempts were made to trick" the strikers, writes Conquest, "but the strike was eventually put down by force, with over 1,000 dead. Executions of 'ringleaders' followed on a mass scale. The rebellion's rank and file were sent for special punishment to Kolyma." About a month later, these prisoners "were sent on to the notorious mines of Kholodnaya. An old inmate describes them marching to their trucks, shouting boasts and sneering at the meeker prisoners who had preceded them and some of them even singing Ukrainian nationalist songs."[105]

We can draw several conclusions from these remarkable events in 1953. By using the strike—the classic tactic of the international workers' movement—the Vorkuta workers indicated that they were a new force to be reckoned with. In the 1930s, the Vorkuta inmates had only moral power on their side. The heroic hunger strikes of the anti-Stalinist socialists had no hope of winning. They were a magnificent statement of a dying generation. By the 1950s, however, the forced labour inmates of Vorkuta had, in additional to moral power, economic power. Two students who had been in Leningrad during the Vorkuta strikes ended up in the Vorkuta pits two months after the strikes ended. "We soon got to know you were on strike," they told Scholmer and other labourers in the camp. "The drop in coal was noticeable at once. We don't have any reserves."[106] The moral power of the 1930s had been reinforced with economic power in the 1950s.

Without question, this flexing of newfound economic muscle hastened the demise of the forced labour system in the Soviet Union. "New strikes kept breaking out through 1954 and 1955," writes George Saunders, "until finally a general amnesty of political prisoners was granted and the camp system partly dismantled."[107] That the strikes could have such great impact was possible because of the changes that had taken place in the Russian economy over a generation. By the 1950s, the conditions that made forced labour economically "rational" for the Russian economy were disappearing. Once the mines had been opened, the canals dug, the dams built, and the roads cut through the tundra, a transition away from forced labour and toward waged labour was clearly on the agenda. Forced labour was less suited to the next stage of industrial development than it had been to the stage of "primary accumulation."[108] A higher technical level required higher skill levels on the part of the working masses and hence greater use of labour by consent rather than by coercion. Importantly, the pool of cheap labour represented by the millions of peasants displaced by war and civil wars was, by and large, used up—millions having been driven off the land either to the cities in search of work or to the Gulag. As such rural reserves disappear, the conditions for systems of formal coerced labour become more constrained.

Certainly, this is a long and difficult process. And certainly, "free wage labour" has elements—sometimes profound elements—of coercion. However, it matters a great deal whether labour is formally coerced (as in the Gulag system) or informally coerced (through wage levels, benefits, and levels of unionization). In the former situation, organizing is difficult in the extreme. In the latter, the difficulties are real but of an entirely different order. The next chapter, in examining the struggles of the emergent "free" wage labouring class in Vorkuta and elsewhere, will reveal this clearly.

So, the events of 1953 represented an economic transformation. Most importantly, however, those events represented the transformation of the mass of forced labourers into a collectivity of proletarians. The proletariat is, in part, formed objectively by capitalism. But it emerges as a class when it subjectively begins defining itself as a class that can act in its own interests. That began to happen in Vorkuta in 1953.

In Scholmer's words, "the most important thing about the strike was that it ever took place at all."[109] Buca later reflected on his feelings at the end of the fourth day of the strike:

> I sat outside one of the huts—out of sight of the guards—and talked and joked with the prisoners, and thought about the changes that had taken place inside the camp during those four days: we had become human beings again.
>
> Anyone who saw those prisoners, from those in the hospital who had no hope of surviving to those who were exhausted from their brutal work, could never doubt that the attempt we had made had been worth while [sic], however it might turn out. I didn't know what was going to happen, but, despite my fears, I was happy.[110]

Shumuk documents the remarkable self-activity that was the foundation on which this kind of new confidence was built. Critical to the conduct of the two-month-long strike in his camp were the regular general meetings pulling together hundreds of striking prisoners.

The general meetings were held in the club, which could accommodate approximately 700 people. Whenever we had to persuade the [strike] committee to follow our lead, our "invisible" self-help organization summoned its supporters to the club where they occupied, according to a prearranged plan, all the available places. As the meeting went through the agenda, and especially when controversial matters were being discussed, our supporters in the audience would speak. There were usually five to seven such speeches, and after each one, all those present would clap and shout their approval.[111]

The self-organization and resulting solidaristic consciousness so clearly visible in the Vorkuta and Noril'sk strikes of 1953 marked the end of one era and the beginning of the next. They marked the end of the era when industrialization could be, and was, conducted on the backs of millions of *zeks*. They marked the beginning of an era when industrialization would increasingly have to rely on wage labour, as it did in the West. And the strikes also served notice that these wage labourers would make an effort to put their imprint on the future of this vast industrial economy. It is to this era that we now turn in order to examine the third and last wave of anti-Stalinist struggle, in which Vorkuta once again played a central role. The making of a new working class, begun by hunger strikes of the Trotskyists in the 1930s, continued with the prison camp strikes of the *zeks* in the 1950s. Although participants in both movements paid a huge price in the short term—mass executions in the 1930s, systematic slaughter of frontline militants in the 1950s—both movements formed indispensable components of the new class-in-the-making that emerged from the rubble of counter-revolution.

3 The Vengeance of History, 1989–91

If the events of 1953 were precipitated by a paralysis at the top of society that set in after the death of Stalin, the events of 1989 were precipitated by a deeper and more thoroughgoing paralysis—a political crisis, signalled by the state's embrace of policies of *glasnost* and *perestroika*, rooted in a profound and prolonged economic crisis. The latter had first manifested itself in a period of sluggish economic growth during the 1970s, followed by half a decade of stagnation, from 1980 to 1985, and then by outright economic decline. *Glasnost* (openness) and *perestroika* (restructuring) were the responses to the economic crisis from the Soviet government of Mikhail Gorbachev. But thousands within the very conservative *nomenklatura*, or bureaucracy, were very resistant to the changes that implementing these policies would have demanded. As in 1953, the resulting paralysis at the top created political openings at the bottom, and the mid to late 1980s were marked by unprecedented political ferment inside the Soviet Union. In this atmosphere, what David Mandel has rightly called the "rebirth of the labour movement" took place between 10 and 24 July 1989—a coal miners' strike involving almost half a million workers.[1] Some seven decades after the creation of what some called a "workers' state" (a term to which we will turn in Part 3 of this book) that state's own workers would undermine its foundations, making real Leon Trotsky's warning, cited in the preface: "The vengeance of history is far more terrible than the vengeance of the most powerful General Secretary."[2]

The depth of the economic crisis gripping the USSR in the 1980s is now well known. The magnitude of this crisis, which will become clear below, created the conditions for a vast proliferation of economic grievances from the working class. The regime's response, under Gorbachev's leadership, was to reintegrate the Soviet economy with that of the West, even if this meant allowing noncompetitive firms to go under. This restructuring was known as *perestroika*. But, in the context of declining living standards, restructuring—described at the time by Michael Burawoy as "a potentially explosive combination of openness for intellectuals and discipline for workers"—was likely to produce social unrest.[3] It is in this sense that *perestroika* and *glasnost* went hand in hand. The intention of the bureaucracy was, through *glasnost*, to legitimize its economic strategy, to open up the political process just enough to allow a greater feeling of participation on the part of the masses, but without conceding anything in terms of control and power. The problem with such schemes is that they can easily get out of control. Millions of people took Gorbachev at his word, and *perestroika* from above became redefined as what Theodore Friedgut and Lewis Siegelbaum termed "*perestroika* from below."[4]

Perestroika from Below

Small groups of *perestroika* enthusiasts began organizing in the mid-1980s. As Friedgut and Siegelbaum note: "In each small group, a start had to be made in introducing democratic change and civic activism. *Perestroika* had to reach up from below to meet the efforts initiated from above."[5] In particular, the workers' movement began pressing its economic demands through initiatives outside the control of both the state and a Stalinist union movement that was completely bound to that state. In the words of worker-activist Aleksandr Utkin: "It was obvious to everyone that the old unions were not defending us. When we sat down for negotiations with the government, the official trade-unions sat with the government opposite us."[6]

In the first half of 1989, these factors resulted in two million worker days lost to strikes, with "an average of 15,000 workers on strike each day."[7] These strikes raised the possibility, for the first time in seventy years, of working-class organizations independent of the state. But so long had the traditions of independent working-class struggle been buried that, at first, the numbers who looked to independent labour organization were relatively small.

The strike of 400,000 coal miners in July changed that dramatically. As Michael Haynes summarizes:

This strike began in July 1989 in the Kuzbass in Western Siberia, the source of one fifth of Soviet coal, and spread to the Donbass where another third was produced. Some 400,000 of the million or so miners of the USSR were involved in the first genuine mass working class action since the revolution.[8]

David Remnick says that this unfolding movement involved "mines all across the country, from Ukraine to Vorkuta to Sakhalin Island,"[9] a truly gigantic workers' action that would have profound political consequences. "The initial demands were economic: more soap, detergent, toothpaste, sausage, shoes and underwear, more sugar, tea, and bread."[10] Workers complained of overcrowded dormitories and buses, a shortage of day-care spaces and schools, miserable life expectancy (for miners, less than fifty years), poor work conditions, industrial pollution, runaway inflation, poor scheduling of holidays, and the arbitrary power and corruption of the local officials.[11] On 10 July, after negotiations had broken down, these grievances exploded in strike action in Mezhdurechensk (three thousand kilometres east of Moscow and less than four hundred kilometres from the border with Mongolia). By 15 July, the strike involved 158 mines and 177,000 workers. On that date, the workers in the Donbass, in Ukraine, more than three thousand kilometres east of the original strikes, began to go out on strike.[12] In all, "100 mines struck in the Donbass with up to 90,000 miners out on a single day.... On 20 July the strike spread to the other mining centres of the Ukraine."[13] As the strikes were reaching their peak there, the Pechora district, twenty-five hundred kilometres north and east of the Donbass, exploded, with thousands going on strike from 19 to 24 July.

Remnick sums up the political consequences of this mass rebellion: "After July 1989, the Kremlin could never again have any confidence at all that it was the master of events. After July 1989, the illusion of a gradual, Gorbachev-directed 'revolution from above' was over."[14] A new force in Russian society was discovering its power. "Everywhere the picture was the same," says David Mandel.

The miners occupied the central squares in permanent meeting. Worker detachments maintained order. In Donetsk [in the Don-bass], veterans of the Afghan war played an important role in this.

... In Kemerovo [near Mezhdurechensk], crime declined by 52% during the strike. The strike committees stopped the sale of alcohol, sealed liquor stores and set up drug inspection points on the main roads. In Donetsk two miners were dismissed for appearing drunk on the central square.[15]

The strikes were relatively short-lived and ended, in each case, with partial but real victories. Vorkuta played a key role, its miners having considerable economic power. Its largest coal pit, Vorgashorskaya, could at the time produce 18,000 tons of coal a day.[16] In Vorkuta, "the miners won concessions from the Government that included an increase in supplies of soap, fresh meat, refrigerators and leather shoes. In addition, the miners were promised pay increases for certain work shifts and some sort of profit sharing."[17] But more important than these concessions was the increase in confidence and level of organization. These were the first sustained, widespread incidences of working-class collective action since the 1953 prison camp strikes. In contrast to the 1953 strikes, however, the workers' organizations, once formed, did not have their leaders dispersed into the prisons of the Gulag. As Mandel notes, "with the end of the strike, the strike committees did not disband but transformed themselves into workers' committees, whose main task was to monitor the execution of the agreements."[18] For the first time in seventy years, organizations based in the working class, independent of the state and powerful enough to avoid instant repression from the regime, were operating in the Soviet Union. A silence more than three generations old was ending.

"There had been strikes before in the Soviet Union," Remnick writes, including "bus drivers in the city of Chekhov, airline pilots who refused to fly until safety standards were improved."

But the symbolism of the miners' strike was extraordinary. The miners embodied the vanguard of the proletariat, a bastion of Bolshevism in the old days. To look out at the great crowd of them in Lenin Square was to see a kind of poster for what had once been called "the masses." And now the masses were walking off the job and declaring that socialism had not delivered anything—not even a bar of soap.[19]

Eighteen months later, the coal miners would again lead a nationwide coal strike against the regime. Between these two actions, smaller but none-theless significant strikes in the coal fields put the working-class struggle front and centre in the unfolding drama of *glasnost* and *perestroika*. In response to the explosive events of July 1989, Gorbachev attempted to all but outlaw strike activity. Vorkuta workers responded with illegal wildcat strikes. On 25 October 1989, Fein writes, a strike by "16,000 of the 24,000 miners in the northern Vorkuta region forced the closing of four of the area's 13 mines."[20] The strike lasted just twenty-four hours. According to *Washington Post* correspondent Michael Dobbs, the workers decided to return after "the local mine association had threatened legal proceedings against 90 to 100 leaders of the strike, accusing them of breaking the new law on resolving labor disputes." However, a return to work did not mean an end to the struggle. A spokesman for the miners said that they "would resume the protest if their demands were not met by year's end."[21]

The strike of Vorkuta workers was part of a wider series of actions by miners in other parts of the Soviet Union. On 1 November, a mas-sive two-hour "warning" strike occurred in the Donbass, the largest coal-producing area of the USSR. The striking miners, who numbered almost one hundred thousand, demanded political change: "In addition to routine economic demands, the strikers in Donetsk in the Ukraine called for abolition of the leading role of the Communist Party and direct election of the Soviet President. Similar political demands have been made by miners in the northern city of Vorkuta."[22] In July 1990, roughly one hundred thousand mineworkers went out on strike again, this time in Ukraine, Siberia, and Vorkuta, with expressly political demands. The *Chicago Tribune* carried the story:

> The strike coordinating committee in the Donetsk basin of the Ukraine issued an appeal that expressed total lack of faith in the government.
>
> "We are of the view that [Soviet prime minister Nikolai] Ryzh-kov's government in the year since it was set up has failed to come up with an effective concept of getting the country out of its present economic crisis," the statement said.

"We cannot sit and wait any longer until our government and the party apparatus dictates its will . . . and leaves us with nothing but hunger, poverty and devastation."

In addition to demanding the resignation of Ryzhkov and his ministers, the miners called for the nationalization of all Communist Party property and the elimination of all party political cells in the government, the army and the KGB.[23]

In the mid-1980s, the activists seeking to rebuild independent working-class organizations after three generations of Stalinism could be numbered in the dozens. Now these activists had an audience of hundreds of thousands. In October 1989, long-time political dissident Boris Kagarlitsky expressed excitement at the possibility that activists could go from the margins to the mainstream. "There are a lot of small groups trying to organise independent trade unions," Kagarlitsky wrote, "but the only serious possibilities lie with Sotsprof"—the Federation of Independent Socialist Trade Unions, launched that summer—"and the strike committees themselves." He went on to note that "there are about 5,000 members of the initiative groups for Sotsprof, and the aim now is to develop it in provincial working class areas."[24]

Sotsprof was just one of many attempts at forming independent working-class organizations. In the coal fields, for instance, a more important role was probably played by the Independent Miners' Union, which in 1991, according to Mandel, had "approximately 55,000 members, though its real influence among the miners was much broader."[25] Given the more than seventy-year absence of independent working-class politics, this re-emergence of independent trade unions, however small in scale relative to the tens of millions who comprised the working class in the Soviet Union, was nonetheless significant.

For all of these independent unions, 1991 was to be a turning point in their history. But for all, it was also to represent, for the moment, the peak of their ability to influence Russian politics. In retrospect, this should have caught no one by surprise. Kagarlitsky had, in 1989, warned enthusiasts in the West: "You mustn't exaggerate the level of class consciousness of the working class. We're only going through the first steps of the working class movement."[26]

The Legacy of the Past

It is impossible to calculate the extent to which working-class consciousness was destroyed by the long years of authoritarianism and Stalinism.
Unable to organize independently, punished at the slightest sign of
independent activity, unable to put forward independent political parties,
and provided with no forums in which to discuss, debate, and hammer
out ideological viewpoints, the political consciousness of the working
class throughout the Soviet Union was driven to an extremely low level.
The 1989 awakening of the class could not help but be marked by this
legacy. The negative aspects of this legacy manifested in different ways.
With respect to the miners, while extremely militant and politicized, they
remained isolated from much of the rest of the working class. In addition,
the vacuum of ideas created by decades of political repression left the
miners open to illusions about Boris Yeltsin and his market-friendly program of reforms. Isolation and Yeltsinism together meant that this initial
attempt at forming independent organizations was to prove incapable,
in the short term, of creating stable, mass working-class organizations.

On 4 March 1991, at the ironically named Bolshevik Mine in Novokuznetsk, a city in the Kuzbass not far from Mezhdurechensk, what was
to have been a one-day walkout in solidarity with striking Ukrainian
miners set off another wave of strikes. The strikes quickly spread to at
least one-third of the country's 580 mines, including those in Vorkuta, and
then settled into a massive, generalized challenge to the regime.[27] Not only
were these strikes larger and more sustained than the 1989 strikes, they
were also more expressly political. "In 1989, it was only the coal miners
of Vorkuta, in the Russian Polar region, who combined radical political
principles with their economic demands," Remnick reported at the time.
"But now, as Gorbachev's economic policies continue to flounder, almost
all of the strikers have proclaimed radical change in political leadership
as central to their position."[28]

Increasingly, however, this political opposition to the Soviet state
transformed itself into political support for Boris Yeltsin, then chair of
the Supreme Soviet of the RSFSR—the Russian Soviet Federated Socialist
Republic. At the start of May, as the second month of the strike drew to
a close, Yeltsin travelled to Novokuznetsk, where, the *New York Times*
reported, he "received a hero's welcome at every stop from miners," some

of them eager to see Gorbachev resign.[29] As one member of the strike committee, Aleksandr Kolesnikov, commented: "So far it's been all hurrah. At the first rally yesterday the miners formally endorsed Yeltsin."[30] The conditions creating this move toward Yeltsin intensified. By 1991, continued economic decline was making life grim for the miners and rendering hollow the "liberals' promises of a bright future from market reform."[31] The decline in their living standards dragged many workers into apathy, which opened the door for Yeltsin and his promises of market reform in a way that was much more pronounced than in 1989.

The miners' enthusiasm for Yeltsin was tempered by the fact that, only the previous week, he had been one of the ten signatories of an agreement reached between Gorbachev and the leaders of nine of the constituent republics of the Soviet Union. Signed on 23 April, the Accord of Ten, as reported by David Mandel, "called on the miners and all other strikers to return to work and to make up the losses, declaring that it was 'unacceptable to try to achieve political goals by inciting to civil disobedience, strikes and appeals to overthrow the political authorities.'"[32] Yeltsin, speaking at a miners' rally, praised their strike to the heavens. "The miners have turned out to be the initiators of the destruction of the old command-administrative system and creators of a new system of economic management," he told the miners. However, Pavel Vashonov, a key member of the Yeltsin camp, expressed a quite different view: "'This wave of strikes cannot give birth to any normal political system,'" he said, going on to argue that the motivation of the workers came from "their instinctive reaction to having been 'robbed and deceived.'"[33]

In the confusion, the strike movement, whose activists had increasingly looked to Yeltsin as an alternative to Gorbachev, came to a halt in city after city, pit after pit. Mandel described "the initial reaction among many of the miners' leaders" as "shock and betrayal," quoting strike leader Aleksandr Kriger as saying, "I think that Yeltsin betrayed us."[34] Whether the miners had been betrayed or not, Yeltsin seemed like a better choice than Gorbachev to many in the movement. In Vorkuta, the strike ended when an agreement was reached to transfer the control of the mines from the USSR and Gorbachev to the Russian Republic and Yeltsin.[35] The workers, in other words, even if disillusioned by the Yeltsin–Gorbachev rapprochement, were looking to Yeltsin and his program of market reforms to solve their deep economic and social grievances. This was expressed in August when hundreds of thousands of working people took to the streets to defend Yeltsin against the reimposition of bureaucratic control in the coup attempted by hard-core Stalinist loyalists that month.

Yeltsin did, of course, prove to be a false saviour. According to Richard Greeman, writing in the early 1990s, Yeltsin's "'low intensity' attack on rights and living standards of working people is demoralizing enough. Planned massive price rises have reduced everyone but the privileged to desperation. Salaries are next to worthless. Pensions are simply not paid on the grounds of a manufactured 'shortage' of money, while 'before our eyes, our systems of free medical care and free universal education are being dismantled without our permission, with no legal basis.'"[36]

The workers' movement, starting from a very low point, proved capable of only momentarily breaking out of its isolation in the mining centres. Except for an explosion in Minsk, wrote Mandel, "the movement failed to embrace the largest Soviet cities, and the miners' attempts to expand the movement in their own regions met with very limited success."[37] In the vacuum of ideas that was the legacy of long decades of Stalinism, and in opposition to Gorbachev, the workers turned to Yeltsin and his pro-market alternative. By 1993, in the wake of the privation and poverty that this "alternative" had led to, the independent union movements of 1991 had retreated from the stage. In the words of Richard Greeman: "For the moment, we have stasis—which the Greeks understood as a violent and degenerative paralysis of a polity in the middle of an unfinished class war."[38]

"They Are Their Sons and Daughters"

In the years following 1993, the situation was not, in fact, one of stasis. If economic decline was the background to *perestroika* and *glasnost*, what ensued in the transition to neoliberalism was economic catastrophe.

It is extremely difficult to measure the state of the economy in the Soviet Union in the 1980s. Government statistics were notoriously unreliable. Working with the statistics we do have and with the most basic measure of the health of an economy—output per capita adjusted for inflation—we find that the economy in the USSR declined 1.27 percent in 1988, 1.47 percent in 1989, 0.76 percent in 1990, and a precipitous 14.6 percent in 1991.[39] No wonder there was such a major strike wave in 1991: the economic decline in that year was similar to that experienced by Greece in the wake of the Great Recession of 2008. However, the years following were even worse. Figure 1 takes the same criterion—output per capita adjusted for inflation—and tracks the performance of the United States, the United Kingdom, and the Russian Federation from 1991 to 2015. The United States and the United Kingdom experienced economic weakness in 1991 and 1992, in the context of the recession that opened up the decade. A sharp decline in 2008 and 2009, during the Great Recession, is also clearly evident. But otherwise, the economies of those two countries grew. By 2007, just before the Great Recession, inflation-adjusted output per capita in the United Kingdom was 43 percent greater than in 1990; in the United States, the figure was 39 percent. By 2015, after recovery from the Great Recession, the output per capita for both countries was 44 percent greater than in 1990.

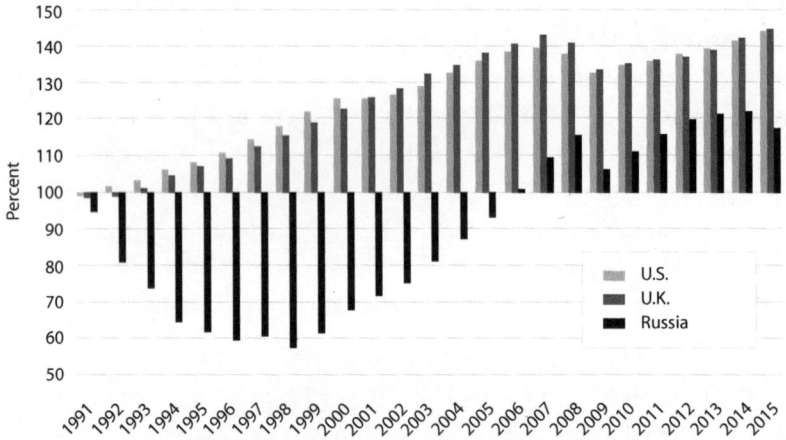

Figure 1. Output per capita in Russia, the U.S., and the U.K. from 1991–2015 (1990=100). Derived from data available in United Nations, "Population" and United Nations, "GDP, at Constant 2005 Prices – National Currency."

But the story in the Russian Federation through the 1990s was catastrophic. As figure 1 shows, inflation-adjusted output per capita dropped so precipitously that, by 1998, it stood at just 58 percent of the 1990 figure. An economic decline of 42 percent is reminiscent of the Great Depression in the United States in the 1930s. A slow recovery began the next year, but only in 2006 did output per capita return to 1990 levels. By 2014, it was up 22 percent from 1990, but it fell back to 17 percent the next year.

Perhaps even more dramatic as an indicator of economic weakness is the trade balance of the Soviet Union and countries of the former Soviet Union in that most basic of commodities: wheat. "Bread, peace, and land!" was the organizing slogan of the 1917 revolution, but, by the late twentieth century, the first of these could not be produced in sufficient quantity to feed the people of the Soviet Union. As Ernest Mandel explained, "the most dramatic expression" of slowing rates of growth in the 1980s in the Soviet Union was "the quasi-stagnation in cereal production, particularly animal feed, which for years has made the USSR dependent on massive imports of agricultural products from capitalist countries (Argentina, Canada, USA, France and Australia)."[40] As figure 2 shows, from the mid-1970s on, the Soviet Union imported more wheat than it exported. By 1984, the trade deficit in wheat stood at a staggering twenty-five million tonnes. The terrible inefficiencies of the system bequeathed by Stalinism are exposed as clearly in this one chart as in any lengthy treatise.

The difficult realities of the early 1990s are also apparent in figure 2. In the first years after the collapse of the Soviet Union, the trade deficit worsened, with 1993 surpassing the twenty-five million tonne mark of 1984. Just as with the earlier figures on output per capita, by the twenty-first century, recovery is visible. But we can also see the sharp economic decline in the first years of neoliberalism. As is often the case in periods of deep and prolonged economic crisis, in the 1990s, the entire energy of the poor and the oppressed turned to survival. Class struggle receded into the background, and the promising beginnings of 1989 to 1991, in terms of the independent organization of workers, became a distant memory.

Again, as in the two periods looked at previously, throughout 1989 to 1991, it was the miners in Vorkuta who were the quickest to press political demands and the most ready to take direct action and who were in the forefront of establishing independent union organizations. According to David Mandel, during the July 1989 awakening of the Russian workers' movement, Vorkuta, of all the coal-mining regions, had the highest "level of politicization." Not only did the miners there demand "the removal of the coal minister and of the chairman of the Union of Workers of the Coal Industry," but "the chairman of the Vorgashorskaya mine strike committee, himself a party member for over ten years," called for the rescinding of the article in the constitution that allotted the Communist Party a monopoly of power in the state.[41]

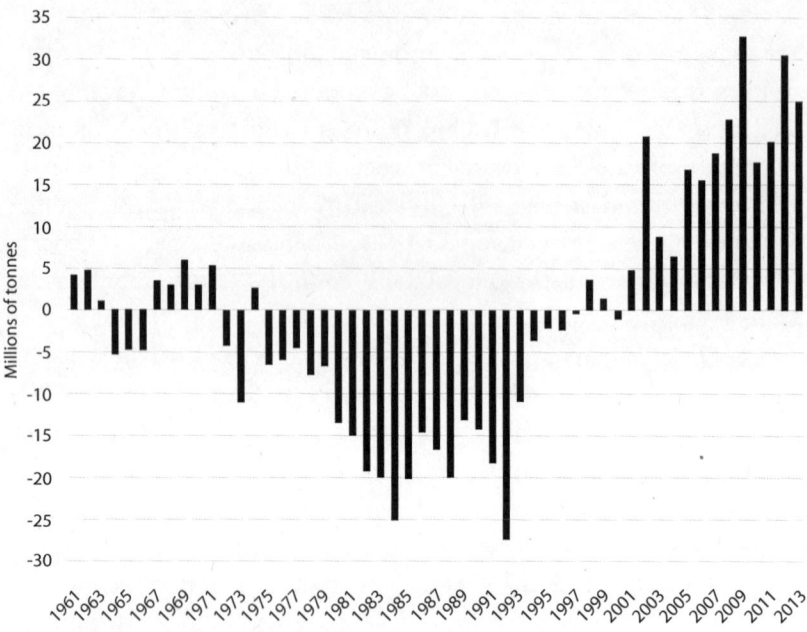

Figure 2. Net exports of wheat in countries of former USSR, 1961–2013. Derived from data available in FAOSTAT, "Crops and Livestock Products, Wheat, Import Quantity, Export Quantity."

In a November 1989 interview, Kagarlitsky was asked why it was the Vorkuta miners who were the most militant and the most politicized.

> "It's important to know that these miners are the sons and grandsons of Stalin's victims. No one other than those in the labour camps ever worked in the mines." Kagarlitsky said today's miners were aware of the Trotskyists who were forced to work in the Vorkuta labour camps during Stalin's purges. "They are their sons and daughters. No one ever moves there, so these are the second and third generation."[42]

This was indeed the revenge of history.

From the Standpoint of the Working Class

A core part of the methodology, for those of us who are historical material-ists, is to listen to the voices of workers in struggle. One of the aspirations of this book is to discern the trajectory of the Russian Revolution of 1917. If we listen to the voices of workers in struggle, that trajectory is revealed with absolute clarity.

Upon invoking a desire to see things from the standpoint of the working class, however, we are immediately confronted with concep-tual difficulties. The term *class*, more often than not, is used to capture an objectively measurable category. We think of it as a statement about differential relations to wealth and power, to status, or to the means of production. These objective measures all have their place. Income levels tell us a considerable amount. Status in a hierarchical economy is very real, and often very offensive. And the question of relation to the means of production is frequently decisive. It is not uncommon for scholars to suggest that for Karl Marx, these objective measures correspond to one half of his class analysis, the half that can fit under the heading of "class in itself"—the objective or structural counterpart to the subjective or struggle-based notion of "class for itself."

Edward Andrew, in 1983, provided a list of those who accept this "class in itself" reading of Marx, a list that includes T. Dos Santos, Nicos Pou-lantzas, Irving M. Zetlin, and Robert Tucker. However, Andrew went on to make the interesting point that, in fact, nowhere did Marx use the term "class in itself."[43] Here is what Marx, as a young man in 1847, actually *did* argue, in *The Poverty of Philosophy*:

> Economic conditions had first transformed the mass of the people of the country into workers. The domination of capital has created for this mass a common situation, common interests. This mass is thus already *a class as against capital*, but not yet for itself. In the strug-gle . . . this mass becomes united, and constitutes itself as *a class for itself*. The interests it defends become class interests. But the struggle of class against class is a political struggle.[44]

There are objective, structural pressures pushing in the direction of class formation. Capital in the cycle of capital accumulation continually calls up and creates a "class as against capital." That is, however, nothing like the structuralist formation implied by the term "class in itself." Structuralist Marxists who emphasize a "class in itself" versus "class for itself" binary risk falling into the same trap identified by Marx, a trap that vitiates all materialisms precedent to historical materialism. The young Karl Marx said, in his famous "Theses on Feuerbach": "The chief defect of all previous materialism . . . is that things [*Gegenstand*], reality, sensuousness are conceived only in the form of the *object*, or of *contemplation*, but not as *sensuous human activity, practice*, not subjectively."[45] Classes are not structures. Classes are collections of human beings with hopes, dreams, ideas, and passions. Marx's interest was not with an inert mass of workers created and recreated by capitalism, but with the dynamic and living mass of workers who, in political struggle, begin to unite and to become a "class for itself." His is a subjective approach with an objective dimension rather than an objective approach with a subjectivist add-on.

More than half a century has passed since the publication of E. P. Thompson's *The Making of the English Working Class* (1963). Thompson is in the company of C. L. R. James, Rosa Luxemburg, and others who remind us in their writings of the human, "class for itself" dimension of serious historical materialist analysis. The emergence of a class "for itself" is not automatically determined. It is a product of struggle.

Thompson chose to use "making" in his title because his book is "a study in an active process, which owes as much to agency as to conditioning. The working class did not rise like the sun at an appointed time. It was present at its own making." As he goes on to explain, "I do not see class as a 'structure,' nor even as a 'category,' but as something which in fact happens (and can be shown to have happened) in human relationships."[46] Writing about class in the context of ancient Greece, G. E. M. de Ste. Croix put it this way: "I am not going to pretend that class is an entity existing objectively in its own right like a Platonic 'Form.'" Similarly, Thompson understood class as "essentially a relationship"—as an expression of the social relations through which human beings enter into the process of production.[47]

The three chapters that constitute part 1 of this book suggest that a Thompsonian approach to class can help us understand class formation in the territories of the Soviet Union in the Stalin and post-Stalin eras. What is sometimes lost in debates about, for example, the "class nature" of the Soviet Union in these eras is the lived experience of the poor, the oppressed, and the exploited. An examination of their struggles—their hopes, dreams, forms of organization, ideas—can shed some light on the working class that did emerge "for itself" on several occasions in the twentieth century and can perhaps give us some insight into the class to emerge for itself at some point in the twenty-first century. The first stage in that process was the heroic hunger strike of the Trotskyist forced labourers—their doomed last stand telling those willing to listen that a new Russian working class "in the making" existed in the Gulag. The second stage was the wave of camp strikes centred on 1953, which led to the dismantling of the forced labour system. The third stage involved the strikes that took place between 1989 to 1991, which sounded the death knell of the Stalinist system. The re-emergence of the working class as a "class for itself" in 1989 to 1991 was a tremendous achievement. The August 1991 coup attempt, when hardline Stalinists attempted to re-establish "communist" rule, was stopped in large part by striking workers throughout the USSR, including, as journalist John Gray notes, "striking miners in most of the Soviet coal fields."[48]

The depression of the neoliberal 1990s drowned the 1989–91 wave in a tsunami of misery. But the story doesn't end there. The economic crisis has eased. Slowly, tentatively, as the figures in this chapter show, the economies throughout much of the former Soviet Union have returned to growth, including returning to being net exporters of wheat. Given that the Black Earth Region that lies in Russia and Ukraine contains some of the most fertile land in the world, it is astonishing that there was ever a moment when these countries had to import wheat on a massive scale. Although the working class in the countries of the former Soviet Union has many obstacles to overcome, it is a class that has covered a tremendous amount of ground in very few years. While it took the Western labouring masses almost two thousand years to progress from the slave rebellions in 71 BC to the struggle for democracy in 1848 AD, in modern Russia, a mere forty to fifty years separated the Spartacus-style revolts of the 1940s and the working-class struggle for democracy in the late 1980s. This struggle for *glasnost* and democracy quickly generated ideas about and the initial attempts at independent working-class organization, which points to a future in which lessons from past struggles can be generalized with much greater rapidity than was the case for the European working-class movement of the late nineteenth and early twentieth centuries. We cannot know in advance the outcome of these struggles, but we do know that they will come.

◼ PART 2

Self-Emancipation Versus Substitutionism

The next chapter and the three that follow are organized around the contrast between the two concepts around which this book is organized: self-emancipation and substitutionism. Their focus falls especially on specific instances of substitutionism and their consequences, both at the time of the 1917 revolution and in the early years of Bolshevik rule.

Chapter 4 examines a kind of substitutionism *sui generis*, in which the mass activity of a temporary new class—the peasants-in-uniform, a temporary class forged by the First World War—substituted for the self-activity of urban workers. This long-ignored analysis has been developed most clearly by Iulii Martov and Raphael Abramovitch, two leading members of the antiwar Menshevik-Internationalists. Both, as well as being Menshevik leaders, had deep roots in the General Jewish Labour Bund in Lithuania, Poland, and Russia—Martov providing intellectual inspiration to the Bund in its infancy, Abramovitch providing years of organizational leadership. In the heat of revolution and civil war, both Martov and Abramovitch pointed to the influence of soldiers and the military army environment on the revolution in Russia.

In chapter 5, I attempt to get at the root of the misunderstanding of the peasants-in-uniform by investigating misunderstandings of the peasantry *per se*. I argue that the largely urban intellectual Left—including, but not limited to, Lenin and the Bolsheviks—had a very formulaic understanding of dynamics in the countryside, on the basis of which they developed abstract schemata that were out of sync with reality. In particular, the overwhelming tendency to see the Russian peasantry as "petit bourgeois" did not mesh with what can only be called the "patriarchal" reality of the dominant institution in the countryside—the *mir*.

Chapters 6 and 7 engage with the early congresses of the Communist International (Comintern)—in particular the recently published proceedings of the Third and Fourth Congresses of the Comintern. Their publication completes the record of the first four congresses of the Comintern, congresses identified by Leon Trotsky as unsurpassed in the manner with which they approached the key political issues of their time. Specifically, these chapters focus on four moments of extreme substitutionism: the Russian invasions of Poland in 1920 and Georgia in 1921 (chapter 6), and the German March Action of 1921 in which a large role was played by leaders of the failed Hungarian revolution of 1919 (chapter 7). Together, these chapters provide a critique of what was known at the time as the "theory of the offensive." The transcripts of the early congresses reveal an incredible tension between substitutionism— acting in a "revolutionary" manner even in the absence of any real prospect of mass support and self-emancipation— and relying on the self-activity of the masses of the working class and the oppressed. Sometimes, it was the leadership of the Comintern who articulated the latter. Often it was not.

4 The Peasant-in-Uniform

Grappling with the problems of substitutionism and searching for a self-emancipationist approach have deep roots in the Russian Left of the era. According to Leopold Haimson, "*samoupravlenie, samostoiatel'nost' samodeiatel'nost'* [lit. self-government, autonomy, self-activity] were terms used by the Mensheviks to express the need for the 'active involvement' of workers in public affairs" and "were developed by the Menshevik editors of *Iskra* following their 1903 split with Lenin."[1] Menshevik leader Pavel Axelrod, in an influential article, of which the first part was published in late 1903 and the second in early 1904, outlined these ideas at some length, arguing that "the development of class self-awareness [class-consciousness] and the self-activity of the proletariat is a process of self-development and self-education of the working class," the indispensable foundation for the "process of social-democratic self-development and self-education."[2]

Leon Trotsky's first major work, *Our Political Tasks*, appeared a few months after Axelrod's article, and was dedicated, by the then twenty-four-year-old Trotsky, to his "dear teacher Pavel Borisovich Axelrod."[3] Trotsky argues that the publication of Axelrod's article marks "the beginning of a new era [epoch] in our movement."[4] I quoted earlier, from this first book of Trotsky's, his scathing deconstruction of what he saw as Lenin's substitutionist methods. The book also offers a positive alternative to substitutionism (*zamestitel'stvo*), deploying all the terms outlined by Haimson and adding a fourth, self-determination (*samopredeleniia*). A term normally deployed in discussions of movements of oppressed nations against imperialism, Trotsky deploys it here to discuss the emergence of an *independent working-class* movement. Tactically, he suggests that participating in elections can be a "starting point for the self-determination of the proletariat"[5]—this in a book that is framed by the idea that the key task facing the Russian movement was to prepare an insurrection against tsarism! He also puts this concept at the centre of his strategic orientation. He takes it as a given that the Russian movement "will triumph as a *workers' movement* or it will not triumph at all." However, he argues, "this exhausts only one side of the question. The other can be formulated as follows: the Russian revolutionary movement must, when it has triumphed as a workers' movement, be transformed without delay into a process of political self-determination of the proletariat," a process that he summarizes as involving "putting the workers forward as the main revolutionary force and making the revolution their political schooling."[6] The unifying concept in all this is the idea of the self-activity of the proletarian masses. Coming out of the devastating split between the Bolsheviks and Mensheviks at the 1903 congress, "the basic task," Trotsky argues, "may in general be formulated as consisting of the development of the self-activity of the proletariat."

> It took the Second Congress, an infinitude of palace revolutions in the Party organisation, and a whole series of bitter frictions in all fields—before the cry (the howl almost) *"Towards the masses! Into the masses!"* burst out from the Party, and the watchword *"self-activity of the proletariat"* became a living and, let us hope, life-giving slogan.
>
> The questions of *social democratic tactics* based totally on politically conscious and active masses, are today placed on the agenda by the whole of the previous development of our Party, a development which. . . . has created all the necessary material and ideological conditions; and one can be assured that now, all publishing or practical work concerned to develop the political self-activity of the working class, will not be without issue and will not be crushed.[7]

The concepts of self-activity and substitutionism can help us navigate the complicated contours of the Russian Revolution. The introduction to this book presented the binary of hope and horror—the hope that exploded in the revolution of 1917, and the horror that has variously been called Stalinism, Thermidorian reaction, and counter-revolution. There is a compelling if grotesque symmetry to these two extremes. Hope crystallized as a mass emotion on 8 March, with the demonstration-turned-strike on Women's Day in 1917. Here, self-activity took centre stage. Horror crystallized as a mass emotion exactly four years later, when Women's Day in 1921 was marked by the opening of the Red Army attack on the rebel sailors of Kronstadt. Here, substitutionism was on full, grotesque—and tragic—display. Isaac Steinberg recounts the details of this initial failed attack, quoting a "Bolshevik historian of that period, N. Pukhoff," who recalled that a blizzard was raging on the night of the attack and "described the Red Armists dressed in long white overalls (like shrouds) to camouflage them in the snow":

> "At the very beginning of the operation," Pukhoff reported, "the Second Battalion refused to go into action. Only with great difficulties, and the help of the Communist Commissars, were they persuaded to step on to the ice. But they no sooner reached the first southern battery of Kronstadt, than an entire company of that battalion surrendered to the enemy, and only the officers returned. . . . Soon it was learned that another military unit, the Third Battalion, had done the same. . . . All, except the Commissar and three or four soldiers, surrendered."[8]

The Bolsheviks turned to drastic measures. They mobilized hundreds of communists from the Tenth Party Congress, then convening in Moscow, to act as agitators. "And to intimidate the rest of the soldiers," writes Steinberg, "the 'revolutionary' tribunals were set working at full speed."[9] The drastic measures worked, and Kronstadt fell to the Bolsheviks. The fortunate rebels escaped, while "the others fell into the hands of the Cheka and military tribunals."[10]

Let us reflect for a minute on the revenge taken by the Cheka on the defeated rebels. "Every night groups of imprisoned sailors were taken from the Petrograd jails and shot," Steinberg tells us.[11] This kind of extrajudicial use of terror and violence had become routine. Victor Serge, who rallied to the Bolshevik cause during the years of civil war, and who makes it very clear that the terror of the counter-revolution was far worse than that of the Bolsheviks, nonetheless maintains that "the formation of the Chekas was one of the gravest and most impermissible errors that the Bolshevik leaders committed in 1918, when plots, blockades, and interventions made them lose their heads." Serge uses the plural, Chekas, because, in reality, throughout the vast expanse of Russia there were many local Chekas, and "these gradually came to select their personnel by virtue of their psychological inclinations." The recruits were "characterized by suspicion, embitterment, harshness, and sadism." As Serge recalls: "In every prison there were quarters reserved for Chekists, judges, police of all sorts, informers, and executioners. The executioners, who used Nagan revolvers, generally ended by being executed themselves. They would begin to drink, to wander around and fire unexpectedly at anybody." As well as being morally degenerate, the Chekas were also (or therefore) a complete failure as a tool with which to build a new society. "All evidence indicates that revolutionary tribunals, functioning in the light of day (without excluding secret sessions in particular cases) and admitting the right of defense, would have attained the same efficiency with far less abuse and depravity," Serge argues. "Was it so necessary to revert to the procedures of the Inquisition?"[12]

In any case, these "procedures of the Inquisition" were used to complete the work of defeating the Kronstadt rebellion, marking the elimination of the last hopes of emancipation emanating from 1917. A state had been consolidated. Tsarism and the old regime were gone, but the new state, from March 1921 on, had nothing in common with anything that could be called a "progressive alternative," let alone a socialist one.

"The Population Slept Peacefully"

Another binary, this one concerning views of the October Revolution, is described in the introduction to this book: the Bolshevik seizure of power in November 1917 is seen either as the final consolidation of soviet power (Trotsky) or as a coup d'état (Souvarine's). Karl Radek, in 1922, offered another interpretation. His analysis begins very much in the manner of Trotsky, by describing November 1917 as a moment "when the working class took power." However, he immediately modifies this notion of workers' power—not by shifting to Souvarine's notion of a coup but by introducing a third, more subtle perspective: "The Revolutionary Military Committee . . . had taken the power in the name of the soviet of the workers and soldiers of Petrograd."[13]

Let us explore this for a moment. The Military Revolutionary Committee (as it is more commonly called) was established in October 1917 by the Petrograd Soviet Executive Committee, its purpose being to organize the defence of the capital from potential right-wing threats. As an institution of the Petrograd Soviet, the committee can be characterized as an instrument of the nascent workers' state. However, because it was in fact dominated by the Bolsheviks, it was an instrument of just one party in that nascent workers' state. It was also the instrument that Trotsky used to direct the insurrection and seizure of power.

What were the elements deployed by the Military Revolutionary Committee to ensure the success of that insurrection? The key to everything was in Petrograd, which, at the time of the revolution, was a wartime city. China Miéville describes it as two cities—"a city of workers, swollen by the war to around 400,000" and "a city of soldiers, of whom 160,000 were stationed there in reserve."[14] The soldiers were not organic to the city: they were present only because of war mobilization. They were also overwhelmingly from rural, peasant backgrounds and had little familiarity with city life. And, finally, they were massively radicalized by the joint effects of the catastrophe of war and the land seizures that were sweeping the empire. These 160,000 peasants-in-uniform understandably played a key role in the revolution. According to Alexander Rabinowitch, they played *the* central role: "The main forces designated to take part in these operations were the Pavlovsky Regiment; Red Guard detachments from the Vyborg, Petrograd, and Vasilevsky Island districts; the Keksgolmsky Regiment; the naval elements arriving from Kronstadt and Helsingfors; and sailors from the Petrograd-based Second Baltic Fleet Detachment."[15]

The relative weight of workers in the active forces is difficult to quantify. The Red Guard described itself as follows: "The workers' Red Guard is an organization of the armed forces of the proletariat for struggle with counterrevolution and defense of the conquests of the proletariat. The workers' Red Guard consists of workers who are recommended by Socialist parties, factory committees and trade-unions."[16] According to William Chamberlin, the sailors were "less numerous" than the Red Guards, but together the two—Red Guards and sailors—"constituted the more active part of the forces of insurrection." Chamberlin describes the Red Guards as "factory workers, who had been drilling and training with special vigor after the defeat of Kornilov. According to the most reliable sources, about twenty thousand Red Guards were available for service on the eve of the uprising."[17]

Raphael Abramovitch paints a very different picture. "The main forces in the 'proletarian' revolt," he writes, "were soldiers and sailors, armored cars and guns. The famed workers' Red Guard acted only as a police force."[18] And, even if the sailors were "less numerous" than the proletarian Red Guards, Chamberlain nonetheless underlines their central importance, noting that the final act of the uprising, "the attack on the Winter Palace, . . . occurred much later than the scheduled time, because the Kronstadt sailors arrived many hours after they had been expected."[19]

Insight into the relative weight of workers and peasants-in-uniform within the Bolshevik movement can be gleaned from the voting statistics related to the ill-fated Constituent Assembly, which is examined in the conclusion to this book. Of the nearly 10.6 million votes won by the Bolsheviks, close to 1.7 million came from sailors and soldiers at the front— evidence, perhaps, of a working-class movement with auxiliary support from peasants-in-uniform.[20] However, Oliver Radkey, from whom these statistics are drawn, says that it is very difficult to determine "whether the garrison vote has been included in the vote for a city. Garrisons did not have their own commissions but they had separate polling stations and so usually the result is totaled up and announced in a bloc. But whether it has then been fused with the civilian vote or left segregated is the question that bedevils the investigator."[21]

Why does this matter? The insurrection of the fall of 1917 has gone down in history as a proletarian revolution that created a workers' state. If the principal force was a proletarian Red Guard, assisted by peasant-soldiers and sailors, then that characterization would make reasonable sense. However, if the proletarian Red Guard was simply a "police force" and the bulk of the heavy lifting was done by the sailors and soldiers, then we have a problem. Is it really possible for peasants from distant rural villages to engage in mass actions resulting in the creation of a proletarian state based in the major urban centres? In stating that the Military Revolutionary Committee took power "in the name of the soviet," Radek acknowledges substitution at one level—the substitution of the committee for the soviet as a whole. However, if the key active element in that taking of power was the peasant-in-uniform, then we have another level of substitution: a workers' state captured *for* the workers *by* thousands of armed peasants.

In later years, both Lenin and Trotsky would develop narratives about the deformation of the revolution. In December 1920, Lenin famously wrote that the very notion of the Soviet Union as a workers' state was "an abstraction." As he went on to point out: "Ours is not actually a workers' state but a workers' and peasants' state." He then added a further qualification: "Ours is a workers' state *with a bureaucratic twist to it*."[22] Trotsky would famously come to analyze the "bureaucratic degeneration of the state"[23] in the Soviet Union, its transformation into a state controlled by a bureaucratic clique rather than through direct democracy exercised by the working class—a degenerated workers' state. Both believed that the revolution had been knocked off the rails after a strong beginning. But if the beginning (at least the October/November beginning) involved substitution on the scale described here—an active element comprising predominantly peasants-in-uniform substituting for a largely passive working-class mass—then we have to incorporate the flawed *beginning* of what came to be called a "workers' state" into the conceptions of both Lenin and Trotsky.

What do we know of the dynamics at work within both the peasants-in-uniform and the urban proletariat? The revolutionary ferment among the peasants-in-uniform was clear—the disastrous summer offensive had broken the Russian army as a fighting force. The overwhelming desire of peasant-soldiers and sailors was to be released from duty and begin the long walk home to participate in these ongoing seizures of land. According to Leonard Schapiro, once the Petrograd Soviet established the Military Revolutionary Committee on 22 October, it soon garnered the support of troops garrisoned in Petrograd, who "were united to a man in their determination to resist any proposal to send them to the front."[24] Schapiro describes what followed:

> By 3 November, when the Commander of the Northern Front
> and Kerensky attempted to transfer some troops from Petrograd,
> a series of conferences of units of the Petrograd garrison passed
> resolutions recognizing the Petrograd Soviet as the only authority
> which had power to issue orders to the troops. It seemed scarcely an

exaggeration to say that the "Provisional Government was on that date already overthrown," at any rate in Petrograd.[25]

But what of the urban working class? It was, after all, their actions that had launched the whole revolutionary process eight months earlier, when workers arose in protest on Women's Day. That a revolutionary ferment still existed among urban workers in Petrograd is clear from the role of the Red Guards in the October insurrection. Nikolai Sukhanov, one of the great chroniclers of the revolution, puts it like this: "The workers' districts of Petersburg were boiling over before everyone's eyes. Only the Bolsheviks were listened to."[26] The question remains, however, whether these workers were prepared for an overnight military action "giving" their class power. The picture that Sukhanov paints needs to be seen alongside others.

Just days prior to the insurrection, Bolshevik delegates from other localities reported on their situation to the Petrograd Committee of their party. Some reports were encouraging: "In the Vyborg region, the masses will support us." In "Obukhov factory: a decisive change in our favour." In "Finland district: the quicker the better." But reports from elsewhere were mixed:

- Krasnoe Selo . . . Out of (our organization of) 5000, 500 will come here, the rest will remain in Krasnoe Selo to see what happens.

- In Kronstadt, morale has dropped considerably. . . . Among the postal and telegraph workers . . . we have few sympathizers.

- In Vasil'evsky Ostrov . . . there is no mood for insurrection.

- Moscow district: the masses will come out at the bidding of the Soviet, but few at the bidding of our party.

- Schlüsselburg district: the masses will rise at the bidding of the Soviet.

- Lettish district: the comrades will come out at the bidding of the Petersburg Bolshevik Committee, but not of the Soviet . . . Estonia: the same.

- Narva district: in general . . . no urge to insurrection.

- Okhta district: there is no mood for insurrection among the workers.

- Trade Unions: in case of a counter-revolutionary attack, the masses will resist, but they will not come out of their own accord.[27]

At a Bolshevik Central Committee meeting just nine days before the insurrection, committee members were equally equivocal. According to Abramovitch, the Bolshevik leader Volodarsky, "who enjoyed great popularity in the factories," said that "in factories in which he had occasion to address the workers, 'the masses received our call with bewilderment.'" Another key Bolshevik, Shlyapnikov, speaking for the steel workers' union, said that "the rising planned by the Bolsheviks is not popular; rumors about an imminent rising even started a panic."[28]

Leon Trotsky addressed an emergency session of the Petrograd Soviet as the insurrection was unfolding. Parts of his statement are riveting. "On behalf of the Military Revolutionary Committee. . . . I declare that the Provisional Government no longer exists." In Rabinowitch's vivid description:

> To storms of applause and shouts of "Long live the Military Revolutionary Committee!" he announced, in rapid order, that the Preparliament had been dispersed, that individual government ministers had been arrested, and that the rail stations, the post office, the central telegraph, the Petrograd Telegraph Agency, and the state bank had been occupied by forces of the Military Revolutionary Committee. "The Winter Palace has not been taken," he reported, "but its fate will be decided momentarily. . . . In the history of the revolutionary movement I know of no other examples in which such huge masses were involved and which developed so bloodlessly."[29]

But another part of his statement is simply astonishing: "The population slept peacefully and did not know that at this time one power was replaced by another."[30] A city's population can sleep while power is transferred from one class to another? Raphael Abramovitch makes a similar point, but puts it in a much more negative light: "The 'proletarian revolution' was accomplished while the working masses of the capital stood by passively. The struggle for the 'world socialist revolution' was won by war-weary peasant lads in soldiers' or sailors' uniforms."[31]

A Temporary New Class

The Russian Revolution has entered the history books as a socialist workers' revolution. And without question, the city that was the centre of the revolution, Petrograd, was also the centre of working-class life in the Russian empire. But a more complex reality was revealed when the first session of the newly formed Petrograd Soviet met in the days after the outbreak of the February (March) Revolution. According to Orlando Figes: "Of the 3,000 delegates, more than two-thirds were servicemen—and this in a city where workers outnumbered soldiers by three or four to one. . . . Most of the soldiers were peasants."[32] It was not for nothing, then, that the full name of the Petrograd Soviet was the Petrograd Soviet of Workers' and Soldiers' Deputies. Some consideration must be given to the similarities—and differences—in the experiences and dynamics essential to, on the one hand, the urban working class, and on the other, the peasants-in-uniform, who, by their thousands, were temporarily housed inside the cities.

A swirl of controversy has developed around the role of these two groups in the revolutionary events of 1917. Richard Pipes argues emphatically that, despite its standard depiction as a workers' revolt, the February Revolution "was, first and foremost, a mutiny of peasant soldiers whom, to save money, the authorities had billeted in overcrowded facilities in the Empire's capital city."[33] Abramovitch places a similar emphasis on the military angle, but he argues that these "peasant soldiers" were unlike ordinary soldiers. Mass war and mass slaughter had led to what he calls "the birth of a new 'class.'"[34] The first years of the war had seen mobilization "on a scale that was unprecedented in Russian history":

> Between 12 and 15 million peasant lads, from villages in remote
> Siberia and other far-flung districts of the vast empire, had been put
> in military uniforms and crowded into urban areas, most of them
> along the northwestern and southern frontiers. . . . Here then, was
> an enormous new social formation—a soldiery that had ceased to be
> peasants in the social and economic sense, that was falling under the
> influence of urban political ideas, and yet had no material roots in
> the working class. Toward the end of 1916, vague ideas of revolution
> and socialism had come to permeate these young men. But their basic
> concern was peace; they wished to be free of the haunting menace of

death or mutilation and to return to normal life, either in the towns or in their distant villages, where their families and land awaited them.[35]

Abramovitch sees this new—and temporary—social formation (or class) as "the main force of the revolution. The pressure from millions of soldiers, the only armed force in the country, proved overwhelming." Indeed, "without or against them, nothing could be done even by those socialist parties which were closest to them—the Mensheviks and the S-R's [Social-Revolutionaries] before the autumn of 1917 and the Bolsheviks thereafter."[36]

Throughout this book, I frequently use the shorthand "peasant-soldiers and sailors." The inclusion of sailors in this shorthand needs to be qualified. Israel Getzler writes that by February 1917, the Kronstadt sailors "were probably the most literate, technically skilled and modern, the most ethnically Russian, least servile and the most disaffected of all Russia's armed forces." Getzler says that the tsarist authorities "faced a recruitment problem and found that 'in view of the special complexity of the modern battleship, the Russian peasant, straight from the *sokha* [wooden plough] cannot immediately become a sailor, while it is the working element that is somewhat prepared for the handling of machines.'"[37] That said, the profound link between the countryside and the sailors was brought into sharp relief during the Kronstadt revolt of 1921. And, for Iulii Martov, the key factor creating a distance between the mass of soldiers and sailors and the working class in the cities was the brutal phenomenon of four years of war.

In a prescient 1919 monograph titled *World Bolshevism*, Martov argues that when Bolshevism first made its appearance as a mass phenomenon in the Russian empire, European left-wing commentators were unanimous in the view that its roots were in the agrarian nature of that empire and that a similar "maximalist" socialist movement was unlikely, if not inconceivable, in the very different urban settings of Germany or France. However, "it became obvious after the experience of the first three months of revolution in Germany that Bolshevism was not *only* the product of an agrarian revolution." He says that "of course, the characteristics of Bolshevism in Russia are largely explained by our agrarian relations," but argues that "World Bolshevism" "must clearly be derived from other social factors."[38]

Martov begins by pointing to the relationship between Bolshevism and wartime mobilization and the resulting "influence of the soldier and the army environment on the revolution in Russia."

> The role that the *army* plays in social life, thanks to the world war, is without any doubt the first common factor that is manifested in the revolutionary processes of countries as socially different as Russia, Germany, England, and France. There is an undeniable connection between the role of soldiers in the revolution and the Bolshevik element in that revolution. Bolshevism is not simply a "soldiers' revolution," but the influence of Bolshevism on the course of the revolution in each country is proportional to the participation of armed soldier masses in this revolution.[39]

Martov goes on to differentiate the socialist consciousness typically associated with the proletariat, which is developed through struggles in the workplace and the socialist consciousness emerging from soldiers in the trenches. "From the very first days of the Bolshevik wave," he writes, "Marxists identified the 'communism of the consumer' as the only social interest binding together social elements that are very different in their class composition and even declassed—that is, detached from their natural social milieu."[40] With the phrases "communism of the consumer" or "consumption communism," Martov is emphasizing the distance between *soldiers* in revolution and *workers* in revolution. For the latter, the central question is control of the means of production in the workplace. This is an absolutely collective concept: modern workplaces, with their complex division of labour, can only be taken over collectively. For the soldier, the emphasis shifts. Soldiers, as such, are divorced from production: their only relationship to the economy consists in the *consumption* of the products of labour. That consumption is overlaid by the horrifying experience of war, an experience putting the oppressed soldier mass up against military hierarchy and officer caste privilege. There is a "band of brothers" communism that does emerge in such circumstances, but its focus is not on controlling the means of production but rather on equalizing or levelling access to consumption.

The soldier's desire for a radical levelling—to make the position of the soldier mass equal to or level with the officer corps—is closely related to

the historical appetite of the Russian peasantry for an end to land privilege and a "levelling" of inequalities in the countryside. For a peasantry
whose orientation is toward subsistence farming, with little opportunity or
motivation to produce a surplus for the market, the impulse toward levelling likewise manifests itself in the realm of consumption, not production.
For both soldier and peasant, the goal is a kind of communism—not the
communism associated with the workers' movement, but a different, more
ancient notion of consumer or consumption communism. Its historical
parallels are to be found in the extreme left wing of the French Revolution
or the English Revolution. It is not the same as the communism associated
with advanced capitalism in the twentieth century.

The Martov/Abramovitch thesis has other critical dimensions. Martov
emphasizes the "social revolutionary psychology" of this new class, "their
peculiar 'anti-parliamentarism.'" Martov sees this as "quite understandable
in a social environment not shaped, as in the past, through the school of
collective defence of its interests, but in the present drawing its strength
and influence exclusively from the possession of weapons."

> English newspapers reported the following curious fact. When
> English troops on the French front were sent ballots during the
> most recent parliamentary elections, in many cases soldiers burned
> masses of them, stating, "When we return to England, we will put
> things right there." In both Germany and Russia we have seen many
> examples of how the soldier masses showed their first active interest
> in politics by expressing their desire to "put things right" through
> force of arms—whether that be "from the Right," as happened in
> the first months of the Russian revolution and the first weeks of the
> German one, or "from the Left."

Martov describes this "anti-parliamentarism" as "a particular corporate
consciousness nourished by the certainty that possession of weapons and
the ability to use them makes it possible to control the destinies of the
state"—an outlook that "comes into fatal, irreconcilable conflict with the
ideas of democracy and with parliamentary forms of government."[41]

In addition, both Martov and Abramovitch call attention to the recomposition of the working class on the home front. Abramovitch argues that
the urban workers of 1917 were very different from the urban workers of

1913. The intervening years had witnessed an exodus of older, experienced militants and an influx of peasants:

> Quite a number of the older workers, who had been part of the Revolution of 1905 or who had been acquainted with the Social Democratic parties or the trade-union movement under the semi-constitutional regime, had been absorbed into the army and lost to industry. Meanwhile, the defense industries, greatly expanded, had received an enormous influx of new workers. Some of these came from among the urban poor, but many more came from the peasantry—a politically unschooled mass which knew little of the traditions of an industrial working class. Nor could such traditions be rapidly acquired, since the working-class movement was stifled in war time.[42]

Martov puts it this way:

> The working masses have changed qualitatively. The old cadres, the most class-educated, spent four and a half years at the front. Detached from productive work, they became permeated with the psychology of the trenches, spiritually dissolved into the social milieu of declassed elements. On their return to the ranks of the proletariat, they brought a revolutionary spirit but, at the same time, the spirit of soldiers' rabble-rousing. During the war, these class-educated cadres were replaced in industry by millions of new workers drawn from ruined artisans and other "little people," rural proletarians, and working-class women. These new proletarians worked under conditions where the political movement of the pro-letariat had completely disappeared and the trade union movement had been reduced to pitiful dimensions. . . . Class consciousness in these new proletarian masses developed extremely slowly, as they had almost no experience in collective struggle alongside more advanced strata of the working class.[43]

Martov takes seriously the demoralizing effects of the war, not only on workers who were transformed into soldiers but also on those called upon to produce the means of destruction:

While those who had lived in the trenches for many years lost their professional skills, were detached from regular productive labour, and were exhausted by the psychologically and physically inhuman conditions of modern warfare, the masses who took their place in the factories expended tremendous energy working overtime to acquire the bare necessities whose prices had increased massively. Most of this exhausting labour was carried out to produce means of destruction, labour that was, from the social point of view, unproductive and could not contribute to generating in the working masses the consciousness of the indispensability of their labour for the existence of society. But this consciousness constitutes an extremely essential element in the class psychology of the modern proletariat.[44]

Martov believed that the combination of these two related phenomena—the formation of a temporary new class through the experience of the war, and the concomitant recomposition of the existing working class—provided the social base, not only for Bolshevism in Russia, but for the "essential features of proletarian Bolshevism as a world phenomenon." So profound was the impact of the trenches that this was even true, according to Martov, in those countries where the armies were not as weighted toward the peasantry as was the Russian army. This "World Bolshevism" had, he says, three features:

The first is maximalism, that is, the desire for immediate, maximum results in the implementation of social improvements without any attention to objective conditions. This maximalism presupposes a dose of naive social optimism, the uncritical belief that the realization of such maximum results may be achieved at any time, that the resources and wealth of the society that the proletariat aspires to acquire are inexhaustible.

The second is a lack of attention to the requirements of social production—the predominance, as with the soldiers, of the consumers' point of view over that of the producer.

The third is the propensity to resolve all issues of political struggle, the struggle for power, by the direct application of armed force, even in relations between different sections of the proletariat. This propensity arises from a skeptical attitude toward the possibilities of finding a democratic solution to social and political problems.[45]

The great vision of self-emancipation embedded in the socialism of Karl Marx, Rosa Luxemburg, and their political generations was based on a profound conviction about the democratic and emancipatory urge essential to the collective working class in the cities. There did exist a parallel emancipatory urge essential to the temporary new class of peasants-in-uniform from the countryside. However, democracy and a respect for rights and justice were completely absent, given the origin of these peasant-soldiers in the patriarchal, cudgel-ruled *mir*, coupled with their long experience in the trenches. The rough and violent instrument chosen by the Bolsheviks to carry out the revolution carried with it the seeds of the destruction of the essence of that revolution.

Coercion and Consent

So far, the emphasis has been on the adjective "new" in the description of this "temporary new class." But equally important is its "temporary" nature. Wars do not last forever. Mass armies are eventually demobilized. There is, at some point, a return to life centred on the means of production, not the means of destruction. For Russia, this transformation happened extremely quickly. If, in October and November 1917, the pivotal role of the temporary new class of peasant-soldiers was indisputable, it was already a class in the process of decomposition. As noted earlier, the overwhelming desire of these soldiers was to return to their villages and take part in rural land seizures. By 1918, they had melted away to such an extent that when the German army resumed its offensive, it encountered almost no resistance. The Russian army had evaporated.

Antonio Gramsci argues that a "dual perspective" exists in political life, one whose manifestations may be relatively simple or complex but that ultimately expresses itself at "two fundamental levels": "the levels of force and of consent, authority and hegemony, violence and civilization."[46] As the temporary new class dissolved, the tens of thousands of peasants-in-uniform left the cities where they had been barracked, and the natural composition of urban populations was gradually restored. Class relations began to return to something resembling normality, and the traditional workers' movement began to reassert itself. The Bolsheviks stood at a crossroads. One road would lead them to strive for consent by adapting their policies to the demands of a movement now returning to normal—that is, a socialist movement committed to pluralism in government, independence of trade unions, convening the Constituent Assembly, and so on. The other road would lead them toward coercion, holding firm to the rule of a minority and enforcing that rule in the only way that any minority can enforce its rule against the will of the majority—by force. We know now that it was the latter road that was taken.

Many at the time knew exactly what was at stake. Just days after the revolution, several members of the newly formed Council of People's Commissars resigned their posts in protest against Bolshevik opposition to a coalition government. Among them was veteran Bolshevik leader Viktor Nogin, who "declared on behalf of the secessionists: 'We hold that it is essential to form a socialist government comprising all the Soviet parties. . . . We consider that beside this there is only one other path: — the maintenance of a purely Bolshevik government by means of political terror. The Council of People's Commissars has entered upon that path.'"[47]

A few weeks later, on 1 (14) December, at an open session of the Soviet Central Executive Committee, an epic confrontation between Steinberg and Trotsky revolved around the same issues. Steinberg reports being in the presence of "some thousand excited delegates—workers, soldiers, sailors—dressed in work clothes, military tunics and peasant garb."[48] At issue was the status of the Kadets—the Constitutional Democrats—a party that, while very much part of the revolutionary bloc in February and March of 1917, had by then become "an outspoken opponent of the October Revolution." On 28 November (11 December), the new Bolshevik-dominated government had proclaimed all leaders of the Kadets "enemies of the people" subject to immediate arrest.[49] Steinberg, when called by the chair of the meeting to speak, argued that "a victorious revolution had no need to condemn its opponents in summary judgement. We, the victors, were strong enough to apply true justice."

> But, I maintained, we could not place an entire group—unspecified anonymous groups of people—outside the pale of human law. We dared not simply and blindly repeat the mistakes of the French Revolution, for after all, we had outgrown it by one hundred and

twenty-five years. Withdraw legal protection from the liberals today, and the same is likely to happen to other political groups tomorrow. It is easy to start the terror, but impossible to stop it.[50]

Steinberg describes Trotsky as he rose to reply: "Pride, power, fury, contempt were in those eyes. He seemed personally insulted."

> "There is not the slightest doubt," he intoned icily, "that the party of the Kadets is organizing the counter-revolution. Every one of its leaders must be made harmless. They complain—and sentimental socialists join them in the complaint—at being thrown into jail! Let them instead be grateful. In past revolutions their kind was dealt with differently. They would have been taken to the Palace Square and there made . . . a head shorter!"
>
> Trotsky threw out the last phrase with vicious fervor—and waited for the storm of applause. Was he not speaking in the name of the people, and for their glory? But the expected did not occur, and the silence spoke louder than any applause. I had the firm impression that there was a murmur of dissent against his bloodthirsty phrases from these simple people, fresh from the battlefields of the revolution. They neither liked nor trusted the bourgeois Kadets, but they disliked no less the vulgarity of their own leader.[51]

How closely balanced were the two positions of Steinberg and Trotsky is evidenced by the fact that, just days later, Steinberg would join the government as People's Commissar of Justice, for a time sitting at the same leadership table as his opponent, Trotsky. In the end, coercion would overwhelm consent as the revolution and then the counter-revolution unfolded, a story to which we will return in the conclusion of this book.

5

The Agrarian Question

To understand fully the role of the peasants as a class, it is imperative to have a clear view of the economic and political contours of the countryside in the Russian empire in the pre-revolutionary years. All such investigations require attention to the writings of Vladimir Lenin. Political economy was a key component of Lenin's epistemology, and central to this political economy were analyses of dynamics in the countryside. According to Tamás Krausz, Lenin's early works "expose the Russian illusions concerning small-holder peasant agriculture."[1] This was clearly still the case in 1907, where in an analysis of Russian agriculture, Lenin wrote:

> Not only is landlordism in Russia medieval, but so also is the peasant allotment system. The latter is incredibly complicated. It splits the peasantry up into thousands of small units, medieval groups, social categories. It reflects the age-old history of arrogant interference in the peasants' agrarian relationships both by the central government and the local authorities. It drives the peasants, as into a ghetto, into petty medieval associations of a fiscal, tax-levying nature, into associations for the ownership of allotment land, i.e., into the village communes.[2]

Here, Lenin condemns as medieval not only large, privately owned estates but also the village communes, which are described as "petty medieval associations." Yet the overwhelming trend in his analysis would be to regard the peasants as "petit bourgeois." This chapter will provide evidence to show that the latter characterization was quite misleading and would have serious consequences both for the peasants and for post-revolutionary Russia overall.

The Patriarchal Commune

The key institution in the countryside was the *mir*, or *obshchina*—two roughly synonymous terms both generally translated as "commune." A centuries-old institution, the *mir* had acquired a new role in the wake of the Manifesto of 1861, which formally abolished serfdom and granted former serfs some of the rights of other citizens. Ex-serfs received land through emancipation, but the *mir* was responsible for allotting strips of land to individual peasant families and, crucially, also responsible for the enormous debt incurred after the transfer of land from nobility to former serfs. Because of this impossibly burdensome debt, the peasants, while legally free, were in fact tied to the land almost to the same extent as they had been before the abolition of serfdom. Their labour was owed to the commune, and this labour was also controlled by the commune—or, more precisely, by the patriarchal village assembly, which controlled everything. The endless cycle of debt meant that there was no incentive for the individual peasant to increase the productivity of labour. It was a life of eternal toil with no possibility of eventual reward.

Russian peasants, around the time of World War I. Courtesy of George Grantham Bain Collection (Library of Congress), Wikimedia Commons.

Rosa Luxemburg clearly understood the manner in which this patriarchal institutional structure enforced economic underdevelopment in the Russian countryside. Citing a statistic from the 1890s, she noted that "70 percent of the peasantry drew less than a minimum existence from their land allotments, 20 percent were able to feed themselves, but not to keep livestock, while only 9 percent had a surplus above their own needs that could be taken to market."[3] Her point was later echoed by Edward Carr: "By far the largest part of the population was engaged in near-subsistence farming, producing food crops primarily for its own consumption and for the satisfaction of its immediate obligations to some superior authority."[4]

Without question the *mir* was economically reactionary. Rosa Luxemburg describes membership in the village commune—the "mark community" (*Markgenossenschaft*), to use her term—as "an iron chain of hunger around the necks of the peasants." But it was also politically reactionary. Many poorer members of the *mir* attempted to escape from their bondage, with sometimes brutal consequences. "Hundreds of fugitives were returned by the police to their communities as undocumented vagabonds," Luxemburg writes, "then made an example of by being beaten on a bench with rods by their mark comrades. But even the rods and the enforcement of passport controls proved powerless against the mass flight of the peasants, who fled from the hell of their 'village communism' to the city."[5]

Lenin was acutely aware of these structures of exploitation and oppression, and he consistently opposed the "utopian" trend within Russian socialism popularized by the Narodniks, who romanticized the *mir* as somehow capable of providing a jumping-off point for postcapitalist communist production.[6] As Krausz observes, "Lenin connected the features of the world market—today it would be called globalization—with the demise of traditional forms of village community."[7] In his first major work, *The Development of Capitalism in Russia*, published in 1899 (with a second edition following in 1908), Lenin forecast a dim future for the *mir*:

Agricultural capitalism is taking another, enormous step forward; it
is boundlessly expanding the commercial production of agricultural
produce and drawing a number of new countries into the world
arena; it is driving patriarchal agriculture out of its last refuges, such
as India or Russia; it is creating something hitherto unknown to

agriculture, namely, the purely industrial production of grain, based on the co-operation of masses of workers equipped with the most up-to-date machinery.[8]

But if Lenin's critique of the feudal character of the commune was clear enough, his prognosis as to its future proved abstract and unrealistic. He considerably overestimated the speed with which this traditional socioeconomic system could make the transition to modern production techniques. He was telescoping historical processes into a foreshortened time frame, a limitation that his analysis, on this point, shared with that of Luxemburg. She also anticipated the relatively rapid disappearance of the *mir*, but, as Peter Hudis points out, she was "considerably overstating the case . . . since the *mir* hardly went out of existence by the time of the end of the 1905 Revolution. Not only did it still exist, in some respects it rebounded in strength immediately following the 1917 Revolution."[9]

Krausz clearly outlines the stubborn survival of the patriarchal *mir*, noting that "the imperialist world war . . . had thrown the already weakened institutions and structures of social solidarity into disarray, breaking the moral checks on murderous instincts and allowing the '*obshchina* revolution' to spread quickly, mediated by the armed peasant soldier in the ranks."[10] The term "*obshchina* revolution" is one that Krausz borrows from Vladimir Buharayev to describe the land seizures that occurred during the 1917 revolution. In Buharayev's description, the *obshchina* community was "pitiless toward anyone who did not use land for its traditional, natural purposes but expected income from it, whether merchants, banks or those who did not cultivate their land themselves."[11] In other words, it is not sufficient to simply say that *peasants* seized the land in 1917; rather, the peasants who seized the land did so not for themselves as individuals, but in the name of the *mir*, their actions serving to reassert its dominance. Those peasants who, laying claim to their individual identity, had managed to escape the *mir* and establish independent family farms were pulled back into the *mir*, their land expropriated along with that of the large landlords.

Krausz also outlines Lenin's expectation of the relentless dissolution of the *mir* under the impact of the insertion of Russia into the world capitalist market. He mentions that this did not happen and that, in fact, the 1917 revolution temporarily strengthened the *mir*. But he doesn't link these two contradictory points—the expectation of the end of the *mir* versus the reality of its stubborn survival and even post-1917 strengthening. He notes, without critical commentary, that Lenin saw only two possible paths to capitalist development in the Russian countryside: the "Prussian" path leading to "big landlord economies," with large landowners hiring rural wage-labourers, and the "American" path of "small peasant economies," in which landed estates would be replaced by individually owned and operated family farms, with rural wage-labour playing a minor role.[12] With the benefit of hindsight, we now know that neither of the two paths envisioned by the young Lenin were taken. It was the very Russian *mir* that proved relatively impervious to either Prussian landlordism or the American family farm. He overestimated the extent to which insertion in the world economy would lead to change in the Russian countryside. The core institution of the countryside—the traditional patriarchal commune—would prove deeply resistant both to the inroads of capitalism and to workers' revolution, posing almost insoluble problems in the coming decades. Petr Stolypin, the prime minister in tsarist Russia from 1906 until his assassination in 1911, tried to encourage the American path, but his experiment was cut short by war and revolution. Lenin, after the revolution, would assume that the Stolypin experiment had opened up the Prussian path, seeing the kulaks as the "big peasants" of his youthful analysis. The reality in the countryside was very different. By the end of the Great War—and certainly by the end of the Civil War—the destruction of life in the countryside had been so thorough that kulaks, understood as a class of rich peasants, had basically ceased to exist.

Petty Producers and the Family Farm

The foundation for all of Lenin's subsequent theorization of the peasantry was laid in *The Development of Capitalism in Russia* and in related writings from the same era.[13] In these early works, Lenin sketched out a schematic political economy with an unrealistic "class against class" projection about the future evolution of agrarian relations in the countryside. This schematic political economy later became encapsulated in Lenin's practice of using the term "petit-bourgeois" to describe agrarian labour in the Russian empire of Lenin's time and to capture the essence of the Russian experience. Given the overwhelming weight of the peasantry in the Russian population, it was just a small step to calling Russia itself "petit-bourgeois," which he did on various occasions, stating: in 1913, Russia is "one of the most petit-bourgeois countries"; in 1914, "Russia out of all the capitalist countries is one of the most backward, most petit-bourgeois"; and in 1917, "Russia is the most petit-bourgeois of all European countries."[14]

Bertram Wolfe suggests that "Russian Marxists, both Bolshevik and Menshevik, tended to view the peasantry with strong reserve as a backward, property-loving, potentially hostile 'petty bourgeoisie.'"[15] Wolfe goes on to identify a profound gulf between the urban left analyzing the peasantry and the peasants themselves: "Most Social Democrats knew so little about the countryside that the issues eluded them. Most Bolsheviks, too, faced the *muzhik* [peasant] with ignorance, and a vague, unconscious dread, or with contempt, enclosed in the formula, 'property-minded, petit-bourgeois.'"[16]

But how well did that formula—"property-minded, petit-bourgeois"—actually describe the Russian peasantry? In the examples from Lenin provided above, "petit-bourgeois" is my translation from the Russian. In all three cases, the translators of *Lenin: Collected Works* (the standard English edition) have instead used "petty bourgeois."[17] Throughout *LCW*, the translators sometimes deploy "petit" and other times "petty" as the modifier for "bourgeois" when translating *melkoburzhuaznyi* and *meshchanskaia*.[18] While both translations are linguistically acceptable, "petit-bourgeois" and "petty bourgeois" are by no means equivalent from the standpoint of political economy. In its most typical usage, the latter word, "petty," signifies "small" in the sense of trivial or unimportant. The former word, "petit," like the "bourgeois" adopted from the French language, very precisely signifies "small" in the sense of "little" and small in size, which is exactly the sense in which the term is employed in political economy—to identify those who engage in production of commodities for sale in the market (hence capitalist or bourgeois), but who do so on a small or restricted scale (hence little or "petit"). That it was the latter meaning—petit bourgeois capitalism understood as small-scale capitalism—that Lenin had in mind is made clear in a major work written in May 1917, where he wrote: "Millions and tens of millions . . . have awakened and reached out for politics. And who are these millions and tens of millions?

For the most part, small-scale proprietors, small-scale bourgeois, people standing in the middle between the capitalists and the wage workers."[19]

But if that was the formal intent when employing the term *petit-bourgeois*—to precisely identify the "small capitalist" nature of life in the countryside—the term was often used by many, including Lenin himself, in a very imprecise manner—to develop not a point of political economy emphasizing the position of peasants in relation to capital accumulation, but a sociological one emphasizing the narrow basis of the peasant economy. Put another way, the English-language translators of Lenin's *Collected Works* were not entirely imprecise in choosing the term *petty* on occasion. It was a sloppy translation choice that directly paralleled a sloppy method in political-economic analysis that was employed by many, Lenin among them, when they used either "petty bourgeois" or "petit bourgeois" not as a scientifically grounded category describing a small accumulator of capital ("property-minded, petit-bourgeois"), but rather as a sociological description of someone whose scale of production is "petty"—that is, trivial and unimportant.

This was by no means an imprecision peculiar to Lenin. Iulii Martov in 1917 was expressing a widely held view that "non-proletarian revolutionary democracy" was the political expression of "the urban and rural petit bourgeoisie," with it understood that the latter (*sel'skaia melkaia burzhuaziia*) was a perfectly accurate descriptor for the Russian peasantry.[20] But again, that section of the Russian peasantry who toiled in the communes—the majority of those in the Russian empire, the vast majority in Russia itself—could in no way merit the "bourgeois" half of the label. Their production was not for the market. It was production to keep body and soul together. They only episodically intersected with the capitalist market forces that could have allowed them to "qualify" as petit-bourgeois producers. Perhaps their labour was "petty." It was not "petit-bourgeois" in any political economy sense.

Karl Radek, in 1922, provided a classic example of this elision between a quasi-scientific category and sociological description when he talked about "the peasants" first as "petty producers of goods" and then, without transition, as "petit-bourgeois."[21] These two categories—petty producer and petit-bourgeois—are by no means identical. If the "petty" labour being engaged in is constantly reduced to subsistence labour—as was the case for the vast majority of Russia's peasants trapped in the prison of the *mir*—then the word "petty" plays merely a descriptive role and is in no way a "scientific" description of the petit-bourgeois or small capitalist. If small-scale, or "petty," production consistently only produces enough for the producers to subsist, then that labour can in no way be called small capitalist—petit-bourgeois. Without the market, products of labour are not commodities for sale—that is, if products of labour are not transformed into commodities through being put on the market, then the labour that produces them absolutely cannot be categorized as "small capitalist."

Lenin was not consistent in his use of the term petit-bourgeois. In 1904, in his pivotal *One Step Forward, Two Steps Back*, while describing what he sees as the petit-bourgeois nature of the intelligentsia, he, in an offhand way, defines "the *conditions of petit-bourgeois existence*" in general as equivalent to "working in isolation or in very small workplaces, etc."[22] This repeats the error of Radek outlined above. The key is not working in isolation or in a small workplace, but doing so in the context of capital accumulation—i.e., while oriented to the market. He does make precisely this distinction in May 1918, in the near aftermath of the revolution, distinguishing the class of small-scale rural capitalists from those engaged in "natural, peasant farming" in the patriarchal context of the *mir*. He goes on to argue: "It is clear that in a small-peasant country the petit-bourgeois element predominates and cannot help but predominate; most, the vast majority of farmers, are small commodity producers."[23] Here, his analysis in the abstract is clear and precise, but his attempt at a concrete assessment of the state of the countryside is wide of the mark. In fact, it was quite clear that small-scale production for the market did *not* dominate the Russian countryside of 1918.

Implicit in Lenin's use of both "petit-bourgeois" (small capitalist) to designate the class position of the peasantry and "commodity" to designate the products of their labour is an assumption that "small capitalism"—the small-scale production of goods (commodities) for the market—predominated in the Russia of his day. The problem confronting the Russian countryside in 1918 was precisely the relative *absence* of a class of "small capitalists"—a petit-bourgeois class. Overwhelmingly, production remained dominated not by small, market-oriented (petit-bourgeois) family farms but by the patriarchal *mir*, where the local ruling elite, consisting of the male heads of households, was intent not on maximizing production through an increase in the productivity of labour but rather on the protection of petty privileges that stemmed from their right to divide and distribute the land cultivated by the *mir*.

There were exceptions to this picture. The dominant role of the *mir* was characteristic of Russia proper (what would later become the Russian Soviet Federated Socialist Republic or RSFSR). As Carr writes: "Once the peasants . . . had broken up the Stolypin holdings and flocked back into the *mir*, an overwhelming proportion of agricultural land in the RSFSR—as much as 98 per cent in some provinces—was held in this form of tenure, and subject to periodical redistribution."[24] The same was not true in many of the eastern European regions to which Russia laid claim. In what was then Byelorussia (today Belarus), "the *mir* was virtually non-existent, and in the Ukraine west of Dnieper it was weak."[25] These peripheral areas did have a large class of family farmers—the "petit-bourgeois element" of Lenin's analysis—that was better able to survive the upheavals of 1917. In Russia itself, however, these farmers were by far the exception rather than the rule.

The characterization of the peasantry as "petit-bourgeois" would have made sense had the schema of Lenin's *The Development of Capitalism in Russia* been accurate and had the patriarchal *mir* in fact been replaced by family farming—the quintessential rural institution of the small-capitalist or petit-bourgeois farmer. However, as we have seen, so tenacious was the *mir* as an institution in the countryside that it took state intervention from Stolypin to protect and encourage the development of a new class of petit-bourgeois family farmers. Prior to the outbreak of war, this new class was increasing in size, but still remained in the shadow of the much larger class working on the commune. With the outbreak of war, the process of transitioning to small-scale family farming was slowed considerably, and then entirely reversed in 1917, when the "land to the peasants" revolution meant the seizure, by a temporarily reinvigorated patriarchal *mir*, of *both* landlord-controlled farms and petit-bourgeois-controlled family farms.

This is complex territory. Stolypin's reforms did find a hearing in the Russian peasantry and did *begin* a process of the dissolution of the *mir* and the emergence of a mass class of family farmers. As Donald Treadgold observes:

The policy of his Government, in his own words, had "for its one object, the establishment of small individual property in land," the destruction of the commune and the foundation of an economic system of free enterprise in rural Russia. As his daughter writes in her memoirs: "The abolition of communal land tenure and the resettlement of the peasants on homesteads (*na khutora*) was the dream of my father from the time of his youth. In this change he saw the principal security of the future happiness of Russia. *To make every peasant a proprietor* and give him the chance to work quietly on his own land, for himself, this must enrich the peasantry."[26]

According to George Tokmakoff, "a Soviet agrarian expert stated in 1918 that the yearning for a *khutor* was a characteristic inclination of peasants in many parts of the country on the eve of the 1917 Revolution."[27]

Regarding the progress achieved by government reforms, Leonid Strakhovsky quotes Stolypin's comments to the State Council in March 1910: "During the three years that the provisions of this law have been in operation, i.e., up to 1 February 1910, over 1,700,000 heads of families have declared their desire to obtain their land in private ownership. This represents about 17 per cent of all peasants in village communes."[28] Strakhovsky adds that, by the end of 1914, "nearly two million heads of families enjoyed private land-ownership, while an additional half million had received certificates entitling them to ownership of their communal lots in villages where there had not been a redistribution of land for the last twenty years. All told, this represented over 25 per cent of peasants in village communes."[29] Even the advent of war and the mobilization of millions of peasant lads into the army did not stop this process. "All through the war the movement continued," writes Wolfe, "so that by January 1, 1916, 6,200,000 families, out of approximately 16,000,000 eligible, had made application for separation." He goes on to note that "if the same trend had been continued at the same rate, all land would have been owned by individual peasants by 1935 or 1936."[30] In short, Stolypin's program of reforms clearly made inroads among a sizeable percentage of the rural population.

Earlier, I outlined Lenin's identification of two potential paths for capitalist farming in Russia: the Prussian path, whereby large landowners hire a wage-labouring rural proletariat, or the American path, the archetype of petit-bourgeois family farming, whereby rural wage-labour plays a marginal role. "Following Lenin," argues Judith Pallot, Soviet historians "identified in the reform a conscious attempt on the part of Nicholas II's government to protect the interests of the large landowners by propelling Russia along a Prussian path of agrarian capitalism."[31] Recall, however, that the 1917–18 agrarian revolution was characterized by seizures of land not by peasants as individual proprietors but rather through the *mir*. It is worth dwelling on this point in some detail. By 1917, Russian peasants formed three principal categories—those working in the *mir*, those working on the large landlord-owned estates, and those who had taken advantage of the Stolypin reform and worked on individual family farms. Let us look at each in turn.

Those working in the *mir* might best be characterized not as petit-bourgeois but as semi-feudal. I have already quoted Lenin to this effect, denouncing the village communes as "petty medieval associations of a fiscal, tax-levying nature" (which, interestingly, was at odds with his general characterization of their labour as petit-bourgeois).[32] Feudalism is characterized by the control of conditions of work and products of labour by an all-powerful lord. No such lord existed as an individual in the *mir*, but the heads of households, meeting in assembly, acted as a patriarchal collective substitute for the feudal lord. Hence the characterization of the *mir* as semi-feudal.

No one would, in the context of actual feudalism, think of calling serfs "petit-bourgeois." They owned no land, and what they produced was not destined for the market but was used partly for their own subsistence and partly to satisfy the conditions of work dictated by the local landlord. In like manner, no one should consider the peasants working in the *mir* "petit-bourgeois." As in the case of serfs, what they produced was similarly used for subsistence and to satisfy the conditions of work, dictated in their case by the local patriarchy-in-assembly. In the patriarchal *mir*, there was little incentive for or possibility of an increase in the productivity of labour. The tendency was, rather, toward stagnation. Under this economic system—very much the opposite of anything resembling "small capitalist"—very little surplus was available for urban consumption.[33]

The term *patriarchal*, however, fits very well, since it captures the power structure ruling the commune—the male heads of households and their cudgels. It was, in fact, the term that Lenin employed in 1918, when he classified the modes of socioeconomic organization that presently existed in Russia, beginning with one he called the "patriarchal, that is, largely natural, peasant farming."[34] Regardless of whether we designate the *mir* as petty medieval, semi-feudal, or patriarchal, however, the key point in terms of political economy is the fact that it was profoundly resistant to the pressures to increase productivity exerted by the capitalist market. The commune was stagnant and unproductive, a terrible institution on which to rely for the production of surplus agricultural goods as commodities for sale to the hungry cities (and, of course, a terrible institution on which to rely for some "leap" into socialism).

The second category was landlord-controlled farming on large estates—the remnants of the old aristocratic holdings of the serf era—that employed agricultural labourers. Here, the conditions of work were very different from those in the *mir*. These peasants were agricultural proletarians in a classic sense, their very existence dependent on selling their labour power. In contrast to the *mir*, the production on these estates was almost entirely oriented toward the market. The landlords required the production and sale of a surplus to sustain their holdings and to accumulate wealth. From the exploitation of these agricultural proletarians, a considerable portion of the food surplus necessary to sustain life in the cities was produced.

The family farms, the great creation of the Stolypin era, accounted for the third category. These family farmers were the one section of the peasantry who were petit-bourgeois in an absolutely classic sense. With ownership of their farm and control over the product of their labour, they had, like the petite bourgeosie everywhere, a huge incentive to increase their production of a surplus for the market. Because the fruits of their labour were theirs to dispose of—crucially, the surplus beyond what was necessary for the sustenance of their family—the more they produced and sold, the more they could accumulate. As George Tokmakoff notes, "private ownership did encourage personal initiative and consequently output."[35] From the family farms, fostered and sustained by Stolypin's reforms, an increasingly important portion of food for the cities was produced. Tokmakoff provides evidence of this increase in output:

> Whereas in 1905, 7,278,000 puds of fertilizer were used, by 1913 this had risen to 34,256,000 puds, a five-fold increase. Mechanization

also proceeded swiftly; in 1911 over 12 million rubles were spent on mechanized agricultural machinery, as compared with the nearly 7 million rubles spent in 1907. These figures reflect the government's drive towards intensive cultivation, as well as the growing feeling on the part of individual families that land might yet prove a good capital investment.[36]

Leonid Strakhovsky agrees that Stolypin's agrarian reforms stimulated the increase in production. He quotes Soviet economist S. M. Dubrovsky from his monumental 1925 analysis of Stolypin's reforms: "Stolypin's legislation was significant because it was staked not on the mere legalization of capitalist processes in the countryside, but on the forcing of them—that is forcing the conversion of the countryside from an extensive to an intensive agricultural economy."[37] As Dubrovsky further noted: "From 1906 to 1915 the total area of land under cultivation increased by 14 per cent; at the same time the development of productive forces in agriculture was the result not only of the increase in cultivated areas but also of a better productivity of the cultivated land, i.e., an increase in the yield of harvests."[38] Strakhovsky goes on to point out that, between 1900 and 1913, the total value of agricultural production in Russia increased by 79.5 percent. As he concludes: "Truly it was said: 'One does not know of such a rapid development of agriculture in the history of any European country.' Its stimulus was Stolypin's agrarian reform."[39]

This process was stalled by the First World War. Earlier, I cited Wolfe saying that applications for separation from the *mir* continued to increase right up to 1916. But the depopulation of the countryside by the call-up of millions of young men made this desire to acquire independent land holdings difficult if not impossible to implement. The shift toward family farming was then completely rolled back by the agrarian revolution of 1917. The land seizures during that revolution virtually eliminated, in Russia proper, two categories of peasant labour: the agricultural proletariat and the agricultural petite bourgeoisie. The *mir*, which was in retreat during the years of the Stolypin reform, massively reasserted itself through the bayonets of the millions of peasant-soldiers returning from the trenches. David Mitrany, in a classic 1951 study of Marxism and the agrarian question, provides a concise summary of the process:

The land settlement of the previous decade was wiped out in many parts by the revival of the *mir*. The total extent of land seized by the communes in 1917–18 for redistribution was put at about 70 million dessiatins (189 mill. acres) from peasants and about 42 mill. dessiatins (114 mill. acres) from large owners. About 4.7 mill. peasant holdings, i.e., about 30.5 per cent of all peasant holdings, were pooled and divided up. The effect of the agrarian revolution, therefore, was in the first place to wipe out all large property, but also and no less to do away with the larger peasant property. In fact, as we have seen, more land was taken away and "pooled" from peasant owners than from large owners, and the levelling and equalizing trend became more marked after October, 1917, and was sanctioned by the law of January, 1918, under which land was socialized.[40]

Lenin's attitude to these developments was contradictory. According to Krausz, "Lenin considered Stolypin's reforms 'progressive' for their destruction of the feudal chains and their acceleration of the evolution of capitalism."[41] Krausz could have added the adverb "grudgingly." In November 1907, just as the Stolypin's reforms were beginning to be implemented, Lenin described them as "progressive in clearing the way for capitalism," but immediately added that "it was the kind of progress that no Social-Democrat could bring himself to support."[42] While the reform was economically progressive, Lenin considered it politically reactionary, because in Lenin's view, Stolypin's aim was to create a conservative, economically prosperous rural class that could act as a counter-revolutionary buffer in the countryside, a role that such a class had already performed admirably in France and England. Thus, while recognizing the economically progressive potential of Stolypin's reforms, Lenin condemned his program as politically reactionary.

Let's look more closely at the analysis Lenin develops. Describing Stolypin's reforms as "avowedly a landlords' programme," Lenin asks:

> But can it be said that it is reactionary in the economic sense, i.e., that it precludes, or seeks to preclude, the development of capitalism, to prevent a bourgeois agrarian evolution? Not at all. On the contrary, the famous agrarian legislation introduced by Stolypin under Article 87 is permeated through and through with the purely bourgeois spirit. There can be no doubt that it follows the line of

capitalist evolution, facilitates and pushes forward that evolution, hastens the expropriation of the peasantry, the break-up of the village commune, and the creation of a peasant bourgeoisie.[43]

However, in spite of Stolypin's reform being "progressive in the scientific-economic sense," he argues that it cannot be supported. He claims that what it will lead to is "bourgeois evolution of the landlord type." Such a path "implies the utmost preservation of bondage and serfdom (remodelled on bourgeois lines), the least rapid development of the productive forces, and the sluggish development of capitalism." He declares that what must be encouraged is "bourgeois evolution of the peasant type," which "implies the most rapid development of the productive forces and the best possible (under commodity production) conditions of existence for the mass of the peasantry."[44]

As we have seen, these two potential paths were characterized by Lenin as the Prussian way (large-scale landlord farms) and the American way (small-scale family farms):

> In the first case feudal landlord economy slowly evolves into bourgeois, Junker landlord economy, which condemns the peasants to decades of most harrowing expropriation and bondage, while at the same time a small minority of *Grossbauern* ("big peasants") arises. In the second case there is no landlord economy, or else it is broken up by revolution, which confiscates and splits up the feudal estates. In that case the peasant predominates, becomes the sole agent of agriculture, and evolves into a capitalist farmer.[45]

There is an important historical parallel to this policy. "Forty acres and a mule" was a phrase that, would, in Eric Foner's words, "echo throughout the south" in the last year of the Civil War in the United States.[46] It was shorthand for the policy of breaking up the former slave plantations and redistributing the land to the newly-emancipated former slaves. Too often reduced to a policy implemented by Union Army General William T. Sherman, it in fact emerged as a demand from within the African American community. On 12 January 1865, Sherman met in Savannah Georgia with twenty leaders of the African American community, seeking advice as to how to cope with the tens of thousands of former slaves now crowding the areas in which the Union Army was operating. At that meeting, Baptist minister and former slave Garrison Frazier defined freedom as "'placing us where we could reap the fruit of our own labor'" and said that "the best way to accomplish this was 'to have land, and turn it and till it by our own labor.'"[47] Four days after this meeting, Sherman "issued Special Field Order No. 15," which set out to implement a version of this policy in parts of South Carolina. This demand was taken up by leaders of what Du Bois called "abolition democracy,"[48] among them Thaddeus Stevens, who in September 1865 said that "each adult freedman should be given forty acres which approximately would dispose of about forty million acres."[49] This policy would ultimately fail, crushed by the counter-revolution symbolized by the terror of the Ku Klux Klan. But the link with the discussion here is clear—"40 acres and a mule" signifying an attempt to replace mass coerced labour—parallel to, in Russia, replacing the semi-coercion and unproductive reality of the *mir* with independent, small family farms.

Lenin saw Stolypin's reforms as leading to a class of wealthy landlord farmers, who he referred to as "Junkers" (an honorific title derived from the German *jung Herr*, or "young lord"). Lenin was, without question, wrong. The effects of Stolypin's reform were more in line with "forty acres and a mule" than with Junker landlords. What was beginning to emerge through these reforms was a class of small family farmers—perhaps "petit-bourgeois," but certainly not *Grossbauern*. "Stolypin headed in the 'American' not the 'Junker' direction," writes Donald Treadgold. "He neither declares for in words, nor provides for in deeds, the strengthening of landlord farming; and the chief authorities do not contest the fact that landlord farming declined more or less rapidly from the emancipation to the revolution."[50] Far from producing a class of *Grossbauern*, the Stolypin reform aligned more closely with the so-called American path.

Mistaken Theory, Catastrophic Practice

Lenin held on to his misleading understanding of the countryside throughout the years of what has come to be known as "war communism." According to Alec Nove:

This term is used to describe and define the period roughly from mid-1918 until March 1921, when the Soviet government, under

Lenin's leadership, adopted a policy of requisitioning farm produce (the so-called *prodrazvestka*), sought to ban all private trade, nationalized almost all industrial establishments and tried to achieve central control over production and allocation of goods, partially replacing money (which was rapidly depreciating) by accounting in kind.[51]

There is a very big debate about the entire collection of "war communist" policies, taken as a whole. Victor Serge sees the 1918–1921 period extremely positively. He says that the label "war communism" was inaccurate and that those years should really be seen as "the first attempt to organise a socialist society."[52] He cites the work of Lev Kritsman, who says in a provocative 1926 book, *The Heroic Period of the Great Russian Revolution*, that those years witnessed "the organisation of the natural economy of the proletariat."[53]

Boris Souvarine, Tamás Krausz, and many others see this very differently. They argue that war communism, and the 1918–21 attempt by the state to "force" the country into socialism, was both impossible and extremely costly. Souvarine says that "driven by the desperate necessities of civil war and by the mystical-romantic strain inherited from anarchism," the Bolsheviks undertook, in the war communist years, to establish socialism "by assault." The Bolshevik-led state "destroyed all private enterprise, though they could not replace it by popular initiative; they confiscated the product of individual labour before they had created collectivist production," and went so far as to think, by 1920, "that they could dispense with money."[54] Krausz makes much the same point, saying that Lenin identified the "nationalization and the administrative liquidation of market conditions with the possibilities for the immediate realization of socialism" and "overestimated the possibilities of socialization, of social supervision within the framework of nationalization, and underestimated the inveteracy of the market and money in a regulating role, a fact he later recognized."[55]

The task here is not to evaluate the policies of war communism in their totality, but to examine only the first one highlighted by Nove—the policy of "requisitioning farm produce" (*prodrazvestka*). The profound misunderstanding of the political economy of the countryside in theory opened the door to a catastrophic mistake in practice that fuelled a civil war between the workers in the cities and the peasants in the countryside.

Lenin's war communism policies were justified—as was Stalin's forced collectivization policy a decade later—through a demonization of the "kulak." Addressing the Moscow Soviet in April 1919, Lenin identified the biggest obstacle to the consolidation of communism in Russia as the "anarchy of the petty proprietors, whose life is guided by one thought: 'I grab all I can—the rest can go hang.'" Lenin labelled these "petty proprietors" as an enemy "more powerful" than the counter-revolutionary generals, such as Kornilov, leading the counter-revolutionary armies.[56] In fact, in order to conjure up this all-important enemy, Lenin in effect collapsed two categories—petit-bourgeois farmer and wealthy landlord (Junker) farmer—into one category, the "petty kulaks," in whom he located the chief obstacle to the consolidation of the workers' state in Russia. This confused political-economic analysis led to a generation of tragically misinformed policies imposed on the countryside.

More than anyone, Isaac Steinberg captures this tragedy. He makes a persuasive case for the idea that, while there were multiple engines of revolution in 1917—the peasants on the land, the workers in the city, national minorities, and the intelligentsia—it was the peasant revolution on the land that was decisive. "The supreme slogan that carried the revolution as a whole," writes Steinberg, "was the peasant call, sanctified back in Populist days: *Zemlya i Volya* ('Land and Freedom')."[57] So powerful was the wave of returning peasant-soldiers, arms in hand, determined to redistribute the land, that nothing could stand in their way. Almost without resistance from either the landlords on the big estates or the so-called Stolypin farmers on the new family farms, they swept all land back under the control of the *mir*, redistributing it to peasant families.

The whole process was codified into law in the remarkable January 1918 Third Peasant Congress, held in Petrograd, "which was the first to merge with the Third Soviet Congress of Workers and Soldiers. Nine hundred proletarian and six hundred peasant deputies established a unity of the Russian working people, a unity symbolized by the 'handshake of Lenin and Spiridonova.'"[58] The latter, Maria Spiridonova, was the revered leader of the Left Social-Revolutionaries, a party to which Steinberg belonged and which briefly shared governmental power with the Bolsheviks. The delegates drafted what Steinberg calls *"their basic law,"* including mandating pensions for all those who could not work, and the distribution of land "in such manner as to assure each family of an honorable, ample and secure existence." The congress deputies remained in the city, waiting for the Central Soviet Executive to ratify their law. Steinberg says that on 27 January (9 February), "this ratification took place in a solemn session."

> Spiridonova's report on the work accomplished left those present shouting with enthusiasm. "No debates! Vote! Vote!" A forest of hands shot up. And still the deputies refused to leave Petrograd until they could hold printed copies of the law in their hands. Two printing presses worked a day and a night, and then the delegates departed, spreading the glad tidings to the far corners of the land.[59]

The euphoria of this moment would not last. Within weeks, peace talks with Germany collapsed, and in the resulting chaos, "the Germans occupied large parts of the food-producing areas, leaving Central Russia cut off from her sources of supply." In that context, "the Government decided to requisition bread from the peasants by force"—the initiation of so-called war communism.[60] "The Bolsheviks could not have called down a greater curse," Steinberg writes. "The village had only just passed through its highest spiritual exultation. It had not only liberated itself from the landowners' yoke, it had also laid the foundations for economic and social equality in its everyday life." Then, suddenly, in what can only have seemed to the peasants a massive act of betrayal, "the Bolshevik state launched something like a *class war* against them."

> In the village itself the Bolsheviks—falling back once more on their outmoded theory—branded the working peasants as "small bourgeois," as men imbued with the psychology of trade, private markets and the instinct for acquisition. They organized the few remaining "paupers" to oppose the overwhelming mass of peasants; they established Soviets of "peasant paupers." They thus set themselves to demolish the foundations of the new revolutionary village. But even that was not enough: into the village they sent thousands of specially mobilized industrial workers for "bread requisitioning." ... These bands, which frequently turned into punitive expeditions against

protesting peasants, corrupted their proletarian participants and led to acts of unbelievable brutality.[61]

This wresting of grain from the hands of the peasants cannot be seen solely as a policy forced onto the Bolsheviks in the context of an emergency. Lenin's "kulak" theory was informing Bolshevik (soon to be Communist) practice *before* the German occupation of the bread-producing regions. On 6 (19) February 1918, immediately after the historic peasant-worker congress and the "handshake of Lenin and Spiridonova," and before his government signed the punitive Treaty of Brest-Litovsk, Lenin addressed a group of activists from both governing parties, the Bolsheviks and the Left SRs, who were about to travel to the countryside to help to advance the revolution. It is a speech in which he repeats the view that the countryside has a large class of wealthy peasants (kulaks), the presumed products of the Prussian path promoted by Stolypin (a path not in fact taken), and assumes that this class had somehow survived the land expropriation movement (it had not). This did not stop Lenin from warning the delegates of the threat that awaited them: "Out there in the countryside, you will come across 'bourgeois' peasants, the kulaks, who will try to upset Soviet power." As he went on to advise:

> You must explain to the people in the villages that the kulaks and sharks must be pulled up short. . . . Ten working people must stand up against every rich man who stretches out his avaricious paw towards public property. . . .
> The external war is over or nearly so. There is no doubt on that score. It is an internal war that is now before us. The bourgeoisie, its plundered goods hidden in its chests, is not worried and thinks: "We shall sit this out." The people must ferret out the sharks and make them disgorge. This is your task in the localities. If we are not to collapse, we must get at them in their hideouts.[62]

Lenin claimed that "every worker and peasant earning his own livelihood feels, deep down in his heart, that there is no salvation from famine and ruin but in Soviet power," and that the peasants in the countryside would therefore clearly see that "it is not punitive expeditions but propagandists that are sent from the centre to bring light to the countryside, to unite those in every village who earn their own livelihood and have never lived at the expense of others."[63] But in fact, every subsequent intervention from city to country would be felt precisely as a "punitive expedition," until, in March 1921, what Krausz calls the "dead end of war communism"[64] collapsed of its own contradictions and gave way to the New Economic Policy (NEP).

The New Economic Policy was economically the opposite of war communism. "Private trade, small-scale manufacture, foreign concessions, even projects for mixed companies with the participation of Russian private capital, the abandonment of free distribution, the turning of state trusts into commercial enterprises—all this followed."[65] Its key provision was the abandonment of forced requisitioning of grain, allowing peasants to sell their grain on the market. However, this economic opening was not accompanied by a political opening. In fact, the political regime became even more repressive.

From the vantage point of the late 1970s, Roy Medvedev persuasively argued that the Bolsheviks should have implemented the New Economic Policy in 1918, rather than "in the much more complicated and difficult situation of early 1921."[66] In fact, well before that policy was adopted, several prominent voices in Russia had called for an end to war communism. Nikolaii Rozhkov, Menshevik and eminent historian, made a personal appeal to Lenin in January 1919—two years prior to the implementation of the NEP—for an end to war communism. A former leading Bolshevik, Rozhkov knew Lenin well.[67] Now, however, he was writing to his former comrade "not because I hope to be heard and understood by you, but because I cannot remain silent, in the face of a situation that to me seems desperate. I must do everything in my power to avert the looming disaster."[68]

According to Krausz, in his letter to Lenin, "Rozhkov gave voice to the most important demand of the New Economic Policy in that he recommended a free market for basic food articles, the organization of the all-Russian market, and shutting down the requisitioning gangs."[69] Indeed, Rozhkov made his case in no uncertain terms. "All your threats of blocking [barrier] units will not help," he wrote, referring to the armed squads mobilized to stop the trade in grain. He argued that Lenin must disband all such squads and "order all local Soviets to lift all bans on imports and exports."[70] Very much along the lines of the NEP policy to come, Rozhkov argued that "without the assistance of private trade initiatives, not you, nor anybody else will be able to cope with the inevitable disaster. If you do not do it [make this policy change] your enemies will." He went on to say: "It is impossible in the twentieth century to turn the country into a conglomerate of closed, local medieval markets. This was natural in the Middle Ages, when the population within present-day Soviet Russia was 20 times smaller. Now it is a blatant absurdity."[71]

For Rozhkov, the looming disaster had two components. First, he feared that in the winter of 1919, half the population of Petrograd would die from hunger. "Under such conditions, even if you were not being directly threatened by the imperialists and the White Army [counter-revolutionaries], you would not hold onto power. You, an economist, should understand this." Second, the emergence of "a counter-revolutionary dictator" would inevitably follow from the stubborn refusal to allow a return to free trade in grain: "There is no such clever dictator yet, but there will be. 'Show me a swamp, and I'll show you the devil.'"[72]

Rozhkov, a supporter of the Mensheviks, was isolated from the levers of power. But in these early years, Leon Trotsky was not. He was among those at the very top of the state hierarchy. In February 1920, one year after Rozhkov's appeal to Lenin, and one year prior to the belated introduction of NEP, Trotsky put forward a proposal to the Communist Party's Central Committee, a proposal that directly paralleled that of Rozhkov's. Noting that "the food resources of the country are threatened with exhaustion," Trotsky argued that the seizure of grain should be ended and replaced by "a levy proportionate to the quantity of production (a sort of progressive tax on agricultural income), set up in such a way that it is nevertheless more profitable to increase the acreage sown or to cultivate it better."[73] According to Erik Landis, Trotsky's proposals "resembled what would be adopted by the party" one year later.[74] They were, however, rejected by the Central Committee, by a vote of eleven to four.[75] Other senior government officials, months before their abandonment, made the case for moving away from the policies we now retrospectively put under the headline of "war communism." One month earlier, on 20 January, at the Third All-Russia Congress of the Soviets of the People's Economy, Yuri Larin proposed ending forced requisitions and moving to a tax in kind, proposals very similar to Trotsky's. Larin was at the time a "member of the Soviet regime's highest economic body, the Supreme Council of the People's Economy (VSNKh)" and "the Communist Party specialist on financial affairs." Although Larin's proposals received serious attention at the congress, they ultimately failed to win approval. Lenin, when informed of the proposals, "pushed for Larin's removal" from his position on the VSNKh.[76]

These critics of war communism had the hard facts of hunger on their side. "Throughout this period," writes Alec Nove, "it was in fact quite impossible to live on the official rations, and the majority of supplies even of bread came through the black market."[77] Leonard Schapiro points out that "in spite of severe repression, right up to 1920 the illegal market accounted for more food supplied to the towns than the legal system of distribution."[78] Nove cites a 1924 article by Kritsman—like Larin, in the early years of the revolution a senior member of VSNKh—reporting that Soviet citizens relied on the illegal market for up to 70 percent of their food needs.[79] We have seen that Rozhkov warned Lenin that half the population of Petrograd was doomed to die of starvation.[80] In other words, had war communism been successful in completely suppressing the trade in bread thousands if not millions more would have starved. But the warnings from Rozhkov, Trotsky, and Larin went unheeded. War communism would drag on until 1921, and along with it the concomitant vilification of the "kulak" in Lenin's writings.

Perhaps no other word in the Russian revolutionary vocabulary has been so abused as the term *kulak*. Originally used to designate those people in the countryside "whose wealth came from usury or trading rather than from agriculture," the word later came to signify a "new stratum of better-off peasants in the Soviet countryside," variously identified with "rural bourgeoisie" and "village capitalists" applied interchangeably.[81] But the notion of the "rich peasants," who sometimes were considered "rich" because they had one or two horses as opposed to none, was completely out of step with the subsistence reality of the Russian countryside. Remember Tito's definition of a kulak—"the test of being a *kulak* was not the size of a man's holding, but whether he was for 'socialism' or against it."[82] This is a reflection not of social science but of political ideology.

More than anything else, *kulak* became a term of opprobrium. From 1918 until his death, Lenin hurled abuse upon what he saw as communism's greatest internal enemy—labelling them in June 1918 as "the criminals who are subjecting the population to the torments of hunger"[83] and in February 1919 as "the shameless rich peasants who fill their money-bags out of the people's need and the hunger."[84] In an August 1918 telegram to the Gubernia Executive Committee in Penza, he argued for "a campaign of ruthless mass terror against the kulaks, priests and whiteguards; suspects to be shut up in a detention camp outside the city."[85] Speaking to a session of the Petrograd Soviet in March 1919, he identified what he saw as a growing class division in the countryside, and argued that "the bulk of the poor peasants, and of the middle peasants who are close to them, are on our side. Against the kulaks, who are our inveterate enemies, we have but one weapon—force."[86]

This anti-kulak discourse was deeply at odds with the reality in the countryside. As we have seen, the Stolypin reform *had* created a new class of family farmers. But as E. H. Carr (echoing many others) notes, the expropriations that had swept through Russia in 1917 were "not confined to landowners' land. Large peasant holdings, created under the Stolypin reform or earlier, were also broken up and distributed—a process afterwards referred to as 'a dekulakization of *kulaks*.'"[87] The seizure of the land by the peasants in 1917 had ended landlordism. It had also virtually ended family farming of the American type, at least in Russia proper.

As indicated earlier, there were exceptions to the above analysis—in what is today Belarus and in western Ukraine, where the *mir* either did not exist or existed on the margins. In those areas, the family farmer was better able to survive the 1917 upheaval, unlike the newly created Stolypin family farmer in Russia proper. In those areas, outside of Russia proper, there *was* a "kulak target" to be found for Lenin's vitriole—if, of course, we persist with the mistake of seeing the family farmer *qua* family farmer as a kulak. But as well as being a mistaken approach, in the context of these non-Russian areas, Lenin's anti-kulak diatribes acquire an especially unsavoury dimension. They can be interpreted as serving to position the kulak as "other," a specifically non-Russian other, against which his largely Russian cadres could be inspired to mobilize.

In sum, it is completely misleading to pin the label "petty-bourgeois" or "petit-bourgeois" on the Russian countryside. The *mir* exhibited no capitalist dynamic for increased productivity or production for profit. Rather, it was an institution that enforced subsistence. There was a brief emergence of a new class of petit-bourgeois family farmers as a consequence of the Stolypin reform. These farmers—freed from the *mir*—were in fact oriented toward profit maximization in a classically petit-bourgeois, or small-capitalist, fashion, and the rise of this class was accompanied by a general improvement in the productivity of agriculture in the Russian countryside. But—and this point cannot be stressed enough—in Russia proper, this small-capitalist class was virtually destroyed by the Great War and the land seizures of 1917, and petit-bourgeois peasants were reabsorbed into the *mir*. Farming in this context was *petty*—the land available for each family was indeed tiny—but it was not in any way *bourgeois*. As Carr points out, "the small peasant with his family lived at subsistence level, and grew for himself and not for the market."[88]

War on the Kulaks and Socialist Consciousness

In the context of forced collectivization and the "war on the kulaks" of the first five-year plan, Trotsky displayed similar confusions as to the nature of the agrarian relations in post-revolutionary Russia. In part 3, in an examination of Trotsky's political biography of Stalin, I review the well-known criterion central to Trotsky's understanding of the class nature of the Soviet Union—the question of nationalized property. In fact, Trotsky develops, in that book, another less well-known criterion. The counter-revolution, in Trotsky's view, had failed to eliminate not only the "nationalization of the means of production and the land" but also "the socialist consciousness of the masses."[89] Where might Trotsky in the 1930s find evidence for the continuing existence of this socialist consciousness, given the horrifying violence directed against the advanced urban workers?

He finds it in the context of Stalin's forced collectivization war on the kulaks, surveyed earlier—the same forced collectivization that led to a horrendous artificial famine and that should in fact be seen as a war on the peasantry as a whole. In Trotsky's view, "the nationalization of the means of production and of the land, is the bureaucracy's law of life and death, for these are the social sources of its dominant position." He then goes on to say that guarding this nationalization of the means of production and the land "was the reason for its [the bureaucracy's] struggle against the *kulak*. The bureaucracy could wage this struggle, and wage it to the end, only with the support of the proletariat."[90]

Millions of peasants died in Stalin's misnamed war on the kulaks. Boris Brutzkus, a leading Russian agricultural economist, describes the brutal process of dekulakization during the winter of 1929–30:

> The local authorities prepared a list of condemned families. Then at night they gathered, armed, together with the members of the local *komsomol* [Communist youth organization] and perhaps a few poor peasants. They invaded the house of their victim; his means of production were confiscated for the local collective farms; a large quantity of consumer goods was usually looted for the private use of the executants of the dekulakization. All members of the family were pitilessly turned out of their homes into the snow-covered streets and it was forbidden to give them any help. The head of the family was generally imprisoned. The instruction was to divide the kulaks into three groups. To the first belonged those who could be considered as active counter-revolutionaries. These were to be shot immediately, without referring their case to the central authorities. The second—usually the most numerous—consisted of those who were destined to be deported to the northern forest regions. They were transported not in passenger carriages, but in railway trucks; the wagons were overcrowded to such an extent that there was no room to sit down. There was no heating, the people were very poorly clothed, and hardly had any food; so it was natural that a great number of them, and especially children, could not stand the long journey and died at a considerable rate. The third group consisted of those kulaks who were allowed to stay in the district, but were banned from admission to the kolkhozes [collective farms]. In this third group the death-rate was also very high because of hunger and cold in the first winter after dekulakization. Many children were parted from their parents; they formed the bands of homeless children which were one of the great social problems of Soviet life.[91]

Trotsky gave his qualified support to this one-sided war against the peasant masses. He saw it as flowing not from the venal needs of a new ruling elite but from the progressive social foundations of a new order. "Thanks to the support of the proletariat," he declared, "it ended with victory for the bureaucracy."[92]

The Soviet state's one-sided war against the peasantry is not evidence of socialist consciousness. To the extent that the proletariat did support what Souvarine rightly calls "the nightmare of collectivization," they became complicit in a mass murder so extreme that some have called it genocide. It resulted in "an agricultural disaster, justly compared to the effects of a major war."[93] And in the end, the disaster in the countryside was accompanied by disaster in the cities—first in 1934, in the purge of Leningrad, and then in 1937–38, in the Great Terror—crushing the remnants of the organized workers themselves. How Trotsky could find evidence of "socialist consciousness" in all of this is unclear.

These atrocities belong to Stalin. But it was Lenin who decisively set Bolshevik policy regarding the peasantry. Lenin never abandoned his "petit-bourgeois" analysis of labour in the countryside, and it led to catastrophic errors in policy. His—and the Bolsheviks'—agrarian policy was premised on the existence of a greedy "peasant bourgeoisie," a so-called kulak class, that was hoarding grain and starving the cities. They declared war on this group, banning free trade and sending armed urban gangs into the countryside to confiscate grain. This "war communism" was an unsustainable policy against which they were warned by many. But it was not abandoned until March 1921, in the context of mass actions by peasants, workers, and sailors in the fateful Kronstadt uprising of March 1921, to which we return in the conclusion.

Earlier, I quoted Bertram Wolfe saying: "Most Social Democrats knew so little about the countryside that the issues eluded them."[94] He was clearly correct. If chapter 4 identified a strategic confusion, manifested in the assumption that a mobilized class of rural peasants-in-uniform can substitute for a self-activated urban working class, this chapter has identified a theoretical confusion—categorizing the labour inside the patriarchal commune as somehow "small capitalist" in nature. It is one thing to observe these kinds of confusions in debates among isolated intellectuals on the fringes of politics. It is quite another when they inform the policies of mass parties and powerful states.

6   Poland and Georgia—The Export of Revolution

The political framework of Bolshevism, sketched in the previous chapters, was built within Russia but would soon impact politics on the world stage. This transition was marked by the second (1920), third (1921), and fourth (1922) congresses of the Communist International (Comintern)—congresses that Trotsky, writing in 1933, singled out as occasions on which key issues were subjected to "a principled analysis that has remain unsurpassed until now."[1] Four events were, overtly or covertly, central to these congresses: the 1919 revolution in Hungary, the 1920 Russian war with Poland, the 1921 attempt at a general strike in Germany (what became known as the "March Action"), and the 1921 invasion of Georgia. We know a little bit about the 1921 March Action. There is some research on the 1919 revolution in Hungary. Both will be examined in the next chapter. Both are classic examples of the problem of substitutionism—bypassing the mass self-emancipation of the working class and attempting to substitute for it the actions of a minoritarian "radical" section of the class. This chapter will examine two events about which we know considerably less, the Russian invasion of Poland in 1920 and of Georgia in 1921. Both were extreme cases of substitutionism—the attempt to substitute for the revolutionary class not a minoritarian party, as was the case in Germany and Hungary, but the bayonets of the peasants-in-uniform organized in the Red Army and Red Cavalry.

In his introduction to the proceedings of the third congress, John Riddell relegates this historical episode to a footnote: "In April 1920, Polish troops launched an offensive in soviet Ukraine. The Red Army was able to push them back into Polish territory and then continued its advance towards Warsaw, where it was stopped. Soviet troops were then forced to retreat. An armistice ending the war was signed in October."² This is true but incomplete. There is much more to the story.

The war did begin with a Polish invasion of Ukraine. By 6 May 1920, the Bolshevik troops had been expelled from Kyiv, "the eleventh time that Kiev had been occupied since 1917."³ Kyiv was a city seen by many as the "birthplace of Russian civilization," and suddenly the Bolsheviks had unfamiliar allies—conservative former monarchists rallying to the defence not of communism but of "Mother Russia."⁴ Within weeks, writes Orlando Figes, 14,000 former officers from the tsar's army "had joined the Red Army to fight the Poles, thousands of civilians had volunteered for war-work, and well over 100,000 deserters had returned to the Red Army."⁵ By mid-July, the Russians had driven the Polish army out of the conquered territory. They then stood on the threshold of a momentous decision—whether to move from a defensive war to an offensive one, which meant an invasion of Poland by Russian troops. This was hotly contested in the Bolshevik Party. Lenin and his supporters won the day: the Russian army invaded Poland, came to the gates of Warsaw, and was thrown out of the country in disarray, suffering horrendous casualties.⁶

"This Should Not Get into the Press"

In the aftermath of the invasion, in a speech to Communist Party members, Lenin explained the thinking of the Central Committee majority, which had thrown its support behind the invasion. As the war against imperialism progressed, he explained, the Central Committee had recognized the existence of "a new, fundamental question"—namely, that of moving from the defensive to the offensive.

> And so, in sum . . . the conviction ripened in us that the military offensive of the Entente against us was over, that the defensive war with imperialism was over, and that we had won. Poland was the stake. And Poland thought that, as a power with imperialist traditions, it was in a position to change the nature of the war. Hence, the assessment was as follows: the period of defensive war was over.

At this point, Lenin interjects a phrase loaded with significance: "I request that you write down less. This should not get into the press."⁷ And indeed it did not get into the press, staying in the closed archives until the collapse of the Soviet Union. Perhaps Lenin's reticence to have his views made known was simply because of the scale of the defeat suffered by the Russian army. We, of course, cannot know his motivations, but keeping this text from public view for several generations had the effect of keeping from public view one of the least attractive aspects of Lenin's epistemology—his belief in the possibility of exporting socialism through military invasion.

> We faced a new task. The defensive period of the war with world-
> wide imperialism was over, and we could and had the obligation
> to, exploit the military situation to launch an offensive war. We had
> defeated them when they advanced against us; we would now try to
> advance against them in order to assist the sovietization of Poland.[8]

He was not reticent on this point. One of the most horrifying aspects of modern warfare is the use of bayonets in hand-to-hand combat—a barbaric relic reminiscent of the militarism of the middle ages, surviving into modernity. Lenin, however, deploys the image of this awful weapon as part of a thumbnail outline of his political objectives.

> We decided to use our military forces to assist the sovietization of
> Poland. Our subsequent overall policy flowed from this [decision].
> We did not formulate it as an official resolution recorded in the min-
> utes of the Central Committee and representing the law for the party
> and the new congress, but we said among ourselves that we must
> probe with bayonets [to discover] whether the social revolution of
> the proletariat in Poland had ripened.[9]

Tamás Krausz recommends treating this speech with some caution, as it "was not intended for the public, and was never edited in its written form," but he then proceeds to do the opposite, treating it very incautiously, investing it with the work of laying the foundation for a Marxist understanding of international relations. The speech, he says, "contains, in a nutshell, Lenin's political and theoretical fundamentals on the links and interconnections between world progress and the international revolutionary transformation."[10] This implies that the interconnections so revealed hold positive lessons. They do not. The "interconnections" revealed here between Russia's internal politics and the "revolutionary transformation" in Poland are nothing more than the interconnections revealed in standard texts of international relations: the borders and government of one state can be changed by another through the use of physical force. Implicit in Krausz's positive gloss on Lenin's speech is that "progressive change" (i.e., socialism) might be the result of such actions. But while it is true that Lenin used the language of revolutionary upheaval to describe his aspirations, the extent to which hopes for socialist transformation were embedded in his speech represented, at best, wishful thinking.

At the level of military strategy, the Russian invasion of Poland resulted in "an enormous defeat," to use Lenin's words.[11] This defeat should have surprised no one. At the level of geopolitics, the thought that the people of Poland, long oppressed by Russia, would welcome an army from Russia entering its territory was absurd. At the level of political theory, the idea that "revolutionary transformation" could be effected by the bayonets of an invading army runs completely counter to the self-emancipation politics outlined by Karl Marx, Rosa Luxemburg, and Luxemburg's close ally and friend, Paul Levi. It was axiomatic to their politics that a country could only be "sovietized" through the self-activity and self-organization of the vast majority of the oppressed and exploited. Luxemburg and Levi were leading figures in the anti-war German left group, the Spartacus League, and would both become founding members and leaders of the German Communist Party (KPD). Luxemburg summarized the core of their politics in 1918: "The Spartacus League will never take over governmental power except in response to the clear, unambiguous will of the great majority of the proletarian mass of all of Germany."[12] This is the opposite of Lenin's grotesque "probe with bayonets" approach.

Like the Spartacists, Iulii Martov "completely rejected an aggressive revolutionary war." On 5 May 1920, he addressed a joint session of the Moscow Soviet and the All-Russian Central Trade Union Council:

> After voicing support for all that Soviet power had done to deflect Polish aggression, Martov expressed concern that the conflict might be transformed from an action to defend the RSFSR into an offensive, cautioned against any adventuring eastward (into Turkey and India), and called for the prompt conclusion of the peace treaty that the peoples of Russia needed so badly.

Martov's, of course, was not a voice to which the Bolsheviks would listen: "There was so much noise in the hall that he could not finish his speech."[13] However, Martov turned out to be correct, and his hecklers wrong. Turning a war to defend Russia against Polish aggression into a Russian offensive war to conquer Poland brought to the fore not the nationalism of an oppressed nation, but rather the ugly patriotism of Great Russian chauvinism. The flood of volunteers who entered the Red Army brought with them traditional Russian patriotism and prejudice. "Many Russians, including former Whites who had fought against the Bolsheviks in the Russian Civil War, opposed the reestablishment of Polish independence, and regarded the war as a traditional conflict between two opposing states," notes Kirsteen Davina Croll. "As a result, numerous former tsarist officers joined the ranks of the Red Army." One of those officers was A. A. Brusilov, who believed that "agitation of national patriotism" was necessary to an army being "strong and battleworthy."[14]

It was one thing to refuse to listen to the voice of the isolated and much abused Martov, but what of the voice of the then-authoritative Leon Trotsky, who was also opposed to invading Poland?[15] Of all the Bolshevik leaders, Trotsky was, without question, the one most experienced in these matters. In 1917, he was head of the Military Revolutionary Committee of the St. Petersburg Soviet when they organized the November seizure of power. From 1919 to 1925, he served as People's Commissar of army and navy affairs and was the pre-eminent political and organizational leader of the Red Army, which would emerge victorious and save Russia from defeat by foreign invasion and internal civil war. Krausz tells us that Trotsky "took a highly skeptical stance regarding a large Soviet military advance on Warsaw."[16] Broué says that Trotsky did not believe "in the export of the revolution at the point of bayonets."[17] But even Trotsky was ignored, and the invasion of Poland proceeded, with little sense of restraint or caution.

The gap between aspirations and reality was starkly revealed during the 1920 Second Congress of the Communist International, which was in session while the invasion was under way.[18] The Poland question received barely a mention during the congress. One of the few exceptions was toward the end of the first session, when Paul Levi brought to the floor a resolution appealing to the workers' movement outside of Russia to block military aid going to the Polish state, a motion that the delegates passed.[19]

Other than that, it hardly figured into the Congress official discussions. Victor Serge, in his participant's account of the Second Congress, lists three issues that were central to the congress: "the necessity for compromise and participation in electoral and Parliamentary politics," "the possibility, and even necessity, of inspiring Soviet-type revolutions in the Asiatic colonial countries," and the need to "work for splits that would break with the old reformist and Parliamentary leaderships" in Europe.[20]

Cover of a 1920 issue of *Communist International* magazine. Tim Davenport Collection, Online Archive of California, Wikimedia Commons.

However, with an air of mystery, Serge adds that there *was* a fourth "even more important" issue, which, however, "was not touched upon in open session." This hidden agenda item was, precisely, the war on Poland—more precisely, the possibility of using the war with Poland to spark revolutions in Western Europe. Serge says that this "fourth problem was not on the agenda and no trace of it will ever be found in the published accounts."[21] In fact, we now know that Lenin and the Bolshevik leadership consciously kept this fourth "even more important" agenda item away from the public eye. Lenin, in his secret speech, is explicit. The Bolshevik leaders "said among themselves" that Poland should be probed with bayonets to see if it was ripe for socialism. However:

> Here we raised a practical question which, as it turned out, was not entirely clear in theoretical terms to the best communist elements of the international community, that is the Communist International. . . . When the Comintern Congress convened in July [1920] in Moscow, we were settling this question in the Central Committee. We could not raise this question at the Comintern congress because that congress had to proceed openly—that was its enormous revolutionary, global political significance, which will become much more evident than has been the case up until now.[22]

If not discussed publicly, Serge says that the sovietization of Poland through Red Army bayonets was "discussed with considerable heat by Lenin, in a gathering of foreign delegates in a small room," where "a map of the Polish front was displayed on the wall." He paints a vivid picture: "Lenin, jacketed, briefcase under arm, delegates and typists all around him, was giving his views on the march of Tukhachevsky's army on Warsaw. He was in excellent spirits, and confident of victory."[23]

Werner Angress describes a similar scene. Lenin gathered Comintern delegates from Germany around a map, asking them where in East Prussia there was likely to be an uprising to greet the victorious Red Army after it had swept through Poland and reached the border with Germany. The Germans, one of whom was Paul Levi, "stared at him in amazement. East Prussia was known as one of the most conservative German regions."[24] Levi, as we saw above, moved the resolution to urge nonintervention in the war with Poland on the part of Western powers. That in no way meant that he expected the residents of traditionally conservative German areas bordering Poland to rise with enthusiasm to greet invading Russian troops.

If it was absurd to expect conservative German peasants to rise up at the sight of Red Army bayonets, it was even more absurd to expect Polish peasants—long the victims of Great Russian chauvinism—to greet a Russian army as their liberators. The Polish nation was just a few months into recovering its independence, after being buried for decades under the oppression of Russian tsars, German kaisers, and Austro-Hungarian emperors. Understandably, Poland rallied to oppose the Russian invasion and defend its newly won independence. Serge points out another reason for Polish workers to oppose the victory of the Red Army. Included on the "Revolutionary Committee that was to govern Poland" was Felix Dzerzhinsky, the feared head of the Cheka, "the man of the Terror."[25] Serge, a leading participant in the Second Congress, writes, "I declared that, far from firing the popular enthusiasm, the name of Dzerzhinsky would freeze it altogether. That is just what happened."[26]

The Russian general leading the invasion—Mikhail Nikolaievich Tukhachevsky—had achieved extraordinary success in the Civil War. In Russia, Tukhachevsky could march his massive armies through land where the peasants would "provide them with supplies and make good his losses in men."[27] The peasants feared the White, counter-revolutionary armies more than they feared the Red Terror. According to Serge, Tukhachevsky's opponents in the Civil War—the White officers—had made "two cardinal errors: their failure . . . to carry out agrarian reform . . . and their reinstatement everywhere of the ancient trinity of generals, high clergy, and landlords."[28] The effect of both errors was to decrease support for the Whites and increase it for the Reds. But Poland was not Russia, and other factors were at work. The relation of Poland to Russia was analogous to that of Ireland to Great Britain. The Polish people were an oppressed nation within the prison-house of nations that had been tsarist Russia. An army of Russian peasants was not going to be greeted as a liberation army any more than a British army would in Ireland.

And what of the instrument chosen to perform this sovietization? Edgar D'Abernon, a British diplomat present in Poland during the war, kept a diary of events and recorded his impression of Russian prisoners of war interrogated by one of his colleagues. He expressed surprise at their "entire lack of enthusiasm or conviction regarding the Soviet Government." He concluded that the only force driving them forward was "the terror which the Tcheka and its network of spies and denunciators inspire. It was apparent that this dread institution was greatly feared by all prisoners, who at once lowered their voices when being questioned regarding it."[29]

An army driven forward by fear of the Cheka is clearly a problem when that army is presumed to be an agent of progressive social change. This was not the only problem. Much of the territory through which the Russian army was marching had a very large Jewish population—part of the historic Jewish Pale of Settlement, "an area in the western border-lands of the empire to which the residence of the Jewish population was almost exclusively confined." At the turn of the century, 95 percent of the Russian empire's Jewish population of roughly five million resided there.[30] Tukhachevsky might very well have been a brilliant general. He also had a history, as a young man, of being an antisemite. In 1917, during World War I, he was a prisoner of war in Bavaria, and there made the acquaintance of French journalist Remy Roure, "one of the most prominent journalists and newspapermen in France in his day, a founder of *Le Monde* and its political editor from 1945 to 1952."[31] In 1928, Roure published, in Paris, a biography of his now famous former cellmate. He records a conversation where Tukhachevsky made vile statements denigrating Jewish people: "The Jews brought us Christianity. That's reason enough to hate them. But then they are a low race. I don't even speak of the dangers they create in my country."[32] Just a few months later, Tukhachevsky was back in Russia and a member of the Bolshevik Party.

Antisemitism was an issue not just for ex-aristocrats like Tukhachevsky, but also for the very poor peasant class that formed the core of the Red Army. Three-quarters of the Red Army soldiers were peasants, and, according to Orlando Figes, "its rank-and-file soldiers frequently became involved in violent looting, especially when passing through non-Russian (particularly Jewish) areas."

> The Red Army, it is important to bear in mind, was predominantly Russian in its ethnic composition. Even units conscripted in the Ukraine and other non-Russian regions (for example the Tatar Republic) were largely made up of Russians. Anti-Semitism was a powerful and growing force in the Red Army during the civil war, despite the fact that a Jew, Lev Davidovitch Trotsky (Bronstein), stood at its political head. Trotsky received hundreds of reports about his own soldiers' violence and looting in Jewish-Ukrainian settlements, some of which he must have known from his youth.[33]

In 1920, this chronic problem became acute when, after being defeated at the gates of Warsaw, the Red Cavalry began retreating in disarray back to Russia. "The men had begun deserting in large numbers," writes Adam Zamoyski, "while those who remained took out their disappointment on the inhabitants of the villages and towns they passed through, particularly the Jews."[34] The political commissars attached to this cavalry were horrified. When the retreat took this military force, now reduced to a rabble, into the heavily Jewish city of Zhytomyr (Zhitomir in Russian) in Ukraine, a telegram dripping with urgency was sent to Lenin:

> In recent days Zhitomir has faced a new task. A new wave of pogroms has swept over the district. The exact number of those killed cannot be established, and the details cannot be established (because of the lack of communication), but certain facts can be established definitively. Retreating units of the First Cavalry Army (Fourth and Sixth Divisions) have been destroying the Jewish population in their path, looting and murdering. . . . Emergency aid is vital. A large sum of money and food must be sent.[35]

The horror of these pogroms was made known to the Russian public through the compelling short stories of Isaac Babel, the famous Jewish-communist writer who accompanied the troops. At the core of the Red Cavalry were the traditionally antisemitic horsemen known as Cossacks. One of the characters in Babel's "The Red Cavalry Stories" says: "The Red Cavalry is a public conjuring trick pulled off by our Party's Central Committee. The curve of the Revolution has thrown the Cossack marauders, saddled with all kinds of prejudices, into the forefront."[36] This understanding of the motley character of the Red Cavalry was echoed by others. "These wild sons of the steppes" might have been "excellent fighters," writes William Chamberlin, but "they included a very small percentage of Communists and listened suspiciously and coldly to the moral lectures of the political workers who were sent into their ranks for purposes of agitation. For many of them booty was a more desirable objective than the triumph of the world revolution."[37] Babel's stories of the crimes committed by the defeated Red Cavalry made things increasingly difficult for him inside Stalinizing Russia, and he eventually paid with his life for telling these bitter truths. But today, his writings make it clear that these

Russian bayonets were not going to lead to liberation in Poland. Using them as a "probe" was not only a mistake, it was a crime.

Photograph of Lenin in Sverdlov Square (now known as Theatre Square) delivering a speech to a group of Red Army soldiers headed to the Polish Front, 5 May 1920. Also pictured are Kamenev and Trotsky, the two men standing on the platform to Lenin's left. Photograph by Grigory Goldstein, Wikimedia Commons.

Trotsky called the invasion of Poland "the catastrophe before Warsaw." Because of the invasion, he argued, "the development of the Polish revolution received a crushing blow."[38] Lenin said, after the fact, "we have suffered an enormous defeat, a colossal army of a hundred thousand is either prisoner of war, or [interned] in Germany. In a word, a gigantic, unheard-of defeat."[39] Despite these words, Lenin only partially confronted the scale and importance of the defeat in this speech, never mind the reasons for it. He did not, for instance, address the fact that it was a defeat preceded by a completely wrong perception of the likely response of the Polish nation and that it could have been avoided had he heeded the advice of Trotsky and Martov. In addition, Lenin was almost certainly understating Russian losses. Adam Zamoyski, in 2008, estimated Russian losses in excess of 200,000. Tukhachevsky, "like his hero Napoleon in 1812 . . . had lost an army." In the days before finally signing a peace treaty, with conditions worse than had been on offer before the Russian invasion, "the road to

Smolensk and Moscow lay wide open."[40] The defeat in Poland, then, not only destroyed prospects for revolution in Poland; it severely jeopardized the very existence of Soviet Russia.

A Tactic or a Principle?

In Trotsky's political biography of Stalin, which I examine in detail in chapters 8 and 9, Trotsky presents a more equivocal position on the Soviet invasion of Poland. Rather than talking of the "catastrophe before Warsaw" or emphasizing the question of Polish national oppression, he makes a much more limited argument, saying that he "was opposed to the march on Warsaw because, considering the weakness of our forces and resources, it could end successfully only on condition of an immediate insurrection in Poland itself, and there was absolutely no assurance of that."[41]

In *Stalin*, Trotsky puts the blame for the defeat in Poland on the shoulders of Stalin, who at the time was in command of the "Western group of the Southern armies" and refused to come to the aid of the army advancing on Warsaw because he "was waging his own war. He wanted at all costs to enter Lvov at the same time that Smilga and Tukhachevsky were to enter Warsaw."[42] But surely this is a side issue. At the time, neither Trotsky nor Karl Radek believed that an invasion could succeed, quite apart from this or that tactical blunder. "Trotsky was convinced," according to Pierre Broué, "that the entry into Polish territory by a Russian army, even under a red flag, would be felt like an invasion in the manner of Tsarism and would provoke a leap in Polish nationalism."[43] William Chamberlin indicates that this is precisely what happened: "To the average Pole of all classes a Russian Army, no matter what glowing proclamations it might issue, was an army of hereditary enemies and oppressors."[44]

> There was a strong nationalist feeling among all classes of the people, not excluding the workers. The peasants, the majority of the Polish population, generally followed the leadership of the priests and of the middleclass intellectuals. And when the Red Army troops were actually within sight of the suburbs of Warsaw they were profoundly discouraged to find Polish workers coming out, not with red flags to greet them, but with rifles to fight them.[45]

Trotsky's opposition to "the export of the revolution at the point of bay-onets," summarized by Broué, represented a *principled* opposition to the invasion, rather than the *tactical* one outlined in *Stalin*.[46] In the immediate aftermath of the defeat in Poland, Karl Radek shared this principled oppos-ition. Tamás Krausz cites a speech by Radek, also delivered at the Ninth All-Russian Conference of the RCP(B), where Radek "underscored that the party and the leadership of the Comintern were vastly over-estimating 'how ripe for revolution' Central Europe was." And he declared: "We must reject the method of 'probing' the international situation 'with bayonets.'"[47]

Radek's views on this are not consistent. According to Serge, at the moment Russian troops were at the gates of Warsaw, Radek declared: "We shall be ripping up the Versailles Treaty with our bayonets!"[48] But in the wake of defeat, his view of the utility of bayonets had changed. His speech at the Ninth Conference drips with sarcasm in his criticism of the party leadership's decision to go to war.

> Now Comrade Lenin shows a new method of collecting informa-tion: not knowing what is being done in a given country he sends an army there. I ask, comrades, do we really have no other methods by which we could get the same results in the sense of becoming fam-iliar with the situation in the country? Vladimir Ilyich argued that we learned about the situation in Germany and England with the help of probing with bayonets. If Vladimir Ilyich had more time to read foreign newspapers, he would have learned without a bayonet. . . . The bayonet will be fine if we have to assist a specific revolution, but in order to find out the situation in this or that country we have another weapon—Marxism, and for this we don't need to send Red Army soldiers.[49]

Much of the discussion at this conference—Lenin's and Radek's speeches included—remained secret until the 1990s. As Krausz writes, "Lenin did not desire a public debate of the issue of 'probing.' In a two-line note of 6 October regarding a piece of writing by Radek that followed up the conference, Lenin reacted, 'I oppose a discussion of the (possible) future assistance we may provide the Germans through Poland; it must be struck out.'"[50]

Surely these are the key issues around which a criticism of the Polish invasion should be debated. In addition to the impossibility of the Russian army being greeted as liberators by the recently independent Poles—an army associated with the long oppression of those very people—in what way can any progress for the Left happen through "probing with bayonets"? Socialism cannot be exported at the point of a gun barrel.

In *Stalin*, Trotsky does not raise these points in his criticism of the Russian invasion of Poland except in countering accusations made by S. E. Rabinovich in his *History of the Civil War* (published as a manual for military schools in the Red Army). Trotsky cites Rabinovich, outlining what he saw as "Trotsky's errors in determining the Polish War, namely that the fundamental political aim of the war on our part was to hasten the revolution in Poland and bring the revolution to Europe from the outside on the bayonets of the Red Army."[51] In response, Trotsky comments:

> In this way the old accusation is turned inside out! As late as 1927, it was recognized that I was an opponent of the March on Warsaw and the crime charged against me was my disinclination to introduce Socialism at the point of a bayonet. But in 1938, it was proclaimed that I advocated the March on Warsaw, guided by my determination to bring Socialism into Poland at the point of a bayonet![52]

This is a point worth emphasizing. Trotsky names Lenin as "the chief initiator" of the Russian invasion of Poland, or "the Polish adventure," as Trotsky calls it.[53] The invasion led to the "catastrophe before Warsaw." Trotsky deals with this invasion and its consequences critically but parenthetically, focusing his attention on a side issue (the role of Stalin). This has the effect of downplaying what were certainly the two main issues— the underappreciation of the long shadow of the Russian oppression of Poland and the horrifyingly wrong perspective of exporting socialism by force of arms.

The armed forces, including their use of bayonets, had of course been a central part of the whole revolutionary experience, as we saw in chapter 4. Trotsky reflects back on that experience: "During the first period, when the Revolution was spreading from the industrial centres toward the periphery, armed fighting detachments of workers, sailors and ex-soldiers were organized to establish the Soviet regime in various localities. These detachments frequently had to wage minor wars." In those circumstances, however, "enjoying as they did the sympathy of the masses, they easily became victorious."[54] Whatever the historical accuracy of this claim, there can be no doubt that in Poland in 1920, the Red Army encountered not the sympathy but the suspicion, distrust, and at times hatred of the Polish masses.

After Poland—Georgia

There was to be a reprise of all these issues in one of the defining moments in the rise of Stalin—the consolidation of Bolshevik rule over his native Georgia. Late in 1922, Lenin became aware of and concerned about a dispute between Stalin and the Central Committee of the Communist Party of Georgia. Stalin wanted to incorporate Georgia into a wider, regional republic. The Georgian Communists were opposed. Lenin endorsed the position of the Georgian Communists and condemned both Stalin and Stalin's key supporters on the question—among them Ordzhonikidze and Dzerzhinskii. As Thomas Twiss notes, Lenin observed that the "centralist and authoritarian actions" of these three men were "typically bureaucratic" and "characteristic of 'that really Russian man, the Great-Russian chauvinist, in substance a rascal and a tyrant.'" Several days later, Lenin "criticized 'Stalin's haste and his infatuation with pure administration, together with his spite against the notorious "nationalist-socialism"', and he denounced Stalin as a 'Great-Russian bully.'"[55]

The words from Lenin quoted by Twiss come from the series of letters he dictated from his sickbed in 1922, letters that collectively have come to be known as his "testament."[56] This testament has become iconic and has spawned much discussion about Lenin charging Stalin with "Great Russian chauvinism." But despite that spotlight on Lenin being the defender of Georgia against Stalin in 1922, very little attention has been paid to Lenin's involvement in the far more important Georgia-related events of 1921. In that year, with Lenin's support, the Russian Red Army invaded Georgia, sending the governing socialists (the Georgian Mensheviks) into exile and reimposing rule from Moscow over a country that had, only three years earlier, emerged from long decades of Russian domination. Lenin's condemnation, in late 1922, of Great Russian chauvinism contrasts sharply with his complicity in the Great Russian expansionism of 1921.

The invasion of 1921 was almost universally opposed by the people of Georgia, who had little inclination to trust the Russian Bolsheviks and a long history of support for the Mensheviks. The ability of the Mensheviks to build a base in Georgia had both general and specific reasons. Stalin, who was originally from Georgia, would be associated with antisemitism throughout his entire career, despite the fact that, in a way almost unique to the Russian empire, Georgia had experienced a relatively harmonious relationship between the dominant nationality and the minority Jewish population. Edvard Radzinsky goes so far as to say, categorically: "Anti-Semitism is not a Caucasian characteristic. From ancient times innumerable peoples have lived in the Caucasus, side by side."[57] Eric Lee makes the same point, specifically about Georgia: "Georgia, almost alone among European countries, had no history of anti-Semitism and was a country where Jews had lived happily for many centuries."[58] There was, therefore, relatively open terrain in Georgia for a group such as the Mensheviks to sink roots, their party having, as we will see in chapter 11, a higher proportion of Jewish members than the Bolsheviks. Some Mensheviks "were also active in the [General Jewish Labour] Bund."[59]

More specifically, Georgia had experienced revolution and local peasant self-rule in the earlier years of the twentieth century, in the little known and little studied Gurian Republic. According to Eric Lee:

> During the nearly seven decades that separated the publication of
> the *Communist Manifesto* in 1848 and the Russian Revolution in 1917,
> there were only two examples of socialists seizing political power
> and attempting to realise their vision of a new society. One was the
> Paris Commune of 1871, which Marx and later Lenin described as
> a kind of prototype for a future socialist society. The other was the
> "Gurian Republic" of 1902–6, widely known at the time but utterly
> forgotten today.[60]

Until brutally crushed in January 1906, the peasants in this little southern section of Georgia, after pushing out the tsarist state, ran their own affairs politically and economically. The local Menshevik organization responded effectively to this revolutionary experiment, which allowed them to build a mass base with which the local Bolsheviks could never compete. Lee describes the response of the Social Democrats to the revolution:

"A year into the rebellion, in May 1903, the Social Democrats in western Georgia held a conference, and took a stand firmly in support of the peasants." This stance by Social Democrats—who, just a few weeks later, would overwhelmingly side with the Mensheviks in the bitter split with the Bolsheviks—led to the "transformation of their party from a small, elitist group based on urban workers into a mass party of the people." Although crushed in January 1906, "unlike the Paris Commune, the Gurian experiment had a second act," which occurred after the Revolution of 1917.[61] The overwhelming strength of the Mensheviks in the region, which was clearly related to their leading role in the Gurian Republic, was revealed in the postwar revolutionary ferment. "By the time the tsarist regime collapsed in March 1917," writes Lee, "there was practically no Bolshevik organisation left in Georgia. The few Bolsheviks in the country put their factional differences with the Mensheviks behind them, and established a joint party committee with their formal rivals."[62] In Transcaucasia, of which Georgia was a part, in the late 1917 vote for the doomed Constituent Assembly, violently suppressed in 1918, "the Bolsheviks received just 86,935 votes compared to 662,000 votes for the Mensheviks."[63] We return in chapter 9 to the question of Menshevik and Bolshevik fortunes in this little country.

Georgia existed as an independent republic for a few short years after the dust had settled from the revolutionary year 1917, its government controlled by the Mensheviks. But this small country of three million was permanently at risk from its far bigger and more powerful neighbour to the north. In November 1919, the Bolsheviks attempted a coup—essentially a rebellion by pro-Bolshevik soldiers. The coup had little support among either peasants or workers in Georgia, and it failed miserably. On 7 May 1920, Soviet Russia and Menshevik Georgia signed a peace treaty, in which the independence of Georgia was formally recognized. At the time, the Red Army was fully engaged in the war with Poland, but the breathing space for Georgia thus created proved to be brief indeed. The Red Army was defeated in its invasion of Poland, marking the end of the civil wars. Russia could now turn its attention toward Georgia and begin a war that clearly falls into a different category—a war of Russian expansionism. In February 1921, under the pretext of supporting a rebellion against Georgia's Menshevik government, a Russian army numbering tens of thousands invaded the country. After several weeks of fierce fighting, Georgia was occupied by Red Army troops, its government forced to flee into exile and its independence quashed by the overwhelming power of Russian armed forces. Souvarine's summation of these events is biting: "What the Red Army could not accomplish in Finland and Poland it did accomplish first in the Ukraine, then in the Caucasus, by methods similar to those adopted by the United States in the annexation of Texas. The Georgian Socialists' dream of creating a new Switzerland between Europe and Asia was nothing but a dream in the circumstances."[64]

While they were militarily victorious, the Bolsheviks were extremely isolated politically. In July 1921, Stalin, on "returning to Tiflis in early July 1921 after many years away from his native Georgia . . . addressed a crowd of more than 5,000 workers in the Nadzaladevi Theatre."

> He began by congratulating the workers on overthrowing the Menshevik yoke. Audience members began to shout. "Lies! There was no Menshevik yoke here! There was no Communist revolution in Georgia! Your troops have removed our freedom!" A furious Stalin responded by ordering a change in the leadership of the local Bolshevik party—and an increase of the Red Terror. This included the shooting of oppositionists at night in Tiflis' Vake Park. There was no trial. In 1923, the Cheka secret police executed ninety-two Georgians in retaliation for the murder of three policemen in Guria. Ordzhonikidze threatened to kill 1.5 million Georgians if necessary.[65]

Despite this repression, organizing against occupation continued, culminating in an uprising in August 1924 that was crushed within three weeks. The uprising was coloured by the shadow of the past: its strongest centre was Guria, the site of the 1902–6 Gurian Republic. It also foreshadowed the terrible years of totalitarianism to come, a key leader of its repression being the "newly appointed deputy head of the republic's Cheka, Lavrentiy Beria."[66] As Lee tells us, the repression meted out to the rebels was horrifying:

> Thousands were killed—according to some estimates, up to 4,000. Many of these were hostages. Some rebels from Imeretia, a province in western Georgia, were stuffed into six railway carriages, taken to a place where graves were dug and there executed, some by Mauser pistols, others by machine guns. Five hundred rebels were shot in

Senaki, a town in western Georgia. Nearly 1,000 men, described as "the cream of Georgia's intelligentsia and nobility," were shot on 1 September.[67]

Beria would climb the ranks until, by the 1950s, he was widely seen as Stalin's successor—a climb that, as we saw earlier, was only terminated with his arrest, trial, and execution after the death of Stalin in 1953.

Stalin's role in these events is clear: he pushed for and supported the use of Red Army bayonets to crush this last stronghold of Menshevism, thus violating the 1920 recognition of Georgian independence. Lenin's role is less clear. He seems to have been at least partially out of the loop, not completely aware of the extent of the military action and mass repression that was taking place. Jeremy Smith says that the invasion "was opposed in the Politburo by Karl Radek," who, along with Trotsky, had also opposed the 1920 invasion of Poland. "The Commissar for War, Trotsky, was absent in the Urals, but was so incensed by the news of the invasion . . . that on his return to Moscow he demanded, unsuccessfully, the creation of a party commission to investigate the events."[68] If Trotsky had any ambivalence in private about the invasion and repression, he hid it well, defending both of these actions publicly in one of his least impressive texts, *Between Red and White*, where he actually characterizes this massively unpopular invasion of a long-oppressed former section of the Russian empire as a "Soviet Revolution."[69] Brian Pearce reminds us that the book was "written on party instructions," and, while it did become "a best-seller in British communist circles in the early twenties," it is probably best filed under the category of propaganda rather than political analysis.[70]

In the aftermath of the invasion, both Lenin and Trotsky became very clear about the problems of Soviet rule over Georgia. We saw above that a key issue in Lenin's late-in-life break with Stalin was what Lenin perceived as the "Great Russian chauvinism" that Stalin was unleashing on the newly occupied Georgia. It was in part over this concern about the repression of Georgia's national rights that Lenin attempted—again, late in life—to form a bloc with Trotsky against Stalin. Trotsky's account of this in his autobiography is riveting:

> It was the beginning of March 1923. Lenin was lying in his room
> in the huge building of the courts of justice. The second stroke was

near; it was preceded by a series of lesser shocks. . . . Vladimir Ilyich
was very much disturbed by Stalin's preparations for the coming
party congress, especially in connection with his factional machinations in Georgia. "Vladimir Ilyich is preparing a bomb for Stalin
at the congress"—that was Fotiyeva's [Lenin's secretary] phrase,
verbatim. The word "bomb" was Lenin's not hers. "Vladimir Ilyich
asks you to take the Georgian case in your hands; he will then feel
confident." On March 5, Lenin dictated this note to me:

"Dear Comrade Trotsky: I wish very much to ask you to take
upon yourself the defense of the Georgian case in the Central Committee of the party. At present, the case is under the 'persecution' of
Stalin and Dzerzhinsky, and I cannot trust their impartiality. Quite
the opposite. If you were to agree to undertake the defense, my mind
would be at rest."[71]

To properly grasp the outlines of Bolshevik policy toward Georgia, it
is insufficient to focus solely on these 1922 and 1923 progressive musings
by Lenin that challenged Great Russian chauvinism. In these musings, we
can perhaps glimpse, in Lenin's last months, the dawning of consciousness
about the problems associated with a politics of violent substitutionism—
of attempting to "impose socialism" from above by force. But if in fact
there was a dawning of such a consciousness, it was too little and too late.
The drift toward totalitarianism was far more powerful than any scruples
from one or two individuals—even leading individuals such as Lenin and
Trotsky.

Stephen Jones maintains that "the 1920s represent one of the brightest
periods in the social and political development of the Soviet national
groups." He bases this claim on some genuinely interesting policies such
as "indigenization" ("an attempt to integrate the nationalities into a new
multi-national state by accommodating national cultural aspirations")
and "policies of 'affirmative action' and wide opportunities for national
self-expression," which "resulted in a new confidence among the native
élites."[72] These are very fine and interesting initiatives, but they need to be
soberly embedded within the history of recurring attempts to challenge
the national rights of historically oppressed nations, such as Georgia and
Poland, through the use of Red Army bayonets—actions that were met
with mass opposition.

Bayonets and Bolshevism

The different perspectives on the invasion of Poland—best crystallized in the contrast between the vehement opposition to invasion articulated by Trotsky and Radek and the naïve and quite wrong support for the invasion by Tukhachevsky and Lenin—reflect tensions at the very heart of the Bolsheviks' understanding of the nature of revolution. Tukhachevsky expresses this naïveté most clearly. In a 1920 account of the debacle, he argues that the defeat "was due, not to politics, but to strategy."[73] He goes on to say that "our western and south-western armies were fighting almost at right angles to one another" and that "lack of co-operation by our Fourth Army tore victory from our hands and led to our catastrophe."[74] This parallels Trotsky's position in *Stalin*, which similarly identified the actions of the southwestern armies—and Stalin in particular—as the cause of the defeat. Trotsky's more *principled* approach summarized by Broué—understanding that bayonets cannot be an instrument for liberation and that the oppressed people of Poland were unlikely to greet their former Russian masters as liberators—exists in an uneasy epistemological tension with his *tactical* approach in *Stalin*. No such tension exists in the approach of Tukhachevsky. In fact, he doubles down and draws from his tactical approach a logical, if completely unrealistic, conclusion.

> There is not the slightest doubt that, if we had succeeded in breaking the Polish Army of bourgeois and seigneurs, the revolution of the working-class in Poland would have been an accomplished fact. And the tempest would not have stopped at the Polish frontier. Like a furious torrent it would have swept over the whole of Eastern Europe. The Red Army will not forget this attempt to carry the revolution outside our frontiers, and if ever the European bourgeoisie braves us to new fights, the Red Army will crush it and spread revolution throughout Europe.[75]

The people of Poland, Hungary, Romania, and East Germany, among other countries, learned from bitter experience that a Red Army conquest of Eastern Europe would bring not socialism but the Stasi and Stalinist totalitarianism.[76]

After the fact, both Trotsky and Radek tried to minimize the extent of the mistake made in invading Poland. In 1921, in a speech in Moscow,

Trotsky insisted that the Bolsheviks did not give the Red Army "any independent significance of its own," but saw it "as an auxiliary force introduced into the struggle of the European forces," a force that "might bring down the landslide of revolution."[77] The same year, in a speech to the leadership of the German party, Karl Radek made much the same point, insisting that

> the aim was not to impose Bolshevism at bayonet point, but only to break through the crust of the military might of the ruling classes. . . . The Executive believed that in Germany things were already ripening for the seizure of political power. It was believed that if we held Warsaw, there would be no further need to advance all the way to Germany.[78]

The next chapter's examination of the March Action will demonstrate that there was no such readiness for revolution in Germany. There was even less readiness in Poland. And the enthusiasm expressed by Tukhachevsky for Napoleon-era military invasions as a vehicle for "revolution" indicates that at least some members of the senior leadership did, in fact, give the Red Army an "independent significance of its own."

Let us return to the account of the war by D'Abernon, which provides a factual foundation for understanding both the military limitations of the manner in which the 1920 Polish–Soviet war was conducted and the political limitations of Tukhachevsky and Lenin. D'Abernon argues that the fighting in Poland should not be classified with other wars of the early twentieth century or even of the nineteenth century. The Polish–Soviet War of 1920, he argues, "should be classified with a totally different period—probably some 200 years earlier."[79] He says that most of the soldiers "were in the fight either through compulsion and fear of being shot at home, or because there was no other immediately available means of livelihood." On both sides, when "outnumbered, outmanoeuvred, or outflanked," the soldiers "either retired or surrendered; authority among their officers was insufficient to induce them to take any other" course. In short, "both the Polish and Soviet Armies were eighteenth century rather than modern in many aspects."[80]

If D'Abernon's analogy with the eighteenth century is correct (and I think it is), then Tukhachevsy and Lenin were operating with a textbook that was two centuries out of date. The great European revolution of the eighteenth century was the French Revolution, and, to some extent, it was able to be exported at the point of a bayonet. Napoleon did leave, in the wake of his invading armies, societies and states more modernized and efficient than they had been, and more capable of developing in a capitalist direction. But the spread of socialism cannot be reduced to these same categories of modernization and efficiency. If socialism is to mean anything at all, its spread has to be both voluntary and associated with the emergence of political organs of mass, democratic self-rule.

Lenin and Trotsky found themselves on opposite sides of the issue of invading Poland. Without question, Trotsky's position was closer to the correct one, while Lenin's was completely wrong. This was not the first moment when Trotsky and Lenin found themselves on opposite sides of an issue. Ian Thatcher characterizes the relationship between Trotsky and Lenin during the war years immediately preceding the 1917 revolutions as "a story of almost continuous opposition."[81] This opposition was not softened with anything resembling diplomacy. In 1914, Lenin wrote, "Trotsky has never had any 'physiognomy' at all; the only thing he does have is a habit of changing sides, of skipping from the liberals to the Marxists and back again, of mouthing scraps of catchwords and bombastic parrot phrases."[82] The previous year, Trotsky had written about Lenin: "The entire edifice of Leninism at the present time is built on lies and falsification and carries within itself the poisonous inception of its own dissolution."[83] We can reject the simplistic explanation for this history of antagonism offered by Stalinist historians, whose purpose is to portray an unbroken line of Trotskyist "crimes" in order to discredit his political legacy. What this antagonism does represent, I would suggest, are quite different understandings of the key aspects of the class struggle in Russia and Europe on which Trotsky and Lenin built their perspectives.

Trotsky, in the manner of Luxemburg and Gramsci—and the much maligned and neglected Iulii Martov—understood the profoundly democratic, self-emancipatory core of the working-class, urban, European workers' movement. It was not for nothing that in both 1905 and 1917, Trotsky was elected chair of the soviet in St. Petersburg. On several occasions before 1917, Trotsky expressed the opinion that Lenin did not always clearly grasp the urban, democratic, proletarian core of the coming

European revolution. Trotsky, in 1915, said that within Lenin, "revolutionary democratism and socialist dogma live side by side without having been amalgamated into a living Marxist whole."[84] This echoes the young Trotsky, who, in the wake of the famous 1903 split in Russian social democracy, argued that Lenin was too much the Jacobin and not enough a social democrat (which, at the time, meant "revolutionary socialist").[85] Jacobinism was the political form appropriate to modernizing antiautocratic revolutions, such as the French Revolution. The leading section of those revolutions was a relatively small layer of the urban petite bourgeoisie, relying in its revolution on the periodic intervention of the urban masses and, in the countryside, on the periodic mass actions of the rural peasantry. From this layer evolved a highly centralized urban core of the Jacobins, with a strong emphasis on militarization, operating with a certain suspicion of the urban and rural masses. For the Jacobins, it was in particular the mass action in the cities that posed problems, as such action tended to push beyond the bounds of a modernizing antifeudal revolution and into the territory of anticapitalism, something the Jacobins were not prepared to countenance.

The Russian revolutions of 1905 and 1917 involved a combination of this kind of Jacobinism—a modernizing revolution against autocratic, tsarist conditions—and something that was completely new and demanded very different strategies and tactics—a workers' revolution against capitalism. Neither revolution could win without the victory of the other. Lenin and the Bolsheviks navigated the difficult project of combining both revolutions, and Lenin openly embraced the incorporation of Jacobinism into the workers' movement. "The Jacobin inseparably connected with the organisation of the proletariat—a proletariat conscious of its class interests—this is the revolutionary Social-Democrat," he said in 1904.[86] This incorporation of Jacobinism into the workers' movement was, however, full of dangers. The tactics appropriate to the modernizing, anti-autocratic revolution are *not* easily imported into the proletariat anticapitalist revolution. Within the latter—at its core, urban, working class, and democratic—forward progress is only possible through mass self-activity. Built into this experience is a high degree of democracy, which takes its highest form in institutions such as the soviet.

Upheavals against premodern autocracy were different. They did, of course, involve furious mass action by the rural peasantry, but they also always necessitated a highly centralized, militarized struggle—for instance, the Roundheads of Cromwell's era and the Jacobins of the French Revolution. The insistence on invading Poland represented a retreat to eighteenth-century tactics in the name of twentieth-century goals. The next chapter will argue that in a parallel sense, the push in Germany for an insurrection during the March Action, even though the KPD represented a small minority of the working class, represented an attempt to sidestep the self-activity of the urban working class. Both the invasion of Poland and the March Action in Germany reflect the extent to which the Bolshevik cadre misunderstood how the European class struggle had evolved from the tactics of an earlier era to those of the mass, democratic self-emancipation appropriate to the class struggle in contemporary capitalism.

7 Germany and Hungary—The United Front

At both the third and fourth congresses of the Communist International, delegates were confronted by the complicated situation in Germany. It was in the cauldron of the German revolutionary years, roughly from 1917 to 1923, that the tactic of the united front crystallized. In a comprehensive review of the recently published *Toward the United Front*, the complete proceedings of the Fourth Congress, Ian Birchall writes that "the central theme of the congress, which recurred under various headings, was the united front.... That meant unity in action with the reformist organisations that still retained the loyalty of the majority of workers in most countries."[1] Today, we might replace "united front" with "coalition-building"—a contemporary term for the politics of self-emancipation. One of the key events of the German revolutionary years was the event that came to be known as the March Action of 1921. A study of the March Action, together with the short-lived 1919 Hungarian revolution—linked to the German events through the person of Béla Kun, who played a leading role in both—brings into sharp relief the catastrophic consequences of *not* basing Left political strategy on serious and sincere coalition building. It also brings into sharp relief the insightful political theories of Paul Levi, whose contributions, in a way not dissimilar to those of Martov's, have been, until recently, either ignored or denigrated.

The March Action

At the time of the March Action, the KPD, despite having more than four hundred thousand members at the time—a genuine mass party—nonetheless had the allegiance of only a small minority of the working class, and was thus far smaller and less influential than the traditional party of German labour, the Social Democratic Party (SPD), which was still many times the size of the KPD. Its minoritarian status notwithstanding, the KPD tried, in its own name, to call a general strike in March of 1921—what came to be known as the March Action. It was an attempt to "force" the German workers into revolution. David Morgan says that, "the essence of the March Action, as it was later described by an admirer, was that 'the party went into battle without concerning itself over who would follow it.' It was a classic attempt to create mass action by sheer act of will. . . . Rather than break off the contrived operation, the leadership increased the pressure on members and used all the means it could think of, including sabotage and faked bomb attacks on Communist property, to bring other workers out on strike."[2]

According to Pierre Broué, between two hundred thousand and five hundred thousand workers chose to participate.[3] Tragically, the former figure is probably the more accurate one, as John Riddell notes in his introduction to the proceedings of the Third Congress. "In Session 5, Heinrich Malzahn of the German opposition estimated that strikers totalled only two hundred thousand—just over half the party's pre-March membership—a figure not challenged in the congress."[4] Strikes are supposed to be actions of the working class, whose members far outnumber the small minority of that class that organizes itself into this or that political party. The fact that the March Action, a so-called general strike, involved at best half of the members of the party that called the strike, is powerful evidence of just how isolated from the mass of the working class the KPD was. Worse, the March Action was associated with numerous acts of violence by the small minority supporting the strike against the vast majority who had chosen not to follow the KPD's call to action. "The strike took on the character of a fratricidal struggle," writes Riddell. "Indeed, in many instances, Communists battled non-Communists among the workforce; in some cases workers were cleared out of the workplace by force."[5]

The party paid an enormous price for its adventurism: it was, arguably, irreparably damaged. Thousands of party members were arrested: by early June, "there were already 400 sentenced to some 1,500 years hard labour, and 500 to 800 years in jail, eight to life imprisonment and four to death."[6] Tens of thousands left the party, many leaving politics altogether, with party membership plummeting from 450,000 to 180,443.[7] Broué documents the very accurate analyses of the Luxemburgists Clara Zetkin and Paul Levi, who, just before the March Action, were absolutely clear that the German Left was in no position to challenge state power, and who were the first to openly oppose the ultra left-wing politics that had led to such a disaster.[8] By contrast, the Comintern leaders—the members of the Executive Committee of the Communist International (ECCI)—pushed hard for the March Action and were proven completely wrong. Lenin and Trotsky, after the fact, provided extremely clear critiques explaining the failure of the March Action—critiques made available in the documents of both the third and fourth congresses. But hindsight is always 20/20, and during the decisive weeks in March, the ECCI's key representatives in Europe were aggressive advocates for this very costly failure. The lessons from this catastrophe are codified in the politics of the united front (hence Riddell's choice of title for the Fourth Congress proceedings, *Toward the United Front*), and in an orientation toward influencing the majority of the working class as opposed to confining left-wing politics to the corridors of small minority organizations (hence Riddell's choice of title for the Third Congress proceedings, *To the Masses*).

The tragedy of the March Action was shaped by what came to be known as "the theory of the offensive." This theory asserts that "offensive," and sometimes insurrectionary, tactics are appropriate, even when communists constitute only a small minority of the working class and the oppressed. It was at the root of not just the 1921 political catastrophe in Germany but also the 1920 military catastrophe for the Russian state in its war with Poland, examined in detail in the previous chapter. In his introduction to *To the Masses*, Riddell links these two episodes.

> the Red Army's Polish offensive inspired an article by Nikolai Bukharin in the Comintern's world journal, headlined "The Policy of the Offensive," which drew on precedents from the French revolutionary wars of the 1790s to make the case that Soviet military advances could spark revolution beyond Soviet borders. In the run-up to the Third Congress, Bukharin's formula was born to a new life in the theory developed by the German party's majority leadership to justify its adventurist policy.[9]

Paul Levi and Béla Kun

A comparative analysis of Paul Levi and his nemesis, Béla Kun, can help bring the issues in question into focus. There is, today, much agreement that the March Action was an irresponsible adventure that shattered the party and isolated it from the mass of the German working class. However, around one key aspect of this experience—the role of KPD leader Paul Levi—there is little unanimity. Levi was clearly correct in opposing the March Action, yet he was expelled from the party on spurious charges of breaking discipline. He has been held in low esteem by many ever since. Those who examine Levi's career will inevitably encounter "the traditional epithets and insults of 'traitor' and 'renegade'" that permeate the bulk of the Stalinist-influenced scholarship on this period, writings that shamefully and inaccurately portray Levi "as no more than a 'class enemy' and a potential traitor, even when he was a leader of the KPD."[10] Levi's "crime," for which he was expelled, was to publish in the nonparty press a pamphlet critical of the party's role in the March Action[11]—a pamphlet whose essential analysis has stood the test of time. Ian Birchall unhelpfully calls Levi's action "political scabbing," which only serves to heighten the emotion around the issue and lessen the possibility of reasoned political inquiry.[12] The expulsion of Levi for the publication of a pamphlet is a sign of the degeneration not of Levi but of the KPD.

To the Masses gives us a tool with which to correct the historical record. Levi, having been expelled from the party, was not allowed to be present at the Third Congress. But in Riddell's book, almost a century later, he returns in spirit. Some of the most exciting content of *To the Masses* can be found in the appendices, which include "Paul Levi Appeals to Third Congress."[13] A carefully worded condemnation of the tactics of the KPD leadership, this piece constitutes an indictment of the actions of the Comintern representative in Germany—the Hungarian Béla Kun. Another appendix contains "Resolution by Clara Zetkin on March Action," a cogent defence of the "to the masses" united front approach.[14]

In a letter to Lenin, also in the appendices of *To the Masses*, we hear the chilling voice of Béla Kun unapologetically defending the March Action: "Beyond any question, the March Action has brought us great political and organisational successes and will bring us many more in the future." This absurd statement flies in the face of the historical record. From Kun's own words, we also gain insight into his use of slander and prevarication. "Levi and Zetkin are utter *hysterics*," he writes, "and what they are saying in the German party right now consists of nothing but lying gossip. No one can believe it contains even a grain of truth." Kun proclaims that Paul Levi is "universally recognised as dangerous." On one occasion, says Kun, "Levi tried to conceal his swinishness and stupidity behind Radek's authority." But his worst venom is reserved for Levi's close comrade, Clara Zetkin: "As for the statements of the aged comrade Zetkin, I would like to say only this: the old woman is suffering from senile dementia. She provides a living proof that Lafargue and his wife acted entirely correctly," he writes, referring to the suicide of Paul Lafargue and Laura Marx.[15]

These words—characteristic not of a serious activist but of a petty, prejudiced bureaucrat—come from what was meant as a private letter to Lenin. Its preservation and publication give us insight into the character and methods of one of the key figures of the era. The impression formed is not flattering. Even worse, we now know that in slandering and denouncing Levi and Zetkin, Kun was attacking the two figures most closely associated with developing the united front/coalition-building method, which is the chief contribution of these congresses to the contemporary Left. Levi, Zetkin, and others developed their politics in that section of the German Left influenced by Rosa Luxemburg, who, from a position of deep respect for the Russian revolutionaries, knew that Bolshevik methods could not be applied without amendment to the very different circumstances of Germany. The Luxemburgist current in the German Left insisted that strategy and tactics shaped by the experience of the revolution in Russia had to be radically modified in order to fit the extremely different conditions prevailing in Germany.[16]

One example can illustrate why we should study Levi's section of the Left and its unique approach to strategies and tactics. An early and important moment in the development of the united front method began with the metalworkers' union in Stuttgart, which, in 1920, called for the uniting of the minority communist workers with the mass of noncommunist workers in "a joint struggle for concrete improvement in the workers' living conditions."[17] This initiative inspired the issuing of an open letter from the KPD calling for the same approach on a national scale.

Clara Zetkin (left) and Rosa Luxemburg in Magdeburg, Germany, for the 1910 congress of the Social Democratic Party. Photographer unknown, Wikimedia Commons.

To the Masses makes available the full text of "Open Letter to German Workers' Organisations," the authors of which "appear to have been Paul Levi and Karl Radek."[18] The letter calls for workers' organizations to work together to achieve various objectives: to "begin unified struggles for higher wages," "raise all payments to victims of the War and pensioners in line with the demanded wage increases," "grant the unemployed across the whole country uniform payments," "distribute foodstuffs at reduced prices to all wage earners and those with low incomes," "confiscate immediately all available habitable spaces," and accomplish other very practical and realizable immediate reforms to improve the conditions of the poor and working-class populations of postwar Germany.[19]

The open letter originated in Stuttgart and illustrates the importance of developments in Germany. As Riddell tells us, "late in 1920, a meeting representing 26,000 Stuttgart metalworkers called for joint struggle for a list of basic demands; the appeal was published 10 December 1920. It was the first formulation of the united front policy that the Comintern was to adopt a year and eight days later."[20] The letter also highlights the central role of Levi and Zetkin. Levi, on returning from the war to Germany in 1918, made Berlin his centre of work, but he "maintained his connections with Stuttgart where Clara Zetkin lived, where the Spartacists had a majority among the local Independent Socialists (USPD), and where Levi helped organize deserters from the armed forces."[21]

The open letter's sensible, careful call for united action—for coalition building—was unfortunately rejected by the leadership of the Social Democratic Party (SPD), the party to which the vast majority of politicized German workers adhered. However, this call was also met with derision from the "left" section of the communists in Germany, who denounced it as reformist. These "lefts" would shortly displace Levi and Zetkin and take the KPD into the catastrophe of the March Action.

If rejected by the SPD leaders and the communist Left, the open letter was greeted with enthusiasm at the base of the workers' movement. As Clara Zetkin wrote, "the demands of the Open Letter had as their result that the masses organised in trade unions drove the union bureaucracy forward."[22] Heinrich Malzahn, a prominent shop steward and KPD member, said that the open letter allowed the KPD to "win a powerful influence before the March Action":

> This Open Letter, together with the slogan of a workers' and employees' united front against the employers' general offensive, won for us the trust of the working class. The best measure of the extent of our trade-union influence is the fact that the union bureaucrats felt that their power was threatened and responded by dismissing union staffers and expelling Communists. That did not harm us, but rather contributed to increasing the party's reputation and influence.[23]

After its publication on 8 January 1921, the KPD "called on the workers to organise democratic assemblies in order to impose their demands on their leaders, and to declare their will to undertake a general struggle to win them."[24] Meeting after meeting took place endorsing the letter's call for unity in struggle.

> On 11 January 1921, the delegate meeting of the workers in the Vulkan naval shipyard in Stettin took place, on 17 January, that of the production workers and office staff at Siemens in Berlin, in the Busch Circus, on the 19th that of the railwaymen in Munich, and in the days which followed, meetings of the metalworkers in Danzig, Leipzig, Halle and Essen, of the railwaymen in Leipzig, Schwerin, Brandenburg and Berlin, the national congresses of the saddle-makers and the carpet weavers, the meetings of the miners in Dorstfeld, and a large workers' gathering in Jena, all fully endorsed the Open Letter, and called for a struggle to be organised around its demands.[25]

To the Masses reveals the uneven response from leading Russian communists to this very fine initiative. It was "quite artificial," according to Zinoviev. "I do not believe that one can call on the workers to form an alliance with other workers' parties."[26] Bukharin agreed, arguing that the open letter approach "does not correspond at all to Communist demands" and "is not revolutionary. After all, we want communism; we want the dictatorship of the proletariat. . . . But what the letter says is that we want the proletariat to live. That is bizarre. Are we living for a new capitalism?"[27] These responses clearly demonstrate that an inability to understand the need for coalition building was not the preserve of irresponsible elements in the German party or of bureaucratic figures like Béla Kun, but went right to the top of the Russian party. Lenin, in contrast, sided completely with Zetkin and Levi and the open letter approach, putting himself in opposition to the German Left and to Zinoviev and Bukharin. In a letter to Zetkin and Levi, he called the open letter "*an entirely correct policy* (I have condemned the contrary opinion of our 'Lefts' who were opposed to the letter)."[28] To the Masses also contains the text of Trotsky's hour-long speech on strategy and tactics, a brilliant refutation of the ultra left-wing position and a defence of the united front/coalition-building approach.[29] Even today, almost a century later, it retains its relevance.

But while there is much to learn from *To the Masses* and *Toward the United Front*, not all of these lessons are about "what to do," but rather are warnings about "what not to do." For example, a vote to endorse Levi's expulsion from the congress was pushed through *before* the debate on the March Action. Surely, in a genuinely democratic organization, the debate on the March Action would have happened first, prior to any discussion of expulsion. Even worse, "Levi's appeal to the congress demanding reversal of his expulsion was apparently not made available to the delegates."[30] Surely, in a genuinely democratic organization, the document of a former leading member, written to that organization, would have been made available to those passing judgment on his fate.

In the end, Levi remained outside the ranks of the KPD and the Comintern, even though his political positions were ultimately endorsed by those organizations. And Kun—whose political positions were thoroughly discredited and rejected—remained a treasured member of the Comintern's leadership. This juxtaposition alone—the banning of Levi and the protection of Kun—indicates deep problems in the Comintern project. One year later, at the Fourth Congress of the Comintern, Zetkin and Kun made back-to-back speeches to mark the fifth anniversary of the Russian Revolution.[31] One can only imagine what Zetkin thought of her placement next to Kun.

The KPD in Germany had become a mass party through its fusion, in December 1920, with the left-wing section of the Independent Social Democratic Party (USPD). At a USPD convention in Halle in October 1920, "a majority of the delegates voted to accept the Twenty-One Conditions and join the Comintern," writes Riddell, going on to say that "Zinoviev gave the main speech in support of Comintern affiliation."[32] This is true, but incomplete. What we can now add is that the critical legwork had been done in the years preceding the Halle Congress by the KPD leadership under Levi. The party he inherited after the assassination of Luxemburg was riven with ultra-left, March Action–style politics. In 1919, he succeeded in separating from these elements through an expulsion of the most ultra-left section of the party, which, while it reduced the party from about one hundred thousand members to about fifty thousand, served to liberate it from what we might call the March Action section of the party. On that basis, he was able to begin negotiations with the left wing of the massive USPD and its eight hundred thousand members.[33] As David Fernbach writes, "Levi approached the leaders of its left wing, who agreed to co-operate on a unifying tactic."[34] Zinoviev did indeed deliver an impressive speech at the Halle Congress, a speech that we now have in English, along with the riveting counter-position by the Russian antiwar Menshevik-Internationalist Iulii Martov.[35] Ben Lewis's comment that "the long hard work of Zinoviev and [the] Comintern yielded a good harvest" minimizes the role of the soon-to-be expelled Levi.[36] Zinoviev's speech would never have had an audience without the careful organizing of Levi in the preceding years.

Hungary 1919

Béla Kun's politics were shaped by his experience in the Hungarian Revolution of 1918–19. On 21 March 1919, Hungary became a soviet republic. The new government "implemented a series of ultraleft measures," writes Riddell, measures that included "refusing to give expropriated land to poor peasants and overhasty collectivisation," and that led to the new republic's increasing isolation.[37] We now have new resources in English to add to our understanding of these events, specifically Paul Levi's critique, written just days after the Communists took power in Hungary. Levi warned that the Hungarian soviet republic came not from proletarian strength but from capitalist weakness and that "the possibility for the dictatorship of the proletariat exists not when the bourgeoisie collapses but when the proletariat rises."[38] He reminded readers of the program of the Spartacists: "The Spartacus League will never take over governmental power except in response to the clear, unambiguous will of the great majority of the proletarian mass of all of Germany."[39]

Kun took power without anything like a majority in the working class. It was estimated that in Budapest, the Communist Party had ten to fifteen thousand members, while in rural Hungary, the membership numbered twenty to twenty-five thousand.[40] This is a good beginning for a left-wing party, but it by no means makes it the mass instrument capable of leading a struggle for workers' power.

In a confusing series of events in early 1919, Kun was jailed as a dangerous radical, but while still in jail, he emerged as the key figure in "unity"
talks with his former opponents, the Social Democrats. Without question, the attraction of Kun, for the Social Democrats, was his association
with the Russian state, from whom they hoped to receive military aid.
Through diplomacy—not the mass action of the workers—Kun and the
Social Democrats drafted a text proclaiming that "a new regime was to
be set up on the Soviet model"—as if workers' power can be established
by diplomacy and decree. Kun did not stop at this. Béla Menczer tells us
what happened next:

> Decrees ordering the "socialisation" of all industrial, commercial
> and landed property employing over twenty persons were published.
> Also decrees to establish "Revolutionary Tribunals" to repress any
> action against the new order, to rename the armed forces and the
> Police "Red Army" and "Red Guard" and fixing the elections for
> "Workers' and Soldiers' Councils" (in Russian: Soviets) for April 7th.
> The Socialist and Communist Parties were merged.[41]

A fledgling communist party that represents, at best, a small minority
of the working class and that assumes "power," not on the back of a mighty
millions-strong movement, but through a back-room deal focused on
issues of geopolitics and international relations that were negotiated in a
prison cell, is clearly going to be in a very weak position. While both Karl
Radek and Paul Levi recognized the weak position of the Hungarian communists, they drew completely opposite conclusions. Radek horrifyingly
maintained that "the Communists should have maintained the gallows
next to the government-buildings in order, if necessary, to demonstrate to
their dear allies the concrete meaning of proletarian dictatorship."[42] Levi's
rejoinder was clear, accurate, and cutting:

> To propose the gallows, at the moment of the establishment of
> soviet-power, as the method of unifying and amalgamating the
> proletariat; to undertake the organisation and consolidation of the
> proletariat not on the basis of the "clear, unambiguous will of the
> great majority of the proletariat", "its conscious affirmation of the
> views, aims, and methods of struggle" of the Communists (accord-
> ing to Rosa Luxemburg), but on the basis of mutual hangings,

all this strikes me—I do not want to use strong words—as a very unfortunate method for the unification of the proletariat.[43]

Just 133 days after Kun's "revolution," Levi's warnings against substitutionist methods—that is, the Left taking power without basing itself on the mass self-activity of the working class—proved tragically correct. The Hungarian communists, by now completely isolated, had to flee for their lives, ushering in years of right-wing dictatorship.

Two Perspectives

Let us return to events in Germany. Two books have been influential in shaping an understanding of the German revolutionary years, both with the March Action at their core: Chris Harman's *Lost Revolution: Germany, 1918–1923* and Pierre Broué's *Révolution en Allemagne: 1917–1923*, available since 2006 in English translation as *The German Revolution, 1917–1923*. While these two books are, in many ways, very similar, they draw very different conclusions when it comes to the March Action of 1921.

Harman and Broué both agree that the March Action was an irresponsible adventure, shattering the party and isolating it from the mass of the German working class. However, around one key aspect of this experience—the role of KPD leader Paul Levi—they diverge sharply. Shortly after the March Action, as we have seen, Levi found himself outside the ranks of the party. Harman characterizes Levi's actions as his "departure from the party," a "resignation barely a week before the Action."[44] This is misleading. Harman is here conflating two quite different episodes. The first occurred on 22 February 1921, when Levi, Zetkin, and three others resigned—not from the party but from the party's leading body.[45] They resigned precisely over the related issues of adventurism and ultra-leftism, issues on which they felt isolated in the leadership; they believed, quite rightly, that they would be able to prosecute their positions more effectively as rank-and-file members. What Harman calls Levi's "departure" from the party happened later, on 15 April, and it was not voluntary. Levi was expelled from the party by the very leading body he had left just weeks before.[46] The verbal move from the highly charged (and accurate) term "expulsion" to the neutral and ambiguous term "departure" minimizes both the error of the KPD leadership and the destructive role of the pro-Russian leadership that took his place. It also seriously distorts Levi's place in this story.

Harman's emotionally charged dismissal of Levi makes it more difficult to assess accurately the political positions of the day. A key precursor to the united front approach—perhaps *the* key precursor—was the previously mentioned open letter, which called for unity in action of Social Democrats and Communists against the threat of the far Right. Levi's role was central in the drafting of this letter, and he was without question its key advocate.[47] According to Broué, the open letter "certainly expresses the political line which Levi had been defending for several months."[48]

Broué devotes two chapters to an examination of Levi's contribution to the German Left.[49] In doing so, Broué usefully highlights the efforts—by Levi, Clara Zetkin, and others deeply influenced by Rosa Luxemburg—to develop an approach to activist politics that was meaningful to their own context. Again, this meant an insistence that strategy and tactics shaped by the experience of the revolution in Russia—a country with pockets of industry surrounded by a sea of peasants—had to be radically modified in order to fit the extremely different conditions prevailing in urban, industrialized Germany.[50] Levi's politics were shaped through years of involvement with the section of the German Left influenced by Rosa Luxemburg, a current that included Levi, Zetkin, and Karl Liebknecht, among others best known for their role in building "the Spartacists," which originated as an antiwar group within the SPD after that party's parliamentary group capitulated to German nationalism and supported the slaughter of the First World War. There is much to learn from these Luxemburgists.

By contrast, Harman says little more about Levi in the period after the March Action, except to indicate that he would end his political life "veering towards the left wing of Social Democracy."[51] Throughout his book, Harman consistently minimizes the role of Levi and all the Luxemburgists, underlining their inexperience, small size, and lack of roots. He completely ignores the scholarship of David W. Morgan, who argues that the Spartacists "had put their advantage as the first outspoken opponents of the war to good use, building themselves strong positions in the party organizations in Stuttgart, Braunschweig, and parts of Berlin . . . and achieving significant minority positions in Düsseldorf, Leipzig, and elsewhere. Spartacist influence was pre-eminent among the antiwar youth."[52] Of particular interest here is the identification of Stuttgart as one of the key bases for the Luxemburgists. This influence of the Luxemburgists—particularly in the person of Clara Zetkin—continued into the early 1920s, which helps us to understand why the open letter, the first big unity-in-action initiative in Germany, came out of Stuttgart in 1920, laying the basis for the united front method. In other words, the emergence of the united front approach from Stuttgart is not the result of Paul Levi's efforts alone, but reflects the approach of an entire Luxemburgist current within the German Left, a current that included Clara Zetkin.

Morgan opens another area of inquiry with the critical observation that to properly understand the united front method, we must take seriously the other large formation on the German Left, the Independent Social Democratic Party. "The term 'united front' is historically associated with the Communist Party," he says, but "in 1921 and 1922 the USPD was *par excellence* the party of united-front tactics. The explicit goal of party policy . . . was to find programs that would override ideological differences and bring the three parties [of the German Left] together in a struggle for the essential requirements of the German proletariat."[53]

Harman's work suffers from an inadequate engagement with some of the key literature on the German revolutionary years. In this chapter, I have sketched out the contributions of three scholars whose works were published before Harman began his research—Pierre Broué, Werner Angress, and David W. Morgan. Harman either ignores these three entirely or uses their research carelessly. Harman does not reference Morgan's research at all. He critiques Angress for minimizing the strength of the KPD during the next great upheaval in class struggle in Germany, in the autumn of 1923.[54] Harman does rely heavily on Broué; indeed, his book has a structure uncannily similar to Broué's. Despite this similarity in structure, he draws completely opposite conclusions from those of Broué concerning Levi and the Luxemburgists. Broué engages with their work carefully and seriously; Harman, by contrast, is quite dismissive. Harman's book is weaker because of his inadequate engagement with the work of these three intellectuals.

For activists in the twenty-first century, the importance of the united front method is, without question, the most meaningful insight from this entire period. The united front approach—what we now might call coalition building—is the way in which minority currents of politicized activists can gather around a defined set of demands and seek unity in action, despite adhering to different politics. The very opposite of the united front approach was exemplified by what came to be known as the March Action of 1921. We have many positive lessons to learn in this regard from Paul Levi, a pioneer of the united front/coalition-building method, and only negative lessons to learn from the ineffective and divisive approach of Béla Kun. Broué's careful approach brings these points out carefully and clearly.

The Teacher–Student Binary

Trotsky in 1933, as we saw above, regarded the first four congresses as "unsurpassed" in their approach to political events of the day. In a 2012 review of *Toward the United Front*, Ian Birchall cautioned against taking such an evaluation too far, reflecting on the dangers of relying too heavily on the Comintern congresses:

> Many years ago, when I was young, it was common to find ortho-
> dox Trotskyists who claimed they based their politics on "the first
> four congresses of the Comintern." (You can probably still find such
> people in the remoter reaches of the Trotskyist blogosphere.) A
> position that made some sense in the 1930s, when Trotskyists were
> insisting that there was a clear break between Lenin and Stalin,
> became less and less relevant as both capitalism and the working
> class went through enormous changes.[55]

This is an important point. An uncritical reliance on the first four congresses inevitably leads to a simplistic understanding of the contrast between the "experienced Russian" leadership of the Comintern, and the "inexperienced, mistake-prone" leadership of the non-Russians. I have already highlighted the "inexperienced, mistake-prone" Russian and Comintern leadership in the March Action, the Hungarian soviet republic, and the invasions of Poland and Georgia. However, an approach to the first four congresses that blurs these mistakes is not limited to the "Trotskyist blogosphere," as Birchall implies.

To illustrate, here is an excerpt from the 1985 history of the Comintern written by the late Duncan Hallas, a founder and, for many years, a central leader of the Socialist Workers' Party in Britain, with which both he and

Birchall were associated for decades: "On the main issues, on the central thrust of its political line, the Comintern leadership was right and *all* its opponents, in their different ways, were wrong. That is precisely why the heritage of the first four congresses, in principles, in strategy and in tactics, is so indispensable to revolutionary socialists today."[56]

This perspective informs Hallas's entire approach. In the introduction of *The Comintern*, he quotes Trotsky: "The International Left Opposition stands on the ground of the first four congresses of the Comintern."[57] He then argues that "the Socialist Workers Party, in Britain, also stands on this ground—which is why the emphasis of this book is on the Comintern's revolutionary period, the period of the first four congresses and immediately after."[58] Two years after the publication of his book, Hallas went on a North American speaking tour to mark the seventieth anniversary of the Russian Revolution of 1917. In an interview published at the time, he spoke "of Bolshevism and of the Communist International in its early years after the Russian Revolution," saying that for himself and others looking to find lessons from that era, "the whole complex of both ideas and experiences that were developed during this period of socialist history are what guide us."[59]

Hallas's book highlights the great accomplishments of the Comintern, including the creation of the united front method. He documents clearly the degeneration of the Comintern after the first four congresses, when it became little more than an extension of the foreign policy of the state-capitalist Soviet Union. And he critiques aspects of its work in the earlier period: "The perspective of the Red International of Labour Unions was mistaken and, by 1921, this should have been recognised and the necessary conclusions drawn."[60] But his overall emphasis is on the key role of the first four congresses and, in those congresses, the superiority of the Russian experience, the Russian political method, and the Russian leadership, all of which he contrasts with the inexperience and political confusion that existed outside of Russia. The March Action story, of course, strains this orientation considerably, and Hallas recognizes the terrible role of the Comintern leadership in that event. But he dilutes this by deflecting the blame toward the German Communist Party, emphasizing that the enthusiasm of the Executive Committee of the Communist International for this adventure was echoed loudly among leading members of the German party. That is true, but it is beside the point. With the evidence he presents, a story could be told of a far-seeing German cadre, trained by Rosa Luxemburg, who had a pretty good sense about what to do in Germany in the early 1920s, but who were muscled out of the way by a well-financed, well-staffed Comintern cadre, who had *no* sense about what to do in Germany in the early 1920s. We cannot schematically separate the "good judgment" of the experienced, well-trained ECCI from the "bad judgment" of the inexperienced, ill-trained German leadership. It is a frame that simply will not work.

Hallas does qualify his close identification with the Russian leadership and their political decisions during the first four congresses, saying, "We cannot simply apply these lessons mechanically without thought to different situations."[61] But an overdrawn portrait of the virtues of the Comintern and the Russian party's leadership makes it difficult to identify and analyze the sometimes serious errors that they made. The Comintern leadership, in the period of the first four congresses, was *not* always right on the main issues. The invasions of Poland and Georgia and the March Action in Germany were not small, tactical blunders; they were mistakes that had historic, and tragic, consequences. Birchall is right: an angular perspective maintaining that "on the main issues . . . the Comintern leadership was right and *all* its opponents . . . were wrong" does open the door to difficulties. But these words and the framework are from Hallas, a central theoretician of Birchall's former party, not someone from the "Trotskyist blogosphere."

Birchall is aware of the limitations of Hallas's book. In his biography of Tony Cliff, Birchall argues that Hallas's work and certain other Trotskyist histories "are valuable in that they defend what was best in the early years of the Comintern . . . while sharply contrasting that early period to the later Stalinist horrors. Yet they remain essentially defensive." He contrasts Hallas's perspective with that of Tony Cliff, who "drew on a different tradition, the work of Alfred Rosmer and Victor Serge, which combined a total commitment to the basic aims and ideals of the Comintern with a recognition of its limitations in practice."[62]

In fact, some of Cliff's criticisms of the actions of the Comintern leadership are very harsh. He says that the March Action, "unlike other defeats," was "not brought about by misdeeds of the local national leadership, but by the adventurist policy imposed on the German party by the leadership of the Comintern."[63] Even worse, this mistake was only partially confronted: the Comintern leaders responsible for the disaster—Zinoviev, Bukharin, Radek, and Kun—were barely reprimanded. Paul Levi—in Cliff's words, "the talented former leader of the KPD, who had been wronged by the central leadership of the Comintern"—would end up expelled and outside the party.[64] With good reason, then, Cliff calls this chapter of his biography of Lenin "The Great Cover-Up."

But remember that Cliff writes about the March Action as an isolated exception to a general rule. That event, he says, was "unlike other defeats." In his four-volume biography of Lenin, the 1920 invasion of Poland— much more serious than the March Action, certainly in terms of lives lost and probably also in terms of its impact on the Russian state—is not even mentioned. He does deal with it in his biography of Trotsky, agreeing that "Lenin's policy turned out to be wrong and costly."[65] But this seriously understates the scale of the catastrophe. The overwhelming emphasis in the bulk of Cliff's many writings on the Russian Revolution is on the superiority of the Russian leadership—of Lenin in particular— when compared with the leaders of the Left outside of Russia. Cliff, in the spirit of Hallas, paints a picture of an experienced, wise Russian leadership interacting with an inexperienced, sometimes foolish non-Russian Left that was prone to errors and mistakes needing to be corrected through a deep study of Russian Bolshevik history. Cliff makes this point very sharply in his biography of Trotsky: "The Congresses of the Comintern were schools of strategy and tactics, and at them Lenin and Trotsky played the part of teachers, while the leaders of the young Communist Parties were the pupils."[66]

This approach is not helpful. The error of the March Action was not a single moment in an otherwise unblemished record. The 1920 catastrophe in Poland was equally destructive to the revolutionary process and equally the result of the "teachers"—in that case, Lenin—making an error of enormous proportions. This error was not a minor, accidental one, but one that exposed crucial flaws in Lenin's and the Bolsheviks' very conception of revolution. As already noted, Lenin outlined the most serious of these flaws in his 1920 speech, examined in the previous chapter, in which he made the case for "probing with bayonets" to discover "whether the social revolution of the proletariat had ripened in Poland."[67] This is a shocking position. The attempt to export the revolution through military invasion is the antithesis of the notion of self-emancipation that underlies any meaningful progressive politics and that was the essence of the Soviet experience at the core of the Russian Revolution.

The invasion of Poland was not just an episodic mistake. On 23 July 1920, "Lenin wrote to Stalin raising the possibility of a thrust through Romania, Czechoslovakia and Hungary with the aim of staging a revolution in Italy. In his reply, Stalin agreed that 'it would be a sin' not to try."[68] This approach was taken up and codified by Tukhachevsky in a theory of the "revolutionary offensive war"—an explicit argument that socialism could be advanced through force of arms.[69] Trotsky furiously combatted these deeply substitutionist notions of socialist transformation; his opposition to these notions, according to Isaac Deutscher, ran "like a red thread through his writings and speeches of this period."[70] In a critique of Tukhachevsky, Trotsky openly links the Russian invasion of Poland in 1920 with the German attempt at a revolution in Germany in 1921. "Since war is a continuation of politics by other means, must our policy be offensive?" he asks. He goes on to answer this question: "This was a very great and criminal heresy, which cost the German proletariat needless bloodshed and which did not bring victory, and were this tactic to be followed in the future it would bring about the ruin of the revolutionary movement in Germany."[71]

If the teacher–student binary is taken to an extreme, the conclusions can be not just wrong but dangerous. In 1978, writing while the Labour Party was in office in the United Kingdom, Cliff wrote: "In our times there is not a single issue which can be decided by ballots. In the decisive class battles bullets will prevail. The capitalists count the machine guns, the bayonets, the grenades at their disposal, and so does the proletariat."[72] These strange and shocking words were embedded in a four-volume biography of Lenin that for a while had some influence in the British and, to some extent, the international Left. It is one thing for Lenin and Tukhachevsky to have mistaken the twentieth century for the eighteenth century. Russia was a kind of hybrid society that did in fact combine premodern rural forms of life with modern twentieth-century industry and science. But when socialists in the West try to draw a straight line from Lenin in 1920 to strategy and tactics in the advanced capitalist world, the results, when not tragic, are embarrassing.

The teacher–student binary is similarly misleading as a framework with which to understand the very core of the Fourth Congress and the key term in the title of the Fourth Congress proceedings, "the United Front." As Birchall pointedly notes: "The united front was not spun out of the skulls of the Comintern's leaders. It was born of the experience of workers in Germany."[73] Let us return to the central role of the Stuttgart workers in the emergence of a united front in Germany. According to Riddell:

> The ongoing need for such a united front was posed by an assembly of Stuttgart's metalworkers in December 1920, acting on the initiative of local KPD activists who were strongly influenced by Zetkin. The metalworkers adopted a resolution calling on the leadership of their union, and of all unions, to launch a joint struggle for tangible improvements in workers' conditions. . . . Although the Social-Democratic leaders rejected this appeal, the Communist campaign in its favour won wide support from union councils.
>
> A month later, in January 1921, the KPD as a whole made a more comprehensive appeal for united action to all workers' organisations, including the Social Democrats. This "Open Letter" reflected the views of party co-chair Paul Levi, working in collaboration with Radek.[74]

It is very significant that it was workers in Stuttgart, Germany who were the first to arrive at the united front approach. As Riddell indicates, it is Stuttgart where Clara Zetkin had her base and where she had influence. As outlined earlier, this base had been built over years by Zetkin, Luxemburg, and the Spartacists. The united front/coalition-building approach thus emerged out of the experience of the German workers themselves—out of the work, in particular, of the politicized workers around Zetkin and the other Luxemburg-influenced members of the KPD. The united front approach was momentarily generalized into the German movement through the open letter, which was, in large part, the initiative of another German leader, Paul Levi. But this open letter encountered almost universal opposition from the representatives of the Comintern working in Germany, and its whole united front/coalition-building approach was tragically derailed through the March Action catastrophe. It was only after this catastrophe that the united front approach was generalized as a method within the Communist International as a whole.

It is true that during both the Third and Fourth Congresses, Trotsky clearly outlined the key principles of the united front, and in this sense, he was the teacher, lecturing to pupils at a school of strategy and tactics. It is true that he articulated a clear opposition to Lenin in the run-up to the Polish invasion and did his best to "teach" the Bolsheviks of their mistake in the months that followed. But it won't help to replace Lenin with Trotsky and retain the frame of "teacher–student" to understand the dynamics of the Comintern. To paraphrase the young Karl Marx, circumstances are changed by human beings, and educators must themselves be educated.[75] The emergence into consciousness of the need for the crucial united front orientation came from the experience of the German workers and was at first argued for publicly by key German socialists such as Zetkin and Levi. It was in the active, organizing experience on the ground, in which serious socialists interacted with advanced workers, that the educators became educated.

The proceedings of the Third and Fourth Congresses published in *Toward the United Front* and *To the Masses*—along with the earlier volumes published by Riddell—complete the record of the early years of the Cominterns and make possible a rounded assessment of the work of these congresses and of the entire era of the Russian Revolution, an assessment that embraces the successes and the failures—the constructive positions that were taken as well as the catastrophic and destructive ones. One of the striking aspects emerging from these volumes is the light they shed on the deep humanity of the participants. As Birchall notes, "these delegates were tough women and men who had lived through an exceptionally demanding decade."[76] A close examination of these proceedings and those of the early congresses enhances the reputation of some militants of that era whose politics reflected a commitment to self-activity (Clara Zetkin and Paul Levi, for instance) and diminishes that of others whose politics were imbued with substitutionism (Grigory Zinoviev and Béla Kun, to name two). That is all to the good. To properly assess the lessons of the past, we need *all* the information from that past, and on the basis of that information, we can draw our own conclusions about how best to use this history in our own work in the twenty-first century.

■ PART 3

The Rear-View Mirror

The Russian Revolution, which began with such hope on Women's Day in 1917, ended with the horrors of Stalinism and counter-revolution. Analysts have been gazing back at 1917 ever since, hoping—in the spirt of the Owl of Minerva cited in the preface—that, now that "the shades of night" have gathered, genuine understanding and wisdom can finally take flight. But recall that the preface also referenced a more pessimistic outcome, that outlined by Marshall McLuhan. Sometimes hindsight is no benefit, and we "look at the present through a rearview mirror" and end up marching "backwards into the future." With both of these possible outcomes in mind, part 3 of this book is organized around two of the key contributions of the twenty-first century that have sharpened our understanding of the Russian Revolution in the years since night has fallen.

This takes us into a time warp. As of this writing, the most recent twenty-first-century contribution to our understanding of the Russian Revolution was in fact drafted more than seventy years ago. But it was only in 2016 that we could acquire, for the first time, a complete published version of all the finished and unfinished fragments of Trotsky's last book—his political biography of Joseph Stalin. In that volume, he articulates, in a manner more compatible with Raya Dunayevskaya and C. L. R. James than with the Trotsky of *Revolution Betrayed*, the notion that the essence of the Soviet Union in the 1930s can be determined by the criterion of control of the surplus product. In placing Stalin's authoritarianism within this classic historical-materialist framework, he omits only the conclusion—that Stalin's elite represented a new class and that nothing progressive remained of what, until then, Trotsky had been calling a "degenerated workers' state." Trotsky's book exists in unacknowledged dialogue with the first great historical-materialist attempt to assess the nature of Stalin's Russia—that of Boris Souvarine, who broke a taboo of Leninist orthodoxy and explored the idea that there was something in the very nature of the Leninist party machine that created a breeding ground for a political "type" such as Stalin. At first, Trotsky vehemently disagrees with Souvarine on this point, but he then quietly and repeatedly returns to it. Chapters 8 and 9 develop and analyze key themes that emerge from Trotsky's analysis.

Chapters 10 and 11 are organized around themes developed in the 2015 intellectual biography of Lenin by Tamás Krausz, the most impressive outline of Lenin's epistemology published in this century. These chapters assert that in order to understand the history of revolution and counter-revolution in Russia, we need to put behind us the quasi-religious reverence toward Lenin that, for more than a century, has been a barrier to sober analysis. Chapter 10 begins with comments on Krausz's introductory biographical chapter and proceeds with a critical examination of Lenin's approach to the Russian Revolution of 1905; an assessment of Nikolay Chernyshevsky, a key influence on Lenin; and a survey of some of the other core subjects taken up by Krausz. I then broach the wider issue of historical materialism and the role of the individual in history, comparing the approaches of Krausz, Georg Lukács, and Leon Trotsky and making a case for the need to move beyond a focus on the individual in history—in particular, one imbued with reverence. Chapter 11 looks at one aspect of Lenin's theory of political organization and challenges a common view that he saw intellectuals as central to that process. In fact, from 1904 on, a profound anti-intellectualism was embedded in the core of Lenin's epistemology. This and other aspects of Lenin's epistemology need to be critiqued and transcended—which is impossible unless we finally develop a historical materialism that rises above the reverence analyzed in the previous chapter.

8 Trotsky on Stalinism—The Surplus and the Machine

Few events capture the tragedy of the Russian Revolution more graphically than the terrible moment in August 1940 when an assassin, operating on instructions from Moscow, mortally wounded Leon Trotsky—the most iconic of anti-Stalinists—by driving an ice-climbing axe into his skull. On Trotsky's desk, in the study where the murder took place, was the unfinished manuscript of a massive political biography titled *Stalin: An Appraisal of the Man and His Influence.*

Charles Malamuth—the translator hired by Trotsky—prepared for publication an English-language version of the work, the first half of which was approved and checked by Trotsky before his death. The remaining portions were in various stages of completion and Malamuth connected these unfinished fragments, writing what he called "extensive interpolations," which he says "in every case" were "set off from the author's text by brackets."[1] Thus edited, the text was ready for publication in 1941, but held back from sale until 1946. There was concern that its publication would jeopardize the war-time alliance with Stalin's Russia—exposing as it did the venal nature of Stalin's rule and the horrifying consolidation of a dictatorial state. When finally published, it "provoked outrage" from mainstream communists, at the time almost entirely under the influence of Stalin.[2] The book found few supporters even among anti-Stalinists. Rob Sewell says that in the preface to certain editions of the book, Trotsky's widow, Natalia Sedova, warned readers to distrust "phrases inserted throughout this book by Charles Malamuth," saying that Malamuth was "a political opponent of Trotsky."[3]

Now, thanks to the diligent work of Alan Woods, we have access to the complete manuscript—the appendix and first seven chapters revised by Trotsky before his death (all but the seventh chapter of the English translation were also checked by him), plus all of the unfinished fragments, including tens of thousands of new words not published by Malamuth. In addition, Woods has removed all of Malamuth's many bracketed insertions. Woods emphasizes this point: "Every trace of Malamuth's interference with the text has been expunged. Where this has created gaping holes in the text, I have added some 'bridging' passages, which are clearly indicated in square brackets."[4] The implication is that we can now, for the first time, gain unfiltered access to the evolving epistemology of one of the great figures of the twentieth century as he attempted to explain one of the great tragedies of the twentieth century—the rise to power of Stalin and the totalitarian system that was constructed on the bones of 1917.

Leon Trotsky in exile in Mexico in 1940, flanked by visiting friends. Photographer unknown. *Leon Trotsky and American Admirers, Mexico,* 1940. Courtesy of National Archives and Records Administration, Wikimedia Commons.

A Voice from Beyond the Grave

Aware since the 1970s of the controversy surrounding this text, I did a detailed "parallel" reading of the two editions, setting out to discover the exact nature of antipathy toward Malamuth. My conclusion was, without question, that this antipathy was unwarranted. A careful comparison of the two editions makes it clear that if Malamuth did "filter" the words of Trotsky to his own ends, the filter deployed was rather porous. Woods says that Malamuth "describes the October Revolution as a 'coup,' which simply repeats the slanders of bourgeois critics," and which "constitutes a gross distortion of the ideas of Trotsky."[5] Woods is undoubtedly correct on the latter point—Trotsky would never have referred to the October Revolution as a coup, and I did find two occasions, in his bracketed interpolations, where Malamuth uses the terms "coup" and "coup d'état" to describe the October 1917 events.[6] Woods has quite rightly removed them from his edition. But—with the exception of one well-worked-over passage examined below—nothing else of substance in the Malamuth translation has been altered. The two editions are, without any question, more similar than different.

The similarity is partially acknowledged by Woods. The portion completed by Trotsky and the translation checked by him—almost half the manuscript—Woods reprints with only incidental changes. As to the half of the Malamuth translation not checked and approved by Trotsky, Woods states that "having examined every sentence of the second half of *Stalin* . . . I consider that in general Malamuth's English translation is not all bad. Although it can hardly be considered a literary masterpiece, it is mostly a correct translation."[7] By Woods's own admission, then, many tens of thousands of the English words published in his edition were translated by Malamuth, not by Woods—to the point that Malamuth really should be listed as co-translator of the book. More pertinent than this question of publication ethics, however, is the question of political orientation. Absent the phrases inserted by Malamuth, and with all the new material from Trotsky translated by Woods, the core epistemologies of the two editions are identical. Malamuth's use of the word "coup" on two occasions may have been a trigger for the emotional responses of Trotsky's supporters, but it was little more than that. I will suggest here that the controversy created by the publication of *Stalin* was caused not by Malamuth but by Trotsky. A significant—and to some, uncomfortable—evolution in his epistemology is clearly evident in both the Malamuth and the Woods–Malamuth translations.

Furthermore, reading both editions brings into focus another work—Boris Souvarine's *Stalin: A Critical Survey of Bolshevism*, published in French in 1935 and translated into English by C. L. R. James in 1939. Nathalie Babel (Isaac Babel's daughter) called Souvarine's *Stalin* "the first biography and historical study of Joseph Stalin."[8] Souvarine, born Boris Lifschitz, was a co-founder of the French Communist Party and, from May 1921 until January 1925, a resident in Moscow—where, writes Michel Surya, he "became a member of three of the leading bodies of the Comintern," exerting what Surya describes as "considerable" influence over Communist Party leadership in the Soviet Union.[9] For a position on one of those three bodies—secretary to the executive of the Communist International—he was nominated by Lenin himself, for whom Souvarine was, in Hella Mandt's words, a "political protégé."[10] Trotsky refers to Souvarine's work repeatedly throughout his own biography of Stalin, criticizing it on key points, but nonetheless describing it as "without doubt the most conscientiously researched work in its selection of facts, documents and quotations."[11] Souvarine was part of the earliest wave of anti-Stalinists, famously labelled "the first disenchanted by communism" by his biographer Jean Louis Panné. In 1924, Souvarine was expelled from the Communist International and therefore from the French party that he had helped to form just a few years earlier.[12] However, he remained a committed activist of the Left, founding, in 1931, what Surya calls "one of the most remarkable journals to emerge from the extreme left between the wars, *La Critique sociale*."[13]

So, in what way does Trotsky's *Stalin* reveal a controversial evolution in the author's epistemology? First, Trotsky emphasizes that to understand the class nature of the Soviet Union, one must not solely employ the concept of state ownership of the economy, the main criterion advanced in his well-known *Revolution Betrayed*. One must also, and in fact primarily, employ a more orthodox, historical-materialist concept—that of control of the surplus product. Second, Trotsky notes that Stalin's rise needs, in part, to be understood in relation to the specific dynamics of the party machine so carefully constructed by Lenin. Both of these ideas are deeply embedded in the Souvarine text as well. At times, the reader of *Stalin* gets the impression that Souvarine is Trotsky's unacknowledged interlocutor.

I argue in this chapter that the *Stalin* biography made Trotsky's followers uncomfortable (it was essentially shunned for more than half a century), not because of the distortions introduced by Malamuth, but because of these two epistemological challenges to what was then historical-materialist orthodoxy. Furthermore, the epistemological evolution represented by these two ideas accompanied a willingness to interrogate and sometimes challenge other key aspects of the Leninist story, an interrogation that was pulling Trotsky the elder back toward positions he had held as Trotsky the youth. This honest questioning and scholarship by one of the key actors in the Russian revolutionary drama provides an indispensable resource for any serious student of that drama. It is important that the shunning be abandoned and that both editions of Trotsky's last work—and Souvarine's pathbreaking 1935 work with which Trotsky was engaging—be studied very seriously.

An Epistemology in Flux

Trotsky wrote *Stalin* while he was bending heaven and earth to hold his followers to the view that in spite of the Thermidor (what others called counter-revolution), about which he was so painfully aware, there remained something progressive about the Soviet Union, something worth defending. In his view, the Soviet Union remained (in the peculiar vernacular of the period) a "degenerated workers' state." However, he was more and more swimming in a milieu that found it increasingly difficult to apply the phrase "workers' state" and the adjective "progressive" to a regime associated with the creation of famine, with forced labour camps, and with purges that together destroyed the lives of millions.

Certainly, Souvarine did not see the Soviet Union as in any sense progressive. In a postscript to the 1939 English translation of his book, he said that counter-revolution had resulted in "a nightmare."

"The expropriation of the expropriators" has led to a sort of bureaucratic feudalism under which the proletariat and the peasantry, debased by officialdom and the mandarinate, have been reduced to a kind of serfdom. If the methods of production are not exactly capitalist, a term which in any case is indefinable, it is only because, for the majority of the Soviet pariahs, the system deserves rather the name of slavery.[14]

This was not the first time that the term *feudal* had been attached to the methods of Stalin. As the regime returned, in 1928, to forcible seizure of grain from the peasants and then began the horror of forced collectivization in late 1929, Bukharin, Rykov, and Tomsky, who were leading Bolsheviks, "accused the Party of pursuing a policy of military-feudal exploitation of the peasantry."[15] This charge was vehemently denied by Stalin in a long speech from which I have already cited extensively.[16]

Souvarine, Bukharin, Rykov, and Tomsky were not alone in trying to identify the mechanisms of exploitation in what was clearly a new, hierarchical, and class-ridden society. One of Trotsky's closest friends and collaborators was Christian Rakovsky, who was exiled to the far north in the late 1920s. Rakovsky clung to the view that the Soviet Union had progressive "survivals," but he saw clearly that it was dominated by a "great class of directors" for whom state ownership was, in fact, a kind of collectivized private property. Souvarine, in an important section of his book, takes Rakovsky quite seriously and quotes him extensively:

> From Siberia, Rakovsky and his deported friends wrote as early as 1930: "From a workers' State with bureaucratic deformations, as Lenin defined the form of our Government, we are developing into a bureaucratic State with proletarian-communist survivals. Under our very eyes has formed and is being formed a great class of directors, which has its internal subdivisions and which increases through calculated co-option and direct or indirect nominations (bureaucratic advancement or fictitious electoral system). The element which unites this original class is a form, also original, of private property, to wit, the State-power." And they took their stand very pertinently on a phrase of Marx, "The bureaucracy possesses the State as private property." Just as the Consulate was neither a republic nor a monarchy, the Secretariat is neither a democracy nor Tsarism, the consequence of a revolution which was neither socialist nor bourgeois.[17]

The English translation of Souvarine's work was done by C. L. R. James while he was writing his masterpiece on the Haitian Revolution, *The Black*

Jacobins. At the time, James was a leading member of the US Socialist Workers Party (SWP), the most important of the political organizations that looked to Trotsky for leadership.[18] In April 1939, he was part of a delegation from the SWP that travelled to Mexico to visit Trotsky in exile, an event principally known for the discussions with Trotsky that helped shape the way in which socialists relate to the struggle against racism.[19] We have no evidence of any views on the trajectory of the Russian revolution expressed by James during that visit, but we do know that just a few months later, James was openly challenging Trotsky's position on Russia. In an article provocatively titled "Russia—A Fascist State," James wrote that the Soviet bureaucracy, while it does engage in the "planning" indispensable to a workers' state, it does so in the manner of "any other capitalist class." He said that the Soviet bureaucracy "plans in order to get as much surplus value as possible from the workers, it plans to preserve itself against other capitalist classes."[20]

We also know that the woman who was soon to become James's close collaborator was in Mexico at the same time. In 1938, Trotsky's staff in Mexico was joined by the then twenty-eight-year-old Raya Dunayevskaya, who for a while served as Trotsky's Russian language secretary.[21] Her collaboration with Trotsky ended abruptly after the Hitler–Stalin pact of 1939.[22] About that pact, she wrote in 1941:

> Because we did not clearly understand the class nature of the present Soviet state, the Soviet Union's integral participation in the Second Imperialist World War came as a monstrous surprise. The Red Army march on Poland, the bloody conquest of part of Finland and the peaceful conquest of the Baltic states proved that the Stalinized Red Army had no more connection with the spirit, purpose and content of October than has the Stalinist state, whose armed might it is. What an abhorrent relapse from the conquests of October are the Stalinist conquests![23]

James and Dunayevskaya would go on to jointly develop the analysis that the Soviet Union under Stalin had degenerated into a form of state capitalism.

The point is that Trotsky's *Stalin* was written at a time when many of his closest collaborators were recoiling from identification with the horrors of Stalinism and looking for new ways of analyzing the postrevolutionary developments. Trotsky did not formally change his characterization of Russia as a workers' state, but without question, *Stalin* indicates a shift in certain of his fundamental points, specifically on two issues—the surplus and the machine.

Control of the Surplus Product

Mapping the different paths taken by Woods and Malamuth in the translation process reveals interesting bits of evidence as to editorial intention. As noted earlier, Woods believed that Malamuth had produced "mostly a correct translation," and as a result, Woods copied hundreds of pages and thousands of paragraphs *verbatim* from Malamuth—not only from the first seven chapters and appendix approved and/or checked by Trotsky, but from all the other portions of the Malamuth text. However, on a very few occasions, Woods did make serious attempts to retranslate. One portion in particular stands out. The Malamuth edition quotes Trotsky as saying:

> The Thermidor rested on a social foundation. It was a matter of bread, meat, living quarters, surplus, if possible, luxury. . . .
>
> The same social motivation is to be found in the Soviet Thermidor. It was first of all a matter of throwing off the Spartan limitations of the first period of the Revolution. But it was also a question of achieving increasing privileges for the bureaucracy. It was not a question of introducing a liberal economic régime. Concessions in that direction were temporary in character and lasted a considerably shorter time than had been originally intended. A liberal régime on the basis of private property means concentration of wealth in the hands of the bourgeoisie, especially its higher-ups. The privileges of the bureaucracy have a different source of origin. The bureaucracy took for itself that part of the national income which it could secure either by the exercise of force or of its authority or by direct intervention in economic relations. In the matter of the national surplus product the bureaucracy and the petty bourgeoisie quickly changed from alliance to enmity. The control of the surplus product opened the bureaucracy's road to power.[24]

The Woods translation makes roughly a dozen changes to this passage, including the following:

- "It was not a question of introducing a liberal economic régime" becomes "It was not a question of introducing a bourgeois economic regime"

- "Concessions in that direction were temporary in character" becomes "Concessions towards capitalism were temporary in character"[25]

The direction of these edits will seem minor to most. However, for those immersed in debates over "the Russian question" their direction is clear. Trotsky's text, as translated by Malamuth, can give the impression that there was a new exploiting ruling class emerging within the Soviet Union. Woods is at pains to keep Trotsky "orthodox" and to indicate that what was emerging was a new *bureaucratic caste*, not a new exploitive *ruling class*. Such a subtle distinction is indispensable to maintaining a view that the counter-revolution was not yet completed, that a new ruling class had not yet emerged, that the Soviet Union remained a "degenerated workers' state."

In a bridging passage in the latter half of his translation, Woods provides a succinct summary of the orthodox position of Trotsky's followers in the 1930s as it concerned the nature of the Soviet Union: "The restoration of limited free trading by the NEP [New Economic Policy] in 1921 was a retreat back to bourgeois expropriation. But in practice the freedom of trade was so limited that it did not undermine the foundations of the regime (the nationalization of the means of production), and the reins of government remained in the hands of the Russian Bolsheviks."[26] In other words, the foundation of the regime—what makes it "postcapitalist"—is the single criterion of "nationalization of the means of production." An afterword to the text by Alan Woods reiterates the decisive, for him, role of this single criterion using the example of the Soviet defeat of Germany in World War II: "Only the colossal vitality of the nationalized planned economy . . . saved the Soviet Union."[27] This is unpersuasive. In 1812, as in 1945, Russia similarly repelled an invading army, one led by Napoleon and not Hitler. In 1812, as in 1945, we don't have to look any further than the old category of patriotism to explain Russia's victory.

That criterion—the nationalization of the means of production—was the key (often the sole) criterion by which to assess the class nature of the Soviet Union for Trotsky and his followers in the 1930s. The problem is that throughout *Stalin*, Trotsky hardly mentions this criterion. Where he does, he is equivocal:

> The counter-revolution sets in when the spool of progressive social conquests begins to unwind. There seems no end to this unwinding. Yet some portion of the conquests of the revolution is always preserved. At any rate, the struggle against equality and the establishment of very deep social differentiations has, so far, neither been unable to eliminate the socialist consciousness of the masses nor the nationalisation of the means of production and the land, which are the basic socialist conquests of the revolution. . . . Thus, in spite of monstrous bureaucratic distortions, the class basis of the USSR remains proletarian. Although it undermines these achievements, the bureaucracy has not yet ventured to resort to the restoration of the private ownership of the means of production.[28]

His invocation of the continuing "socialist consciousness of the masses" was analyzed earlier, in chapter 5. If, as was argued in that chapter, there is little evidence of the continuing "socialist consciousness of the masses" in the 1930s, then indeed the only remaining criterion for claiming the continuation of socialism in the USSR would be nationalization of the means of production. Importantly, however, Trotsky concludes his point with the following caveat: "But let us bear in mind that the unwinding process has not yet been completed, and the future of Europe and the world during the next few decades has not yet been decided."[29] Trotsky then proceeds—in the paragraph that Woods so painstakingly revised from the Malamuth translation and throughout the book in other nonrevised sections—to suggest and develop a completely different criterion by which to assess the class nature of the Soviet Union—the control of the surplus product.

Trotsky asserts that "the substance of the Thermidor was, is and could not fail to be social in character. It stood for the crystallization of a new privileged stratum, the creation of a new substratum for the economically dominant class. There were two pretenders to this role: the petty bourgeoisie and the bureaucracy itself."[30] The petty (or petite) bourgeoisie (by this, he means primarily the so-called rich peasants) is clearly a class designation, but here he is putting the bureaucracy in the same category, which suggests that, in his thinking, it too was becoming a class.

In the latter half of *Stalin*, in notes that are slightly different versions of early material in the book, Trotsky writes: "Possession of the surplus produce opened the bureaucracy's road to power."[31] Developing a class analysis on the basis of control of the surplus product is, of course, the essence of Marx's method—and of historical materialism. However, Trotsky does not draw the conclusion that this control of the surplus product by a state elite results in a new class. Rather, he suggests that "the introduction of a liberal economic regime was out of the question. . . . A liberal regime based on private property means the concentration of wealth in the hands of the bourgeoisie and its upper layers. But the privileges of the bureaucracy did not flow from the automatic development of the existing economic relations."[32] True enough. But students of capitalism are all too aware that while aspects of capitalism's present might be "liberal," there was nothing liberal about its origins in state-directed mercantilism and the completely illiberal trans-Atlantic slave trade.

Souvarine makes many of the same points that Trotsky does, but does not hesitate to conclude that the Soviet Union is no longer in any way progressive or that it constitutes some kind of a workers' state. "So-called Soviet society rests on its own method of exploitation," he writes, "of man by man, of the producer by the bureaucracy, of the technician by the political power."

> For the individual appropriation of surplus value is substituted a collective appropriation by the State, a deduction made for the parasitic consumption of functionaries. Stalin reckoned for 1933 about 8,000,000 functionaries and employees, whose precise income it is impossible to estimate. But official documentation leaves us no doubt: the bureaucracy takes an undue part of the produce, corresponding more or less to the old capitalist profit, of the subjugated classes, which it submits to an inexorable sweating system. There has thus been formed around the Party a new social category, interested in maintaining the established order, and perpetuating the State of which Lenin predicted the extinction with the disappearance of classes.[33]

Souvarine does not give the resulting class society an official designation. But if he will not say what it is, he is absolutely clear what it is not:

> Stalin denies "State socialism" in the USSR on the ground that the means of production are collective property. But the appropriation of profit has an unquestionably private character, and it is this which matters. Private profit is apparent in the growing social inequality, which is more revolting in its arrant injustice than in the capitalist countries where it is diminishing, more intolerable in the terminology of hypocritical equalitarianism. No society, it is true, has ever existed without a hierarchy, without authority, without natural and artificial privileges. But the socialist dream of founding one has in Russia turned into a nightmare.[34]

His polemic here is directed against Stalin's view of the "progressive" nature of the Soviet Union. It could equally be directed at Trotsky.

"With the Aid of an Impersonal Machine"

The second area where Trotsky is carving out new territory, challenging an orthodoxy he helped create, has to do with theorizing a link between the rise of Stalin and the history of and nature essential to the Leninist party machine of professional revolutionaries (or to use contemporary language, professional staff). Very early on in the text, he makes this explicit:

> Stalin took possession of power, not with the aid of personal qualities, but with the aid of an impersonal machine. And it was not he who created the machine, but the machine that created him. That machine, with its force and its authority, was the product of the prolonged and heroic struggle of the Bolshevik Party, which itself grew out of ideas. The machine was the bearer of the idea before it became an end in itself. Stalin headed the machine from the moment he cut off the umbilical cord that bound it to the idea and it became a thing unto itself. Lenin created the machine through constant association with the masses, if not by oral word, then by printed word, if not directly, then through the medium of his disciples. Stalin did not create the machine but took possession of it.[35]

He comes back to this idea frequently throughout the text. Calling Stalin by his frequently used party nickname "Koba," Trotsky says the following:

- "Koba was protecting 'the *apparat*' [political machine] against pressure from below."[36]

- "Koba preferred to have firm ground under his feet. He prized the apparatus more than the idea."[37]

- "In all those instances when it is necessary for him to choose between the idea and the political machine, he invariably inclines toward the machine."[38]

- "Pulling wires from behind the scenes, relying on the illegal apparatus. In that activity Stalin undoubtedly proved himself more apt than anyone else."[39]

What Trotsky presents is a very strong claim that the party machine—disconnected from "the idea," his shorthand for the theory and program of Russian social democracy, and without the hand of its creator, Lenin—becomes the perfect breeding ground for authoritarianism and dictatorship. Critically, he does not see this as an aberration emerging late in the party's history, but as something embedded in its very nature, in that the "negative aspects of Bolshevism's centripetal tendencies" were making themselves apparent as early as 1905 at the Third Congress of the Russian Social-Democracy.

> The habits peculiar to a political machine were already forming in the underground. The young revolutionary bureaucrat was already emerging as a type. The conditions of conspiracy, true enough, offered rather meager scope for such of the formalities of democracy as electiveness, accountability and control. Yet, undoubtedly the committeemen narrowed these limitations considerably more than necessity demanded and were far more intransigent and severe with the revolutionary workingmen than with themselves, preferring to domineer even on occasions that called imperatively for lending an attentive ear to the voice of the masses.[40]

This is as scathing an indictment of the conservative tendencies of Leninist staff-driven centralism as any written by Luxemburg or Martov. Trotsky is, however, hesitant to draw too sweeping a conclusion:

> In this connection it is rather tempting to draw the inference that future Stalinism was already rooted in Bolshevik centralism or, more sweepingly, in the underground hierarchy of professional revolutionists. But upon analysis that inference crumbles to dust, disclosing an astounding paucity of historical content. Of course, there are dangers of one kind or another in the very process of stringently picking and choosing persons of advanced views and welding them into a tightly centralized organization. But the roots of such dangers will never be found in the so-called "principle" of centralism; rather they should be sought in the lack of homogeneity and the backwardness of the toilers—that is, in the general social conditions which make imperative that very centripetal leadership of the class by its vanguard.[41]

Here, his logic becomes confusing. Cultural backwardness requires centralism in the formation of a party. That centralism creates a conservative apparatus that privileges the place of the full-time staff of professional revolutionaries and that becomes a petri dish for the creation of bureaucrats in the Stalin mould. The negative effects can be offset by "the idea" and the presence of Lenin. But without Lenin, "the idea" disappears, and the authoritarian bureaucrat (Stalin) comes to prominence. If all this is true, then what possible justification could there be for such austere, staff-driven centralism in the first place? The whole schema only works, apparently, if we have access to a Lenin—to one great individual. A political program that embeds into its schema the necessity for one great individual is, to say the least, unsatisfying.

At one point, Trotsky links this analysis to his first major work, the 1904 book cited earlier, a book he wrote that provided a scathing criticism of Leninist centralism.[42] He says that the book "contains not a little that is immature and erroneous in my criticism of Lenin," but that it does contain "pages which present a fairly accurate characterization of the cast of thought of the 'committeemen' of those days."[43] However, in the context of criticizing Souvarine for focusing too much on the conservative nature of the machine and the professional revolutionaries, he is much harder on this 1904 work, calling its approach "a logical reduction to absurdity."[44]

> In the recently published book by Boris Souvarine entitled *Stalin*, Stalin's moral standing is deduced from his "belonging to the order of professional revolutionists." Souvarine's generalization in this case as in others is superficial and arbitrary. . . . He attempts to deduce the whole evolution of the Soviet Republic from certain original sins he attributes to the nature of Bolshevism—as if Bolshevism operated in an empty space or with an amorphous mass; as if Bolshevism were a demi-god of history which sculptures human material in its own image and likeness; and as if there were no interaction with the social environment.[45]

Trotsky says that Souvarine's "mind is formalistic and utterly devoid of historical penetration and intuition. He does not see the phenomena in three dimensions," only looking for "literary precedents and not the inherent laws of development."[46] Even a short examination of Souvarine's impressive book shows that this is completely unfair. I have relied as much on Souvarine as on Trotsky for analysis and for concrete and material-historical (i.e., not formalistic) examples with which to sketch out the social and material foundations of war, revolution, and counter-revolution in the Soviet Union. Both Trotsky and Souvarine are indispensable in such a project, and both often take the same approach to key historical issues. Take just one example—the role played by Lenin in advancing the career of the future dictator, Joseph Stalin. Souvarine's discussion of Stalin at the time of his 1912 co-optation onto the Central Committee is virtually identical to that of Trotsky:

> The Mensheviks had excluded this "professional revolutionary," the Bolsheviks advanced him. Unknown to the Party of which he was the instrument, he became one of the leaders solely by the decision of the other leaders. He was never elected; at all stages from the local and provincial committees in the Caucasus, up to the supreme All-Russian Committee he rose patiently and gradually in the hierarchy of the organisation without requiring the confidence of the masses or thinking of responsibility to them. He belonged exclusively to the "clandestine group of organisers" who imposed him on

the organised. The Party knew nothing about him at the time of his nomination and was to remain in ignorance for a long time. . . . In contrast to a Trotsky, independently developed, ripened in dispute and in controversy with Plekhanov, Lenin, and Martov, and associated with the representatives of international socialism, Stalin was a product of the Party, grown up under its tutelage; but this was only a section of the Party which was itself incorporated in the directing organisation.[47]

Trotsky's account of the same issue—Stalin's rise in the ranks of the party—is as follows. At the Prague conference in 1912, "Stalin wanted to become a member of the Central Committee" and "Lenin deemed it necessary to have him elected to the Central Committee." However, "Lenin . . . met with serious opposition. There was but one thing he could do: wait until the conference came to an end and then appeal to the small leading circle, which either relied on Lenin's recommendation or shared his estimate of the candidate. Thus, Stalin for the first time came into the Central Committee through the back door."[48] The point to underline here is that it was a back door held open by Lenin.

Not only are Souvarine's and Trotsky's approaches to this issue more similar than different, but they both show that what is at stake is not centralism per se (organizing underground against autocracy imposed a kind of centralism on all political currents), but rather *undemocratic* and *unaccountable* centralism.

For Souvarine, who had come to the conclusion that the authoritarianism of the Stalin era had roots in the authoritarianism of the Lenin era, such an approach was straightforward. Trotsky, though, was writing as an orthodox Leninist, for whom the key organizing idea is the need for a centralized party of professional revolutionaries. For him to so clearly identify the party machine as the breeding ground for Stalinism was not straightforward. His antipathy toward Souvarine is explicable as antipathy toward the conclusions drawn by Souvarine—that it was the Leninist era that created the conditions for Stalinism. But it is not explicable as antipathy toward Souvarine's analysis itself. In all key respects, Souvarine's line of analysis parallels that of Trotsky. We have already seen that Trotsky was obliquely moving back toward his 1904 analysis of the limits of Leninism. Perhaps his antipathy toward Souvarine comes from the fact that Souvarine is not at all oblique about this analysis, but synthesizes the twenty-four-year-old Trotsky's arguments clearly and without embellishment—an analysis that Trotsky, now an orthodox Leninist, would find uncomfortable. In the polemics against emergent Leninism in 1904, Souvarine says this:

> The most violent, if not the most effective blows, were dealt by Trotsky in the pamphlet *Our Political Tasks*, in which he described Lenin as "head of the reactionary wing of our Party" and the "dull caricature of the tragic intransigence of Jacobinism." Leninist methods, said Trotsky, would lead to a situation in which "the organisation of the Party takes the place of the Party itself, the Central Committee takes the place of the organisation, and finally the dictator takes the place of the Central Committee." They would in the end impose on the Party the discipline first of the barracks, and then of the factory.[49]

Or, as Trotsky put it, "Rigour of organisation as opposed to our opportunism is simply another form of political stupidity."[50]

9   A Movement's Dirty Linen

Some two decades before the young Souvarine became a protégé of Lenin, a young Trotsky had played that same role. In 1902, after his first escape from exile, the twenty-three-year-old Trotsky arrived in London, and his first destination was the apartment of Lenin and Nadyezhda Krupskaya.[1] Krupskaya and Lenin had a long political and personal partnership, beginning in the 1890s, that would last until Lenin's death in 1924. By contrast, this first moment in the comradeship between Trotsky and Lenin would last less than a year. In 1903, when Lenin created the Bolsheviks from a split in the Russian Social Democratic Labour Party (RSDRP), Trotsky sided with Lenin's Menshevik opponents, soon to separate from them as well, and, until 1917, took a "non-factional" position, arguing for the building of a united Left in Russia.

This divide between Trotsky and Lenin was bridged in July 1917, symbolized by the merger between the four-thousand-strong Inter-District Committee (or Mezhraionka, the non-factional group Trotsky had joined after arriving in Russia) and the now mass Bolshevik Party. From that point forward, Trotsky saw himself as both a Bolshevik and a Leninist, and after Lenin's death, while he prosecuted his long battle against Stalin, Trotsky's followers proudly took the name "Bolshevik-Leninist," a name proposed to them by Zinoviev when he, Kamenev, and Krupskaya were briefly part of what was called the United Opposition.[2] This claim to orthodox Leninism did not prevent Trotsky, in the pages of *Stalin*, from engaging in a deeply honest and at times highly critical analysis of the Russian Revolution and the role in that revolution played by Lenin and the Bolsheviks.

One key issue was the Bolsheviks' use of criminal and often violent methods by which to raise money. This approach to fundraising was rooted in the defeat of the 1905 revolution (the story of which will be detailed in chapter 10), which was also, not coincidentally, the moment when the figure of Joseph Stalin first indistinctly emerged onto the pages of history, under the alias of Ivanovich.

The "Muddy Wave" of Bolshevik Expropriations

In April 1906, in the wake of the suppression of the 1905 revolution, at a party unification congress held in Stockholm, Ivanovich (Stalin) declared, "We are on the eve of a new explosion. . . . On that all of us are agreed." In 1907, Lenin repeated this prediction: "Ahead is a new, an even more menacing . . . revolutionary crisis." As Trotsky notes: "This conclusion proved erroneous. Although the revolution was still strong enough to leave its impress on the arena of Tsarist pseudo-parliamentarism, it was already broken." Stalin and Lenin's mistake led inexorably to deep problems. It was the basis for advancing a "policy of attack," which "became increasingly the policy of guerrilla clashes and scattered blows. The land was widely inundated with so-called 'expropriations'—armed raids on banks, treasuries, and other repositories of money."[3]

The story of these expropriations is one of the most depressing narratives in the history of the Russian Left. Armed actions had an honourable enough origin as actions of self-defence against tsarist reaction. As Souvarine writes, in the reaction against the 1905 revolution, "the authorities shot rebels in the army and the navy without mercy, crushed rural rioting by punitive expeditions on a considerable scale."[4] This state terror was opposed by the "*drujiny*—fighting squads of the various revolutionary parties." However, the armed actions of these fighting squads were being carried out not in the context of a rising tide of mass action, but in a context of retreat, decline, demoralization, and mass passivity. In other words, as the mass movement retreated, small bands of armed rebels tried, for a while, to continue to attack in a futile attempt to substitute for the mass action of the now passive peasants and workers. In Souvarine's words, "the *boyeviki* (armed militants, sharpshooters, guerrillas) turned to the offensive. . . . Murderous attacks on policemen, Cossacks and government agents, armed expropriations of public and private funds began to multiply."[5] An attempt by an armed minority to substitute for the now demoralized working class and peasantry degenerated into actions of common criminals:

> The flying squads were mixed up with mischievous elements which were not disinterested but indisciplined and operating on their own account. Signs of degeneration, cases of common assault, acts of terrorism against the inhabitants, soon threw great discredit on the movement. Robbers and bandits, who made it their business to hold the population to ransom rather than to annoy the authorities made the "war of the partisans" suspect. It became difficult to distinguish between "ex'es" of all sorts and various forms of brigandage.[6]

Souvarine quotes Rosa Luxemburg characterizing these "innumerable thefts and robberies on private persons," which "passed like a muddy wave over this period of depression when the revolution was temporarily on the defensive."[7]

This was all a departure from Russian social-democratic policy. The same 1906 Stockholm Congress of the Russian Social Democratic Labour Party where Ivanovich / Stalin made his entrance into party history voted against the use of armed terrorism.[8] The party subsequently divided into warring camps, with one half of the schism, the Mensheviks, holding to that position and the other half, the Bolsheviks, abandoning it.

A disproportionate percentage of the expropriations took place in the Caucasus, which includes Stalin's native Georgia. Between 1904 and 1908, the Bolsheviks had "a large share" in the 1,150 "acts of terrorism" (to use Souvarine's phrase) committed in the Caucasus.[9] However—returning to an issue broached in chapter 6—in that region the Bolsheviks were simultaneously responsible for only a risible share of political activists. The Georgian Bolshevik Filipp Makharadze admitted "in bitter terms" that "at the beginning of 1905 the Social-Democratic organization . . . underwent a schism," and in the Caucasus, "the directing organs of the Party passed entirely into Menshevik hands. This circumstance made the rally of the masses to the Menshevik position inevitable."[10] The weakness of the Bolsheviks in Georgia was underlined by the 1906 Stockholm unification congress. Tiflis, the main city of Georgia, elected eleven delegates to the conference—ten Mensheviks and only one Bolshevik, Stalin, travelling under the alias Ivanovich.[11] This puts the armed actions of the Bolsheviks in the Caucasus in an even worse light. They were not solely the sub-stitution of a left-wing minority in the context of passivity of the mass movement. They were also armed actions being carried out by a minority within that minority, activists with no mass base in the area in which they were operating.

Bolshevik political isolation in the city notwithstanding, Tiflis was the location for the most spectacular—and most notorious—of the Bolshevik expropriations. On 23 June 1907, ten members of a Bolshevik armed group hurled bombs at a government mail coach. As Isaac Levine describes it: "When the smoke had cleared away, an appalling scene was revealed. Around the central Pushkin Park scores of bodies were swimming in pools of blood. Many were writhing in pain. The harvest totalled fifty dead and wounded."[12] The bombers escaped with 341,000 rubles, roughly equiva-lent (in 2015) to USD$10 million.[13] As Souvarine wrote: "The Tiflis affair exploded (the word is justified) like a bomb"; it took place just three weeks after the closing of the Fifth Congress of the Russian Social Democratic Labour Party, held in 1907 in London, where the delegates had voted unanimously to disband all fighting squads associated with the party.[14]

For years, this bombing and other unsavoury fundraising activities undermined the reputation of Lenin and the Bolsheviks in the eyes of the international Left. One of their more distasteful undertakings involved assigning two young male members to seduce two sisters, heirs to the for-tune of a wealthy supporter, N. P. Schmidt, who had died in 1907. The goal, which was achieved, was to redirect the sisters' inherited fortune into Bol-shevik coffers.[15] At one point, proceeds from a variety of these unsavoury activities were handed over to "three German social democrats, Franz Mehring, Klara Zetkin and Karl Kautsky, as trustees."[16] This occurred at a plenum of the Central Committee, held at the beginning of 1910, which, in the words of Nikolai Popov, author of the official "high Stalinist" history of the Communist Party, "was dominated by the influence of those who favoured union" between the Bolsheviks and the Mensheviks.[17] At that plenum, it was decided that "all factional centres were charged to transfer their funds to the general party treasury."[18]

In response, Lenin convened what he called a "conference" of the entire party in Prague in 1912. In a clever fictionalized biography of Krupskaya, Jane Casey writes that in January of that year, "spies and thugs were flocking in droves to Ilyich's [Lenin's] all-Russian Party Conference."[19] Leaving aside Casey's unflattering characterization of the delegates, she is certainly wrong as to the quantity. It was a "conference" in name only and attended by very few, although the exact number varies in different reports. Robert Williams puts the number at fourteen, "twelve Leninists and two Mensheviks"; Trotsky claims it was fifteen.[20] Popov lists, besides Lenin and Krupskaya, thirteen delegates: one was a representative of the Mensheviks, two were police spies, and the rest were virtually unknown but loyal Leninists.[21] James White says eighteen attended, sixteen Bolsheviks and two Mensheviks—and by his account, three of the eighteen were police spies.[22] The RSDRP aspired to be a party for the entire Russian empire. However, there were no representatives present from any of the oppressed nations that made up that empire. All the delegates were from Russia proper. According to Abraham Ascher, the conference delegates "at best represented one-fifth of the membership of the Social Democratic movement."[23] This tiny gathering called itself the "Sixth All-Russia Conference" of the RSDRP and met in session for twelve days, passing almost two dozen resolutions.[24]

One resolution characterized the vast majority of those who were not in attendance as "liquidators" and declared them outside the party. Twenty percent of the party, in other words, had, through a bureaucratic manoeuvre, expelled the other 80 percent.

A subsequent resolution, titled "Property in the Hands of the Former Trustee, and Financial Reports," argued in essence that: a) the German trustees (represented by Klara Zetkin) were holding funds and trying to determine to which wing of the party they should be delivered; b) with the exclusion from membership of the 80 percent, the 20 percent now constituted the entire social democratic movement; and, c) therefore there was now only one party to which the funds could be returned (the party of the 20 percent). With this syllogism in hand, they passed the resolution, which instructed "the Central Committee to take all measures immediately to obtain the property of the Party from Comrade Zetkin."[25] That obtaining control of these funds was the goal of the 1912 conference was made fairly evident the following month. Lenin travelled to Berlin, met with Kautsky, and "demanded the money held by the trustees. Failing in this, Lenin began legal proceedings." In May 1912, he was still pursuing the matter, seeking counsel from his legal representative. "'I myself was a lawyer,' mused Lenin. 'I studied French law and German law, regulating arbitration court relations. I have no doubt that Zetkin is completely wrong.'"[26]

It has been widely assumed that Stalin was a key player in the criminal activities that generated the funds in dispute, although it is something about which Stalin always remained silent. Trotsky, bizarrely, calls this a mysterious "romantic period" in Stalin's life.[27] Others saw it more negatively. According to Trotsky:

> On the eighteenth of March, 1918—that is, a few months after the founding of the Soviet regime—the Menshevik leader, Iulii Martov, wrote in his Moscow newspaper: "That the Caucasian Bolsheviks attached themselves to all sorts of daring enterprises of an expropriatory kind should be well known to the same citizen Stalin, who in his time was expelled from his Party organization for having something to do with expropriation." Stalin deemed it necessary to have Martov brought before the judgment of the revolutionary tribunal.[28]

Whatever the exact nature of Stalin's role, it was during this complicated, distasteful period of robberies and criminal activity that he first entered the leadership of the party.

Martov Versus Lenin

In 1911, Iulii Martov penned an explosive pamphlet titled *Saviours or Destroyers?* that documents the recourse by Lenin and the Bolsheviks to criminal activities to finance their operations.[29] In the pamphlet, Martov deals with the aforementioned 1907 Tiflis robbery, which, as we saw, injured and killed numerous innocent bystanders. "All those arrested in this connection were more or less well-known Bolsheviks." Their participation in these activities was against party policy, and they were thus expelled and "barred from membership of any other party organ."[30] These criminal activities continued, however, and Martov decided to publish the complete record because "the methods by which it [the Leninist group] maintains its supremacy in underground circles and which it is seeking to impose on the overt workers' movement are introducing confusion and dissension into the latter."[31]

The pamphlet was not well received. Clara Zetkin called it "grubby."[32] In 1914, Lenin published a lengthy journal article, "The Bourgeois Intelligentsia's Methods of Struggle Against the Workers," in response to a second charge from Martov—that a senior Bolshevik, Roman Malinovsky, was in fact a police agent. Referring to the earlier scandal, Lenin commented: "When Martov, in collaboration with and on the responsibility of Dan, wrote the special libellous pamphlet, *Saviours or Destroyers*, even the mild and cautious Kautsky . . . called it 'disgusting.'"[33] More precisely, Kautsky condemned it as the "washing of dirty linen in public."[34] Lenin linked the first scandal (exposing the Bolsheviks' "fund-raising methods") to the second (claims that Malinovsky was a police agent), drawing general conclusions. "Scandal-mongering," he said, was the characteristic method not just of Martov, but of an entire "social stratum" of what he called "intellectualists." "Every social stratum has its own way of life, its own habits and inclinations," he wrote.[35]

As it turned out, the charge of scandalmongering was spurious, at least as it concerns Malinovsky. In the spring of 1917, the provisional government opened the tsarist-era secret police files, which clearly documented Malinovsky's long-standing role as a police agent infiltrating Lenin's inner circles. Lenin's attitude toward Malinovsky, in the words of R. C. Elwood, "changed abruptly," a considerable understatement given that the new information led to Malinovsky's execution "before a Soviet firing squad in the early morning hours of 6 November 1918."[36]

Lenin was actually wrong on all matters of substance. Martov and the Mensheviks were correct not only about Malinovsky, but also about the Bolsheviks' criminal activities. In later years, many who had, with high emotion, distanced themselves from Martov's 1911 exposé began to change their minds. Kautsky, for one, "much later, told the Menshevik Boris Nicolaevsky that his scathing assessment had been mistaken."[37] In fact, from the very beginning, while Martov's pamphlet might have been attacked because it was seen to be in poor taste, it could not be challenged as to its factual basis. Souvarine writes that "the sincerity and truthfulness of his [Martov's] testimony cannot be contested" and that "other sources provide details and facts which confirm his allegations."[38]

The "airing of dirty linen" is always controversial in the heat of the political moment. For historians reflecting back on events and developing analyses of an arc of history, all dirty linen, controversial or not, must be brought into the light of day and examined. Trotsky does not shy away from this: he openly deals with the prehistory of Bolshevism brought to light by Martov in 1911, as well as with the practice of Bolsheviks once they were in power.

Adventurism, Staff, and the Political Volunteer

Trotsky says that at the time of the Tiflis bank robbery, Lenin's support for criminal activities was opposed by "the majority of the Bolshevik faction."[39] He provides little insight as to why Lenin would lead in such a damaging direction, except to say that in the case of the Tiflis expropriation, he "could not resist the temptation." Trotsky does not pass judgment on the period, except to say that the robbery "contained in it a goodly element of adventurism, which as a rule was foreign to Lenin's politics."[40] This is a very understated, almost muted, critique of events that were, in their time, controversial and destructive.

Trotsky wasn't always so understated in his critiques. At the peak of the controversy in 1910, while travelling to the Eighth World Congress of the Second International in Copenhagen, Trotsky told Lenin that in a forthcoming article in the main newspaper of the German Social Democratic Party, he had criticized the Bolsheviks on the issue of expropriations. Trotsky knew that, as he put it in his autobiography, "the most prickly question in the article was that of so-called 'expropriations.' After the defeat of the revolution, armed 'expropriations' and terrorist acts inevitably tended to disorganize the revolutionary party itself." The article, which was to appear that morning, led to what Trotsky characterized as the "sharpest conflict with Lenin in my whole life." Lenin tried, unsuccessfully, to get him to send a telegraph asking that the article be pulled. Plekhanov sought to bring Trotsky to trial. In the end, the affair blew over. In 1929, Trotsky repudiated his 1910 position, saying that "as a matter of fact, the article was not right."[41] But as I have outlined here, by 1940, he was more willing to portray the whole expropriations episode in a negative light, as he had in 1910.

Trotsky said little else about the money question. "Prior to the Constitutional Manifesto of 1905," he writes, "the revolutionary movement was financed principally by the liberal bourgeoisie and by the radical intellectuals. That was true also in the case of the Bolsheviks, whom the liberal opposition then regarded as merely somewhat bolder revolutionary democrats."[42] It is Souvarine who links the decline in funds from these sources after the defeat of 1905 to the increasing dependence on criminal activity: "Party subscriptions were insignificant. . . . The revolutionary profession, extended to a Party, or at all events to its officials, required more funds, and the 'ex'es' were the main source of supply for the Bolshevik Centre."[43]

According to Souvarine, "the money question was disastrous."[44] The Tiflis episode and the whole era of Bolshevik fundraising through crime was representative of "the eternal and disgusting question of cash," which had "acquired so much importance for international Bolshevism."[45] He links the addiction to criminal enterprise to more than adventurism, arguing that it was tied directly to Lenin's commitment to maintaining a party machine staffed by what Lenin called "professional revolutionaries": the "money question," then, was "the invariable corollary of the idea of professional revolutionaries."[46]

Raising funds played out differently for the Mensheviks, whose activists were "very rarely supported by the party": each "had to earn his living as best he could."[47] To use contemporary language, the Bolsheviks were like a staff-driven NGO, while the Mensheviks were more like a coalition run by political volunteers.[48] To finance their activities, the Mensheviks relied largely "on the infinitesimal subscriptions" (dues) from their members. In the period of reaction after the defeat of the 1905 revolution, these subscriptions declined drastically for both parties. Despite this decline, the Bolsheviks were able "to maintain a legion of militants, to send emissaries to all quarters, to found journals, to distribute pamphlets."[49]

These resources also facilitated the inflation of Bolshevik presence at party congresses. Souvarine writes that one participant in these expropriations "relates in his memoirs that his group paid to the Bolshevik Central Committee 60,000 roubles; 40,000 roubles to the Regional Committee, providing, among other things, for the publication of three newspapers; and in addition subsidised the journeys of delegates (certainly Bolsheviks) to the London Congress."[50] The cost of attending this 1907 congress in London was, of course, a huge burden for anyone coming from the difficult conditions prevailing in Russia during the years of reaction after the suppression of the 1905 revolution. There are conflicting accounts as to the relative size of the party's component parts at that congress. Souvarine says that in 1907, at the time of the Fifth Congress, the Mensheviks had more members than the Bolsheviks—43,000 compared to 33,000.[51] Later research indicates that Souvarine has the poles reversed: J. L. H. Keep writes that at the time of that congress, the party's total membership was in excess of 148,000, of which 46,000 were Bolsheviks, 38,000 were Mensheviks, 25,000 were part of the Polish section, another 25,000 were part of the Jewish Bund, and 13,000 were from Latvia.[52] By either set of figures, the Bolsheviks were far from a majority in the party, yet unlike the congress in 1906, they were usually able to win majorities. In 1911, Martov claimed that this capacity "was due solely to their command of secret financial resources."[53] The Bolsheviks were much more staff-oriented than other portions of the party, and staff did play a large role at the Fifth Congress. Souvarine says that "the statistics state" that the 312 delegates included "56 'professional revolutionaries' and 118 delegates 'living at the expense of the Party.'"[54]

At one level, the entire drama here is simply grotesque. On the big questions of the day (such as opposition to imperialist war), Leon Trotsky, Vladimir Lenin, and Iulii Martov were in complete agreement, but they nonetheless engaged, for years, in the most extreme polemics, one against the other. Revulsion at the criminal exploits of Bolshevik armed bands certainly fuelled the emotion behind these divisions. It all came to a head in the summer of 1914, when a special conference of the Second International was scheduled. Pavel Axelrod and Rosa Luxemburg, writes Martov, "were charged with drawing up a manifesto on the necessity of unity, directed against the splitting policies of the Bolsheviks. Lenin's faction was thus completely isolated."[55] As Ruth Fischer notes, Luxemburg and Axelrod were perfectly aware that Lenin's group would not countenance a forced unity with the rest of the Russian Left and that the "unification would have meant, in effect, the expulsion of the Bolsheviks from the International."[56] This sordid piece of history is rarely mentioned in discussions of either Lenin or Luxemburg. According to Martov, "the World War, breaking out after a few weeks, brought the unity effort thus begun to an end."[57] With the outbreak of war and the subsequent revolution and counter-revolution, squabbles that would otherwise have been inconsequential and forgotten (except, of course, for the victims of the robberies, seductions, and related activity) now became part of the prehistory of one of the big stories of the twentieth century.

Trotsky does not shrink from confronting this sordid history. The machine built by Lenin was, in part, rooted in the "muddy wave of expropriations," a key by-product of which was the emergence into leadership of Joseph Stalin.

The Muck of Ages I: Orientalist Discourse

The youthful collaborators Karl Marx and Frederick Engels, while still in their twenties, were realists about the human material with which their hoped-for new world would be created, as is clear from their writing in *The German Ideology*:

> Both for the production on a mass scale of this communist consciousness, and for the success of the cause itself, the alteration of men on a mass scale is necessary, an alteration which can only take place in a practical movement, a *revolution*; the revolution is necessary, therefore, not only because the *ruling* class cannot be overthrown in any other way, but also because the class *overthrowing* it can only in a revolution succeed in ridding itself of all the muck of ages and become fitted to found society anew.[58]

Some of that "muck of ages"—prejudices and stereotypes inherited from the society in which they lived—sullied the work of the young men who penned this warning. Marx's eleven theses on Feuerbach—written in 1845, when Marx was not yet thirty—contain many brilliant observations (most famously the last: "The philosophers have only *interpreted* the world in various ways; the point is to *change* it"). Yet in the first thesis—in which Marx criticizes Feuerbach for conceiving material reality only in the form of objects, rather than subjectively—he argues that, in *The Essence of Christianity*, Feuerbach "regards the theoretical attitude as the only genuinely human attitude, while practice is conceived and defined only in its dirty-Jewish [*schmutzig-jüdischen*] form of appearance."[59] This latter portion of the first of the theses is cited with far less frequency than the well-known portion that precedes it. The words appeared in a manuscript never published in Marx's lifetime, and we can only speculate about whether he would have retained the expression "dirty-Jewish" in a version of the "Theses on Feuerbach" intended for publication. However, this is not the only occasion where Marx uses what Abigail Bakan calls "highly problematic formulations." Regardless of "the common assumptions of the period," Bakan argues, "the generalization of ethnic stereotypes is hardly an inspiration for contemporary activists."[60] A complete appreciation of the theses and of the legacy of Marx and Engels demands that we confront both the insights into social life that they offer and the insights into the prejudices of nineteenth-century European society—prejudices from which Marx was not immune.[61]

The "muck of ages" also sullies, to varying degrees, some of the literature from the Russian Revolution, even before the rise of Stalin and Stalinism. Let's be clear: Lenin, Trotsky, and the key representatives of the Russian Left were far in advance of their contemporaries on many key issues. While many of their liberal contemporaries, for instance, were buried in this or that apology for the "progressive" nature of imperialism, the year before the outbreak of the Great War, Lenin prophetically wrote a passionate condemnation of "backward Europe" and a hymn of praise to "advanced Asia." He argues that in Europe, "the commanding bourgeoisie, fearing the growth and increasing strength of the proletariat, comes out in support of everything backward, moribund and medieval." As an example of "this decay of the entire European bourgeoisie," he cites "the support it is lending to reaction in Asia." He goes on to contrast this with Asia, where, he says, "a mighty democratic movement" is emerging. "*Hundreds* of millions of people are awakening to life, light and freedom," all while "'advanced' Europe . . . is plundering China and helping the foes of democracy, the foes of freedom in China!"[62] Leon Trotsky is famously identified with the related theories of Uneven and Combined Development, and Permanent Revolution.[63] Both theories focus on areas of the world that most of his contemporaries regarded as "backward"—Asia, Africa, and Latin America, in particular. Trotsky argued that, quite to the contrary, these areas of the world were the key to human progress, since they were the likely arenas for mass movements against imperialism, war, and capitalism. Given the horrors that transpired in the twentieth century—two world wars, the rise of fascism, and European and American military debacles in Indochina, Algeria, Korea, the Philippines, and elsewhere—and given the anticolonial movements that reshaped world politics, in particular after World War II, we can now see that Lenin and Trotsky were both on the right side of history in their analyses.

However, being progressive in policy orientation was not always reflected in their choice of language or argument. Whatever their merits (and they have many), the biographies of Stalin by Trotsky and, to a lesser extent, Souvarine occasionally resort to a casual discourse in the category of what Edward Said would call Orientalism.[64] Although they employ this discourse rarely, each occurrence is jarring and offensive to modern readers. On the very first page of his biography of Stalin, Trotsky writes: "The late Leonid Krassin . . . was the first, if I am not mistaken, to call Stalin an 'Asiatic.'" Trotsky does show an awareness of the problematic nature of the use of this word and tries to excuse its use:

> He [Krassin] had in mind no problematical racial attributes, but rather that blending of grit, shrewdness, craftiness and cruelty which has been considered characteristic of the statesmen of Asia. Bukharin subsequently simplified the appellation, calling Stalin "Genghis Khan," manifestly in order to draw attention to his cruelty, which has developed into brutality. Stalin himself, in conversation with a Japanese journalist, once called himself an "Asiatic."[65]

But this "essentialist" digression is no justification at all. Both the use of the word "Asiatic" and the essentialist apology with which its use is excused are offensive on their face.

Elsewhere, Trotsky uses Orientalist discourse without qualification. Explaining why Stalin wrote so little in the public press, Trotsky says: "Sluggishness and inordinate cautiousness, utter lack of literary resourcefulness, and, finally, extreme Oriental laziness combined to make Stalin's pen rather unproductive."[66] Describing generations of Russian occupation of Stalin's homeland Georgia, Trotsky writes that "in two centuries the Petersburg bureaucracy could not replace the old Asiatic barbarism with a European culture." Georgia's "semifeudal social structure was based on a low level of economic development and was therefore distinguished by the traits of Asiatic patriarchy, not excluding Asiatic cruelty."[67] Even worse, he goes on to speculate about "southern" and "northern" personality types:

In the countries of the Mediterranean Sea, in the Balkans, in Italy, in Spain, in addition to the so-called Southern type, which is character-ized by a combination of lazy shiftlessness and explosive irascibility, one meets cold natures, in whom phlegm is combined with stub-bornness and slyness. The first type prevails; the second augments it as an exception. It would seem as if each national group is doled out its due share of basic character elements, yet these are less happily distributed under the southern than under the northern sun.

Again, he tries to draw back from this offensive approach, saying: "We must not venture too far afield into the unprofitable region of national metaphysics."[68] But the damage has already been done.

Let us turn to Souvarine. He speaks of Stalin's "oriental dexterity in intrigue, unscrupulousness, lack of sensitiveness in personal relations, and scorn of men and of human life," his predisposition to "a typical Ori-ental method of avoiding a definite decision," and "his oriental method of dividing in order to rule."[69] This use of a casual Orientalist discourse casts its shadow into post–World War II scholarship as well: even the esteemed Isaac Deutscher, in his own political biography of Stalin, writes of "a relative eclipse of European Russia in favour of the backward Asiatic and semi-Asiatic periphery."[70]

Again, this casual Orientalist discourse occurs very infrequently in Trotsky's writings. In the magnificent work of his youth—his history of the 1905 revolution—the term "Asian despotism" occurs twice: "Tsarism represents an intermediate form between European absolutism and Asian despotism, being, possibly, closer to the latter of these two," and, similarly, "our autocracy, placed between European absolutism and Asian despot-ism, had many features resembling the latter."[71] This use of "Asian" to form a contrast with "European," in an attempt to make generalizations about aspects of the underlying political economy, parallels Deutscher's use of the term. Tamás Krausz also treats the term in this fashion, saying, without other comment, that "Trotsky placed Russian tsarism after 1907 some-where between European absolutism and Asiatic despotism."[72] In Trotsky's three-volume history of the Russian Revolution, his use of "Asiatic" is infrequent and has a similar tenor.[73]

Not all in the Russian socialist movement were as restrained in the use of an Orientalist discourse. One of those who showed less restraint was

Vladimir Lenin, the man to whom both Trotsky and Souvarine had once looked for inspiration. A casual use of Orientalist discourse is prevalent throughout Lenin's writings.

Sometimes, as with Trotsky, Lenin's use of Orientalist terms is clearly intended as a literary shorthand to contrast feudalism with capitalism, autocracy with democracy. In 1905, he wrote: "The democratic reforms in the political system, and the social and economic reforms that have become a necessity for Russia . . . will, for the first time, really clear the ground for a wide and rapid, European, and not Asiatic, development of capitalism."[74] And two years later he referred to the necessity of "a 'clearing' of the medieval agrarian relationships and regulations, partly feudal and partly Asiatic."[75] Not only do these references remain offensive, despite their innocuous function, but they are exceptions to his usual practice, described quite accurately by Bertram Wolfe, who says that "the word 'Asiatic' was frequently used as a term of opprobrium concerning Russia's past and institutions."[76] This is such a pervasive and little appreciated literary device in Lenin's work that it is worth providing examples from two decades of his writing:

- 1894—"Asiatic abuse of human dignity"[77]

- 1897—"from autocratic and semi-Asiatic Russia to cultured, free and civilised England";[78] "Asiatic backwardness"[79]

- 1901—"Asiatic-barbarian"[80]

- 1902—"Asiatic reaction";[81] "the Asiatically barbarous way in which the many-million-strong peasantry is dying out"[82]

- 1905—"Asiatic bondage";[83] "the accursed heritage of serf-ownership, Asiatic barbarism, and human degradation";[84] "all the infamy, viciousness, Asiatic barbarity, violence, and exploitation that pervade the whole social and political system of Russia";[85] "wildly Asiatic . . . autocracy";[86] "all the savagery of the Asiatic";[87] "with us despotism is Asiatically virginal";[88] "the Asiatic conservatism of the autocracy";[89] "in Russia purely capitalist antagonisms are very very much overshadowed by the antagonisms between 'culture' and Asiatic barbarism, Europeanism and Tartarism, capitalism and feudalism"[90]

- 1906—"Asiatic despotism";[91] "the accursed Asiatic canker and serfdom which is poisoning Russia";[92] "a ruthless mass struggle against Asiatic despotism and feudal landlordism";[93] "the clumsy, dull-witted and Asiatically corrupt Russian officials"[94]

- 1907—"Asiatic despotism";[95] "Asiatic semi-decay"[96]

- 1908—"the most backward farming methods and of all that Asiatic barbarism which is called patriarchal rural life"[97]

- 1911—"an ability to conceal . . . Asiatic 'practices' behind glib phrases, external appearances, poses and gestures made to look 'European'";[98] "an absolutism impregnated with Asiatic barbarity"[99]

- 1913—"slave, Asiatic, tsarist Russia";[100] "hardened, Asiatic philistinism";[101] "lovers of Asiatic scandal-mongering";[102] "Asiatic primitiveness";[103] "bureaucracy and Asiatic barbarism"[104]

- 1914—"what a great difference there is between Vandervelde, the true European, who attaches no importance to Asiatic gullibility or rule-of-thumb methods but collects the facts, and the Russian, liquidationist and liberal-bourgeois windbags, who pose as 'Europeans'!"[105]

Suddenly, in 1914, Lenin's use of an Orientalist discourse virtually disappears from his writings. One of his last uses of the term "Asiatic" displays, for the first time, the kind of qualification as to its use that we saw earlier in Trotsky's writing: "Knowing full well that there is much in the relationships and frontiers created or fixed by this class that is un-European and anti-European (we would say Asiatic if this did not sound undeservedly slighting to the Japanese and Chinese), the Cadets, nevertheless, accept them as the utmost limit."[106] That this was written in a journal article on the right of nations to self-determination is highly significant. Building solidarity between the Great Russian Left and the nations of Asia oppressed by Great Russian imperialism would be made more difficult by using "Asiatic" as a literary device to signify backwardness in contrast to "European" to signify progress and civilization. With the outbreak of war that same year, Lenin distinguished himself and his section of the Left with an insistence on the importance of the right of national self-determination, which might well explain the abandonment of his earlier practice. But for twenty years, he relentlessly used the term "Asiatic" in a completely Orientalist fashion. If the use of Orientalist discourse is an issue when reading Trotsky and Souvarine in the twenty-first century, it is a much more serious issue when reading Lenin.

Lenin, Trotsky, and Souvarine must of course be put in their context. All were part of a Left that paid a heavy price for its willingness to combat racism and prejudice within Eurasia. But that Left also suffered, as did most European ideologies at the time, from an unexamined modernist prejudice that, with little reflection, equated Europe with civilization and progress and Asia with barbarism and backwardness. It is a warning to the modern reader to avoid any inclination to put any of these authors on a pedestal and treat their writings as holy writ. They were all taking on difficult and important work, but they were doing so with all the strengths and weaknesses of the culture of which they were a part.

"An Old Buggy with a Leaky Roof, That's Lost Its Wheels"

Trotksy's *Stalin*, in its honest grappling with the legacy of Lenin and the rise of Stalin, can help us in the task of putting things in their proper context, and of *not* putting any one individual on a pedestal. There is no essential difference between the 1941 and 2016 translations of the book, the first by Malamuth and the second by Woods (the latter incorporating virtually unaltered the bulk of Malamuth's work). Certainly, the two places where Malamuth uses the word "coup" to describe the Bolshevik seizure of power would annoy followers of Leon Trotsky. But these in no way define the essence of the text. The "hue and cry" over Malamuth is a distraction. The high emotions associated with this unfinished classic have to do with the uncomfortable challenge to 1930s orthodoxy, a challenge clearly evident in Trotsky's loyal but highly critical treatment of the Leninist machine, and in his emphasis on control of the surplus product as a key criterion by which to assess the class nature of the Soviet Union. Trotsky's epistemology was in flux, and that posed a huge challenge to those who had been trained in his writings from the early 1930s.

Woods, in his 2016 work, fully accepts the inherited prejudice against Malamuth, repeating some of the claims made against him, but then concludes that Malamuth's translation is "not all bad" and in fact "is mostly a correct translation." He uses tens of thousands of words from Malamuth's translated text in his own translation, but he leaves Malamuth's name out of the credits. We need to move beyond this old factional squabble and get to the substance of the analysis.

In spite of his protestations to the contrary, Trotsky was being influenced by a younger generation—certainly including Souvarine, and probably also including James and Dunayevskaya—leading to his emphases on the surplus and the machine, notable departures from his previous writings. As a true intellectual, his ideas were evolving. We will never know where that evolution would have taken him, since he became one of the counter-revolution's millions of victims, stopped dead by a cowardly Stalinist assassin. But we need no longer be stopped from engaging with the text because of prejudice over the role of Malamuth. Woods, his unfortunate treatment of Malamuth aside, has done us a service by making the whole text available for study and reflection in the context of the centennial of the Russian Revolution. Both Trotsky and Souvarine wrote serious classic texts grappling with the horror of Stalinism, texts that are an important resource for new generations of scholars and activists in the twenty-first century.

One of Souvarine's best friends was the famous communist poet Isaac Babel, who we encountered in chapter 6. In the early 1920s, Babel was one of the most famous literary figures in Russia, but, by the end of the decade, he had become *persona non grata*. Cynthia Ozick says that "Babel's publications grew fewer and fewer. He was charged with 'silence'—the sin of Soviet unproductivity."[107] In 1939, he mysteriously disappeared, and "his name was not officially heard again until 1954," his daughter writes.[108] "As we now know, his trial took place on January 26, 1940, in one of Lavrenti Beria's private chambers. It lasted about twenty minutes. The sentence had been prepared in advance and without ambiguity: death by firing squad."[109] The execution was carried out the following day, "and his body was thrown into a communal grave."[110] Babel's fate mirrored that of the revolution itself, a metaphor for the tragic analyses outlined by Trotsky and Souvarine.

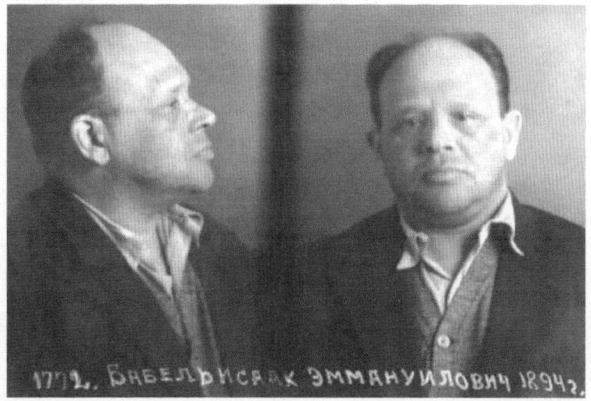

Mug shot of Isaac Babel taken in May 1939 by the NKVD or the People's Commissariat for Internal Affairs. Photographer unknown, Wikimedia Commons.

In 1932—before the worst of the forced collectivization famine hit in 1933; before the expulsion of tens of thousands (maybe hundreds of thousands) from Leningrad in 1934; before the Great Terror of 1937–38—Babel, having been away for three years, returned to Paris, where his wife and daughter lived. There, he visited his friend Yuri Annenkov and spoke of his concern for the future:

> "I have a family: a wife and daughter," said Babel. "I love them and have to provide for them. Under no circumstances do I want them to return to Sovietland. They must remain here in freedom. But what about myself? . . . Should I return to our proletarian revolution? Revolution indeed! It's disappeared! The proletariat? It flew off, like an old buggy with a leaky roof, that's lost its wheels."

> "Now, dear brother," he continued, "it's the Central Committees that are pushing forward—they'll be more effective. They don't need wheels—they have machine guns instead. All the rest is clear and needs no further commentary."[111]

10   Lenin—Beyond Reverence

In this chapter and the next, we turn from Trotsky's *Stalin* to Tamás Krausz's monumental intellectual biography of Lenin. Published in 2015, only months before Woods's translation of *Stalin*, Krausz's *Reconstructing Lenin* is based on the author's "40-year immersion in the study of the specifics and historical contexts of Lenin's thoughts."[1] Paul Buhle's response to the publication of the Krausz volume was enthusiastic. Referencing the experience of the United States in the late 1960s, Buhle says that members of the New Left movement were not particularly into Lenin. They were more taken with Marcuse, but did not look "reverentially at either," instead seeking "a third solution."[2] It is from this critical, nonreverential standpoint that Buhle approaches Krausz's work and concludes by giving it high praise. Krausz "gives us a Lenin who is deeply relevant for the present," he writes, ending his review with: "We need more 'leaps,' and this volume will help us."[3]

Buhle suggests that Krausz's book has succeeded in its professed aim—to reconstruct the intellectual biography of Lenin and, in doing so, to approach Lenin dispassionately and without reverence. As Krausz puts it, he was "looking for a path between the 'cult' and 'anti-cult.'" The "cult" glorified Lenin's singular and indispensable role as the founder of a party and a state. The "anti-cult" replaced what Krausz calls "uncritical glorification" with a focus on Lenin's thought "purely as an ideology of legitimization."[4]

Finding a path beyond reverence, between the cult and the anti-cult, is a very worthwhile project. The Lenin personality cult will be familiar to any who watched with horror as Lenin statues were built by the thousands in a Soviet Union dominated by totalitarian Stalinism and the Gulag. But when the Soviet Union collapsed, writes Krausz, "the legitimizing ideology of Leninism sank into the pits of history along with the system itself."[5] The anti-cult of personality became prominent in the Soviet Union in the 1980s and accelerated in the post-Soviet era as a "new system cried out for a legitimizing ideology."[6] Krausz's book is impressive, and its goal laudable. My own book has on many occasions relied on Krausz's scholarship. But this scholarship sometimes veers off of the nonreverential path. This chapter will look at three such moments—the approach Krausz takes to Lenin's biography, to Lenin's analysis of the 1905 revolution, and to Lenin's relationship to nineteenth-century novelist and social analyst Nikolay Chernyshevsky.

A Biographical Cul-de-sac

The signs that Krausz's approach will have difficulty rising above the stance of reverence are revealed in the book's first section, a seventy-page introductory biography of Lenin. Here, Krausz obsessively sketches trivial details of Lenin's personal life that are of no conceivable use to the project of dissecting Lenin's epistemology. He notes that Lenin liked cats and enjoyed singing songs of revolution as well as the occasional aria, that he "picked mushrooms passionately," that he had a humble diet ("soup, bread, fish, and tea"), that he "enjoyed the company of children, perhaps because he could have none himself due to his wife's autoimmune deficiency," that he went hunting a few days before his death. "It would have naturally crossed his mind," Krausz writes, "that he was saying goodbye to the life from which he had received fulfillment: revolution. Yet he was disappointed as his death approached, for the *work* remained a torso and not an entire body."[7]

Other reviewers have called this biographical chapter "excellent" and "sparkling."[8] But if Krausz's project is to navigate the middle waters between cult and anti-cult, the chapter is in fact distracting, too closely related to the long history of reverential treatment of every aspect of Lenin's life story.

From 1970 to 1982, the Institute of Marxism-Leninism embarked on a multivolume publishing project (twelve volumes in total) on Lenin's life, "in which the whole of his life can be traced year after year, by day, and sometimes by hour."[9] We are introduced to this publishing project with a description of Lenin as "the greatest revolutionary and theoretician of Marxism, the creator of the Communist Party of the Soviet Union, the leader of the Great October Socialist Revolution and the founder of the world's first socialist state." Apparently, "millions of people around the world" are eager to know every possible detail about him and "his theoretical and revolutionary-transformational activities."[10] A critical researcher, on reading this panegyric, will be suspicious about the quality and reliability of material written through such a lens of reverence.

The Krausz text, far from distancing itself from this kind of effusive praise, at times embraces it enthusiastically. Krausz insists that the "unity and coherence" in Lenin the mature politician were already visible in Lenin as a youth: "The theoretical and methodological coherence of his investigations is surprising, given that Lenin had not even finished his university education when he had already emerged from his first study of Marx."[11] He castigates "those who . . . deliberately or unwittingly overlook the coherence of Lenin's political and historical-theoretical analyses."[12] At times, the unrestrained encomium is almost embarrassing:

> Lenin embodied all that was necessary in the Russian Revolution for its survival: his organizational drive focused on decisive fields; he was inspiring to the masses; he had great political flexibility, uncompromising, plebeian and internationalist commitment, and stamina; he was self-sacrificial. . . . His energy, strength of will, and his passion for life infused his surroundings and became a sort of incitement to significant masses of workers, which was partly instrumental in the party's, or the Soviet government's ability to suddenly change tack in its politics whenever this proved necessary.[13]

Both the emphasis on the trivial and the overly effusive praise are symptomatic of an incomplete break from the stance of reverence, and might explain some of the limitations in Krausz's sketch of the development of Lenin's epistemology.

The 1905 "Dress Rehearsal"

Krausz argues, in essence, that self-emancipation was at the core of Lenin's epistemology. For Lenin, says Krausz, "*dialectical materialism* (and epistemology) incorporates the *self-movement* in things, phenomena, processes, as well as the *conscious human activity to transform society*.

Thus, it is not a matter of the historical dialectic of ideas, but rather the self-movement and self-creation of history through social classes and individuals."[14] It was the historical event of the 1905 revolution that actualized this theoretical approach, bringing to the stage of history the self-active urban proletariat organized in workers' councils (soviets)—the institutional embodiment of workers' self-activity. Lenin famously called 1905 a "dress rehearsal" for "the revolutions of 1917—both the bourgeois, February revolution, and the proletarian, October revolution."[15] Krausz asserts that "Lenin was the first, along with Rosa Luxemburg, to realize that in historical terms a new form of revolution had taken place in 1905."[16]

The equation of Lenin and Luxemburg in their understanding of the 1905 events will not hold up to sustained analysis. Krausz is, of course, right to include Luxemburg as a key theorist of the 1905 events. Her "Mass Strike" remains a classic text, shaped by the great events of which 1905 was the culmination.[17] So also does Leon Trotsky's *1905*, which is not mentioned by Krausz but which also rates as a classic.[18] Luxemburg and Trotsky, in fact, approach 1905 in ways quite different from Lenin. Their views reflect an epistemology quite different to that of Lenin's, and these views (along with their epistemology) have stood the test of time much more than have Lenin's.

Luxemburg saw 1905 as the culmination of years of interaction between economic and political struggle, years during which, through mass strikes, the Russian workers developed the consciousness and organization to challenge the autocracy. She traces an unfolding process of class struggle in the Russian empire, from the strike of St. Petersburg textile workers in 1896 right up to the outbreak of the revolution in 1905.[19]

The trigger for the Russian Revolution of 1905 occurred on 22 January. As Luxemburg describes it: "The demonstration of 200,000 workers ended in a frightful bloodbath before the czar's palace. The bloody massacre in St. Petersburg was, as is well known, the signal for the outbreak of the first gigantic series of mass strikes which spread over the whole of Russia within a few days." She goes on to say: "This January mass strike was without doubt carried through under the immediate influence of the gigantic general strike which in December 1904 broke out in the Caucausus, in Baku, and for a long time kept the whole of Russia in suspense."[20]

Luxemburg then traces the history of economic struggle underpinning the entire movement. March 1902 saw a strike in the Caucasus. In November of that same year there was a general strike in Rostov-on-Don. In 1903, "the whole of South Russia in May, June and July was aflame. Baku, Tiflis, Batum, Elisavetgrad, Odessa, Kiev, Nikolaev and Ekaterinoslav were in a general strike in the literal meaning of those words." The foundation of these great protests was economic. "In Tiflis the strike was begun by 2000 commercial employees. . . . In Elisavetgrad a strike began in all the factories with purely economic demands. . . . In Odessa the movement began with a wage struggle. . . . In Kiev a strike began in the railway workshops on July 21. Here also the immediate cause was miserable conditions of labor, and wage demands were presented. . . . In Nikolaev the general strike broke out under the immediate influence of the news from Odessa, Baku, Batum and Tiflis."[21]

"Thus," concludes Luxemburg, "the colossal general strike in south Russia came into being in the summer of 1903. By many small channels of partial economic struggles and little 'accidental' occurrences it flowed rapidly to a raging sea, and changed the entire south of the czarist empire for some weeks into a bizarre revolutionary workers' republic."[22] The now "raging sea" of workers' protests became general. First in Baku, "due to unemployment," a general strike broke out, the working class "again on the field of battle." Finally, "in January 1905 the mass strike in St. Petersburg broke out."

> Here also as is well known, the immediate cause was trivial. Two
> men employed at the Putilov works were discharged on account
> of their membership in the legal Zubatovian union. This measure
> called forth a solidarity strike on January 16 of the whole of the
> 12,000 employees in this works . . . in a few days 140,000 workers
> were on strike.[23]

The defining basis of Luxemburg's analysis, then, is the powerful foundation of confidence and organization built up in the economic struggle that underpinned the emergence of a political movement.

The young Leon Trotsky approached 1905 from a different but complementary angle. He emphasized the role of the soviets, which came about through "the revolutionary struggle of the Russian proletariat" finding "its culmination—and, at the same time, its tragic conclusion—in the activities of the Petersburg Soviet of Workers' Deputies."[24]

> The Soviet grew as the natural organ of the proletariat in its immediate struggle for power as determined by the actual course of events. The name of "workers' government" which the workers themselves on the one hand, and the reactionary press on the other, gave to the Soviet was an expression of the fact that the Soviet really was a workers' government in embryo. . . . The Soviet was, from the start, the organization of the proletariat, and its aim was the struggle for revolutionary power.[25]

Without question a new form of revolution had taken place. It was the introduction, to the world, of workers' council democracy through the institution of the soviet. Pierre Broué captures this brilliantly:

> The first soviet made its appearance at Ivanovo-Voznessensk, the "Russian Manchester." It was born from a strike committee and daily assemblies of strikers during the seventy-two days of the conflict. The form of the elected council of delegates, controlled by their constituents and recallable at any time, had appeared on Russian soil and was rapidly adopted in all the working-class areas. It seems that it was on the initiative of the print workers that the St. Petersburg soviet was born. It quickly expanded to include factory delegates from all the workers of the capital, representatives of non-working-class unions, and of the different factions of social democracy. It was the soviet that led the general strike and took responsibility for keeping order while simultaneously managing transportation and other public services whose functioning was indispensable for the strike's success. It was the soviet that . . . imposed the eight-hour day in workplaces. The soviet took the initiative to publish the daily *Izvestiia* (News); organized a boycott of taxes; launched the celebrated manifesto warning creditors that the revolution would not pay interest on Russia's debts; and imposed, against rising inflation, the payment of wages in gold coin. The soviet gave impetus to the organization of unions, organized workers' self-defence groups that repressed an attempted pogrom by the Black Hundreds [right-wing terrorists]. The St. Petersburg Soviet, by

example and through the publicity that was made about it, led to the formation of soviets in all the large cities.[26]

Trotsky responded to the soviets in a manner that put him ahead of his time. "Placed at the heart of the St. Petersburg Soviet experience," writes Broué, Trotsky "drew up the balance sheet of its actions, and concluded: 'There is no doubt that at the next revolutionary explosion, similar councils of workers will form in every country. A pan-Russian soviet of workers, organized by a national congress . . . will assume leadership.'" That future pan-Russian soviet, Broué quotes Trotsky as saying, would be able to organize "revolutionary collaboration with the army, the peasantry and the plebian sections of the middle classes," and would organize the abolition of absolutism, the police, and the bureaucratic apparatus. It would be in a position to initiate "the eight-hour day; the arming of the people and, above all, the workers; the transformation of the soviets into revolutionary organs of self-government in the cities, the formation of peasant soviets to direct, on the spot, the agrarian revolution," and finally, it would be able to ensure "elections to the Constituent Assembly."[27]

Trotsky, in 1905, worked closely with the Mensheviks—a faction of the Left that Lenin strongly opposed, but that, like Trotsky, had a clear sense of the importance of the soviets. According to Broué: "The Mensheviks, whose propaganda willingly advanced watchwords such as 'popular state,' 'self-government' or 'commune,' supported the creation of the soviets and in them played a not insignificant role."[28] Israel Getzler says this more forcefully. Placing a strong emphasis on the elective principle in both the party and the wider workers' movement, he writes:

It may not be unreasonable to suggest that by May 1905 [Menshevik leader Iulii] Martov's thinking and Menshevik thinking in general had already established the principles which in October 1905, were to become the organization and ideological basis of the Petersburg Soviet, i.e. a representative council of the entire working class elected in industrial plants, factories and workshops by democratic vote.[29]

By contrast, Lenin's wing of the Left—the Bolshevik faction—was completely sectarian. Pierre Broué says that the Bolsheviks "were much more reticent [than the Mensheviks] with regard to the soviets. Some among them saw in the soviets an attempt to develop an informal and irresponsible organism in competition with the authority of the party. The Bolsheviks of St. Petersburg began by refusing to participate" in the soviets.[30] According to Trotsky: "The part of the Bolshevik Central Committee then in St. Petersburg resolutely opposed an elected non-party organization because it was afraid of competition with the party."[31]

The extent to which Lenin shared this sectarian position is not clear. He did challenge it in a letter written from exile to the Bolshevik leadership on the ground: "I think it inadvisable to demand that the Soviet of Workers' Deputies should accept the Social-Democratic programme and join the Russian Social-Democratic Labour Party."[32]

This certainly shows Lenin pushing back against the sectarianism of the local Bolshevik leadership. But Lenin was very tentative, very unsure of himself, prefacing his remarks with the comment: "I may be wrong, but I believe (on the strength of the incomplete and only 'paper' information at my disposal) that politically the Soviet of Workers' Deputies should be regarded as the embryo of a *provisional revolutionary government*."[33] This is in sync with a caveat he introduces very early in the letter: "I consider it absolutely necessary to make a most important reservation. I am speaking as an onlooker. I still have to write from that accursed 'afar,' from the hateful 'abroad' of an exile."[34] Most significantly, the letter was not published in the Bolshevik press of 1905, lying dormant in the archives until 1940, years after Lenin's death. The fact that a letter from Lenin, written in the midst of revolution and suggesting a complete change of course for the Bolsheviks, should have remained unpublished speaks volumes.

Trotsky sharply differentiates Lenin's position from that of the local leadership: "The sectarian attitude of the Bolshevik leaders toward the Soviet lasted until Lenin's arrival in November."[35] Others present a different picture. James White says that Lenin "was rather dismissive of soviets as a means of mobilising the workers."[36] According to Broué, "Lenin himself did not seem to give the Soviets either the importance or the significance that he would give them in 1917."[37]

A survey of Lenin's writings in subsequent years shows clearly that he did not emphasize the mass strike movement, à la Luxemburg, or the soviet experience, à la Trotsky, but rather focussed on an event that has now receded into the obscurity of history: the armed uprising of two thousand militant fighters in Moscow in December (perhaps five hundred of them either Bolshevik or Menshevik).[38] "The December action in Moscow," wrote Lenin, "vividly demonstrated that the general strike, as an independent and predominant form of struggle, is out of date, that the movement is breaking out of these narrow bounds with elemental and irresistible force and giving rise to the highest form of struggle—an uprising."[39] The same emphasis can be found in a piece by Lenin marking the five-year anniversary of the 1905 revolution.[40] So focused on armed insurrection was Lenin that in volume 8 of his collected works, which covers the first six months of 1905, the word "insurrection" appears 44 times, "dynamite" twice, "bomb" 4 times, "revolver" 4 times, and "uprising" 202 times, 40 of which are part of the phrase "armed uprising."[41]

The 1905 uprising had no chance of success. It was crushed by the overwhelmingly superior armed strength of the tsarist state, leading to a horrific reaction. In February 1907, according to Trotsky, "Lenin characterized the political situation of the country in the following words: 'The most unrestrained, the most brazen lawlessness . . . The most reactionary election law in Europe.'"[42] Trotsky argued that "Lenin's prestige was decidedly lowered by the December defeat."[43] It took years, however, for Lenin to admit that the moment for armed uprising had passed. Through 1906 and 1907, Lenin and his Bolshevik comrades, in the face of continuing fierce reaction from the tsar, had not abandoned armed insurrection as an immediate objective.

Today, few looking back on the events of 1905 would identify the failed uprising of two thousand armed workers in Moscow as the highest form of struggle in 1905. Most would identify—à la Luxemburg and Trotsky—the mass strike of hundreds of thousands and the emergence of a network of workers' councils across the Russian empire as the highest forms of struggle. Certainly in 1906, Lenin had not yet come to this conclusion, calling the general strike "out of date" and identifying the armed uprising as "the highest form of struggle."[44] A January 1917 lecture by Lenin on the 1905 revolution is more rounded: he incorporated some of Luxemburg's emphasis on the importance of mass strikes and the interaction between the economic and the political, and he at least noted the emergence of "the famous Soviets of Workers' Deputies," which he refers to as "a peculiar mass organization."[45]

Broué provides a summary of the evolution of Lenin's thinking about 1905 that parallels the summary given here. In the heat of revolution in 1905, Lenin supported the conservative position of the St. Petersburg Bolsheviks, "in whose eyes the soviet was 'neither a workers' parliament, nor an organ of workers' self-government,' but only a 'combat organization for attaining certain definite aims.'"

> In 1907 he admitted that it was necessary to scientifically study the question to understand if the soviets truly constituted "a revolutionary power." In January 1917, at a conference on the 1905 revolution, he only mentioned the soviets in passing, defining them as "organs of struggle." It was only in the course of the following weeks that he would modify his analysis, under the influence of Bukharin, the Dutch socialist Pannekoek, and above all the role played by the new Russian soviets.[46]

Clearly, then, Lenin's position on the 1905 revolution did evolve and mature. By 1917, he was clearer as to the real significance of the event, the importance of the mass strikes, and the importance of the institution of the soviet. But this evolution was painstaking, took years, and lagged far behind the positions of both Luxemburg and Trotsky. Krausz's claim that "Lenin was the first, along with Rosa Luxemburg, to realize that in historical terms a new form of revolution had taken place in 1905" is simply wrong.

What Is to Be Done . . . with Chernyshevsky?

If great historical events, such as the 1905 revolution, can be foundational to epistemologies, so can influential works of literature. In this regard, Lenin scholars, Krausz among them, inevitably reference the nineteenth-century figure of Nikolay Chernyshevsky when sketching Leninist epistemologies. Krausz points out what many others have noted—that Lenin's favourite book as a youth was Chernyshevsky's novel *What Is to Be Done?* Lenin paid explicit homage to this novel, borrowing its title for his famous 1902 pamphlet on party organization.[47] Krausz argues that Chernyshevsky's novel, "in which the protagonist, Rakhmetov, is a revolutionary," can be "held responsible for Lenin becoming a revolutionary. . . . During one summer he read the book five times." Krausz then goes on to make a very strong claim: "Throughout his life, Lenin declared that next to Marx, Engels, and Plekhanov, Chernyshevsky had the greatest influence upon his thinking."[48]

Krausz is not alone in this emphasis on Chernyshevsky. China Miéville, in his contribution to books published on the centenary of the revolution, begins his account with a reference to "the trenchant Nikolai Chernyshevsky" and returns to the novel in his epilogue.[49] Tariq Ali, in his contribution to the centenary literature, frequently references Chernysehvsky and, like Krausz, makes strong claims as to the novel's influence on Lenin, saying that "the book that changed him was not *Capital*, as official hagiographers would later maintain, but Chernyshevsky's novel *What Is to Be Done?*"[50] At the same time, both Miéville and Ali display some ambivalence about the literary value of Chernyshevsky's novel, which Miéville calls a "strange book."[51]

As an artifact of a moment in Russian history, *What Is to be Done?* is worth reading and studying. Chernyshevsky's novel was part of the literary ferment against tsarist oppression that was so characteristic of nineteenth-century Russian literature. However, those who tackle it in the current period will not encounter an easy book.[52] As a work of literature, the novel is laborious and tedious, reminiscent at times of high Stalinist "socialist realism" and at others of writings by the rational egoist Ayn Rand, one of the twentieth century's most prominent anticommunists. However, a reverential approach to Lenin too often spills over into a reverential silence about these aspects of his favourite author.

Written while the author was imprisoned, completed in 1863, and serialized in the publication *Sovremennik* (Contemporary), the novel proved "quite too liberal" for the tsarist authorities. As the translators of the 1886 English edition stated in their preface, the novel "was hardly brought out in book form before it was ruthlessly suppressed." Nonetheless, they wrote, it "made an immense sensation throughout Russia. It is said that hundreds of young girls living in disagreeable circumstances started to follow Véra Pavlovna's example, and hundreds of young men, to live honorable, lofty, philosophical lives in the fashion of the types represented by Lopukhoóf and Kirsánof."[53]

Richard Peace describes the novel's protagonist, Rakhmetov, as "Chernyshevsky's answer to Bazarov," the nihilist protagonist of Ivan

Turgenev's *Fathers and Sons*.[54] Writing in the introduction to the 1989 English translation of *What Is to Be Done?* Michael Katz and William Wagner characterize Bazarov's world view as "destructive at best. He aims only 'to clear the ground' and has absolutely no positive program in mind."[55] In Turgenev's novel, Bazarov sums up his philosophy by proclaiming to his friend Arkady, "Give us fresh victims! We must smash people!"[56] Bazarov fails miserably at love and dies a tormented death after recklessly poisoning himself with typhus during a needless autopsy on a peasant. There is little to learn from his example.

As a role model, Rakhmetov has moved beyond this all-embracing nihilism and is, in that sense, an improvement. But Rakhmetov's alternative to nihilism has its own problems. He is guided by "a set of original principles to govern his material, moral, and spiritual life," Chernyshevsky writes. "He said to himself, 'I shall not drink one drop of wine. I shall not touch any women.'" Although he had been "brought up on a sumptuous diet," he "gave up white bread and had only black bread at his table. For weeks at a time he never put a lump of sugar into his mouth; for months at a time he ate no fruit, no veal, and no poultry."[57]

Apart from the avoidance of women, these ascetic predilections might be understood as a young activist's desire to live like the "common people." In Rakhmetov's words: "Anything the common people eat on occasion, I too can eat on occasion. Anything that is never available to them, I too must never eat. That is essential so that I can appreciate how difficult their life is compared to mine." But not all of his dietary choices can be so categorized. We learn that "he needed to eat beef, a great deal of beef. . . . He ordered his landlady to purchase good quality beef, the very best cuts for him." He also had one habit about which he felt "remorse"—his smoking: "Out of his 400-ruble income, almost 150 went for cigars."[58]

The puritanical traits listed to this point strike us as quaint but harmless. Others, though, are bizarre and abhorrent. One morning, Kirsanov (earlier spelled Kirsánof) is summoned by Rakhmetov's landlady, who senses something amiss. He goes in haste to his friend's apartment. "Rakhmetov unlocked the door with a broad, grim smile," and Kirsanov was confronted with a terrible sight.

> The back and sides of Rakhmetov's underclothes . . . were soaked
> in blood; there was blood under the bed; the felt on which he slept

was also covered with blood; in the felt were hundreds of little nails, heads down and points up sticking out almost half a vershok [nearly an inch]. Rakhmetov had been lying on them all night. "What on earth is this, Rakhmetov?" cried Kirsanov in horror. "A trial," he replied. "It's necessary. Improbable, of course, but in any case necessary. Now I know I can do it."[59]

This was the man that Chernyshevsky labelled "extraordinary."

According to Katz and Wagner, Chernyshevsky "drew heavily on British utilitarianism to explain human behavior and to refute idealist conceptions of morality. The resulting theory of rational egoism enabled him to reconcile the individual's need for personal self-fulfillment with the collective interests of the community."[60] So strong is this rational egoist component of Chernyshevsky that a widely cited defence of Ayn Rand—Chris Matthew Sciabarra's *Ayn Rand: The Russian Radical*—sees a direct link between Chernyshevsky and Rand. According to Sciabarra, the ethics of Chernyshevsky amount to "a form of psychological egoism, where each person always acts selfishly," a stance perfectly in sync with Rand's *Atlas Shrugged* and *The Fountainhead*.[61]

Krausz surmises that it was during "the summer that followed his expulsion from Kazan University" that Lenin read *What Is to Be Done?* five times. That would have been the summer of 1888, when Lenin was eighteen years old. What was it that drove the young Lenin to consume this novel over and over again that summer? Lenin's student activism, for which he was expelled from Kazan University in December 1887, came only months after the death of his elder brother, Aleksandr, who was arrested and executed in May for his involvement in a plot to assassinate Alexander III. This might well have drawn a grief-stricken teenage Lenin toward Rakhmetov. According to Nathan Haskell Dole and S. S. Skidelsky, "nearly all the characters" of the Chernyshevsky novel "are supposed to be drawn from real life," including Rakhmetov, who "is considered by many Russians to be a true picture of Karakózof, who in 1866 attempted to assassinate the Emperor Alexander II."[62] Dole and Skidelsky are not speculating about a hidden meaning planted by Chernyshevsky; the novel was finished three years prior to the assassination attempt. It is, rather, a reflection of the way in which the novel was so aligned with the spirit of the time that its readers could easily leap to such a conclusion.

We can have some patience for Lenin's fascination with the peculiar figure of Rakhmetov. Lenin was young and grieving the loss of his brother. We should have less patience with Lenin's biographer, who leaves the reader with the false impression that it is Chernyshevsky the novelist who stayed with Lenin all his life—alongside Marx, Engels, and Plekhanov.

Except for the homage to the novel embedded in the title of Lenin's own *What Is to Be Done?* Lenin never refers to Chernyshevsky the novelist in the *Collected Works.*[63] He writes with respect about Chernyshevsky "the materialist," who "ridiculed the petty concessions to idealism and mysticism that were made by the then fashionable 'positivists.'"[64] He praises Chernyshevsky the "revolutionary democrat," who "approached all the political events of his times in a revolutionary spirit and was able to exercise a revolutionary influence by advocating . . . the idea of a peasant revolution, the idea of the struggle of the masses for the overthrow of all the old authorities."[65] He cites Chernyshevsky's careful analysis of the Peasant Reform of 1861. Chernyshevsky, Lenin writes, saw that so-called reform as "*vile.*" From its inception, "he clearly saw its feudal nature, he clearly saw that the liberal emancipators were robbing the peasants of their last shirt."[66] This "emancipation" of the peasants included punitive "land redemption payments," which were so extreme that "for half a century the peasants have languished in hunger, and have died on those land allotments, weighted down by such payments."[67]

A genuine intellectual biography of Lenin demands that we separate Chernyshevsky the mediocre, Rand-like novelist from Chernyshevsky the dedicated political activist. We should similarly separate the teenage Lenin grieving for his elder brother from the adult Lenin trying to organize a socialist movement. Such separations, however, become impossible once the biographer loses objectivity through an attitude of reverence and deference.

Historical Materialism and the Role of the Individual in History

Paul Buhle says that "Krausz might well be regarded as successor to Georg Lukács," referring to a 1924 book on Lenin by another philosopher from Hungary.[68] Krausz agrees. "The subject of this book," he writes in the preface to *Reconstructing Lenin*, "is not unprecedented within the Hungarian field of Lenin research. A publication by Georg Lukács of what he called 'an occasional study' on the 'unity of Lenin's thought' came out as early as 1924. His 100-page essay is an autonomous philosophical work of extraordinary value, and as such still has its own independent life."[69]

But this puts a whole lot of weight onto a little pamphlet that, as Martin Jay points out, was "hastily written in February 1924, to commemorate the loss" of what Lukács called "the greatest thinker to have been produced by the working-class movement since Marx."[70] The pamphlet is replete with panegyrics of the same type: Lenin was a "genius" who saw "the true essence, the living, active main trends . . . behind every event of his time."[71]

This is compatible with a tradition, already visible before Lenin's death, of treating him with a reverence that had the flavour of religion (or of a Chernyshevsky novel). In an article titled simply "Lenin," to mark the twenty-fifth anniversary of party organizing in Russia, the always florid Karl Radek wrote: "All revolutionists amongst the proletarians of every country are filled with the thought and the wish that this Moses, who has led the slaves from the land of bondage, may pass with us into the promised land."[72] Reaching back more than two thousand years to find a mythical biblical character as a reference point for a biographical sketch of a living person is both unnecessary and embarrassing.

In the immediate aftermath of Lenin's death, Trotsky, usually more measured, also wrote in quite florid terms, calling Lenin "the great leader, Lenin, Ilyich, the unique, the only one." He went on to say, "Lenin is no more. These words fall upon our mind as heavily as a giant rock falls into the sea. . . . The party is orphaned; and so is the working class." And finally: "How shall we go forward? Shall we keep to the road, shall we not go astray? For Lenin, comrades, is no longer with us."[73]

We can perhaps understand Lukács's and Trotsky's emotional responses to the death of a head of state and of a comrade, but we need to put these responses in their context. Part of that context was politics—deadly serious politics that must be appreciated in our reading of both Lukács and Trotsky from that year. Trotsky's little pamphlet titled "Lenin Is Dead," as Bertram Wolfe notes, "was written hurriedly because Lenin had just died. . . . It was rushed to the press because Stalin had cunningly deceived Trotsky about the day of Lenin's burial to convince the ailing Trotsky that he could not possibly arrive from a sanitarium in the Caucasus in time for the funeral."[74]

Martin Jay says something similar about Lukács's *Lenin*, which was "probably designed to head off the accusations of heresy stimulated by *History and Class Consciousness*," Lukács's attempt at a philosophical defence of Bolshevism published the year before Lenin's death. In the small pamphlet to commemorate Lenin, Lukács purged "virtually all references of his ultra-leftist sectarianism."

> Instead, Lenin's "Realpolitik" . . . was invoked as an antidote to the utopian musings of the Left sectarians. . . . He praised Lenin's theory of the vanguard party with few of those Luxemburgist qualifications evident in at least the early essays of *History and Class Consciousness*. Although the soviets were still lauded as the locus of dual power under a bourgeois regime and the means by which the split between economics and politics was overcome, they were severed entirely from any notion of majoritarian democracy, for "it must always be remembered that the great majority of the population belongs to neither of the two classes which play a decisive part in the class struggle, to neither the proletariat nor the bourgeoisie."[75]

This is awkward territory for both Lukács and Trotsky—and of course, for Krausz. A method by which to analyze the role of the individual in history does not automatically flow from the categories central to historical materialism, a paradigm that is focused on the intersection between political economy, social movements, and class struggle and that consciously disparages the liberal approach (and the Chernyshevsky approach), which fetishizes the role of "great men" (and they are usually *men*). Yet these hastily written eulogies—and Krausz's twenty-first-century recapitulation of the same themes—feel much more rooted in either that disparaged liberal tradition or the unexamined Chernyshevsky tradition rather than in historical materialism.[76]

There are much better attempts at situating the individual—including the individual named Vladimir Lenin—within the wider dynamics of political economy and class struggle. Compare Trotsky's grief-stricken approach in 1924 to his more dispassionate approach a decade later.

In 1934, Trotsky eschewed the "genius" category employed in Lukács's 1924 panegyric. "Lenin was not a demiurge of the revolutionary process," writes Trotsky. "He merely entered into a chain of objective historic forces. But he was a great link in that chain."[77] For Trotsky, that link is one that includes the collective institutional actor, the Bolshevik Party. The October Revolution "was inferred from the whole situation," but could not have happened "without a party. The party could fulfill its mission only after understanding it. For that Lenin was needed." Trotsky identifies the equivocation of authoritative leaders such as Lev Kamenev and Joseph Stalin, who were "tossed by the course of events to the right. . . . Inner struggle in the Bolshevik Party was absolutely unavoidable. Lenin's arrival merely hastened the process. His personal influence shortened the crisis."[78]

This is a much deeper analysis than that provided by Lukács. It does not deny the role of the individual: in fact, Trotsky writes that "the role of personality arises before us here on a truly gigantic scale." However, "it is necessary only to understand that role correctly, taking personality as a link in the historic chain."[79] However one evaluates the actions of Lenin, Trotsky, and the Bolsheviks, at the plane of understanding class struggle dynamics, this analysis is head and shoulders above that put forward by Lukács—and Trotsky—in 1924.

A Plural, Not a Singular, Left

Krausz argues that "it is impossible to excavate the legacy of Lenin without steady determination and strict analysis."[80] However, imbued with the very reverence against which he warns us, his book falters on both counts. In fact, the very existence of one more biography of Lenin (we already have hundreds) poses its own questions. Too much of the Left's long engagement with the Russian Revolution has been coloured by a counter-intuitive focus on the role of the lone figure of Vladimir Lenin—counter-intuitive because historical materialism, the method claimed by most who focus on 1917, points us not toward individuals but toward political economy and social classes.

In the Russian revolutionary era, probably the key test for any notion of party building was posed by the necessity of opposing an imperialist war. Perhaps the key moment in creating an antiwar movement was the famous Zimmerwald conference of 1915. Krausz implies that it was principally

Lenin who pushed for this conference.[81] In fact, it was the product of a much wider layer in the antiwar Left than just the Bolsheviks.[82] Israel Getzler notes that "though the original initiative came from the Italian socialists," a key mover was Lenin's nemesis, Iulii Martov. When leading Italian socialist Odino Morgari was in Paris in April 1915, five months before Zimmerwald, Martov, in the words of Getzler, "worked on" him and "appealed to Robert Grimm to replace what was planned as a conference of socialists of neutral countries only, by an international conference of all socialists pledged to peace."[83]

To this point, Lenin and the Bolsheviks had advocated a peculiar and divisive policy known as "revolutionary defeatism." Sometimes this policy focused only on Russia. A resolution "adopted by the foreign (i.e., outside Russia) sections of the Bolshevik party at their conference in Berne in March 1915" called the defeat of Russian tsarism "under all conditions, the lesser evil."[84] At other times, the policy implied that such an approach should be applied by all socialists to all countries involved in the Great War. In 1915, Lenin and Zinoviev, in their pamphlet *Socialism and War*, argued that "the Socialists of *all* the belligerent countries should express their wish that *all* 'their' governments be defeated."[85] Besides being difficult to understand, this position was prone to extreme misinterpretation. In Brian Pearce's words, there was the "danger of a sterile nihilistic conclusion being drawn from his presentation of the way to fight against the war." Noticing that Lenin was calling for the defeat of Russia in the war, a Ukrainian nationalist approached him in January 1915 to seek a working agreement, asking for the Bolsheviks to work openly with those allied with Russia's wartime enemies. Lenin, notes Pearce in his succinct account, had to "rebuff" these "hopeful overtures," telling the anti-Russian Ukrainian: "We are not travelling the same road."[86] Both Luxemburg and Trotsky saw Lenin's position as simply social patriotism in reverse. Whereas the "social patriots" lined up with the militarism of their own state, Lenin's policy would be used by those who were lining up with the militarism of the opposing states—but *all* militarisms had to be opposed.

At Zimmerwald, Lenin's position on revolutionary defeatism was supported by just eight delegates. Trotsky, who was with the majority, argued that the Leninist position, sectarian and confusing, pushed a program of action too far into the future. It was not sufficiently organized around activism in the here and now for an immediate peace. Trotsky proposed a manifesto that put the question of an immediate peace at the centre and that provided a socialist analysis as to the causes of the war. In contrast to Lenin putting "defeatism" to the fore, Trotsky advanced the position of "the struggle for peace . . . a peace without annexations or war indemnities and based on self-determination for *all* peoples."[87] Lenin, knowing that he was isolated, decided to not vote against this, and Trotsky's position was carried unanimously and without amendments. But Lenin did not immediately change his mind. "After Zimmerwald," writes Pearce, "Lenin continued for just over a year to plug away at his 'defeatism' thesis." And, at the next antiwar gathering in Kienthal, in April 1916, he again attempted, without success, to have his defeatist views adopted as the standpoint of the movement. After Kienthal, he published two more pieces defending the defeatist standpoint, but these appear to be his last statements on the matter.[88] In their work on the ground, many Bolsheviks, in practice, came around to the more concrete position of Trotsky, Martov, and the majority of the Zimmerwaldians.

Pierre Broué calls Zimmerwald a "decisive turning point" in the construction of a New Left from the ashes of the Second International.[89] The pressure of the wider movement pushed Lenin and the Bolsheviks away from their sharply formulated, confusing, and extremely sectarian positions, around which no mass movement could be built, toward more concrete, comprehensible slogans, around which a "peace now" mass movement *could* be built. It was this internationalist Zimmerwald platform—and its corollary emerging from the follow-up conference at Kienthal—that provided the basis for the creation of a united Left, however temporary, in Russia. This united Left included the fusion, in July 1917, of the four-thousand-strong Mezhraionka (Inter-District Committee) and the Bolsheviks, a union that brought not only Trotsky into the party, but also many prominent activists.[90] The anonymous author of "Memoirs of a Bolshevik-Leninist" goes so far as to say that these new recruits "became the ideological and organizational backbone of the Bolshevik Party."[91]

The Zimmerwald perspective, shaped by Trotsky, was not, in other words, a momentary step on the road toward Bolshevism but a defining and enduring reorientation of the Left, away from the too strident positions of the Bolsheviks—a reorientation that laid the basis for future unity, not shaped by Lenin the helmsman. It was an emergent, collective Left of which Lenin was a part, but which had many other key players, including Iulii Martov, Leon Trotsky, Clara Zetkin, and Robert Grimm—not to mention Rosa Luxemburg, who had a powerful impact. This decisive moment in the story of the Left and the social movements of the twentieth century was made possible by a plural, not a singular, Left, which is a significant lesson for us from this period.

It is worth reiterating a key point from this narrative. Lenin and the Bolsheviks were pressured into this change of position by developments in the wider movement; they did not think their way toward them on their own. In fact, Lenin's thinking on the whole question of socialists, imperialism, and war had been, if anything, oblique and confusing. In a series of letters to Inessa Armand, he tried to outline the key points of his theory, saying that socialist policy in the second decade of the twentieth century had to be different from socialist policy in the last decade of the nineteenth century, because: "In 1891 there was no imperialism at all . . . and there was not, nor could there have been, an imperialist war on the part of Germany."[92] Imperialism was absent from the world stage in 1891? Not only does Lenin's comment disregard the unlikeliness of such a great change in international political economy occurring in only twenty-five years, but it also ignores the vast expanse of the British Empire, which was at the peak of its power in the very decade when the world had supposedly not yet arrived at imperialism!

Living as we are in the shadow of the hundredth anniversary of the Russian Revolution, it is timely to attempt to reconstruct Lenin. Krausz's reconstruction, which was "four decades in the making," is an impressive, meticulously researched book spanning the decades that marked the end of the cult of Lenin and the entrenching of the anti-cult.[93] But it is part of an emergent discourse not yet able to separate itself from a reverential attitude, which, as I have tried to show in this chapter, stands as a barrier to clarity and understanding. While Krausz's attempt at an epistemological reconstruction of Lenin is a welcome contribution to a necessary conversation, this reconstruction itself requires considerable deconstruction.

11 Intellectuals and the Working Class

The Leninist story has its roots in an attempt, at the turn of the twentieth century, to gather the scattered left-wing groups across the Russian empire and organize them into a single unified party. Alexander Potresov, a person central to this process, wrote that "at the end of our deportation, we established what Lenin called the 'Triple Alliance' (Lenin, Martov, and I), with the aim of creating an illegal literary centre of the movement around the paper *Iskra* [Spark] and the magazine *Zaria* [Dawn] and to make of these publications a tool to build a truly all-Russian, unified and organized party."[1]

At one level, the history of this project is well known, including the launch of these two publications (*Iskra* in 1900, *Zaria* in 1901), the theorizing of their use in Lenin's *What Is to Be Done?* and the unexpected split that broke the unity of the "Triple Alliance" at the end of the 1903 Congress, putting Lenin at odds with Martov and Potresov. At another level, it is virtually unknown. At best, our received wisdom is partial. First, the "publication as organizer" concept is universally credited to one person—Lenin. In fact, as Potresov tells us, Lenin had two intimate collaborators—Martov and Potresov. Second, the concept is universally associated with the newspaper *Iskra* as the publication around which the organization would be built. In fact, the project envisaged a newspaper for popular consumption (*Iskra*) along with a theoretical journal for in-depth history and theory (*Zaria*). The eclipse of two of the three collaborators speaks to the long habit of elevating the role of Lenin and minimizing (or erasing) the role of others—the theme of the previous chapter. The eclipse of the theoretical journal from the "publication as organizer" concept speaks to the anti-intellectualism that is the theme of this chapter. Krausz's scholarship helps us open the door to this aspect of Lenin's thought.

The Turn to Anti-intellectualism

Navigating the relationship between the left and the intelligentsia was a critical task in Lenin's time as much as it is in our own. Tamás Krausz and many others highlight the centrality to Lenin, at the time of the launch of *Iskra* and *Zaria*, of a theory of political organization in which intellectuals—or intelligentsia—would play a crucial role. In the early 1900s, Lenin believed that socialist "consciousness had to be injected from the outside," as Krausz notes.[2] Therefore, he ascribed a central role to intellectuals coming into the movement from outside the working class. In 1902, Lenin articulated his views in *What Is to Be Done?*:

> The theory of socialism . . . grew out of the philosophic, historical, and economic theories elaborated by educated representatives of the propertied classes, by intellectuals. By their social status the founders of modern scientific socialism, Marx and Engels, themselves belonged to the bourgeois intelligentsia. In the very same way, in Russia, the theoretical doctrine of Social-Democracy arose altogether independently of the spontaneous growth of the working-class movement; it arose as a natural and inevitable outcome of the development of thought among the revolutionary socialist intelligentsia.[3]

Whatever the merits of this argument, it was not one unique to Lenin. It is well-known (and documented within Lenin's text) that his view that the socialist movement required the uniting of working-class militants with radical intellectuals outside the working class leaned heavily on the writings of Karl Kautsky.[4] It is not well-known that in 1900, Iulii Martov, who was later to become Lenin's principal critic, had published the book *Red Banner in Russia: An Essay on the History of the Russian Labor Movement*, which was organized around a thesis almost identical to that of Lenin's.[5] Savel'ev and Tiutiukin summarize the focus of Martov's book: "From an initial premise that the contemporary international socialist movement resulted from the unification of two elements that had long been developing separately (the workers' economic struggle and the ideological and theoretical activity of socialist intellectuals), Tsederbaum [Martov] studied the merger of these two currents, specifically in the Russian context."[6] Lenin spoke favourably of Martov's book at the time of its publication.[7]

A photograph of Lenin (centre, sitting behind table), Martov (to Lenin's left, elbow on table), and other young intellectuals taken after a meeting of the St. Petersburg chapter of the League of Struggle for the Emancipation of the Working Class, February 1987. Photograph by Nadezdha Konstantinovna Krupskaya, Wikimedia Commons.

That said, Lenin decisively parted company with Kautsky's and Martov's views from 1903 until his death, making a hard turn toward anti-intellectualism. The trigger for this turn was the split in the Russian Left in 1903. Krausz suggests that Lenin saw "sociological and psychological reasons" for the split. This line of argument was developed in Lenin's polemical work titled *One Step Forward, Two Steps Back*, where he "entertained a digression about the 'significance of the mentality of the intelligentsia.' According to him, differences in mentality were bound to hamper consolidation, at least until the time the workers took control of the party."[8] Krausz goes on to argue that "a certain degree of anti-intelligentsia bias was characteristic of Lenin's political disposition. It stemmed from his approach to class (the interests of intellectuals being different from that of the working class)." Lenin's "political experiences" showed him that, "due to its 'individualist' traits, a significant majority of the intelligentsia would not subject itself to the 'social order and discipline' of the Soviet system."[9] Krausz is outlining what can only be called a problematic and simplistic sociology and, at the same time, minimizing the significance of this simplistic sociology to Lenin's thought. This "anti-intelligentsia" bias, based on an essentialist sociology, was more than a diversion: it became embedded in the core of Lenin's writings and lasted until his death.

Lenin's *One Step Forward, Two Steps Back* crystallizes this turn to anti-intellectualism. In that work, his characterizations of the intellectual can be placed into two categories: (a) the economic reductionist sociology summarized by Krausz; and (b) invective and insults. Let's begin with the latter, which set the tone for his entire book. He counterposes "the individualism of the intellectual, with its platonic acceptance of organisational relations" to "the proletariat," which "is trained for organisation by its whole life, far more radically than many an intellectual."[10] He declares: "Onward! That's what I understand! That's life! Not the endless, tedious intellectual talk, which comes to an end not because people have resolved the issue, but because they are tired of talking."[11] These outbursts are in no way isolated. Lenin denigrates "the mentality of the radical intellectual, who has much more in common with bourgeois decadence than with Social-Democracy."[12] *One Step Forward, Two Steps Back* contains many more similar instances of invective.

- "intellectual feebleness," "flabby whimpering of intellectuals," "the instability and feebleness of the intellectual"[13]
- "the 'flabby whimper' of defeated intellectuals"[14]
- "opportunism and intellectualist instability," "the intellectualist instability of the minority," "the intellectualist instability of certain comrades"[15]
- "unstable intellectuals"[16]
- "the dissolute intellectual"[17]

When Lenin leaves the terrain of insult and invective, the level of his analysis rises only slightly. The key to the rightward drift outside the Bolsheviks, he argues, is "the minority's intellectualist individualism."[18] He claims that "to the individualism of the intellectual," with "its tendency to opportunist argument and anarchistic phrase-mongering, all proletarian organisation and discipline seems to be serfdom."[19] He describes "the political complexion of this typical intellectual, who on joining the Social-Democratic movement brought with him opportunist habits of thought."[20] He contrasts "the psychology of the unstable intellectual and that of the seasoned proletarian, between intellectual individualism and proletarian cohesion."[21] He invokes the categories of the French Revolution to make his case, counterposing "the Girondist timidity of the bourgeois intellectual" to the Jacobinism of his faction. "The Jacobin inseparably connected with the organisation of the proletariat—a proletariat conscious of its class interests—this is the revolutionary Social-Democrat," he declares. The next sentence then fully combines the two approaches—insult followed by sociological reductionism: "The Girondist yearning for professors and school boys, who is afraid of the dictatorship of the proletariat, and who sighs about the absolute value of democratic demands, this is the opportunist."[22]

In a leaflet written in July 1904, but published only in 1923, the invective, insults, and reductionist sociology again blur together:

> We are fighting in the interests of the working-class movement in Russia against émigré squabbling. We are fighting on behalf of the revolutionary proletarian trend in our movement against the opportunist intellectualist trend. . . . We are fighting for a united party organization of our working-class vanguard and against intellectualist licentiousness, disorganization, and anarchy. We are fighting for respect for party congresses and against flaccid recklessness, against divergence of word and deed, against contempt for agreements and decisions adopted by common consent.[23]

The anti-intellectual diatribes continued through 1905, dropped off in 1906, then reached a crescendo in 1907. Samples from the latter year follow, organized by month.

January: "a gang of intellectual phrase-mongers";[24] "the musty atmosphere of intellectualist politicking";[25] "vague, intellectualist pretension";[26] "unstable intellectual opportunists";[27] "arrogant Menshevik intellectuals"[28]

February: "the Russian Marxist intellectuals, who are debilitated by scepticism, dulled by pedantry";[29] "an intellectual philistine who moralises";[30] "The Russian intellectual is limp and despondent";[31]

"the plaints of the miserable, frightened and faint-hearted intellectuals";[32] "The spinelessness and political short-sightedness, characteristic of the petty-bourgeois intellectuals and philistines"[33]

April: "the whining of petty-bourgeois intellectuals";[34] "genuine, impotent, intellectualist grumbling";[35] "The intellectualist Menshevik hens have hatched out ducklings";[36] "intellectualist-philistine weariness with the revolution";[37] "An 'intellectual' who cannot find himself an audience that is not indifferent to those problems as much resembles a 'democrat' or an intellectual in the best sense of the word, as a woman who sells herself by marrying for money resembles a loving wife. Both are variations of officially respectable and perfectly legal prostitution";[38] "whining intellectualist trash"[39]

May: "idle dreams of an idle intellectual";[40] "As an intellectualist party, bourgeois liberalism is impotent"[41]

August: "the intellectuals who have wormed themselves into the Social-Democratic movement . . . display such cowardice and spinelessness in the struggle, such a shameful epidemic of renegade moods, such toadyism towards the heroes of bourgeois fashion or reactionary outrages—so let our proletariat derive from our bourgeois revolution a triple contempt for petty-bourgeois flabbiness and vacillation"[42]

October: "the boundless servility of intellectualist philistinism";[43] "the green mould of intellectualist opportunism"[44]

December: "intellectualist tittle-tattle";[45] "intellectualist-bureaucratic chatter"[46]

What was the context for this torrent of verbal abuse? The initial anti-intellectual tirade in 1904 was directed toward his new opponents in the party, Iulii Martov and the Mensheviks, from whom he had divided in 1903. Again in 1907, Menshevik intellectuals were his major target, but the context is one sketched out earlier—what Luxemburg called the "muddy wave" of Bolshevik expropriations, actions whose most vocal critics were, again, Martov and the Mensheviks. The most notorious of these expropriations—the Tiflis bank robbery—occurred in 1907, corresponding to the crescendo of insults documented here. Hurling insult and invective is a classic method by which to deflect attention from unsavoury actions, which the "muddy wave" period certainly saw in abundance. The anti-intellectualist theme appears again and again in Lenin's writings in the years that follow.

Rosa Luxemburg was solicited by Martov and the other editors of *Iskra* "to analyze the split between the Mensheviks and Bolsheviks in the Russian Social-Democratic Party."[47] What resulted was a careful, systematic, and devastating rebuttal of Lenin's views. In her article—published in the German theoretical journal *Neue Zeit*, edited by Karl Kautsky—Luxemburg critiqued Lenin's denigration of the intellectual and sociological glorification of the proletariat, linking both to his extreme emphasis on military-like discipline and centralism inside the party. What Luxemburg found "surprising," she wrote, was his "conviction that all the preconditions for the realization of a large and highly centralized workers' party are already to hand in Russia."

> When he optimistically exclaims that it is now "not the proletariat but certain intellectuals in Russian social democracy who are lacking in self-education in the spirit of organization and discipline," and when he praises the educational significance of the factory for the proletariat in making it completely ripe for "discipline and organization," this once again betrays an over-mechanistic conception of social democratic organization. The "discipline" that Lenin has in mind is instilled into the proletariat not just by the factory but also by the *barracks* and by modern bureaucracy—in a word, by the entire mechanism of the centralized bourgeois state. . . . It is not through the discipline instilled in the proletariat by the capitalist state, with the straightforward transfer of the baton from the bourgeoisie to a social democratic Central Committee, but only the defying and uprooting this spirit of servile discipline that the proletarian can be educated for the new discipline, the voluntary self-discipline of social democracy.[48]

Lenin wrote a response in which he abandoned invective altogether and did his best to bolster the sociological side of his argument, contrasting "the intellectual-opportunist and proletarian revolutionary trends" in the Russian Left, and elsewhere altering this slightly to "a proletarian-revolutionary and an intellectual-opportunist wing of our

Party."[49] But his reply fails to address the points of substance raised by Luxemburg, which may explain why it was never published in *Neue Zeit* and remained unpublished until 1930, when the drive to construct a Lenin cult was in full swing.

Much has been written about Lenin's epistemology as it concerns the relationship between radical intellectuals and the working class.[50] However, it is only the young Lenin's pro-intellectual views that have been examined in detail; very little attention has been paid to the "mature" Lenin's turn to anti-intellectualism. At the very least, in order to properly arrive at an appreciation of the merits and demerits of Lenin's approach, we need to incorporate Luxemburg's critique, which carefully links the two questions of the role of the intellectual and the building of a political organization, avoiding both anti-intellectualism and sociological reductionism.

One more point needs to be added. In part, the dichotomy between "intelligentsia" and "proletariat," so evident in Lenin's writings, reflected a class analysis that had not come to grips with the increasingly important role of mental labour within the proletariat. Theodor [Fedor] Dan, in his last book published in 1946, presented a characteristic analysis of the Russian intelligentsia of his era, an analysis in sync with what both Lenin and Martov had written at the turn of the last century (but not of course in sync with Lenin's turn to anti-intellectualism). Dan says that "intelligentsia" is a "specifically Russian word" and it "does not mean a professional group of the population but a special group united by a certain political solidarity." Like educated people everywhere, he says, they tend to come from the "upper classes," but do not identify with these "upper classes." He says that "what is common to all the educated people included in it [the intelligentsia] is their political and social radicalism," and that this has to do with the specificities of Russian economic and social development. This means that "in other languages there is no adequate expression for the Russian word 'intelligentsia' because outside Russia there was and is no such social phenomenon."[51]

The identification of a special role for a group of intellectuals whose origin is outside either the peasantry or the proletariat (understood narrowly as the manual working class) is important. But there are limitations to such an approach. First, if by upper classes we mean the aristocracy and the bourgeoisie (which in a strict class analysis is the only thing that "upper classes" can mean), it by definition cannot account for the presence within the Russian intelligentsia of people such as Dan himself—the son of a pharmacist and a representative of that portion of the intelligentsia that was Jewish. In an environment as antisemitic as the old Russian empire, Jews were completely excluded from both "upper classes," whether aristocrat or bourgeois.[52] A sketch of the background of Martov, another outstanding Jewish member of the Russian intelligentsia, can help us understand the intelligentsia more precisely. Martov's biographer says that Martov's great-grandfather was "the enlightened watchmaker of Zamosc." His grandfather "was the founder and editor of the first Jewish journals and newspapers in Hebrew, Yiddish, and Russian." One uncle was "headmaster of the famous Odessa *Talmud Torah*." Another "financed his medical studies at the university of Berlin by translating Turgenev's works into German." His father was "secretary-general of the Russian Steamship Company" and "the Eastern correspondent of the *Peterburgskie vedemosti* (the *Petersburg Record*)."[53] Perhaps "secretary-general" of a steamship line would qualify as being part of the managerial class, and in this limited sense qualify as "upper class." But the rest of Martov's background—comprised of watchmakers, editors, headmasters, translators, newspaper correspondents and medical doctors—clearly does not.

Too often our understanding of "the proletariat" is restricted to manual labourers, excluding the white-collar section of the proletariat, those who we might classify as "mental labourers." Too often, these white-collar mental labourers are put into the elastic and ill-defined category of "middle class" or "petit-bourgeois," and through this conceptual back door are shoved into the category of "upper class." Such a conceptual move perhaps would be understandable a century ago, when much manual labour was in fact menial labour—when in other words, the "lifestyle" divide between manual and mental labourers was extreme. Today, that divide is much diminished. Many who would qualify as "manual labourers" are in fact highly skilled, deploying training and education indispensable in an increasingly complex economy. By contrast, many who would qualify as "mental labourers" are doing far more work formerly offloaded to others in the workforce. To give just one simple example—the typing pool has been absorbed into the personal computer and word processing software used daily by every contemporary professional.

If our understanding of the working class is broadened to include mental labourers, if we permit ourselves to mix together collars both blue and white, then this changes our understanding of the intelligentsia dramatically. With that perspective, the experience of Russia looks less *sui generis* and more anticipatory—a precursor to a phenomenon that has become increasingly widespread. The New Left student movement of the 1960s and 1970s is an excellent example. A small—a very small—number from among the New Left might have been considered "children of the bourgeoisie." Some were "children of the proletariat" narrowly understood as the blue-collar workforce. Most were "children of the proletariat" properly understood as comprising both manual and mental labourers. This late twentieth-century New Left intelligentsia, just like the early twentieth-century Russian intelligentsia, often "stood outside" their place of origin (identifying with the peasants in Vietnam, for instance, and not with the US working class army with which they were at war) and were very much united by a sense of political and social radicalism. But saying that they came from the "upper classes" (which many conservative analysts did, in order to label, ridicule, and dismiss them) can only be maintained if the white-collar working class is designated as "upper class"—a position that is less and less tenable. To properly embrace both manual and mental labour within the working class demands a rejection of all politics based on anti-intellectualism.

The Muck of Ages II: Anti-Intellectualism and Antisemitism

A discussion on anti-intellectualism, left here, would be incomplete. Lenin was writing in the context of tsarism and the Russian empire—a society imbued with a host of prejudices. In the context of the upheaval of 1917, one of those prejudices was directed against the intelligentsia. Orlando Figes writes of the "deep anti-intellectualism that was widely shared by the rank and file who had joined the [Bolshevik] Party since 1917." This anti-intellectualism could, in part, be seen as a component of anti-capitalism. Derived from *bourgeois*, "the popular term *burzhoois* . . . was used as a general form of abuse against employers, officers, landowners, priests, merchants, Jews, students, professionals, or anyone well-dressed, foreign-looking or seemingly well-to-do." Students and other "intellectuals" were thus painted with the same brush as the "other" privileged people who oppressed the lower classes. Ominously, the one word that stands out in this list is "Jews."[54] The anti-intellectualism of the crowd had a sinister dimension.

Anti-Jewish racism—by convention, usually referred to as antisemitism—was one of the most divisive and pervasive of the prejudices that corrupted the culture from which the revolutionary movement emerged.[55] Marc Ferro recounts that as Kerensky fled Petrograd after the Bolshevik seizure of power, he saw graffiti "painted in enormous letters, 'Down with the Jew Kerensky, Long Live Trotsky.'"[56] Kerensky was, of course, not Jewish, while Trotsky was. Raphael Abramovitch, a participant in and chronicler of the revolutionary process, notes something similar, remarking on the "odd combination of social demagogy, revolutionary mood and anti-Semitism" one would encounter on the streets of Petrograd in 1917. "As the days of October approached, the more openly one could hear the same groups of people on the street that shouted for peace, also talking about Kerensky, saying that he was Jewish and that his real name was Kerenson."[57] The point is not simply to highlight this irony, but rather to point out the equation in popular consciousness of "the other" with "the Jew"—the essence of anti-Jewish racism. Russian political activists were swimming in a milieu where casual antisemitism was pervasive, even among the revolutionary urban crowds that overthrew tsarism.

Early twentieth-century Russia was not the only place where anti-intellectualism became enmeshed with antisemitism. Writing in the early 1960s about the Cold War, Richard Hofstadter challenged the anti-intellectualism of the McCarthyite Cold Warriors:

> Arthur Schlesinger, Jr., in a mordant protest written soon after the election, found the intellectual "in a situation he has not known for a generation." After twenty years of Democratic rule, during which the intellectual had been in the main understood and respected, business had come back into power, bringing with it "the vulgarization which has been the almost invariable consequence of business supremacy." Now the intellectual, dismissed as an "egghead," an oddity, would be governed by a party which had little use for or understanding of him, and would be made the scapegoat

for everything from the income tax to the attack on Pearl Harbor. "Anti-intellectualism," Schlesinger remarked, "has long been the anti-Semitism of the businessman."[58]

The key takeaway here is Hofstadter's observation that anti-intellectualism can be a kind of disguised antisemitism. The overlap between these two forms of prejudice, whether intentional or not, was a factor in the Lenin-era disputes.

This is a complex subject. Antisemitism became a dominant aspect of life in Stalin's Russia. By contrast, the Bolshevik Party, while Lenin was alive, was famous for combatting antisemitism in Russia. Early in his career, Lenin emphatically made the case for what we might, in the twenty-first century, call an intersectional approach to political activism. He thought that, too often, activism was defined in narrow class-reductionist and trade-union terms, an approach that would prevent the union of the many strands of opposition developing against tsarism and capitalism. He asserted: "It cannot be too strongly maintained . . . that the Social-Democrat's ideal should not be the trade-union secretary, but *the tribune of the people*, who is able to react to every manifestation of tyranny and oppression, no matter where it appears, no matter what stratum or class of the people it affects."[59] These words were backed up by practice. Before 1917, tsarist oppression took its sharpest form in the periodic pogroms organized against the oppressed Jewish population of the Russian empire. Opposition to these pogroms was central to the activity of Lenin and the Bolsheviks. To cite just one example, in the run-up to a party congress in 1905, Lenin wrote: "We have been promised the report of a comrade who helped organise *hundreds* of workers for armed resistance in the event of an anti-Jewish pogrom in a certain large city. . . . It is of the highest importance that the greatest possible number of comrades undertake such and similar work *at once*."[60]

This commitment to combatting antisemitism was systematically eroded as the Stalinist bureaucracy cemented its authority. This did not happen overnight. Mikhail Baitalsky—a survivor of Vorkuta, an activist in the anti-Stalinist opposition, and a keen opponent of antisemitism— argued that a commitment to combatting antisemitism still left traces into the 1930s:

Even in the varied camp atmosphere of the time, I still did not sense any distinct expressions of anti-Semitism. More precisely, the attitude existed in graduated intensity. In the world of the criminal scum, anti-Semitism was openly expressed. Among the higher social layers, I did not notice it. It turns out that the lower depths were better at anticipating the coming change.[61]

The "coming change" was the new turn to repression, which began in 1947, lasted until Stalin's death in 1953, and included state-sanctioned antisemitism under the guise of a campaign against "cosmopolitanism." Baitalsky's point about the early 1930s notwithstanding, the signs of this shift could be seen much earlier. The economist Yuri Larin held a seminar on antisemitism in 1928. Vadim Rogovin, quoting Larin's 1929 account, described the meeting:

> Here the worker-propagandists who had gathered from all corners of the nation cited typical questions asked at various meetings. In a number of these questions, which reflected the traditional formulations of anti-Semitism ("Why do Jews always manage to get good positions?", "Why don't Jews want to do heavy labor?", "Won't the Jews betray if there is a war?", and so forth), an important place too was occupied by "new" questions of the type: "Why was the party opposition made up of 76 percent Jews?"[62]

This presaged the manner in which Stalin would deploy antisemitism as a weapon in the years of the Great Terror. The Moscow Trials, held from 1936 to 1938, were the portion of this terror visible to outside observers. These were, of course, trials in name only; they have been clearly exposed as judicial frame-ups based on confessions extracted under torture. At these so-called trials, writes Rogovin, "a disproportionately high number of the defendants were Jewish. At the first show trial, ten (out of sixteen) of the defendants were Jews, at the second, eight (out of seventeen). . . . In all this, Trotsky saw an attempt by Stalin to exploit the anti-Semitic moods that still existed in the country in the struggle against the Opposition."[63]

In a 1937 article, "Thermidor and Anti-Semitism," Trotsky analyzed in detail the antisemitism emerging under Stalin, underlining the pre-existing widespread antisemitism in tsarist Russia. While the revolutions of 1917 had removed antisemitism from law, "legislation alone does not change people," he argued.

> Their thoughts, emotions, outlook depend upon tradition, material conditions of life, cultural level, etc. The Soviet regime is not yet twenty years old. The older half of the population was educated under tsarism. The younger half has inherited a great deal from the older. These general historical conditions in themselves should make any thinking person realize that, despite the model legislation of the October Revolution, it is impossible that national and chauvinist prejudices, particularly anti-Semitism, should not have persisted strongly among the backward layers of the population.[64]

This latent antisemitism was increasingly deployed as a divide-and-conquer tool to inflame passions against the Opposition and deflect criticism from the regime. Trotsky saw this as a sign of the reactionary nature of the regime in the 1930s, pointing out: "History has never yet seen an example when the reaction following the revolutionary upsurge was not accompanied by the most unbridled chauvinistic passions, anti-Semitism among them."[65]

Suzanne Rosenberg lived through the period of state-sponsored antisemitism, from 1947 to 1953. "Venom and abuse were hailed upon the 'rootless cosmopolites,'" she wrote, going on to describe the campaign as "directed mostly against Jewish professionals and intellectuals."[66] In 1952, a friend of Nadezhda Joffe travelled to Moscow on vacation. As Joffe recalls: "When she returned, she described how the situation there was terrible: the anti-Semitism bordered on an atmosphere of pogroms."[67]

Mensheviks and Bolsheviks

The question of antisemitism hit different "registers" depending upon the wing of the Russian Left in which one resided. Lenin's key opponents were the Mensheviks. The trigger for his turn from being pro-intellectual to anti-intellectual was the 1903 RSDRP congress, where the Mensheviks and Bolsheviks divided. The Mensheviks continued to be a focus for Lenin's anger in the years that followed the congress—and the Bolsheviks and the Mensheviks came from distinctly different social strata. Philip Mendes points out that "15 out of the 17 Mensheviks who attended the 1903 RSDLP

Congress were Jews." This close connection between the Mensheviks and the radicalization in the Jewish community would continue in later years. "Eight out of the 17 members of the Menshevik Central Committee in June 1917 were Jews," writes Mendes. "Leading Jewish Mensheviks prior to and after the Bolshevik revolution included Julius [Iulii] Martov, Pavel Axelrod, Fyodor Dan, Raphael Abramovitch, Mark Liber, Eva Broido, David Dallin and Solomon Schwarz." Mendes makes a point outlined earlier: "A number of Mensheviks were also active in the [General Jewish Labour] Bund."[68] The Menshevik and Bund stories repeatedly overlap throughout this whole period.

Writings by Martov, the leading figure of the Menshevik Left, had been instrumental in the founding of the Bund in 1897.[69] When the Bund left the RSDRP in the fractious year of 1903, this was a damaging blow to the party because the Bund was a far larger operation than all the rest of the RSDRP combined. Just before the outbreak of the 1905 revolution, for instance, the party in Russia, Bolsheviks and Mensheviks combined, had 8,400 members, while the Bund on its own had 23,000.[70] Its work was focused on the Jewish Pale of Settlement, where, as noted earlier, 95 percent of the empire's roughly five million Jews resided at the turn of the century.[71] Concentrated thus, the Bund was—at the time of the 1903 fracturing of the RSDRP—the one section of the Left in the Russian empire that would qualify as a party with roots and influence. (A contemporary parallel might be the several thousand members of Québec solidaire, little known in the rest of Canada, but with real influence in Québec.) The Bund rejoined the RSDRP in 1906. At the congress held during that year of reunification, Jewish delegates from the Bund constituted 20 percent of the three hundred in attendance. The Menshevik delegation was 20 percent Jewish, twice the percentage of Jews among the Bolsheviks. From that point on, the Mensheviks would be intimately connected with the Bund. In fact, according to Abraham Ascher, "there was such intimate collaboration between the two groups that several men prominent in the Bund were also leaders of Menshevism."[72]

The Bolshevik story is quite different. According to Leonard Schapiro, "in historical origin and in ideology bolshevism is an essentially Russian movement."[73] This, of course, does not mean non-Jewish, since many Jews were also Russian, but it does highlight the fact that Bolshevik influence was centred in the "Great Russian" European part of the Russian empire. The twenty-five provinces that made up the Pale were concentrated in what is today Poland, Belarus, and Ukraine, and were "thus largely outside the major areas of ethnic Russian settlement," and largely outside the influence of the Bolsheviks.[74]

A Question of Discourse

As with the earlier "muck of ages" discussion on Orientalism, understanding the contours of antisemitism requires examining the contours of discourse, in particular the casual use of language or research that has the effect of othering a section of humanity. Isaac Deutscher, writing in the late 1940s, said that at the 1907 party congress, "there were few genuine Russians among the moderate Socialists [the Mensheviks]—most of whom were Jews or Georgians."[75] The implication that "Jews or Georgians" were not "genuine Russians" is misleading. However, a report on the 1907 party congress by Joseph Stalin takes us from the misleading to the offensive.

> No less interesting is the national composition of the congress. The figures showed that the majority of the Menshevik group were Jews (not counting the Bundists, of course), then came Georgians and then Russians. On the other hand, the overwhelming majority of the Bolshevik group were Russians, then came Jews (not counting Poles and Letts, of course), then Georgians, etc. In this connection one of the Bolsheviks (I think it was Comrade Alexinsky) observed in jest that the Mensheviks constituted a Jewish group while the Bolsheviks constituted a true-Russian group and, therefore, it wouldn't be a bad idea for us Bolsheviks to organise a pogrom in the Party.[76]

Deutscher characterizes this invocation of pogrom as a "heavy jocular aside" and maintains that "anti-semitism could hardly be read into this . . . because nobody had been more blunt than Koba in the condemnation of racial hatred."[77] This is beside the point. Racist jokes are not always told by people who are about to engage in racist actions. It does not change the fact that they are nonetheless racist. Contrast Deutscher's approach with that of Robert Tucker, who writes:

[Stalin's] heavy-handed treatment of this theme and his lack of embarrassment about quoting Alexinsky's anti-Semitic remark add credibility to Arsenidze's memory of his speaking as follows to Georgian workers in Batum in 1905: "'Lenin,' Koba would say, 'is outraged that God sent him such comrades as the Mensheviks! Who are these people anyway! Martov, Dan, Axelrod are circumcised Yids.'"[78]

Tucker's point is not that Lenin himself would have actually used such language, but that there were unscrupulous and antisemitic members of his organization who would.

By the 1930s, Stalinists would frequently use an antisemitic discourse in their fight with Leon Trotsky by invoking the biblical figure of Judas. As Jeffrey Brooks explains:

By 1937 the contrast between good and evil was fully developed, and the forces were personified in the supreme hero and the supreme enemy. Trotsky was assigned the role of Judas, and Stalin, by implication, that of Christ and God combined. *Pravda*'s editors employed this contrast during the second purge trial in January 1937, and it suited the anti-Semitic undertone of the campaign against Trotsky in particular and the trial in general.[79]

There is considerable literature identifying the use of the name "Judas" as a form of disguised antisemitism. Vladimir Lenin, for example, said: "The most important fact about Judas, apart from his betrayal of Jesus, is his connection with anti-Semitism. Almost since the death of Christ, Judas has been held up by Christians as a symbol of the Jews: their supposed deviousness, their lust for money, and other racial vices."[80]

Nonetheless, Lenin was not averse to using "Judas" in his polemical writings. In 1933, one of these polemical writings—an unpublished draft of an article from 1911—began to circulate. Trotsky called it "a new bit of gossip emanating from Moscow," gossip saying that "Lenin had declared that Trotsky was a 'Judas.'" Trotsky explains that "in one of the moments of accentuation of the emigrant struggle, Lenin angrily called Trotsky a 'yudushka' in a note that he wrote."[81] The Russian "*Iudushka*" (often translated as "Judushka") is a diminutive form of "Judas." The proper translation, then, is "little Judas," which brings out clearly both the racialized reference and the patronizing tone. The standard English translation of the article in question airbrushes the diminutive from the record. I have restored it in the following extract, the title of which is properly translated as "The Little Judas Trotsky's blush of shame." Lenin writes: "At the Plenary Meeting, the little Judas Trotsky . . . vowed and swore that he was true to the Party." He then describes what happened after the plenum:

> The little Judas expelled the representative of the Central Committee from *Pravda* and began to write liquidationist articles in *Vorwärts*. In defiance of the direct decision of the School Commission appointed by the Plenary Meeting to the effect that no Party lecturer may go to the *Vpered* factional school, the little Judas Trotsky did go and discussed a plan for a conference with the *Vpered* group. . . . And it is this little Judas who beats his breast and loudly professes his loyalty to the Party, claiming that he did not grovel before the *Vpered* group and the liquidators. Such is the little Judas Trotsky's blush of shame.[82]

Trotsky rebuked the Stalinists for unearthing it and circulating it out of context. He argued that the term appears in a writing of Lenin's that "was not even an article, but a note written in a moment of anger," and that, like other "polemical letters" from Lenin, it contained "unavoidable exaggerations." The note was written, says Trotsky, "a number of years before the October Revolution, the civil war, the building of the Soviet state, and the founding of the Communist International." To get at "the true relations between Lenin and Trotsky" would involve quoting from "more authoritative documents than that of a note resulting from a conflict in emigration."[83] This is true enough, but Trotsky sidesteps the issue of the racially charged nature of *any* use of the term "Judas," let alone "little Judas." Robert Service suggests that "Lenin or his editorial board had second thoughts about [the] publication" of Lenin's article "because Yudushka or little Judas had a possible anti-Semitic connotation."[84] Hence, the article remained in the archives until it was dug up in the highly charged context of Stalin's contest with Trotsky.

Adam Ulam claims that in 1911 and 1912, Trotsky was "regularly called 'little Judas Trotsky'" by Lenin.[85] He does not, however, provide evidence, and in Lenin's published works, the use of the term "little Judas" does not recur as a term of abuse directed toward Trotsky. But elsewhere in his published works, both "Judas" and "Judushka" are on more than one occasion deployed as descriptors for others with whom he has a dispute.

In 1894, he described the state bureaucracy as "made up mainly of middle-class intellectuals," who he described as "Judushkas who use their feudal sympathies and connections to fool the workers and peasants."[86] In 1901, he described the typical landlord as "a usurer and a robber, a beast of prey, like any village bloodsucker" possessed with "an ability to conceal his Judas nature under a doctrine of romanticism and magnanimity."[87] That same year, he said that the tsarist government was pursuing a "Judas policy of taking bread from the starving."[88] In 1906, in the wake of the 1905 revolution, he mocked liberals who called for unity: "Why fight, why this internecine strife? wails Judas Cadet."[89] In 1912, he characterized the liberal publication *Novoe Vremia* as both "nationalist" and "Judas-like."[90]

Frequently, he would use a less direct designation for his opponents—deploying the literary figure of Porfirii "Little Judas" Golovlyov, a character in Mikhail Saltykov-Shchedrin's nineteenth-century novel *The Golovlyov Family*. In 1901, he used this figure to denigrate official declarations of the Russian government.[91] In 1902, he dismissed the positions of the newspaper *Finlandskaia gazeta* as "unctuous twaddle in the spirit of 'Judas' Golovlyov."[92] In 1907, he said: "This Judas Golovlyov of a Cadet . . . really does throw dust in the eyes of the people and stupefy them."[93] In 1908, he criticized a speech by the liberal Mikhail Kapustin, saying, "Judas Golovlyov falls far short in comparison with this parliamentarian."[94] And in 1922, he said that so-called left-wing opponents of the Soviet state "try to conceal their malicious glee and behave mostly like Judas Golovlyov."[95]

Trotsky asserts that it was this fictional character that Lenin was invoking when he called him "little Judas," a fictional character with "no relation at all to the Judas of the Evangel."[96] Perhaps, but invoking the "Judas" Porfirii Golovlyov is not unproblematic. I. P. Foote describes the character Golovlyov this way:

> He is not a villain in the conventional sense. He performs no grand acts of wickedness. Such evil as he does is on the mean level suggested by his family nicknames "Judas" and "the bloodsucker." The enormity of Porfirii lies in his hypocrisy. His life is a grotesque ritual in which any act of meanness is permissible provided that some

aphorism, text or proverb can be invoked to justify it. He nauseates
chiefly by his incessant moralising and empty talk.[97]

Saltykov-Shchedrin wrote in an era when those labelled "liberal" in
terms of their aspirations to move beyond tsarist autocracy were often
simultaneously antisemitic. As David Aberbach points out, "Russian literature prior to the 1880s was full of . . . anti-Semitic stereotyping." He
includes famous writers in this category, like Lermontov, Turgenev, Gogol,
Dostoyevsky, and Tolstoy, whose works at times "betray prejudice and
hatred nourished by the church and kept alive in the popular imagination.
. . . Pre-1881 Russian writers fell short of their liberal, humanistic ideals
when they wrote of Jews."[98] Saltykov-Shchedrin worked closely with the
populist poet Nikolai Nekrasov, who, in 1866, published a horrifying poem
called "Ballet." In describing the practicality of "our girls," the poet writes:

Their ideal is the golden calf
Embodied in the grey-haired Jew,
Whose filthy hand causes these bosoms
To quiver with gold.[99]

No commentary is necessary.

According to Shmuel Ettinger in his book *A History of the Jewish
People*, in the 1870s, the decade when *The Golovlyov Family* was written, Saltykov-Shchedrin "had joined Nekrasov and others of the same
camp in savagely denouncing the Jews." By the early 1880s, the violence
of anti-Jewish pogroms was forcing many to shift their positions. To his
credit, Saltykov-Shchedrin was one of these: in the summer of 1882, he
published "a passionate article defending the persecuted Jew."[100] It was
too late, however: by this time, his offensive character Porfirii "Judas"
Golovlyov had taken on a life of his own in the discourse of other writers.

In explaining the reference to Judas Golovlyov, N. P. Kolikov, who was
responsible for the index of names in volume 6 of the fifth edition of Lenin's
Russian-language complete collected works (*Polnoe sobranie sochinenii*),
ignores all this. He writes a general note about Saltykov-Shchedrin, who he
describes as "a great Russian writer-satirist and revolutionary democrat."
He mentions the poet Nekrasov as a member of Russia's "democratic intelligentsia," but makes no further comment. He says that Lenin thought the

portrayal of the character Judas Golovlyov was "immortal" and that he "repeatedly used this character . . . to expose social groups and political parties hostile to the people." Lenin also "used others" from the novelist's works, asserts Kolikov, but he gives no specifics.[101] There are, in fact, many occasions where Lenin makes allusions to Saltykov-Shchedrin's works in his writings, but only one character—Judas Golovlyov—is mentioned repeatedly. Kolikov's editor's note is insufficient. In the antisemitic atmosphere of the Russian empire, there could have been no innocent manner with which Lenin could have deployed the words "Judas," "little Judas," or "Judas Golovlyov."

The point here is not to pin the label of antisemite on Lenin. His periodic vulgar literary outbursts and his sometimes careless choices of literary references, crude and unacceptable though they may be, are at odds with much of (early) Bolshevik political practice, which made combatting antisemitism a principle of the socialist movement. The point is to identify the way in which the iconic figure of Lenin was, no more than any of his generation, insulated from "the muck of ages." Revealed here, as in the discussion of Orientalism, are unexamined prejudices inherited from the society of his day, leading to a recurring habit of casually using epithets that played on old and deep prejudices in Russian culture. More significant is Lenin's profound anti-intellectualism, on display from 1904 until his death, which led him into a cul-de-sac and helped nurture an environment where his less scrupulous cadre—for instance, Stalin—could, with little effort, drift from anti-intellectualism into the state-sanctioned antisemitism of 1947 to 1953. Honestly confronting these issues underscores the point that was central to chapter 10: we can learn from the life and work of Lenin, but only if we avoid adopting an attitude of reverence.

Conclusion

Ends and Means

In 1918, a few months after the October Revolution, Lenin succinctly and honestly outlined his approach to the challenges facing the new regime.

> While the revolution in Germany is still slow in "coming forth," our task is to study the state capitalism of the Germans, to spare *no effort* in copying it and not shrink from adopting *dictatorial* methods to hasten the copying of it. Our task is to hasten this copying even more than Peter [the Great] hastened the copying of Western culture by barbarian Russia, and we must not hesitate to use barbarous methods in fighting barbarism.[1]

This captures precisely the essence of Lenin's political methods, characterized by a firm belief that ends justified means. He presided over the "muddy wave" of expropriations, serene in the conviction that it did not matter how money was acquired, only how it was used once acquired. Similarly, while committed to the "dictatorship of the proletariat," he saw no contradiction in using as his principal agents in achieving that proletarian state the very non-proletarian soldier and sailor peasants-in-uniform—the temporary new class so clearly analyzed by Martov and Abramovitch. Illustrative of Lenin's willingness to lean on non-working-class forces was his outburst days before the insurrection, at a meeting of the Petrograd Bolshevik Party Committee. When it looked for a moment as though he would be outvoted by his comrades, he offered this as a response: "If you want a split, go ahead. If you get the majority, take power in the Central Executive committee and carry on. But we will go to the sailors."[2] He was fully prepared, in other words, to bypass the working-class of Petrograd and to jump-start the workers' revolution through the deployment of sailors from outside Petrograd.

However, means *do* shape ends. The temporary new class of peasants and workers in uniform was a rough and violent instrument, one that would shape its Leninist leaders as much as they would shape it. A January 1918 incident illustrates this. Early on the morning of 7 (20) January, Isaac Steinberg, then serving as People's Commissar of Justice, received a phone call from a shaken Lenin. In what Steinberg describes as a "hoarse voice," Lenin told Steinberg that during the night two elderly prisoners—F. F. Kokoshkin and A. I. Shingaraev, both former cabinet ministers and members of the Kadet (liberal) Party—had been murdered in their hospital beds by "unidentified sailors." The two had been taken to the hospital the previous evening, and the murder had occurred a few hours later. When, later that morning, Steinberg joined Lenin in his office, the latter "looked dejected, even though several hours had passed since the event" and "without a word he pushed a typewritten sheet toward me. It was a directive to all Government offices to institute a strict investigation of the crime and to arrest the guilty sailors."[3]

Upon hearing of the situation, Pavel Dybenko, then the People's Commissar of Naval Affairs, "showed no surprise and said calmly, 'Very well, I shall write an appeal to the sailors not to do such things again and to bring the culprits to justice.'" What Dybenko said next was a harbinger of things to come. "His voice was even, but a little flame played in his eyes as he added, 'Of course, they [the sailors] will take this merely as an act of political terror.' It was the first time that I heard a Bolshevik that day describe the plain murder as an act of 'political terror,' thus giving it a kind of sanction."[4] Dybenko was proven correct, and, by the evening, it had become clear that the sailors in the fleet were sheltering the two murderers and that any attempt to capture them would involve a confrontation and possibly a rupture with them. Lenin's attitude toward the murders underwent a complete reversal. Steinberg "raised the question in the Council of People's Commissars. With his customary coolness, Lenin simply handed us a few papers which began to circulate the room."

> They were wires from sailors on warships anchored in Reval and in Finnish waters. In forthright terms they informed Lenin that they would not permit the case to be pursued, that they regarded the

murder of the liberal ministers as an act of political terror which the Soviet Government would not dare oppose. And Lenin, with no effort to suppress a cynical smile, asked, "Well? Would you have us go against them?"

"Certainly," I replied. "If we don't do it now, it will be the more difficult later to appease any thirst for blood. This was a heinous crime, not political terror."

"The Bolsheviks," says Steinberg, "sat silent, as was their custom in delicate situations, and let Lenin do the talking. . . . Lenin had already forgotten the impression the murder had made on him that first morning, when he had at least recognized the explosive nature of the deed. . . . Was it worth incurring the displeasure of some of the sailors? Lenin decided that it was not."[5]

There are multiple versions of exactly how the murders took place. According to a contemporaneous account by Andrej Kalpašnikov, Dybenko and several associates were directly involved in the murder. These men "awakened the head guard, forced him to show them the rooms of their victims, and then, in the presence of everyone, shot them down."[6] John Spargo, also writing at that time, paints Dybenko's role differently. Spargo writes that, in response to the murders, Dybenko "published a remarkable order condemning the assassins as 'having murdered their helpless enemies, rendered harmless by imprisonment.'" But if Dybenko appears in a better light by this account, the Cheka does not, because "the sailors and Red Guards" according to Spargo "had gone straight to the hospital" from Cheka offices. Spargo claimed that it was "generally believed" that the Cheka "had some connection with the murders."[7]

Just hours before the transport of the two liberals to the hospital where they were murdered, the Constituent Assembly had been dispersed after holding its one and only session in a tense atmosphere replete with threats and preceded by a violently suppressed demonstration. This coincidence was noted at the time. One liberal of the era wrote in his secret diary: "How tragically Kokoshkin died; he perished on the day of the existence of that very Constituent Assembly whose law he wrote."[8] The two events—the murder of the liberals and the dispersal of the Assembly (which will be examined below)—are two moments in the use of violence against what the Bolsheviks called "bourgeois democracy." In both cases, the instruments of repression were the "revolutionary sailors."

"The Very Cruelest Revolutionary Terror"

By mid-1918, state-sanctioned Red Terror came to define the Bolshevik regime. What do we know about the terror deployed by the Bolshevik state? We know that the state justified it as a response to the terror of the Bolsheviks' opponents, the White Armies—and that those White Armies did engage in the most appalling atrocities. China Miéville quotes an "unlikely source, Major General William Graves, who commanded US forces in Siberia," as saying that he "considers himself 'well on the side of safety when I say that the anti-Bolsheviks killed one hundred people in Eastern Siberia, to every one killed by the Bolsheviks.'"[9] During the Civil War, Elias Heifetz was the chair of the All-Ukrainian Relief Committee for the Victims of Pogroms, and with those pogroms still fresh in his mind, he published, in 1920, the extraordinary *Slaughter of the Jews in the Ukraine*.[10] His chronicle of murder, rape, and humiliation unleashed by the counter-revolutionary armies in Ukraine against that country's Jewish population is almost unreadable, the deeds are so horrible. Those events would stand as the most horrific moment in the history of Jewish oppression, until the Nazi holocaust of World War II.

> If we assume that 120,000 deaths were due directly to the pogroms, we shall not be guilty of exaggeration. To these must be added the injured and wounded, those suffering from nervous and mental shock and the violated women. The pogroms swept the Ukraine like a hurricane, and it was impossible to undertake a census of such cases. The number, however, must be prodigious, running into the tens of thousands.
> . . . The Jewish population of the villages and hamlets visited by the pogroms left everything behind as it was, and fled without further thought to a larger place. The roads were covered with the bodies of old men, women and children, and in the larger places the same horrible death awaited the fugitives.[11]

The pro-Bolshevik forces were not all innocents in this process. "To the nightmare of Jewish pogroms in the Ukraine belong also the anti-Jewish excesses and pogroms by bands calling themselves 'Reds' and belonging . . . to the Ukrainian Red Soviet army," Heifetz tells us.[12] He gives an unflattering portrayal of the Soviet rank and file, composed, for the most part, of "insurrectionist bands of freebooters" who had an "antipathy to strangers, especially Jews."[13] However, Heifetz clearly differentiates the Reds from the Whites: "In proportion to the entire number of Jewish persecutions the excesses of these people play an insignificant role."[14] The Red Terror was in very large part a reaction to the horrendous terror of the counter-revolutionary forces.

But it was also in part an inevitable product of the terrible oppression and suffering experienced for generations by a downtrodden, impoverished people, a point developed persuasively by Orlando Figes: "The Terror erupted from below. It was an integral element of the social revolution from the start. The Bolsheviks encouraged but did not create this mass terror."[15]

If our goal is simply to explain the terror, we can leave our discussion here. But if our goal is to assess the attitude that political actors should take to terror, we have to go further. There is the question of how to approach terror as a matter not of strategy and tactics but of *principle*. Steinberg quotes from the January 1919 program manifesto of the fledgling German Communist Party, a manifesto written by Rosa Luxemburg: "The proletarian revolution requires no terror for its aims. It hates and despises killing. It does not need these weapons because it does not combat individuals but institutions."[16]

Let us return to the issue of the death penalty, that horrifying instrument of state policy whose restoration for use at the front in 1917 did so much to undermine confidence in the Kerensky government and led directly to mass radicalization and the events of the October Revolution. By the summer of 1918, Iulii Martov was denouncing the death penalty not of Kerensky and the right-wing generals but of the Bolsheviks and the workers' state:

> The death penalty had been declared abolished, but in every city, in every county, various "Extraordinary Commissions" [Chekas] and "Military-Revolutionary Committees" ordered the shooting of hundreds and hundreds of people. Some were killed as counterrevolutionaries, others as speculators, and yet others as robbers. No

court established whether those sentenced were really guilty, nobody can know whether the person executed was really guilty. . . . How many innocent people have been killed like that all over Russia! With the tacit approval of the Council of People's Commissars, nameless individuals are sitting in Chekas passing death sentences. Among these individuals giving orders for executions, we from time to time discover criminals, bribe-takers, people who themselves are on the run from the law, and former tsarist provocateurs.[17]

Clearly, Martov had a moral objection to the Red Terror and to capital punishment. We can feel it in the passion of these lines. His opposition, like Luxemburg's, was also one of political principle.

> We social-democrats are opposed to all terror, both from above and from below.
> Therefore, we are against the death penalty—this extreme means of terror, to which all rulers resort to intimidate people when they have lost their trust.
> The struggle against the death penalty was inscribed on the banners of all those who struggled for the freedom and happiness of the Russian people, all those who struggled for socialism.[18]

Lenin's view was the opposite. He saw terror, including recourse to the death penalty, as an embedded part of the transition to socialism. This at first put him in opposition to his own comrades. One of the first, if not *the* first, decrees of the Military Revolutionary Committee after the seizure of power was to abolish the death penalty for troops at the front. Trotsky was present at the vote, but Lenin was not. According to Trotsky, when Lenin heard of this decision, "his anger was unbounded. 'Nonsense,' he kept on repeating. 'How can one make a revolution without firing squads?'"[19] In the introduction to this book, I outlined the despair and shock that engulfed the Russian masses when the death penalty was reintroduced for use by the officer corps against the peasants-in-uniform, who were their cannon fodder. Lenin's fierce embrace of precisely this instrument as essential to his revolution was a sign of the problems embedded in his approach. It was a position from which Lenin never flinched, and that Trotsky was shortly to embrace. When, in early 1918, the German army resumed its offensive, Trotsky drafted an appeal, which, as Steinberg notes, included "the threat that all who opposed Government orders would be 'destroyed on the spot.'" Steinberg, still the People's Commissar for Justice, "objected that this cruel threat killed the whole pathos of the manifesto. Lenin replied with derision, 'On the contrary, herein lies true revolutionary pathos. Do you really believe that we can be victorious without the very cruelest revolutionary terror?'"[20]

Lenin was not alone among the Bolshevik leadership in his embrace of the necessity of terror on a mass scale. One of the most chilling statements of that time came from his chief lieutenant, Grigory Zinoviev. In a September 1918 speech, Zinoviev said: "To overcome our enemies we must have our own socialist militarism. We must carry along with us 90 million out of the 100 million of Soviet Russia's population. As for the rest, we have nothing to say to them. They must be annihilated."[21] But Zinoviev is a handy scapegoat, someone who today has very few followers. Lenin, by contrast, is still an icon in sections of the Left. That icon frequently exhorted his comrades to intensify the terror. When Bolshevik rule was threatened in one region, he urged the local communists to "organise immediately mass terror, shoot and deport the hundreds of prostitutes who are making drunkards of the soldiers, former officers and the like."[22] In August 1918, he sent a telegram to communists in Penza, saying: "Essential to organise a reinforced guard of selected and reliable people, to carry out a campaign of ruthless mass terror against the kulaks, priests and whiteguards; suspects to be shut up in a detention camp outside the city."[23] After the assassination of Volodarsky, he rebuked the communist authorities who had tried to restrain the crowds from vigilante "justice" in Petrograd: "I protest most emphatically! We are discrediting ourselves: we threaten mass terror, even in resolutions of the Soviet of Deputies, yet when it comes to action we obstruct the revolutionary initiative of the masses, a quite correct one. This is im-poss-ible! The terrorists will consider us old women."[24]

This cannot be reduced to a position to which Lenin had been pushed by force of circumstances. Already in the context of the 1905 revolution he had a very clear position that mass terror would be a necessary, embedded part of any revolution in Russia. In February 1905, he wrote: "All the forces of every party should be mobilised. All should have a single technical plan of action. Bombs and dynamite, individual and mass terror— everything that can help the popular uprising."[25] And in August of the following year, he declared, "Social-Democracy must recognise this mass terror and incorporate it into its tactics." He did qualify this conception of mass terror, saying that a key task would be "organising and controlling it . . . subordinating it to the interests and conditions of the working-class movement and the general revolutionary struggle, while eliminating and ruthlessly lopping off the 'hooligan' perversion of this guerrilla warfare."[26] But that is not the point. For Lenin, the use of mass terror in the transition to socialism was a principle. For Luxemburg and Martov, *opposition* to the use of mass terror by the socialists was a principle.

The key organ for administering the terror was the infamous Cheka, the predecessor to the KGB. An important insight into the psychology of this instrument of terror comes from articles printed in a short-lived publication known either as *Cheka Weekly* or *Bulletin of the Cheka*, which for six weeks in 1918, "was openly intended to vaunt the merits of the secret police and to encourage 'the just desire of the masses for revenge."[27] A letter that makes for chilling reading was published in its September 1918 issue. "In times of fierce civil war you cannot be soft," said the several high-ranking officials from Nolinsk in Vyatka Province who authored the letter. "We declared mass terror against our enemies and . . . we decided to make this mass terror not a paper thing, but a reality. Mass shootings of hostages took place in many cities after this. And this was good." It gets worse. The authors chastise one regional Cheka for releasing British diplomatic representative Bruce Lockhart. "Tell us," they remonstrate. "Why didn't you subject this Lockhart to the most refined tortures, in order to get information and addresses? . . . Do you suppose that to inflict terrible tortures upon a man is more inhuman than to blow up bridges and food stores in order to find in the pangs of hunger an ally for the overthrow of the Soviet regime?"[28] The editors of *Cheka Weekly* did not denounce this open advocacy of torture. In fact, they were at pains to point out that they did not object "in substance to this letter." Their only objection was that such terror was "not at all in our interest."[29] However, the letter's matter-of-fact call for torture led to the editors being rebuked by the Central Committee. *Cheka Weekly* was discontinued.[30] Innumerable other sources indicate that, in fact, torture was part of the toolkit of Cheka-organized terror. Steinberg's cataloguing of just some of these, quoting from "a series of peasant reports and Government documents for the year 1919," makes for grim reading.[31] In the village of Uranj in the province of Kostroma, "the beating of petitioners in the Soviet was customary and flogging was carried on in all villages of the province. In Beryozovka, for instance, peasants were beaten with fists as well as sticks. They were forced to take off their boots and sit for hours in the snow." Steinberg reports a Red Army soldier saying: "Makhov gave us orders to give it good to the arrested peasants, that is to whip them thoroughly. Instead of dragging them along with us, he said, whip them and let them remember the Soviet regime." The stories of abuse go on and on. "In some villages," Steinberg writes, "the Cheka locked masses of peasants in cold warehouses, stripped them and beat them with gun butts."[32]

"Let this be enough," Steinberg concludes. "We have not reached the limit, but then we never shall. Such descriptions could be continued indefinitely: they are so many, so varied, so cruelly eloquent. We shall not return to them. Let our memory, retaining these words and these acts, help our minds and our consciences later to draw the final conclusions about terror, the Bolshevik terror."[33]

Bolsheviks Against Workers

In late 1917 and early 1918, as the temporary new class of peasants-in-uniform melted into the countryside, there was a return in the cities to something approaching "normal" class relations. This re-emergence of a "traditional" workers' movement is a story steeped in obscurity. Tony Cliff notes that, immediately after the November revolution, the Bolsheviks "had to deal with another enemy no less dangerous" than the counter-revolutionaries who were set to march on the capital. He refers to this enemy as "the saboteurs within." Cliff was a lifelong supporter of workers' action and strikes. However, without commenting on the irony of his observation, he attaches the term "saboteur" to the story of a mass strike movement:

> On 27 October (9 November) a general strike of all state employees was called in Petrograd, and almost all the officials and clerks of public institutions came out.
>
> The employees of the Ministries of Agriculture, Labour, Posts and Telegraphs, Food, Finance and Foreign Affairs went on strike.

So did the teachers. By 15 (28) December, more than 30,000 Petrograd teachers were on strike. They were joined by the workers in the public libraries and the People's Houses and by 50,000 bank clerks. These strikes confronted the new rulers with grave difficulties.

The telegraphists and telephonists also stopped work. Telegraphy was the only quick means of communication across the huge distances of Russia. These workers were very much under the influence of the Mensheviks and Socialist [Social] Revolutionaries. Most of the telegraphists refused to work for the Bolshevik intruders.[34]

Steinberg, one of the harshest critics of the Bolsheviks, similarly saw this strike in a very negative light. "In the first months after October, 1917," he writes, "large sections of officialdom and the professional intelligentsia sabotaged the new Government. Under the influence of the embittered moderates (to say nothing of the open reactionaries), they sacrificed the interests of country and people to their hatred of the new regime. They stayed away from their offices or refused to carry out their functions in public institutions."[35]

Others describe this "general strike of white-collar personnel (*sluzhashchie*)," as Richard Pipes calls it, with a completely different emphasis.[36] George Leggett says that within hours of the Bolshevik seizure of power, "the Committee for Salvation of Country and Revolution (KSRiR) had been formed in the City Duma Building, with the participation of members of the Executive of Peasants' Soviets, and of Menshevik and SR leaders such as Dan and Gotz."[37] The strike that ensued was "co-ordinated by the Union of Unions," which "disposed of formidable financial resources, out of which the strikers were advanced wages up to 1 January 1918."[38] Richard Pipes devotes considerable attention to this strike action, calling it "a grandiose, non-violent act of protest by the nation's civil servants and employees of private enterprises against the destruction of democracy," and going on to describe its participants and structure:

> It quickly acquired an organizational structure, first in the shape
> of strike committees in the ministries, banks, and other public
> institutions and then in a coordinating body called the Committee
> for the Salvation of the Fatherland and the Revolution (*Komitet
> Spaseniia Rodiny i Revoliutsii*). The committee originally consisted

of Municipal Duma officials, members of the Central Executive Committee of Soviets dissolved by the Bolsheviks, representatives of the All-Russian Congress of Peasant Soviets, the Union of Unions of Government Employees, and several clerical unions, including that of postal workers. Gradually, representatives of Russian socialist parties, the Left SRs excepted, also joined.[39]

After the Union of Unions of Government Employees in Petrograd called on its members, on 29 October, to join the strike, "work in all the ministries in Petrograd ground to a halt. Except for porters and some secretarial staff, their personnel either failed to come to work or came and sat doing nothing."[40] Pipes describes the growth of the action in the ten days that followed:

> The strike spread to non-governmental institutions. Private banks had shut their doors as early as October 26–27. On November 1, the All-Russian Union of Postal and Telegraph Employees announced that unless the Bolshevik Government gave way to a coalition cabinet it would order its membership to stop work. Soon telegraph and telephone workers walked out in Petrograd, Moscow, and some provincial towns. On November 2, Petrograd's pharmacists went on strike; on November 7, water transport workers followed suit as did schoolteachers. On November 8, the Union of Printers in Petrograd announced that if the Bolsheviks carried out their Press Decree they, too, would strike.[41]

At the core of these protests was a simple political position—against the imposition of a one-party state and for the creation of a pluralist, multiparty socialist government. This, in fact, represented the overwhelming common sense of the Left. At the Second Congress of the Soviets, which convened as the Military Revolutionary Committee insurrection was underway, the Bolsheviks were in a strong but not overwhelming position. Out of 670 delegates, they had 300—a plurality but not a majority.[42] Furthermore, according to China Miéville, in matters of voting, their influence was bolstered by "somewhat lax organisational arrangements that had given them more than their proportional share."[43] As John Gooding points out, "of the 366 soviet committees represented at the congress," just over two-thirds "had sent delegates on the assumption that power would be shared among the various socialist groupings."[44]

But with the exception of the brief coalition between the Bolsheviks and the Left Social-Revolutionaries, there was to be no multiparty government. The new government used force to end the strike, in which the call for a coalition socialist government had been the principal demand. From mid-November on, the Bolsheviks operated "a counter-offensive," writes Pipes. "The Bolsheviks now physically occupied, one by one, every public institution in Petrograd and compelled their employees, under threat of severe punishment, to work for them."[45] The strikes were defeated, and along with them, any hopes for a pluralist, multiparty, socialist government.

This is a confusing story. Without question, the call for a coalition socialist government animated much of the strike movement, but it is also true that sections of the leadership of this strike movement comprised open reactionaries who were determined to overthrow the new regime by force. The Committee for Salvation of Country and Revolution included in its leadership individuals who, according to Alexander Rabinowitch, "drew up plans to coordinate an uprising in Petrograd with the entry into the capital of Krasnov's Cossacks, expected momentarily." A successful entry of Cossack troops into Petrograd would have undoubtedly ended in bloodshed and repression. In the end, only a thousand troops could be mustered for the effort, and they confronted a pro-Bolshevik "motley army approximately ten times larger, made up of workers' detachments, soldiers of the Petrograd garrison, and Baltic sailors."[46] The Cossacks were beaten back, and the military threat, for a time, receded. But in our assessment of these events, we need to engage with both aspects of the post-insurrectionary turmoil—the reactionary attempt to use military force against the new regime and the democratic urge of much of the strike movement, animated by a sense of the need for coalition and compromise.

The Cheka and Strikebreaking

The Bolshevik response to this strike movement played a critical role in shaping the institutions of terror that were to corrupt Bolshevik rule in subsequent years. The Military Revolutionary Committee (MRC), the central institution that organized the November insurrection, became the key force repressing the strike movement. "On 9 November, the MRC ordered the arrest of KSRiR [Committee for Salvation of Country and Revolution] members," writes George Leggett. Eleven days later, "the MRC took steps to wind up the dissolved Duma and the KSRiR. And on 26 November, the MRC declared all employees of public departments who sabotaged the national economy to be 'enemies of the people'. The MRC effort to suppress the strike was directed by [Felix] Dzerzhinsky."[47]

As the MRC was winding down its operations in December, reports reached the government's leading body, the Council of People's Commissars (Sovnarkom), of new threats on a country-wide scale. Minutes from a 7 (20) December meeting of the Sovnarkom indicate that council members were concerned with "the possibility of a Russia-wide postal and telegraph strike and about the possibility of a Russia-wide general strike of all government agency employees."[48] The Sovnarkom thus "resolved 'to charge Comrade Dzerzhinsky to establish a special commission to examine the possibility of combating such a strike by the most energetic revolutionary measures, and to determine methods of suppressing malicious sabotage.'"[49] As Leggett writes: "The urgency of the public service strike crisis was such that, at its meeting on 7 (20) December (attended by Lenin as chairman, by Stalin, Petrovskii, and others), the Sovnarkom decided not to disperse until Dzerzhinsky's improvised special commission, then still in session, had presented its proposals. That same evening, Dzerzhinsky made his report to the Sovnarkom."[50] Dzerzhinsky proposed the creation of the All-Russian Extraordinary Commission for Combating Counter-Revolution and Sabotage, the institution that we now know as the Cheka, and the Sovnarkom approved his recommendation. Pipes agrees that it was in an effort "to break the resistance of financial personnel that Lenin initially created, in December 1917, his security police, the Cheka."[51] Nicolas Werth describes the Cheka's first action, breaking "a strike by state employees in Petrograd":

The method was swift and effective—all its leaders were arrested—and the justification simple: "Anyone who no longer wishes to work with the people has no place among them," declared Dzerzhinsky, who also arrested a number of the Menshevik and Socialist [Social] Revolutionary deputies elected to the Constituent Assembly. This arbitrary act was immediately condemned by Isaac Steinberg, the people's commissar of justice, who was himself a left Socialist Revolutionary.[52]

The anti-strike mandate of the Cheka was not explicit in the records of its birth, which outlined the liquidation of "all counterrevolutionary and sabotage politics throughout Russia" as its raison d'être.[53] The official announcement in the daily press, however, was explicit: "The commission is to watch the press, saboteurs, strikers, and the Socialist [Social] Revolutionists of the Right."[54] Surely it is important to know that this repressive institution had its origin as a tool of strikebreaking.

Perhaps the actions of these white-collar workers can be put in the category of "backward consciousness." The strikers were almost all in the category of "mental labourers," a category that most socialists at the time incorrectly called "petit-bourgeois" and did not consider part of the working class. We now know, however, that this distinction between mental labourers and manual labourers is unhelpful in characterizing the proletariat, at the forefront of whose ranks are frequently literate mental labourers—in an earlier period, typesetters and printers, postal and telegraph workers; in the contemporary movement, teachers, civil servants, and nurses. But in analyses of the Russian Revolution, there is an embedded bias that restricts the notion of "the proletariat" to manual factory labourers and categorizes mental labourers as "middle class" or "petit-bourgeois." Laura Engelstein, in her very helpful history of the 1905 revolution in Moscow, makes exactly this mistake.

> Another group that made a vital contribution to the labor movement in 1905 was the white-collar employees in the non-manufacturing sector. They identified with the working-class cause, provided organizational guidance, and joined their blue-collar fellows in the meeting hall and on the street. Without them, no coherent movement would have emerged among either railroad workers or municipal employees, two groups indispensable to the success of the revolution in Moscow.

However, rather than saying that this shows how our understanding of the working class must change to incorporate mental labourers, Engelstein says that this shows how our understanding of the revolution must change to incorporate "non-working class" forces. "The Moscow labor movement of 1905 was not, strictly speaking, a 'proletarian' affair" because "it depended for its success on the support and participation of non-working class groups."[55] A more reasonable conclusion would be that our notion of the working class must expand to include manual *and* mental labourers.

Earlier, I cited Victor Serge, who on most issues was a strong supporter of the Bolsheviks, insisting that "the formation of the Chekas was one of the gravest and most impermissible errors that the Bolshevik leaders committed in 1918."[56] But here we see that the first Cheka was called into existence in 1917. This displacement of one year is perhaps explained by the fact that Serge, too, labelled the 1917 anti-Bolshevik strikers as petit-bourgeois (or, in his words "middle class"). He in fact devotes an entire chapter in his *Year One of the Russian Revolution* to the subject, titled "The urban middle classes against the proletariat."[57] He characterizes the strike movement of the autumn and winter of 1917 as being part of a revolt by the "middle classes in the towns," who he describes as "the students of the military colleges, the youth of the high schools, the officials, the senior staffs, the technicians, the intellectuals, the socialists, all of them people of the middling sort, more or less exploited but highly privileged within the system of exploitation and participating in it."[58] Left there, this is quite unpersuasive. The category "people of the middling sort" is extremely imprecise. His approach does become more precise when, invoking Kritsman, he suggests that the "technical intelligentsia" is "*simultaneously the organiser of production and of exploitation*: it is thereby led to identify itself with the system, and to conceive of the capitalist mode of production as the only one possible."[59] But does this accord with the facts?

It is in fact extremely difficult to argue that the mass opposition to the Bolsheviks was restricted to middle-class, petit-bourgeois forces. Serge himself acknowledges that big sections of workers were a part of the strike movement—16,000 municipal employees and a "number of sections of skilled workers."[60] Among those skilled workers would be, presumably, the telegraph operators listed earlier. The telegraph—the indispensable connecting tissue linking the far-flung cities of the Russian empire—was intimately connected with the railways. The communication network depended on the physical transportation network, with the telegraph lines typically following the miles of track winding their way through the empire. Although undeveloped by Western European standards, the rail system was enormous and growing. Roger Pethybridge, the expert on this question, notes that "by October 1916 there were no less than 1,001,522 personnel employed on the Tsarist railways, as compared with 432,000 in 1898."[61] The workers on the rails were also central to the union movement: "the Railway Union became the largest of the workers' organizations prior to 1917, embracing manual, clerical and administrative staff."[62] We saw in the introduction to this book the critical role the rail workers played in the events of that revolution. In Trotsky's account of the events of 1917, he points out that when General Kornilov attempted to march on Petrograd and overturn the provisional government, "the railroad workers tore up and barricaded the tracks in order to hold back Kornilov's army."[63] Steinberg saw this through a wider lens: "As on a signal, workers, soldiers, railway men, postal officials armed themselves, occupied all danger points, cut off the military headquarters from the rest of the country and forced them to complete capitulation."[64]

Without question, the label "petit-bourgeois" cannot be used for the rail workers, who quickly became the main group of workers opposed to the Bolshevik seizure of power, as Leggett tells us: "On 29 October [11 November], *Vikzhel*, the Menshevik-influenced All-Russian Executive Committee of the Union of Railwaymen, delivered an ultimatum demanding—under threat of a general rail strike—that all socialist parties should negotiate for the formation of a widely based coalition government."[65] These critical members of the working class did not strike, as the mental labourers did, but they did threaten a general strike, with the same demand as their white-collar counterparts—for a multiparty, as opposed to one-party, state. Theirs was a force that the Bolsheviks could not ignore. *Vikzhel* mediated talks in order to try and transition toward a multiparty state. Leggett provides some details:

> Under threat of a strike that would halt the delivery of food to Petrograd, *Vikzhel* demanded the creation of a democratic coalition government (often called in those days a homogenous socialist government) that ranged from the Popular Socialists to the Bolsheviks. Martov was not only the soul of this undertaking but actually extracted an agreement to hold talks from the Central Committee of

the RSDLP (Unified), which up to that point had been denying that any agreement with the Bolsheviks was even feasible.[66]

The response from the Bolsheviks was to split the union. Unable to win a majority at the Railwaymen's Congress, Bolshevik rail workers divided from *Vikzhel* and formed "a new Bolshevik-controlled executive body, *Vikzhedor*, composed from the unsuccessful minority at the Railwaymen's Congress." The job of supervising the railways was given to this new body. Economically, it was a disaster, resulting in what Pethybridge calls "chaos on the railways."[67] Politically, however, it was a success, creating a lever for the Bolsheviks among the rail workers that was capable of deflecting their threat.

Steve Smith argues that "most groups of workers—with the exception of certain 'labor aristocrats' and white-collar workers" supported the Bolshevik seizure of power.[68] "Labor aristocrats" presumably refers to the rail workers, and "white-collar workers" to the public-sector strikers. Perhaps this is an adequate characterization of these big events—this class struggle against Bolshevism of late 1917 and early 1918. Perhaps, however, we need to say more. Perhaps this working-class opposition to Bolshevism can be seen as the attempt to reassert workers' agency over a revolution that had taken an increasingly substitutionist turn. Perhaps this was the attempt of the workers at the point of production to put their stamp on a revolution that had been initiated by the "temporary new class" described by Martov and Abramovitch, and that was increasingly under the control of the Cheka and other institutions of terror emanating from the minoritarian Bolsheviks.

There is a compelling logic to this latter interpretation, especially when we examine working-class support—or lack thereof—for Bolshevik rule in the subsequent years and months. Grégoire (Grigorii) Aronson describes the process of weakening support for the Bolsheviks within the working class:

The October Revolution was barely a month and a half old, when large masses no longer believed the slogans and promises of the Bolsheviks. Any sympathy for them was gone, and the benevolent neutrality of the previous weeks gave way to growing opposition. The dissolution of the Constituent Assembly (and local government

Table 1. Percentage of total votes cast in the Constituent Assembly elections of November 1917

		SR	LSR (est.)	Bolshevik
Total votes cast	44,219,000	34.2	4.4	23.9
Urban, industrial areas				
Petrograd, Moscow	1,707,000	3.6	8.9	46.3
Other Industrial	5,864,000	33.2	7.2	47.0
Armed Forces				
Sailors	165,000	13.3	18.8	46.1
Soldiers at Front, North and West	1,817,000	23.7		61.9
Soldiers at Front, Other	2,153,000	50.0		22.0
Russian peasant areas	12,886,000	52.6	4.5	17.6
Key non-Russian regions				
Ukraine	8,167,000	4.8	9.4	10.6
Transcaucasia (incl. Georgia)	1,887,000	5.6		4.6
Belarus	2,264,000	28.0		55.5
Baltic States	436,000	0.7		50.0
Other	6,872,000	53.7		9.6

bodies), in early January 1918, had almost everywhere the effect of estranging the mass of workers from the Bolsheviks and changing their attitude towards them. After the conclusion of the Treaty of Brest Litovsk, the convening of the Constituent Assembly became a popular slogan. The need for a democratic state authority qualified to speak for the whole country became increasingly felt. And in the working class areas, sympathy for the Mensheviks and SRs, previously in decline, began to revive.[69]

The Constituent Assembly has been referred to periodically throughout this book. The convening of such an assembly had been a demand of the anti-tsarist movement for a generation—to gather democratically elected representatives from every region of the empire, to formally construct a new political order, and to address and try to solve the great problems of that empire, in particular the agrarian or land question. The election happened in November 1917, just three weeks after the Bolsheviks

Menshevik	Kadet	Ukrainian	Other parties
3.3	4.7	12.2	17.2
3.0	29.9	0.2	8.1
2.4	6.9		3.3
1.2		7.9	12.7
0.9	1.7	9.6	2.3
5.4	1.7	16.5	4.5
1.2	4.0	0.0	20.0
1.3	2.9	58.4	12.6
30.2	1.3		58.3
2.1	2.8		11.7
1.3			47.7
3.8	3.9	1.0	27.9

NOTE: Percentages do not add up to 100 because there were many smaller categories of parties that are not included in this table.

SOURCE: Compiled from statistics available in Oliver Henry Radkey, Russia Goes to the Polls: The Election to the All-Russian Constituent Assembly, 1917, 148–60.

seized power. The assembly held one session on 5 (18) January, but was dispersed by armed sailors and never allowed to meet again. Oliver Radkey is the indispensable source for any study of this assembly. He argues that: "The election to the Constituent Assembly has two outstanding features: a uniqueness without parallel in the fortunes of other great peoples, and a death that makes it all but impossible to reassemble its shattered fragments."[70] To the extent that it is possible, Radkey has reassembled those fragments. Table 1 provides a summary of his key findings.

No party won a majority in the election. The Social-Revolutionaries received the greatest share of the vote (38.6 percent), but they put forward their lists of candidates *before* that party divided and the Left Social-Revolutionaries (Left SRs) emerged as a separate party. It is impossible to tell what portion of the overall SR vote would have gone to the Left SRs. Based on Radkey's research, I have made a very rough approximation for areas we know were Left SR strongholds, thus reducing the SR totals to 34.2 percent. Still, this certainly overstates SR support and understates Left SR support. The Bolsheviks came second, with 23.9 percent.

As important as the overall totals are the votes by region. In the two great urban centres of the Russian empire, St. Petersburg and Moscow, the Bolsheviks were dominant, winning close to half the vote. Their big rival in these cities was the liberal party—the Constitutional Democrats, or Kadets—which captured one-third of the vote. In the other industrial areas of the country, the Bolsheviks were similarly dominant, and the Kadets a non-factor. The sailors in the fleet voted 45.9 percent for the Bolsheviks, and the peasants-in-uniform on the northern and western fronts gave the Bolsheviks an astonishing 61.9 percent support. Soldiers on fronts further away from urban and industrial Russia backed the Social-Revolutionaries. The SR was also overwhelmingly dominant in the Russian peasant villages, outpolling the Bolsheviks 52.6 percent to 17.6 percent.

The non-Russian parts of the empire require separate treatment. Two of them—the areas that are today Belarus and the Baltic states—strongly supported the Bolsheviks. But in two others—today, Transcaucasus and Ukraine—Bolshevik support was risible: 4.6 percent and 10.6 percent, respectively. In Transcaucasus, of which Georgia is a part, national parties classified as "Turko-Tatar" by Radkey won 24.3 percent of the vote, and the Mensheviks—hegemonic among Georgian-speaking people—polled 30.2 percent.

Any democratic government to emerge from this complex election would have had to take the form of a coalition. Could the Bolsheviks have positioned themselves at the centre of such a coalition? Certainly, a portion of the SR vote would have been willing to participate—that portion that was, in essence, Left SR, a party whose program was almost identical to the Bolsheviks. In table 1, I have identified 4.4 percent of the vote as going to the Left SR. That figure is based as much on guesswork as on statistical analysis and without question underestimates the Left SR's real support, which was certainly far higher. And, interestingly, the very large bloc of votes that went to nationalist parties in Ukraine cannot, by any means, be written off as "bourgeois nationalist." In at least three places—Poltava, Kharkiv, and Kherson—the Ukrainian Social-Revolutionaries mounted a joint list with the Bolsheviks' closest allies—the Left SRs—and these joint lists polled well over one million votes.[71] In other words, a whole section of the Ukrainian nationalist vote should, in theory, have been amenable to coalition with the Bolsheviks and the Left SRs. It would, of course, have required a staunch defence of Ukraine's national rights—something that, as we have seen, was not to characterize Bolshevik rule. It might, however, have led to an unfolding of different Russia–Ukraine relations than the appalling near genocide and artificially produced famine whose story was outlined in the introduction to this book.

In any case, coalition was not the road chosen. The Bolsheviks argued that the vote was illegitimate because its candidates were selected before the overthrow of the provisional government and before the emergence of the Left Social-Revolutionaries as a separate party. Rosa Luxemburg, from her prison cell, puzzled over why "such clever people as Lenin and Trotsky" didn't pursue a different path:

> Since the Constituent Assembly was elected long before the deci-
> sive turning point, the October Revolution, and its composition
> reflected the picture of the vanished past and not of the new state of
> affairs, then it follows automatically that the outgrown and therefore
> still-born Constituent Assembly should have been annulled, and
> without delay, new elections to a new Constituent Assembly should
> have been arranged.[72]

No new elections were called, however, and the assembly was forcibly suppressed. The manner in which it was suppressed became itself a factor in working-class opposition to the Bolsheviks. A demonstration of some thousands, "workers with banners, office workers, and intellectuals," marched to welcome the delegates to the Constituent Assembly, only to be fired upon by soldiers. The official death toll from this incident was twenty-one.[73] Inna Rakitnikov, in a report on the demonstration prepared for the International Socialist Bureau, said: "On all the streets leading to the palace, groups of Red Guards had been established; they received the order, 'Not to spare the cartridges.' On that day at Petrograd there were one hundred killed and wounded."[74]

When the assembly finally did convene, the Bolsheviks were in a distinct minority, and, as Chamberlin writes, "the soldiers and sailors in the galleries were the deciding force," interrupting speeches from other parties "with hoots, jeers and hostile interjections."[75] Until stopped by Lenin, "impatient sailors in the gallery amused themselves by aiming their guns" at the head of SR leader Viktor Chernov.[76] In the wee hours of the morning, after just one sitting, the assembly was dispersed, never to reconvene. Ironically, it was sailors from Kronstadt—the same Kronstadt that three years later became iconic as the last stand against one-party Bolshevik rule—who played a key role in dispersing the assembly. According to Israel Getzler, six hundred Kronstadt sailors were dispatched to be present when the assembly met. Kronstadt veteran Pavel Dybenko, who, as we earlier saw, was implicated in the assassination of the Kadet ministers, spoke for the sailors at the assembly. Another leader from Kronstadt, Fiodor Raskolnikov, led the walkout by the Bolshevik delegates. And it fell to Kronstadt sailor Anatolii Zhelezniakov to order the Assembly members to get out "because the guards are tired."[77]

Contrary to some reports, this dispersal of the assembly by armed soldiers, and the violence that preceded it, did not go unnoticed. William Rosenberg writes of a "major outbreak of worker protest in Petrograd. . . . Thousands had gathered at the Obukhov works in the southeastern district of the city and at nearby plants in the Nevskii district, including the important Aleksandrovsk locomotive works. There were also protests at several plants in the Vyborg district, and at the Trubochnyi works on Vasil'evskii Island."[78]

Rosenberg tells us how this working-class opposition to Bolshevism took organizational form:

It is largely in this context that one needs to understand the emergence of the Conference of Factory and Plant Representatives as a center of worker dissidence. In mid-January [1918] a meeting described in the press as a "Workers' Conference of the Union to Defend the Constituent Assembly" took place in Petrograd, organized in the main, apparently, by self-described "Right" Mensheviks disaffected from their Central Committee over the question of cooperation with the Bolsheviks. They were determined to build a new, representative movement "from below," shedding formal party affiliations. Workers from a number of plants soon joined them in forming the conference as a broad-based assembly, hoping among other things to counter what one observer lamented as the Petrograd workers' new "passivity and indifference." The first "extraordinary" meeting of the conference convened in Petrograd on March 13 in the midst of new protests over the evacuation, which occurred most intensively just before Brest Litovsk, when it seemed the city might fall under German control.[79]

This working-class opposition also took political form. Vladimir Brovkin says that: "The Menshevik platform—which insisted that the unions must be independent from the employer, be it a 'workers' state' or a private entrepreneur; that the soviets had to remain what they had been in 1917: workers' political organizations and not agencies to run municipal services—was gaining wide popular support."[80]

Finally, the working-class opposition took the form of direct action—strikes, demonstrations, and campaigns to take control of local soviets. The response from the Bolsheviks was increased repression. "In 1918," writes Brovkin, "a wave of general strikes rolled across European Russia."

> General strikes took place in Tula, Nizhnii Novgorod, Kaluga, Tver', Iaroslavl', and other cities. The Bolsheviks arrested strike committees, imposed curfews, and declared a state of emergency. Violent clashes took place between the Cheka and the workers. The general pattern in the escalation of conflict between the Bolsheviks and the workers repeated itself over and over: the workers, angered by the Bolsheviks' disbanding of the newly elected soviet, where the opposition had won, or by the postponement of elections, resorted to strikes and protest marches. The Bolsheviks responded with arrests and shootings, which in turn led to general strikes and uprisings, and on the part of the Bolsheviks to mass arrests, the complete shutdown of the opposition press, and terror by August 1918.[81]

Working-class anger at the Bolsheviks coincided with growing peasant discontent:

> By June [1918] the peasants, who in October had welcomed the redivision of land, were angered by grain requisitioning. The army had disintegrated, and the soldiers, formerly the backbone of Bolshevik support, had become peasants, bagmen on the roads, and unemployed—groups not friendly to the Bolsheviks. Even the sailors, whose intervention into politics had been decisive for the

Bolshevik victory in October, had begun to turn against the Bolsheviks. This was the beginning of a long road that was to lead to the sailors' revolts in 1919 and Kronstadt in 1921.[82]

The story of the great Kronstadt revolt of 1921 has been told eloquently elsewhere.[83] It was the culmination of mass peasant and workers' movements against Bolshevik policies. Orlando Figes documents the great peasant uprising against forced requisitioning, an uprising centred in Tambov, which began in August 1920 and was not finally suppressed until the summer of 1921. In Tambov and elsewhere, "much of the rural state infrastructure was swept aside by a huge tidal wave of peasant anger and destruction."[84] Jonathan Aves puts the uprising in Kronstadt in the context of a working-class uprising in Petrograd that was rooted in deep disaffection with Bolshevik rule. "By the end of 1920," writes Aves, "a mood of extreme hostility amongst workers to the Communist Party dictatorship was developing." This hostility was well-known to the leadership of the party. The Workers' Opposition had proposed that a Congress of Producers should run the economy; Zinoviev, in March 1921, suggested that if such a plan went forward, "the Communist Party would receive only one per cent of the delegates."[85]

The workers' protests in Petrograd in the run-up to the Kronstadt rebellion have often been characterized as a "go slow," or *volynka*, movement. But Aves maintains that "the industrial unrest of February-March 1921" needs to be seen as "a strike movement," and that "the decision to abandon the policy of grain requisitioning was first made public" in response not to the Kronstadt rebellion but to this movement.[86] However we evaluate these events, the fact of massive subaltern unrest against the Bolsheviks seems undeniable. The repression against the Kronstadt rebels was fierce. And while economic concessions were made (in particular, abandoning war communism and allowing free trade in grain), they were accompanied by a harsh political clampdown, "what Martov denounced as ... 'purely economic concessions without a change in the political order.'"[87] Israel Getzler's judgment is harsh. The suppression of Kronstadt, he says, "marked a turning point, if not the terminal point, in the history of the Russian revolution. Lenin's response blocked what was still left of the revolution's political open-endedness, completed the formation of the highly centralized and bureaucratized single-party dictatorship, and put Russia firmly on the road to Stalinism."[88] By 1921, the new state carved out of the old Russian empire bore no resemblance to that envisaged by any of the participants in the 1917 revolution. "Barbarous methods" had not proved fruitful in achieving any of the ends imagined by that generation.

Their Ethics and Ours

The question of ethics—of interrogating the relationship between ends and means—is deeply related to the tension between self-emancipation and substitutionism. Put another way, the constant evacuation of self-emancipation from the criteria by which political means are selected, and the resulting drift into substitutionist methods, has a clear ethical or moral dimension, on exactly the same plane as an "end justifies means" ethic. Self-emancipation is a means to an end—but for the Machiavellian, it is only one of many possible means. If that end can be achieved through other means, however unethical, so be it.

Unless of course, the ends we achieve are *completely* shaped by the means we employ. In fact, this is almost self-evident common sense. It takes a sophisticated theorist to make the opposite case. One who made the attempt was Leon Trotsky. His oft-cited *Their Morals and Ours* provides a coherent and digestible summary of what he saw as a historical-materialist approach to ethics. He accepts the charge, levelled at the Bolsheviks, that they saw the means employed as justified by the ends achieved. He denies, however, that this involved an expulsion of ethics from the question of political activity:

> A means can be justified only by its end. But the end in turn needs to be justified. From the Marxist point of view, which expresses the historical interests of the proletariat, the end is justified if it leads to increasing the power of humanity over nature and to the abolition of the power of one person over another.[89]

Rather than being sophisticated, this is just sophistry. Specifically, it is not clear at what point we would identify the "historical interests of the proletariat" as being served by the actions taken during the revolution. Their historical interests were certainly not served by mass internment in the

Gulag. They were also not served by the mass depopulation of Leningrad in 1934 and 1935, nor by the Great Terror of 1937 and 1938. The historical interests of the German proletariat in 1921 were ill-served by the instrument created by the Russian Revolution, the Communist International. More generally, Trotsky's claim that actions in the present can be ethically justified by results that make themselves visible only in the future perhaps provides a "rear-view mirror" standard for historians by which we can assess the justness of means employed, but it provides very little help for assessing actions in the present. But surely the very reason we have a field of study called "ethics" is because we realize that even if understanding is always retrospective, that is of little help when we peer into the future and try to assess what actions to take now. The Owl of Minerva and the rear-view mirror will do when we are writing our memoirs, but not when we are contemplating party or state policy.

Put it this way—we do not and cannot know the long-term, or even immediate term, consequences of our actions. The very nature of ethics is to provide guidance as to what actions to take in the present, precisely when we are not aware of how things will work out in the future. This dilemma can only be resolved by resorting to a *deus ex machina*— displacing one's own assessment of future possibilities to a far-seeing, omnipotent being. But whether this displacement is to an oracle, as in ancient times, or to a party or party leader in the modern era, it is a solution to the ethical dilemma in form only and is unsatisfying to any with an interest in self-determination and self-emancipation.

For the One Who Thinks Differently

In chapter 8, we saw that Souvarine and Trotsky assessed the evolution of the Russian Revolution within two key frameworks: the control of the surplus and the dynamics essential to a hierarchical political party machine. In chapter 4, we saw Martov and Abramovitch introduce another, namely, the dynamics essential to the temporary new peasant-soldier class created from the horrors of the Great War. The essence of the politics within the industrial workers' movement on which the socialist project had been based in Marx's time was a battle for the extension of democracy—hence the name "social democracy." In contrast, the politics within the movement characteristic of the temporary new peasant-soldier class had, at its core, impatience with democracy and a tendency toward "direct action" through force of arms to settle disputes. This core aspect of the Martov/ Abramovitch thesis enriches our ability to understand the tragic degeneration of the revolution of 1917—the move from hope to horror.

Rosa Luxemburg, in 1918, wrote a piece specifically to criticize the Bolsheviks' forcible suppression of the Constituent Assembly:

> Freedom only for the supporters of the government, only for the members of one party—however numerous they may be—is no freedom at all. Freedom is always and exclusively freedom for the one who thinks differently. Not because of any fanatical concept of "justice" but because all that is instructive, wholesome and purifying in political freedom depends on this essential characteristic, and its effectiveness vanishes when "freedom" becomes a special privilege.[90]

Martov was one who was not afraid to "think differently"—opposing the governments of his day, opposing the leadership of his own party when it collapsed into pro-war social patriotism, opposing the Bolsheviks' use of barbarous methods to try and achieve socialist ends. Luxemburg's defence of "the one who thinks differently" and Martov's historical-materialist exploration of the role of the temporary new class of peasants-in-uniform, along with the view they both shared, that ends cannot be separated from means—these can allow us to understand the big events we call the Russian Revolution.

The fact that Martov and Luxemburg are historical materialists in a classic sense is critically important. It means that we need not be restricted to "psychological factors" in explaining the Leninist distrust of self-activity and embrace of terror. It is helpful, in this regard, to return to the previously cited January 1919 program manifesto of the young German Communist Party and quote it at greater length.

> During the bourgeois revolutions bloodshed, terror, and political murder were an indispensable weapon in the hands of the rising classes.
>
> The proletarian revolution requires no terror to realize its aims. It hates and despises killing. It does not need these weapons because it does not combat individuals but institutions, because it does not enter the arena with naïve illusions whose disappointment it would

seek to revenge. It is not the desperate attempt of a minority to mold
the world forcibly according to its ideal, but the action of the great
massive millions of the people, destined to fulfill a historic mission
and to transform historical necessity into reality.[91]

These were some of the last published words of Luxemburg, and they remain
to this day one of the best short summaries of the key self-emancipation
lessons from the Russian revolutionary era.

The very framing of this excerpt from Luxemburg takes us back to
a theme touched on in part 2 of this book. The Russian revolutionaries
aspired to straddle two revolutionary processes: the bourgeois (or, to use
more contemporary language, "modernizing") revolution against tsarism,
and the working-class socialist revolution against capitalism. Oliver Cromwell and Maximilien Robespierre both became agents of their respective
country's modernizing revolutions; both ended up being covered with the
blood of victims from their own use of terror. Lenin, as a modernizing
revolutionary, is in their company. We can make that historical parallel
and in that sense understand what happened in the years following 1917.
But doing so—putting Lenin and Trotsky at least to some extent in the
same category as Cromwell and Robespierre—should serve as a warning
sign should we attempt to look uncritically at these historical figures as
models for contemporary, urban social movements. Clearly, the approach
of Cromwell and Robespierre are of historical interest only. And this is
how we should approach Lenin and the Bolsheviks. Clearly, their attempt
to combine mass terror with a transition to socialism ended in abject
failure—not to speak of moral degeneration on a colossal scale.

The Bolshevik Jacobins proved adept at constructing a weapon with
which to raise money and build a party, and later, to overthrow the provisional government and build a new state. But Luxemburg's point in the
manifesto quoted above is the theme of this concluding chapter—*what* is
achieved from certain actions depends very much on *how* those actions
are carried out.

It is not a matter of indifference that making a fetish of professional
staff as the core of a party, with all that implies, created a belief in
hierarchy inside the Bolshevik Party. That approach to party-building
reflected a conspiratorial approach to politics and a distrust of openness
that would repeatedly be an obstacle to the forward movement of the

Left. The distrust of the soviets in 1905 is a clear example of this. It was not the staff-driven Bolsheviks who were able to respond in a positive manner, but rather the scholar-activists (or journalist/scholar/organizers) in and around the Mensheviks. The "money question" that flowed from the staff model intersected with the emphasis on hierarchy to create the catastrophe of the period of expropriations, almost wrecking the party in the process. All of this generated a "bureaucratic type," of which Stalin was the epitome. He could not consolidate his rule until the entire generation with which he had grown up had been eliminated. However, his political physiognomy was shaped by the particularly negative features of that generation's experience.

Part 1 of this book suggested that to get to the heart of that experience, we have to let ourselves listen to the experience of workers' struggles that, at key moments, have defined the future of post-revolutionary Russia. Part 2 suggested that we have to put aside anti-Menshevik prejudices and read and study the great contributions of Martov and Abramovitch. Part 3 suggested that, throughout this whole process, we cannot tolerate either a casual or a systematic anti-intellectualism that puts a wall of prejudice and shunning between ourselves and the subjects of our research—an anti-intellectualism into which Lenin descended after his divide from the Mensheviks in 1903. We have to let ourselves read Trotsky's last book and try to let his intellectual journey speak to us on its own terms. We have to read Solzhenitsyn—perhaps disagree with him politically, but listen to his story of *zek* resistance to the hell of the Gulag. And we have to fully abandon a standpoint of reverence in our approach to Lenin—and for that matter, to all individuals associated with the Russian experience—and let history speak to us dispassionately and without filters of preconception. If we do so, we can see, for instance, the debates inside the Comintern as real debates reflecting real tensions between a substitutionist politics (which, if attempted in the twenty-first century, would end as badly as they did in the twentieth) and a politics of self-emancipation. In the end, it is the latter that is the only meaningful approach to social progress in this or any generation.

Notes

Preface: On Forgetting to Read Solzhenitsyn

1. Anne Applebaum, *Gulag: A History*, xv.
2. Aleksandr I. Solzhenitsyn, *The Gulag Archipelago*, 1:x.
3. The word *zakliuchennyi* means prisoner or detainee, and during the construction of the White Sea Canal in the 1930s, the forced labourers who worked (and died) in their thousands on the project were euphemistically labelled *zakliuchennyi kanaloarmeets*—canal army prisoners. Official records often abbreviated this as ZK or z/k, and prisoners who saw these abbreviations turned the abbreviations into a slang word, *zek* or *zeka*. The former, *zek*, has entered into common use and is now, effectively, a synonym for prisoner. See Lilia Pal'veleva, "Arestantskie slova" [Convict terms].
4. Solzhenitsyn, *Gulag Archipelago*, 1:x.
5. Michael E. Allen, *The Gulag Study*, 26.
6. Alan Barenberg, *Gulag Town, Company Town: Forced Labor and Its Legacy in Vorkuta*, 3. The river camp (*Rechnoi lager'*) was established on 27 August 1948. See Allen, *The Gulag Study*, 26. Throughout this book, "Vorkuta" will be used frequently as a shorthand to refer to the entire camp complex.
7. Barenberg, *Gulag Town*, 7.
8. Ibid. Barenberg's reference is to Lynne Viola's introduction (subtitled "The Other Archipelago") in *The Unknown Gulag: The Lost World of Stalin's Special Settlements*.
9. Barenberg, *Gulag Town*, 9. Barenberg cites Sheila Fitzpatrick, "War and Society in Soviet Context," 41–47; Donald Filtzer, "From Mobilized to Free Labour," 158; as well as Filtzer, *Soviet Workers and Late Stalinism*, 39–40.
10. Viola, *Unknown Gulag*, 32.
11. Suzanne Rosenberg, *A Soviet Odyssey*, 191–90.
12. Applebaum, *Gulag*, 580–81.
13. See the discussion in ibid., 581–83.

14. Solzhenitsyn, *Gulag Archipelago*, 3:445.

15. Ibid., 1:19 and 1:134.

16. Ibid., 1:134.

17. Ibid., 3:421.

18. Ibid., 3:526.

19. Ibid., 1:xi.

20. See Ian D. Thatcher, "The St Petersburg/Petrograd Mezhraionka, 1913–1917: The Rise and Fall of a Russian Social Democratic Workers' Party Unity Faction." Some commentators use RSDLP (based on the English translation) rather than RSDRP.

21. Only from 2009 available in complete form, retitled as *In the First Circle*.

22. W. E. B. Du Bois, *Black Reconstruction: An Essay toward a History of the Part Which Black Folk Played in the Attempt to Reconstruct Democracy in America, 1860-1880*. See in particular, chapter I, "The Black Worker" and chapter IV, "The General Strike." Thanks to Dr. Anthony Bogues, director of the Center for the Study of Slavery and Justice at Brown University, for drawing this to my attention.

23. These memoirs and accounts include those by Paul Barton, Mikhail Baitalsky, Edward Buca, Brigitte Gerland, Maria Joffe, Nadezhda Joffe, Hryhory Kostiuk, Suzanne Rosenberg, Joseph Scholmer, and Danylo Shumak, as well as the collections gathered together in George Saunders, ed., *Samizdat: Voices of the Soviet Opposition*; Pierre Frank, ed., *Renaissance du bolchévisme en U.R.S.S: mémoires d'un bolchévik-léniniste*; Commission internationale contre le régime concentrationnaire, *Livre blanc: Sur les camps de concentration soviétiques*; and David Rousset, Gérard Rosenthal, and Théo Bernard, *Pour la vérité sur les camps concentrationnaires (Un procès antistalinien à Paris)*. The memoirs by both Maria and Nadezda Joffe are available in their original Russian, part of a collection of more than 2,500 maintained by the Sakharov Center (see https://www.sakharov-center.ru/asfcd/auth/?t=list).

24. Elsewhere, the numbered pits are sometimes described as numbered Camps.

25. Solzhenitsyn, *Gulag Archipelago*, 3:283. This strike will be described in greater detail in chapter 2.

26. Shumuk, *Life Sentence: Memoirs of a Ukrainian Political Prisoner*, 239 and 242.

27. Solzhenitsyn, *Gulag Archipelago*, 3:258.

28. Ibid.

29. Mikhail Baitalsky, *Notebooks for the Grandchildren: Recollections of a Trotskyist Who Survived the Stalin Terror*, 15–21.

30. Solzhenitsyn, *The Gulag Archipelago*, 2:232.

31. Baitalsky, *Notebooks for the Grandchildren*, 19–20. In referring to "camp criminals," Baitalsky alludes to a division in the camps between "political" prisoners (of whom he was one) and "criminal" prisoners. His evident antipathy for the latter reflects a legacy of bitterness over the abuse that political prisoners often suffered at the hands of the "criminals," violence sometimes encouraged by the camp authorities themselves.

32. Leon Trotsky, "Stalinism and Bolshevism: Concerning the Historical and Theoretical Roots of the Fourth International" [1937], 423.

33. Victor Serge, "A Letter and Some Notes" [1939], 54.

34. See, for example, Slavoj Žižek, "Afterword: Lenin's Choice." For a critique of Žižek's approach, see Paul Kellogg, "The Only Hope of the Revolution Is the Crowd: The Limits of Žižek's Leninism."

35. V. I. Lenin, "Five Years of the Russian Revolution and the Prospects of the World Revolution," report to the Fourth Congress of the Communist International, 13 November 1922, *Lenin: Collected Works* [hereafter *LCW*], 33:430, 431. Lenin's address was published in *Pravda* two days later.

36. The Economist, "Northern Lights-Out: Russia."

37. Leon Trotsky, *Stalin: An Appraisal of the Man and His Influence*, ed. and trans. Alan Woods, 689. The translation by Charles Malamuth omits the word "far." Leon Trotsky, *Stalin: An Appraisal of the Man and His Influence*, ed. and trans. Charles Malamuth, 383.

38. I sketched out early versions of some of the points raised in chapters 6 and 7 in review articles of *To the Masses* and *Toward the United Front*: Paul Kellogg, "Grappling with Our History: The March Action, the Russo-Polish War, and the United Front" and "Coalition Building, Capitalism and War: Review Article of John Riddell, *To the Masses: Proceedings of the Third Congress of the Communist International, 1921.*" *To the Masses* and *Toward the United Front* have been the subject of numerous discussions and debates around the world, some of which have been filmed during meetings in Toronto, New York, and London. For Toronto, see Socialist Project's *Book Launch: Toward the United Front* and *Luxemburg, Lenin, Levi: Rethinking Revolutionary History*, and Taghabon, *Book Launch—To the Masses: Proceedings of the 3rd Congress of the Communist International* (1 of 6); for New York, see GC–ISO, *The Comintern Debate on Workers' Unity: NYC Book Launch for John Riddell's "To the Masses"*; for London, see SocResVideo, *John Riddell—United Fronts in the 20th and 21st Centuries*.

39. Marshall McLuhan, *The Medium Is the Message*, 74–75.

40. Georg Wilhelm Friedrich Hegel, preface to *Philosophy of Right*.

41. Rosa Luxemburg, "The Russian Revolution" [1918], 305.

42. Maria Joffe, *One Long Night*, 40–41. For the Russian original, see Joffe, *Odna noch': Povest' o pravde*, 24.

43. Applebaum, *Gulag*, 311.

44. Edward Buca, *Vorkuta*, 143–44.

45. The complete text of this note can be found in his daughter's memoirs: Nadezhda Joffe, *Vremia nazad: Moia zhizn', moia sud'ba, moia epokha* [Back in time: My life, my fate, my epoch], 62–72; translated in Nadezhda Joffe, *Back in Time: My Life, My Fate, My Epoch—The Memoirs of Nadezhda A. Joffe*, 55–63.

Introduction: Hope and Horror

1. Karl Marx, "Provisional Rules of the Association" [1864], 14.

2. Leon Trotsky, *Our Political Tasks* [1904], 72. Compare with Trotsky, *Nashi politicheskie zadachi (takticheskie i organizatsionnye voprosy)* [Our political tasks (tactical and organizational questions)], 50.

3. Until February 1918, Russia used the Julian calendar, whose dates were thirteen days behind the Gregorian. According to the Gregorian calendar, what has gone down in history as the "February Revolution" actually began on 8 March, while the "October Revolution" began on 7 November. In this book, dates refer to the Gregorian calendar, although, for reasons of context, I will occasionally provide both, putting the Julian date first, followed by the Gregorian in parentheses.

4. Orlando Figes, *A People's Tragedy: The Russian Revolution, 1891–1924*, 308.

5. Ibid., 310.

6. Ibid.

7. Georgakas, "October Song." Paul Le Blanc, in homage to Georgakas, gave the same title to his centenary history of the revolution. Paul Le Blanc, *October Song*.

8. Raphael R. Abramovitch, *The Soviet Revolution: 1917–1939*, 7–34.

9. Isaac Nachman Steinberg, *In the Workshop of the Revolution*, 44.

10. P. Iu. Savel'ev and S. V. Tiutiukin, "Iulii Osipovich Martov (1873–1923): The Man and the Politician," 67. See also Israel Getzler, *Martov: A Political Biography of a Russian Social Democrat*, 1.

11. P. Iu. Savel'ev and S. V. Tiutiukin, "Iulii Osipovich Martov (1873–1923): The Man and the Politician," 67.

12. Haimson, *The Making of Three Russian Revolutionaries: Voices from the Menshevik Past*, 19.

13. These three terms—"*revoliutsiia*" [revolution], "*perevorot*" [overthrow] and "*vosstanie*" [uprising]—are used differently today than they were

in Martov's time. "Many of the distinctions" between these three words "typical of modern usage, turn out to be uncharacteristic for the use of these words at the beginning of the 20th century . . . there have been significant shifts in their meaning over the last hundred years." Dobrovol'skii and Peppel', 99.

14. Martov, "Deklaratsiia fraktsii men'shevikov-internatsionalistov i evreiskoi sotsialisticheskoi rabochei partii poalei-tsion, zachitannaia Iu. O. Martovym" [Declaration of the Menshevik-Internationalist and Jewish Socialist Labour Party (Paole-Tsion) fractions, read out by Iu. O. Martov, 1917]. Compare with Leopold Haimson, *Russia's Revolutionary Experience, 1905-1917: Two Essays*, 101.

15. Martov, "Mirovoi bol'shevizm" [World Bolshevism], 413. Portions of the latter book were published in the journal *Mysl* [Thought] in 1919. Four years later, a complete version was published posthumously in Berlin, but it was never available inside Russia. See Martov, *Mirovoi bol'shevizm* [World Bolshevism]. Only in 2000 was a Russian-language excerpt legally published in Russia. Translations from *World Bolshevism* are those of Mariya Melentyeva and Paul Kellogg, and the page numbers are from the 2000 version.

16. Malcolm E. Falkus, *The Industrialisation of Russia*, 17.

17. Edward Hallett Carr, "The Russian Revolution and the Peasant," 69.

18. Ibid., 70.

19. Gorky, "On the Russian Peasantry," 21.

20. Figes, *People's Tragedy*, 232–33.

21. Matteo Ermacora, "Rural Society." Raphael Abramovitch indicates that the number of peasant lads mobilized might have been as high as fifteen million. Abramovitch, *Soviet Revolution*, 20.

22. Roger Pethybridge, *The Social Prelude to Stalinism*, 81.

23. This is a rough estimate based on the assumption that peasants comprised 80 percent of the population and applying to all of the Russian empire at the time of the war, an age-distribution survey from a nineteenth-century village in rural, post-emancipation Russia. Richard Pipes, *Russia Under the Bolshevik Regime*, 492; Herdis Kolle, "The Russian Post-Emancipation Household: Two Villages in the Moscow Area."

24. Boris Souvarine, *Stalin: A Critical Survey of Bolshevism*, 143.

25. Richard Pipes, *The Russian Revolution*, 236.

26. My calculations are based on Souvarine, *Stalin*, 313, and the editors of the English-language edition of V. I. Lenin, *The Development of Capitalism in Russia*, 1899, in *LCW*, 3:71n1.

27. Pipes, *Russian Revolution*, 245.

28. Marcel Liebman, *The Russian Revolution: The Origins, Phases and Meaning of the Bolshevik Victory*, 100.

29. Pipes, *Russian Revolution*, 244.

30. George Tokmakoff, "Stolypin's Agrarian Reform: An Appraisal," 128.

31. Steinberg, *In the Workshop of the Revolution*, cover copy.

32. Ibid., 31. I have chosen to follow Steinberg (and some others) in preferring "Social-Revolutionaries" to "Socialist-Revolutionaries"—and not solely because Steinberg was, himself, a leading member of the Left Social-Revolutionaries. Using the term "socialist" tends to blur the distinction between this unique section of the Russian Left and the sections that came to dominate the revolution. There was a strong ethical component to the politics of the Social-Revolutionaries, which, according to Steinberg, included ideals such as "the liberation of mankind" and "love for the neighbor." The goal, he says, was "not only to gain freedom *from something*, but also to gain freedom *for something*. And that something is always more than personal, civil or political freedom." As with French workers in 1848, Steinberg's party "demanded the *social* Republic"—that is, "far-reaching changes in the structure of society, changes that would alter the relationship between man and man *spiritually* and *morally* as well as governmentally and economically." See Steinberg, *In the Workshop of the Revolution*, 11–12. Given this, I think "Social-Revolutionaries" is the most accurate English rendition for the name of this interesting and important section of the Russian Left.

33. Ibid., 32.

34. Ibid., 33.

35. Ibid., 34.

36. Ibid.

37. Ibid., 38–39.

38. Pethybridge, *The Social Prelude to Stalinism*, 81.

39. Souvarine, *Stalin*, 159.

40. Pipes, *Russian Revolution*, 127.

41. In this text and elsewhere, by convention, the years 1918 to 1921 are often characterized in the singular as "the Civil War." However, there were in fact multiple civil wars, most importantly that between the Bolshevik-controlled cities and the non-Bolshevik countryside, as well as the more well-known war of Bolshevik (Red) armies versus counter-revolutionary (White) armies. See Geoffrey Swain, *The Origins of the Russian Civil War*.

42. Steinberg, *In the Workshop of the Revolution*, 296.

43. Raphael Abramovistch [Abramovitch], Vassily Suchomlin, and Irakli Zeretelli [Tsereteli], *Der Terror gegen die Sozialistischen Parteien in Russland und Georgien* [The Terror against Socialist Parties in Russia and Georgia], 49.

44. Steinberg, *In the Workshop of the Revolution*, 296, 300.

45. Trotsky, *Stalin*, ed. and trans. Charles Malamuth, 408. In his translation, Alan Woods uses "bureaucracy" instead of "substratum." See Trotsky, *Stalin*, ed. and trans. Alan Woods, 717.

46. Abramovitch, *Soviet Revolution*, 337.

47. Lynne Viola, *The Unknown Gulag: The Lost World of Stalin's Special Settlements*, 6.

48. Donald W. Treadgold, "Was Stolypin in Favor of Kulaks?" 11n24, citing a report in the London *Times*. The report, written by a *Times* correspondent, quotes a speech delivered by Josip Broz Tito, the long-serving communist leader of post-World War II Yugoslavia. In that speech, delivered following a visit to the Macedonian People's Republic, Tito notes that even a man owning a mere twelve hectares of land might well be considered a kulak. See "Marshal Tito's Land Policy," *The Times* (London), 9 August 1944. The threshold of twelve hectares (just under thirty acres) was, to say the least, a very low bar, not exactly meriting the terms rich, capitalist, bourgeois, nor any other of the many descriptors often attached to the word kulak.

49. Souvarine, *Stalin*, 552.

50. Ibid., 670.

51. "About Us: History," *Forward*, n.d., https://forward.com/about-us/history/.

52. Vera Broido indicates that the "correct name" for the delegation "was the Delegation of the RSDRP Abroad—*Zagranichnaia delegatsia RSDRP*." The writings of two of these three, Abramovitch and Martov, figure prominently in this book. The third, Eva L'vovna Broido, is one of the unsung heroes of the Russian Revolution. In 1920, she was one of the first to enter exile in Europe (because of her health), and in 1927 was one of the last to clandestinely return to the Soviet Union to help organize the dwindling band of socialist oppositionists to totalitarian rule. After six months of work in the socialist underground, she was arrested and imprisoned. From 1936 on, her family received no word from her. It was only with the collapse of the Stalinist state, and the opening of the archives, that her daughter Vera learned that "Mother had been tried by a military tribunal in 1940 and sentenced to death … She was shot on 14 September 1941." Like many tens of thousands of political prisoners from that era, Eva Broido was posthumously rehabilitated. See Vera Broido, *Lenin and the Mensheviks*, 121, and Vera Broido, *Daughter of Revolution*, 184 and 208–11.

53. Sidney Hook, "Introduction" to Abramovitch, *Soviet Revolution*, ix.

54. Associated Press, "Moscow Denies Famine Deaths."

55. *Weekly People*, "The World News in Brief."

56. Jay Lovestone, "The Meaning of the Soviet Purges," 304.

57. Walter Duranty, "Russians Hungry, but Not Starving," quoting "a British source."

58. Ibid.

59. H. R. Knickerbocker, "Famine Grips Russia Millions Dying, Idle on Rise, Says Briton."

60. Quoted in ibid.

61. Quoted in ibid.

62. Muggeridge, "The Soviet's War on the Peasants," 564. While Muggeridge would go on to fame and some notoriety, living into his eighties, Jones would die young. While on assignment for the *Manchester Guardian* in China in 1935, he was kidnapped by bandits and executed. For unknown reasons, German newspaper correspondent Herbert Mueller, kidnapped along with Jones, was released unharmed. There has been much speculation in the years since that Mueller was a Stalinist agent working with the bandits and that the kidnapping was staged—its whole purpose being to eliminate a key eyewitness to the famine. Ray Gamache, *Gareth Jones: Eyewitness to the Holodomor*, 3, citing Margaret Siriol Colley, *Gareth Jones: A Manchukuo Incident*.

63. R. J. Rummel, *Lethal Politics*, 107n46.

64. Mark B. Tauger, "The 1932 Harvest and the Famine of 1933," 89.

65. Quoted in Gareth Jones, "Russia—Land of Starvation."

66. Gareth Jones, "Fate of Thrifty in U.S.S.R."

67. Gareth Jones, "Soviet Collective Farm Move Caused Famine in Russia, Says Gareth Jones."

68. Rummel, *Lethal Politics*, 104.

69. N. M. Dronin and E. G. Bellinger, *Climate Dependence and Food Problems in Russia, 1900–1990: The Interaction of Climate and Agricultural Policy and Their Effect on Food Problems*, 152.

70. Stephen F. Cohen, *Bukharin and the Bolshevik Revolution: A Political Biography, 1888–1938*, 317, quoting Nikolai Bukharin from sources listed on 455n200.

71. Ibid., 330.

72. Ibid., 331.

73. Alec Nove, *An Economic History of the U.S.S.R.*, 169.

74. Joseph Stalin, "Dizzy with Success: Concerning Questions of the Collective-Farm Movement" [1930].

75. Nove, *Economic History of the U.S.S.R.*, 171.

76. Ibid., 172.

77. Cohen, *Bukharin and the Bolshevik Revolution*, 339.

78. Quoted in N. I. Nemakov, *Kommunisticheskaya partiya—organizator massovogo kolkhoznogo dvizheniya (1929–1932 gg.)* [Communist party—organizer of the mass collective farm movement (1929–1932)], 259. Little known today, Rudzutak was once a prominent person in the Soviet Union. In 1924, for instance, he, along with Stalin and six others, was a pallbearer at Lenin's funeral. However, just three years after delivering the report quoted here, he became one of the many thousands arrested and shot for allegedly being a "counter-revolutionary." Years later, again like many of these thousands of unfortunates, he was posthumously rehabilitated. See Robert Service, *Stalin: A Biography*, 219; Roy Medvedev, *Let History Judge: The Origins and Consequences of Stalinism*, 180, 193.

79. Nove, *Economic History of the U.S.S.R.*, 173.

80. Ibid., 178.

81. Ibid., 179, quoting Iu. A. Moshkov, *Zernovaia problema v gody sploshnoi kollektivizatsii* [The grain problem in the years of complete collectivization] (Moscow: Moscow University, 1966), 217.

82. Ibid., 399n46, quoting Moshkov. See also Bojko et al., *Holodomor: The Great Famine in Ukraine 1932–1933*, 301.

83. Ibid., 180.

84. Stanisław Swianiewicz, *Forced Labour and Economic Development: An Enquiry into the Experience of Soviet Industrialization*, 98.

85. Ibid., 114.

86. Ibid., 116–17.

87. Ukrainian National Association, "30 U.N. Member-States Sign Joint Declaration on Great Famine," 20.

88. Joseph Stalin was not alone in pursuing policies that manufactured famine. In the decade that followed the Holodomor, the Bengal region of the Indian subcontinent was the epicentre of an equally horrific famine—the product of a "scorched earth" policy backed by Winston Churchill's War Cabinet. See Madhusree Mukerjee, *Churchill's Secret War: The British Empire and the Ravaging of India During World War II*, 63–67. In this context, if we justifiably cringe when, in a typical mid-twentieth-century article, Stalin is proclaimed the "leader of progressive mankind," we might wonder at the lack of cringeing when an early twenty-first-century movie portrays Churchill "as the greatest Briton of all time." G. M. Malenkov, "Comrade Stalin—Leader of Progressive Mankind"; Jonathan Teplitzky, dir., *Churchill*, 1:33:22.

89. Solomon M. Schwarz, *Labor in the Soviet Union*, 152.

90. Ibid., 171.

91. Roy A. Medvedev, *Let History Judge*, 165.

92. Ciliga, *The Russian Enigma*, 71. In 1924, following Lenin's death, Petrograd (formerly St. Petersburg) was renamed Leningrad.

93. Souvarine, *Stalin*, 598.

94. Aleksandr I. Solzhenitsyn, *The Gulag Archipelago*, 1:58.

95. Medvedev, *Let History Judge*, 230.

96. Ibid., 192–235; quotation from 233.

97. Ibid., 234.

98. Suzanne Rosenberg, *A Soviet Odyssey*, 59.

99. Souvarine, *Stalin*, 628.

100. Medvedev, *Let History Judge*, 239.

101. Nadezhda Joffe, *Back in Time: My Life, My Fate, My Epoch—The Memoirs of Nadezhda A. Joffe*, 210.

102. Medvedev, *Let History Judge*, 239.

103. J. Arch Getty, Gábor T. Rittersporn, and Viktor N. Zemskov, "Victims of the Soviet Penal System in the Pre-War Years: A First Approach on the Basis of Archival Evidence," 1023. Michael Haynes and Rumy Husan accept this figure, as does Steven Rosefielde, who gives annual figures of 353,074 and 321,618 for 1937 and 1938, respectively. See Haynes and Husan, *A Century of State Murder? Death and Policy in Twentieth-Century Russia*, 70; Rosefielde, *Red Holocaust*, 58.

104. Souvarine, "Postscript: The Counter-Revolution," 669.

105. Nove, *Economic History of the U.S.S.R.*, 180.

106. Tatjana Lorkovic, "Microform Collection: The All-Union Population Census, [1937 and] 1939."

Chapter 1: One Long Night, 1936–38

1. From Anonymous, "Mémoires d'un bolchevik-léniniste," 152.

2. Anonymous, "Memoirs of a Bolshevik-Leninist," 165.

3. Hryhory Kostiuk, "The Accursed Years from Lukianivka Prison to the Tragedy at Vorkuta (1935–40)," 169.

4. Anonymous, "Memoirs of a Bolshevik-Leninist," 165.

5. Kostiuk, "Accursed Years," 169.

6. Anonymous, "Memoirs of a Bolshevik-Leninist," 165.

7. George Saunders, foreword to *Samizdat: Voices of the Soviet Opposition*, 10. There were of course people from many different political stripes interred in the Gulag. Most, certainly, had no party affiliation. But for those who were deemed "political" prisoners, the vast majority were on the left. If from 1917 until 1937 you had been an Anarchist, a Menshevik, a Social-Revolutionary, a follower of Trotsky, or Zinoviev, or Kamenev, and, finally, even if you had been a follower of Stalin, you were likely to end up in the camps, labelled

a "counter-revolutionary," and shot. There were hundreds of thousands of these left-wing political prisoners. There is no good single adjective to describe this collection of prisoners. I have chosen "socialist" as the adjective with the most meaning for a contemporary audience.

8. Vorkuta is situated at a latitude of 67°30'N, at the northeastern tip of what was formerly the Komi Autonomous Republic of the Russian Federation and is today the Komi Republic, one of twenty-two semi-autonomous republics within the Russian state.

9. *The Economist*, "Northern Lights-Out: Russia."

10. Tom Balmforth, "Vorkuta: Gulag Is Gone, but a Virtual Prison Has Taken Its Place."

11. *The Economist*, "Northern Lights-Out."

12. Joseph Scholmer, *Vorkuta*, 55.

13. Ibid., 56. Nicholas I reigned from 1825 to 1855.

14. J. Arch Getty, Gábor T. Rittersporn, and Viktor N. Zemskov, "Victims of the Soviet Penal System in the Pre-War Years: A First Approach on the Basis of Archival Evidence," 1022.

15. Alan Barenberg, "From Prison Camp to Mining Town: The Gulag and Its Legacy in Vorkuta, 1938–1965," 51. The NKVD was one of the many iterations of the Soviet Union's notorious secret police force. From 1934 to 1946, the NKVD was the commissariat responsible for state security, including the secret police. The original incarnation of the secret police was the "Cheka" about which more will be said below.

16. Robert Conquest, *The Great Terror: Stalin's Purge of the Thirties*, 122.

17. Igor' Petrov, "Nastoiashchee imia respondenta #440" [The real name of respondent #440].

18. M.B. [Ivan Khoroshev], "Trotskyists at Vorkuta (An Eyewitness Report)," 216. M.B.'s account was first published by the *Socialist Courier* in 1961. Khoroshev's other most frequently used synonym was Mikhail Nil'skii.

19. Mikhail Baitalsky, *Notebooks for the Grandchildren: Recollections of a Trotskyist Who Survived the Stalin Terror*, 225.

20. Roland Gaucher, *Opposition in the U.S.S.R., 1917–1967*, 90–91.

21. Pierre Broué, *Communistes contre Staline: Massacre d'une génération*, 35.

22. Ibid., 37.

23. Gaucher, *Opposition in the U.S.S.R.*, 105.

24. Boris Souvarine, *Stalin: A Critical Survey of Bolshevism*, 492.

25. Gus Fagan, introduction to *Selected Writings on Opposition in the USSR, 1923–30*, by Khristian Georgievich Rakovskiĭ, 54.

26. Michal Reiman, *The Birth of Stalinism: The USSR on the Eve of the "Second Revolution*," 19.

27. Ibid., 22.
28. Mikhail Nil'skii [Ivan Mitrofanovich Khoroshev], *Vorkuta* (Samizdat edition, 1986), 74–75.
29. Saunders, "Currents in the Soviet Opposition Movement," 10.
30. Aleksandra Chumakova, "Memoirs of Aleksandra Chumakova," 190–91.
31. Joseph Berger, *Shipwreck of a Generation: The Memoirs of Joseph Berger*, 90.
32. Maria Joffe, *One Long Night: A Tale of Truth*. I borrowed the title of this gripping memoir when I named this chapter.
33. Ibid., 91.
34. Ibid., 94.
35. Broué, *Communistes contre Staline*, 257.
36. Berger, *Shipwreck of a Generation*, 94.
37. Conquest, *Kolyma: The Arctic Death Camps*, 13.
38. M.B. [Ivan Khoroshev], "Trotskisty na Vorkute" [Trotskyists at Vorkuta], 201. George Saunders translates this statement as "the Trotskyists formed a quite disparate group at Vorkuta; one part of them kept its old name of 'Bolshevik-Leninists.'" M.B., "Trotskyists at Vorkuta," 206. While I generally quote from Saunders's translation, the translation here seems to me closer to the spirit of the original.
39. M.B. [Ivan Khoroshev], "Trotskyists at Vorkuta," 206.
40. Ibid.
41. Ibid., 207.
42. Ibid., 210–12.
43. Berger, *Shipwreck of a Generation*, 97.
44. Aleksandr I. Solzhenitsyn, *The Gulag Archipelago*, 2:319.
45. M.B. [Ivan Khoroshev], "Trotskyists at Vorkuta," 211. M.B. mentions two further demands, one that women and prisoners who were elderly or ill not be incarcerated in Arctic camps and the other that "affairs relating to political opposition to the regime must not be judged by special NKVD tribunals, but in public judicial assemblies" (211).
46. Ibid., 213.
47. Solzhenitsyn, *Gulag Archipelago*, 2:319.
48. Anonymous, "Memoirs of a Bolshevik-Leninist," 142.
49. Solzhenitsyn, *Gulag Archipelago*, 2:319.
50. Elinor Lipper, *Eleven Years in Soviet Prison Camps*, 104.
51. Ibid., 106.
52. Ibid., 107. The anonymous memoirist whose *samizdat* account was first published in 1970 seems to have conflated Kashketin and Garanin. He writes that Kashketin, before he began his work at Vorkuta, "annihilated

more than fifteen thousand Communists at Kolyma." Anonymous, "Memoirs of a Bolshevik-Leninist," 172.

53. Vadim Z. Rogovin, *Stalin's Terror of 1937–1938: Political Genocide in the USSR*, 284.

54. Solzhenitsyn, *Gulag Archipelago*, 2:387.

55. Rossi, *The Gulag Handbook: An Encyclopedia Dictionary of Soviet Penitentiary Institutions and Terms Related to the Forced Labor Camps*, 488. From 1921 until 1930, such a prison was designated a "special purpose isolator" (*izoliator spetsial'nogo naznacheniia*, or simply *spetsizoliator*). From 1930 until 1937 this was changed to "OGPU special detention centre" (*izoliator osobogo naznacheniia OGPU*). Both are often referred to simply as "political isolator" (*politizoliator*). See Rossi, *The Gulag Handbook*, 139–40, 450, and 488.

56. This is translated as "newspapers" in the English translation of Ciliga's book. However, the Russian original is *zhurnala*, which means "journal" or "publication." See Ciliga, *The Russian Enigma*, 211; Ciliga, "Verkhneural'skii politizoliator" [Verkne-Uralsk political isolator], 362.

57. Ciliga, *Russian Enigma*, 211 and 199. The first part of Ciliga's book was originally published in French, in 1938, under the title *Au pays du grand mensonge*, which translates as "In the country of the great lie," a phrase picked up in the 1977 French-language edition, *Dix ans au pays du mensonge déconcertant*. The phrase "great lie" is much more evocative than "enigma," chosen by the English-language translators, and is, I think, closer to the intent and theme of the Ciliga volume.

58. Ibid., 211.

59. Alexander Fokin, "Tetradi verkhneural'skogo politicheskogo izoliatora: Predstavlenie istochnika i razmyshleniia o ego znachenii [The Notebooks of the Verkhne-Uralsk political isolator: Introduction of a source and reflections on its significance].

60. "Fashistskii perevorot v Germanii" [The Fascist coup in Germany].

61. Ciliga, "Verkhneural'snii politizoliator" [Verkne-Uralsk political isolator], 362.

62. Baitalsky, *Notebooks for the Grandchildren*, 220.

63. Nil'skii [Khoroshev], *Vorkuta*, 91. Compare with Nil'skii [Khoroshev] "Vorkutinskaia tragediia" [The Vorkuta tragedy], 296; M.B. [Ivan Khoroshev], "Trotskyists at Vorkuta," 215–16.

64. Nil'skii [Ivan Khoroshev], "Vorkutinskaia tragediia" [The Vorkuta tragedy], 308.

65. Baitalsky, *Notebooks for the Grandchildren*, 47, 225.

66. Berger, *Shipwreck of a Generation*, 96, 98.

67. Broué, *Communistes contre Staline*, 320.

68. Roy A. Medvedev, *Let History Judge: The Origins and Consequences of Stalinism*, 234.

69. Abramowitsch [Abramovitch], Suchomlin, and Zeretelli [Tsereteli], *Der Terror Gegen Die Sozialistischen Parteien in Russland Und Georgien [The Terror against Socialist Parties in Russia and Georgia]*.

70. Broido, *Lenin and the Mensheviks*, 159–62.

71. Ibid., 164.

72. Ibid., 165.

73. Anton Antonov-Ovseyenko, *The Time of Stalin: Portrait of a Tyranny*, xv. Antonov-Ovseyenko's father, Vladimir, held diplomatic posts in Stalin's government until the fall of 1937, when he was arrested, interrogated, and subsequently executed, in February 1938. His son was also arrested, initially in 1940, and went on to spend a total of nearly thirteen years in Gulag forced labour camps, including Vorkuta.

74. Stephen F. Cohen, "Introduction" to Antonov-Ovseyenko, *The Time of Stalin*, x.

75. Ibid., 319 and 329. Mikoyan was also the Politburo member who, in a speech delivered at the Twentieth Congress, "rehabilitated" Antonov-Ovseyenko's father, officially proclaiming him innocent.

76. Ibid., 145–46.

77. Leon Trotsky, "To the Bulgarian Comrades, October 4, 1930," 53.

78. Ibid., 54.

Chapter 2: Striking Against the Gulag, 1947–53

1. Alan Barenberg, "From Prison Camp to Mining Town: The Gulag and Its Legacy in Vorkuta, 1938–1965," 20.

2. Anna M. Cienciala, Natalia S. Lebedeva, and Wojciech Materski, eds., *Katyn: A Crime Without Punishment*, 343.

3. Stanisław Swianiewicz, *In the Shadow of Katyn: Stalin's Terror*, 80–83.

4. Benjamin B. Fischer, "The Katyn Controversy: Stalin's Killing Field." See also Stanisław Swianiewicz, *In the Shadow of* Katyn, 80–83, 147–50.

5. Institute of National Remembrance, "Decision to Commence Investigation into Katyn Massacre."

6. Swianiewicz, *In the Shadow of Katyn*, 147–50.

7. Ibid., 214–15.

8. Ibid., 215.

9. Ibid., 77.

10. Formally the "Vecheka (*Vserossiiskaia Chrezvychainaia Komissiia po borbe s kontrrevoliutsiei i sabotazhem*)—All-Russian Extraordinary Commission for combating counter-revolution, speculation and sabotage, colloquially known as Chrezvychaika or Cheka." See Broido, *Lenin and the Mensheviks*, 30.

11. Stanisław Swianiewicz, *Forced Labour and Economic Development: An Enquiry into the Experience of Soviet Industrialization*, 15.

12. Swianiewicz, *In the Shadow of Katyn*, 131–32.

13. Aleksandr I. Solzhenitsyn, *The Gulag Archipelago*, 1:24–92.

14. Swianiewicz, *Forced Labour and Economic Development*, 114–21; Anne Applebaum, *Gulag: A History*, 45; Lynne Viola, V. P. Danilov, N. A. Ivnitskii, and Denis Kozlov, eds., *The War Against the Peasantry, 1927–1930*.

15. Solzhenitsyn, *Gulag Archipelago*, 1:24.

16. Ibid., 1:25.

17. Ibid.

18. Roman Serbyn, "The First Man-Made Famine in Soviet Ukraine: 1921–1923," 5.

19. Ibid., 9.

20. Ibid., 5–12.

21. Swianiewicz, *Forced Labour and Economic Development*, 113–14.

22. Applebaum, *Gulag*, 87.

23. David Mandel, *Perestroika and the Soviet People: Rebirth of the Labour Movement*, 196.

24. Joseph Scholmer, *Vorkuta*, 212.

25. For the standard English translation as "primitive accumulation," see Marx, "The So-Called Primitive Accumulation" [1867]. This standard translation is misleading both conceptually and linguistically. Invoking the word "primitive" for a term deployed to describe the transition from pre-capitalist to capitalist social relations might fit well with the stage-ist modernism so widespread in the nineteenth and twentieth centuries, but it does not fit well with any reasonable translation from German to English. The German original is "Ursprüngliche Akkumulation." See Marx, "Die Sog. Ursprüngliche Akkumulation" [The so-called primary accumulation]. One might translate this as "original" or "initial" accumulation but only rarely as "primitive" accumulation. Some have suggested the term "originary." See Rosalind Morris, "*Ursprüngliche Akkumulation*: The Secret of an Originary Mistranslation." But this is a little awkward for use in everyday English. "Primary" is, I think, best as it implies any or all of first, foundational, and ongoing.

26. Robert Miles, *Capitalism and Unfree Labour: Anomaly or Necessity?* 36.

27. Abigail B. Bakan, "Review of *Capitalism and Unfree Labour: Anomaly or Necessity?* by Robert Miles," 236.

28. Evgeny Preobrazhensky, *The New Economics* [1926], 83n1.

29. Ibid., 88.

30. Ibid., 124. The passage is italicized in the original.

31. Stalin, "Industrialisation and the Grain Problem: Speech Delivered on July 9, 1928," 165–66.

32. Preobrazhensky, *New Economics*, 5–6 and 124.

33. Stalin, "Industrialisation and the Grain Problem," 167.

34. Alec Nove, introduction to Preobrazhensky, *The New Economics*, xiv.

35. Ibid., xv.

36. See Martin McCauley, *Stalin and Stalinism*, 76–88.

37. Scholmer, *Vorkuta*, 224.

38. Edward Buca, *Vorkuta*, 202.

39. Alan Barenberg, *Gulag Town, Company Town: Forced Labor and Its Legacy in Vorkuta*, 15–16. As the source of Chernov's reference to "mining engineers of Ukhta," Barenberg cites Georgii Aleksandrovich Chernov, *Iz istorii otkritiia pechorskogo ugol'nogo basseina* [From the history of the discovery of the Pechora coal basin], 2nd ed. (Syktyvkar: Komi knizhnoe izd-vo, 1989), 94.

40. P. I. Negretov, "How Vorkuta Began," 569. Negretov, whose article appeared in 1977, goes on to discuss the use of forced labour at Vorkuta, pointing out that "in the thirties Vorkuta was in the domain of the NKVD (until 1934—OGPU), and its labour force came from the camps" (570). He also notes that, while "the use of convict labour in industry and construction, especially in remote parts of the USSR, was never (except, perhaps, in the forties) a secret" (570), it was rarely mentioned in literature intended for public consumption.

41. Mikhail Mikhailovich Prigorovski, *The Coal Resources of the USSR*, 4, 7.

42. Ibid., 7.

43. Ibid., 14.

44. Ibid., 15.

45. Maria Joffe, *One Long Night: A Tale of Truth*, 38.

46. Ibid., 17.

47. Ibid., 17n.

48. Ibid., 38.

49. Globe and Mail, "250,000 Slaves Strike in Red Camp."

50. Brigitte Gerland, "Student Intellectuals and Religionists Form Backbone of Resistance in Soviet Slave Camps."

51. In Brigitte Gerland's "Rare Eyewitness Report of Soviet Labor Camp Given by 'Graduate,'" the date given for the circulation of the manifesto is 1949.

52. R.M. Tashtemkhanova, *Nemetskaia shkola sredneazievedeniia i kazakhstaniki: Uchebnoe posobie dlia studentov istoricheskikh fakul'tetov* [The German school of Central Asian and Kazakh studies: A Manual for history students].

53. Brigitte Gerland, "Vorkuta (1950–53): Oppositional Currents and the Mine Strikes," 222–23.

54. Pierre Broué, *Communistes contre Staline: Massacre d'une génération*, 178–79.

55. Gerland, "Vorkuta (1950–53)," 222–24.

56. Ibid., 225.

57. Brigitte Gerland, "500,000 Live in Huts Beneath Arctic Snow, Glad of Free Speech." Given the similarity of the ITL program to the analysis of the Left Opposition in the 1930s, it is hard not to speculate about there being a "physical link" between the two. We do know that some of the children survived the exterminations in Vorkuta (those under the age of twelve), and we can certainly surmise that the hellish conditions of their parents' deaths would have had a radicalizing effect on them. Evidence for this is the fact, cited above, that some children were involved in the hunger strike in Vorkuta of 1936–37. We also know, as of the 1970s, that some Left Oppositionists survived the purges and lived to publish their experiences in *samizdat* form. George Saunders speculates along these lines but, given the paucity of the evidence, can say no more than that "many of these young Leninists had been children of 'enemies of the people,' i.e., their parents had been prominent in the party, government, and military but had been purged in 1936–38." See George Saunders, "Introduction: Currents in the Soviet Opposition Movement," in Saunders, ed., *Samizdat: Voices of the Soviet Opposition*, 19.

58. Gerland, "Vorkuta (1950–53)," 227.

59. The literal translation of the words *suki* and *blatnoy* would be "bitches" and "thieves," although I think "collaborators" and "irreconcilables" captures their role in the camp system more accurately. The words of Ivan, a member of Vorkuta's *blatnoy*, clarify the antagonism between these groups:

> The underworld has its own traditions and strict codes. The first rule is that no member of it is ever allowed to co-operate in any way with the authorities. When a criminal is in a prison or camp, he can work with an axe, a pick, a hammer or a spade, but never in administration or the kitchen. Nor must he ever take part in building anything to be used against the prisoners, such as fences, watch-towers or isolation cells. He

isn't allowed to take any part in supervising other prisoners. Those of us who follow these rules are called *blatnoy*. But there are traitors among us who co-operate with the authorities, and betray their own brothers, and we call them *suki*—bitches. They're already dead men, sentenced by the rest of us, and at the first opportunity some *blatnoy* will kill them. We have our leaders and our courts. Quoted in Buca, *Vorkuta*, 59–60.

60. Ibid., 175.

61. Ibid.

62. Ibid., 178.

63. Dimitri Panin, *The Notebooks of Sologdin*, 88–90.

64. Saunders, "Introduction: Currents in the Soviet Opposition Movement," 21. For a report on the Kolyma battle, see Varlam Shalamov, "Major Pugachov's Last Battle," 241–56. The Kolyma revolt was more on the scale of a break-out than a collective rebellion.

65. Panin, *Notebooks of Sologdin*, 319.

66. Gerland, "Vorkuta (1950–53)," 228.

67. Panin, *Notebooks of Sologdin*, 309–20.

68. Buca, *Vorkuta*, 80.

69. Gerland, "Vorkuta (1950–53)," 224.

70. Buca, *Vorkuta*, 198, 199.

71. Ibid., 229.

72. Scholmer, *Vorkuta*, 187.

73. Beria is a prime example of the personal corruption that accompanies violence and totalitarian rule. Dmitri Volkogonov captures this starkly: "He worshipped only violence. He often gratified his sadistic needs by conducting interrogations himself, many of them ending in tragedy. . . . Beria's chief of personal security . . . would bring him any young girl who took his fancy, and the slightest resistance would bring tragic consequences for both the girl and her family." After the death of Stalin, Beria's peers "found the courage and perspicacity to render the monster harmless." They had him arrested and put on trial. When sentenced to death on 23 December 1953, "he fell to his knees in tears, writhing and begging for mercy." His peers—including Krushchev—listened to the whole thing "on a specially installed link." See Dmitri Volkogonov, *Stalin: Triumph and Tragedy*, 333.

74. Scholmer, *Vorkuta*, 188.

75. Anne Applebaum, *Iron Curtain: The Crushing of Eastern Europe 1944–56*, 436.

76. Beria quoted in Mark Kramer, "The Early Post-Stalin Succession Struggle and Upheavals in East-Central Europe: Internal-External Linkages in Soviet Policy Making (Part 1)," 23, quoted in ibid., 437.

77. Applebaum, *Iron Curtain*, 439.

78. Ibid., 442.

79. Scholmer, *Vorkuta*, 196.

80. Gerland, "Vorkuta (1950–53)," 231.

81. Ibid., 232.

82. Scholmer, *Vorkuta*, 213, 205. Alan Barenberg reports that, according to an official estimate, 15,604 prisoners—roughly 40 percent of the total camp population—were on strike by 29 July. See Barenberg, *Gulag Town, Company Town*, 131, 134.

83. Gerland, "Vorkuta (1950–53)," 233.

84. Ibid.

85. Buca, *Vorkuta*, 255.

86. Ibid., 243–47.

87. Ibid., 247.

88. Scholmer, *Vorkuta*, 232. In Scholmer's view, their vulnerability stemmed in part from the fact that the organizers chose to hold their meetings not in the depths of the mines—"the exclusive preserve of the prisoners"— but rather in the camps themselves, where they could be overheard by informers, thereby allowing the NKVD to identify and isolate "the most active elements in the strike" (232).

89. Buca, *Vorkuta*, 268–70. Solzhenitsyn also provides an account of these events from which I quoted in the preface, but he gives a date of 11 August rather than 1 August (*Gulag Archipelago*, 3:283).

90. Buca, *Vorkuta*, 270.

91. Ibid., 271.

92. Ibid., 271–72.

93. Ibid., 272.

94. Scholmer, *Vorkuta*, 227.

95. Gerland, "Vorkuta (1950–53)," 234.

96. Scholmer, *Vorkuta*, 228.

97. Ibid.

98. Gerland, "Vorkuta (1950–53)," 234.

99. Shumuk, *Life Sentence: Memoirs of a Ukrainian Political Prisoner*, 192.

100. Ibid., 209.

101. Ibid., 197.

102. Ibid., 209.

103. Ibid., 212.

104. Robert Conquest, *Kolyma: The Arctic Death Camps*, 100.

105. Ibid., 100. The "old inmate" was Michel Solomon, who later recorded his experiences in *Magadan*.

106. Scholmer, *Vorkuta*, 234.

107. Saunders, "Introduction: Currents in the Soviet Opposition Movement," 22.

108. Frustration with the extent to which this bitter reality remained invisible is commented on by survivors of the Gulag. Henry Wallace, then vice president of the United States, visited Kolyma during the war. Elinor Lipper, a survivor of the prison camps, describes Wallace's enthusiasm for the 350-kilometre Kolyma Road and then notes: "He does not say—or does not know—that this highway was built entirely by prisoners and that tens of thousands gave their lives in building it." See Elinor Lipper, *Eleven Years in Soviet Prison Camps*, 111–16. In 1971, then prime minister of Canada Pierre Trudeau visited Noril'sk and "praised the Soviet Union's 'achievement' in constructing such a wonderful city." See Shumuk, *Life Sentence*, 389n1.

109. Scholmer, *Vorkuta*, 234.

110. Buca, *Vorkuta*, 259.

111. Shumuk, *Life Sentence*, 217.

Chapter 3: The Vengeance of History, 1989–91

1. David Mandel, *Perestroika and the Soviet People: Rebirth of the Labour Movement*. Mandel's outline of the background to this crisis is succinct and compelling (51–78).

2. Leon Trotsky, *Stalin: An Appraisal of the Man and His Influence*, ed. and trans. Alan Woods, 689. The translation by Charles Malamuth omits the word "far." See Leon Trotsky, *Stalin: An Appraisal of the Man and His Influence*, ed. and trans. Charles Malamuth, 383.

3. Michael Burawoy, "Reflections on the Class Consciousness of Hungarian Steelworkers," 26.

4. Theodore Friedgut and Lewis Siegelbaum, "Perestroika from Below: The Soviet Miners' Strike and Its Aftermath."

5. Ibid., 17.

6. Quoted in David Mandel, "The Independent Miners' Union: Three Interviews," 148.

7. Mandel, *Perestroika and the Soviet People*, 55.

8. Michael Haynes, *Russia: Class and Power, 1917–2000*, 187.

9. David Remnick, *Lenin's Tomb: The Last Days of the Soviet Empire*, 223.

10. Ibid., 224.

11. Mandel, *Perestroika and the Soviet People*, 52–53.

12. Ibid., 55–56.

13. Ibid., 57.

14. Remnick, *Lenin's Tomb*, 223.

15. Mandel, *Perestroika and the Soviet People*, 56.
16. The Economist, "Northern Lights-Out: Russia."
17. Esther B. Fein, "Soviet Miners Strike in Defiance of Ban."
18. Mandel, *Perestroika and the Soviet People*, 58.
19. Remnick, *Lenin's Tomb*, 224–25.
20. Fein, "Soviet Miners Strike in Defiance of Ban."
21. Michael Dobbs, "Soviet Miners Vote to End 1-Day Strike."
22. Michael Dobbs, "Miners Strike Is 'Warning' in Ukraine."
23. Vincent J. Schodolski and Thom Shanker, "Soviet Coal Miners Stage Big 1-Day Strike."
24. Boris Kagarlitsky, "USSR—A Voice of the Socialist Opposition."
25. Mandel, "The Independent Miners' Union: Three Interviews," 141.
26. Kagarlitsky, "USSR—A Voice of the Socialist Opposition."
27. Serge Schmemann, "Strike by Soviet Miners Spreads in Rising Challenge to Kremlin."
28. David Remnick, "Striking Soviet Miners Push Radical Demand for Political Change."
29. Serge Schmemann, "Yeltsin Has an Offer for Striking Miners."
30. Quoted in ibid.
31. Mandel, *Perestroika and the Soviet People*, 161.
32. Ibid., 186.
33. Daniel Sneider, "Yeltsin's Deal with Strikers Tests Pact with Gorbachev."
34. Mandel, *Perestroika and the Soviet People*, 187.
35. Ibid., 186.
36. Richard Greeman, "The Death of Communism and the New World Order," 59–60, quoting Nikolai Preobrazhensky, of the Petersburg Party of Labor.
37. Mandel, "Strike Wave of March–April 1991," 193.
38. Greeman, "Death of Communism and the New World Order," 61.
39. CIA, *CIA World Factbook 1987, 1989, 1990,* and *1991.*
40. Ernest Mandel, *Beyond Perestroika: The Failure of Gorbachev's USSR*, 5. On several occasions, while presenting aspects of this research, I have been challenged on this point. The deficit in the trade of grain, according to some, was solely a product of the deficit in animal feed, which resulted from the shift to beef consumption in the 1970s and 1980s. This evades the point that other "breadbasket" countries—Canada, for example—were capable of producing sufficient quantities of grain for both human and animal consumption and of being a net exporter of each during this same period of time.
41. Mandel, *Perestroika and the Soviet People*, 60.
42. Quoted in John Rees, "Gorbachev Defied as Miners Strike Again."

43. Edward Andrew, "Class in Itself and Class Against Capital: Karl Marx and His Classifiers," 577.

44. Karl Marx, *The Poverty of Philosophy* [1847], 211; emphasis added.

45. Karl Marx, "Theses on Feuerbach" [1845], 3.

46. E. P. Thompson, *The Making of the English Working Class*, 9.

47. G. E. M. de Ste. Croix, *The Class Struggle in the Ancient Greek World: From the Archaic Age to the Arab Conquests*, 32.

48. John Gray, "Three Yeltsin Supporters Killed Outside Russian Parliament."

Chapter 4: The Peasant-in-Uniform

1. Leopold Haimson, *The Making of Three Russian Revolutionaries*, 482n13.

2. Pavel Axelrod, "Ob'edinenie rossiiskoi sotsial-demokratii i ee zadachi" [The unification of Russian social democracy and its tasks] [15 December 1903 and 15 January 1904]. An abridged version of this article exists in English translation, but does not include the section quoted here. See Abraham Ascher, ed., *The Mensheviks in the Russian Revolution*, 48–52.

3. Leon Trotsky, *Our Political Tasks*, 1.

4. Leon Trotsky, *Nashi politicheskie zadachi* [Our political tasks], 25; compare with Trotsky, *Our Political Tasks*, 39.

5. Trotsky, *Nashi politicheskie zadachi* [Our political tasks], 51; compare with Trotsky, *Our Political Tasks*, 71.

6. Trotsky, *Our Political Tasks*, 8.

7. Ibid., 68. A slightly edited version of the English-language translation of Trotsky's book can be found at https://www.marxists.org/archive/trotsky/1904/tasks/. The Russian language original—available in only a handful of libraries—formed the core for a widely circulated article by Tony Cliff, written in 1960 and republished in 1973. See Cliff, "The Revolutionary Party and the Class, or Trotsky on Substitutionism" and Cliff, "Trotsky on Substitutionism."

8. Isaac Nachman Steinberg, *In the Workshop of the Revolution*, 291, quoting A. S. Pukhov, *Kronshtadtskiy myatezh v 1921 godu* [The Kronstadt rebellion of 1921] (Leningrad, 1931). Steinberg uses "Pukhoff" instead of the more usual "Pukhov" and uses the initial "N." rather than "A. S."

9. Ibid., 293.

10. Ibid., 295.

11. Ibid., 296.

12. Victor Serge, *Memoirs of a Revolutionary* [1951], 94

13. Karl Radek, "The Paths of the Russian Revolution" [1922], 70.

14. China Miéville, *October: The Story of the Russian Revolution*, 39.

15. Alexander Rabinowitch, *The Bolsheviks Come to Power: The Revolution of 1917 in Petrograd*, 274.

16. "Articles of Service of the Workers' Red Guard in Petrograd, Adopted at a City Conference of the Red Guard on November 4, 1917," articles 1 and 2, quoted in William Henry Chamberlin, *The Russian Revolution, 1917–1921*, 1:465.

17. Chamberlin, *Russian Revolution*, 1:307. "Kornilov" is General Kornilov, whose late-August attempt to overthrow the provisional government was mentioned in the introduction.

18. Raphael R. Abramovitch, *The Soviet Revolution, 1917–1939*, 88.

19. Chamberlin, *Russian Revolution*, 1:311.

20. For the precise figures, see table 1, in the conclusion. See also the discussion in Oliver Henry Radkey, *Russia Goes to the Polls: The Election to the All-Russian Constituent Assembly, 1917*, 148–60.

21. Ibid., xvii.

22. V. I. Lenin, "The Trade Unions, the Present Situation and Trotsky's Mistakes." Pamphlet, 1920, in *Lenin: Collected Works*, 32:24; emphasis in the original.

23. Leon Trotsky, *The Revolution Betrayed* [1937], 170.

24. Leonard Schapiro, *The Origin of the Communist Autocracy: Political Opposition in the Soviet State, First Phase, 1917–1922*, 63. In the Julian calendar, 22 October was 9 October, the date on which the Executive Committee of the Petrograd Soviet first voted to establish the Military Revolutionary Committee.

25. Schapiro, *Origin of the Communist Autocracy*, 63–64. Schapiro quotes from Nikolai Nikolaevich Sukhanov, *Zapiski o revoliutsii* [Notes on the revolution] (Berlin, St. Petersburg, and Moscow: Z. I. Grzhebin, 1923), 7:94–97. See also the abridged English translation of Sukhanov's seven-volume original, *The Russian Revolution, 1917: A Personal Record*, 587–89. There, the passage reads: "By October 21st [that is, 3 November] the Provisional Government had already been overthrown, and was non-existent in the territory of the capital" (587).

26. Sukhanov, *Russian Revolution, 1917*, 562.

27. Schapiro, *Origin of the Communist Autocracy*, 55, quoting *Pervyi legal'nyi peterburgskii komitet bol'shevikov v 1917 g. Sbornik materialov v protokolov zasedanii peterburgskogo komiteta RSDRP(b). . . . za 1917 g.* [The first Petersburg Bolshevik committee of 1917: Collection of materials and minutes of meetings of the Petersburg committee of the RSDRP(b). . . . for 1917] (Moscow and Leningrad, 1927), 312–15.

28. Abramovitch, *Soviet Revolution*, 80.

29. Rabinowitch, *Bolsheviks Come to Power*, 278.

30. Trotsky, quoted in ibid.

31. Abramovitch, *Soviet Revolution*, 89.

32. Orlando Figes, *A People's Tragedy: The Russian Revolution, 1891–1924*, 325.

33. Richard Pipes, *The Russian Revolution*, 278.

34. Abramovitch, *Soviet Revolution, 1917–1939*, 18.

35. Ibid., 20.

36. Ibid., 21.

37. Israel Getzler, *Kronstadt, 1917–1921: The Fate of a Soviet Democracy*, 10, quoting from A. Drezen, "Baltiiskii flot v gody pod"ema" [The Baltic fleet in its heyday], *Krasnaia letopis'* [The Red chronicle] no. 3 (36) (1930): 145, and from K. F. Shatsillo, *Russkii imperializm i razvitie flota: Nakanune pervoi mirovoi voiny* [Russian imperialism and naval development: On the eve of the first world war] (Moscow: 1968), 77.

38. Iulii Osipovich Martov, "Mirovoi bol'shevizm" [World Bolshevism], 394.

39. Ibid.

40. Ibid., 395.

41. Ibid.

42. Abramovitch, *Soviet Revolution: 1917–1939*, 20.

43. Martov, "Mirovoi bol'shevizm" [World Bolshevism], 396–97.

44. Ibid., 397.

45. Ibid., 396.

46. Antonio Gramsci, "The Modern Prince," 169–70.

47. George Leggett, *The Cheka: Lenin's Political Police—The All-Russian Extraordinary Commission for Combating Counter-revolution and Sabotage, December 1917 to February 1922*, 5, quoting *Protokoly zasedanii vserossiiskogo tsentral'nogo ispolnitelnogo komiteta sovetov rabochikh, soldatskikh, krest'ianskikh i kazach'ikh deputatov II sozyva* [Minutes of the meetings of the All-Russian Central Executive Committee of the Soviets of Workers, Soldiers, Peasants and Cossack Deputies, 2nd Convocation], Moscow, 1918, 27.

48. Steinberg, *In the Workshop of the Revolution*, 57.

49. Ibid., 58.

50. Ibid., 59.

51. Ibid., 60; ellipses in the original.

Chapter 5: The Agrarian Question

1. Tamás Krausz, *Reconstructing Lenin: An Intellectual Biography*, 86.

2. V. I. Lenin, "The Agrarian Programme of Social-Democracy," in *LCW*, 13:424. As Lenin notes in a postscript to the 1917 edition, his treatise was first published in St. Petersburg in 1908, but the copies were "seized and destroyed by the tsarist censor" (430), with only a single, not-quite-complete copy surviving.

3. Rosa Luxemburg, "Introduction to Political Economy" [1910], 222.

4. Edward Hallett Carr, "The Russian Revolution and the Peasant," 69.

5. Luxemburg, "Introduction to Political Economy," 224. A "mark comrade" is another member of the "mark community," the *Markgenossenschaft*.

6. Narodism (from the Russian word *narod*, or "people") was a populist movement that became influential in the late nineteenth century and in which the Social-Revolutionaries found inspiration. On Lenin's opposition to Narodism, see Krausz, *Reconstructing Lenin*, 80–84.

7. Ibid., 89.

8. V. I. Lenin, *The Development of Capitalism in Russia*, in *LCW*, 3:339.

9. "Editor's Note," in Luxemburg, "Introduction to Political Economy," 300n185.

10. Krausz, *Reconstructing Lenin*, 235.

11. Ibid., 510–11n99. Krausz quotes Vladimir Buharayev, "1917—Az obscsina-forradalom pirruszi gyözelme" [1917—The Pyrrhic victory of the obshchina revolution], in *1917 és ami utána következett* [1917 and what followed], ed. Tamás Krausz (Budapest: Magyar Ruszisztikai Intézet, 1998), 47–48.

12. Krausz, *Reconstructing Lenin*, 106, quoting V. I. Lenin, "Old and New," *Zvezda*, 10 December 1911, in *LCW*, 17:390.

13. James White has suggested that Lenin's approach to the agrarian question, outlined in these writings, might well have been influenced by the ideas of Lenin's elder brother, Aleksandr, who—before his execution in 1887, at the age of only twenty-one—was deeply immersed in studying the economics of the countryside. See James D. White, *Lenin: The Practice and Theory of Revolution*, 21–40.

14. "*Rossiia—odna iz naibolee melkoburzhuaznykh stran*" in V. I. Lenin, "Zaputavshiesia bespartiitsy" [Bewildered non-party people], *Za pravdu*, 4 October 1913, in *Polnoe sobranie sochinenii* [The complete collected works; hereafter *PSS*], 24:66; "*Rossiia iz vsekh kapitalisticheskikh stran odna iz naibolee otstalykh, naibolee melkoburzhuaznykh stran*" in "Ideinaia bor'ba v rabochem dvizhenii" [The ideological struggle in the working-class movement], *Put' pravdy*, 4 May 1914, in *PSS*, 25:133; "*Rossiia naibolee melkoburzhuaznaia strana iz vsekh evropeiskikh stran*" in *Zadachi proletariata v nashei revoliutsii* [The tasks of the proletariat in our revolution], 28 May 1917, in *PSS*, 31:156.

15. Bertram D. Wolfe, "Lenin, Stolypin, and the Russian Village," 52.

16. Ibid., 53.

17. See *LCW*, 19:436; 20:279; and 24:61.

18. See *LCW*, 19:436; 20:279; 20:269; and 24:61–62; and *PSS*, 24:66; 25:122; 25:133; and 31:156.

19. Lenin, *Zadachi proletariata v nashei revoliutsii* [The tasks of the proletariat in our revolution], 28 May 1917, in *PSS*, 31:156, "*Bol'shei chast'iu melkie khoziaichiki, melkie khoziaichiki, melkie burzhua, liudi, stoiashchie posredine mezhdu kapitalistami i naemnymi rabochimi*" in the Russian original. In the standard English translation, the last sentence reads: "For the most part small proprietors, petty bourgeois, people standing midway between the capitalists and the wage-workers." See *LCW*, 24:61.

20. Iulii Martov, "O politicheskom polozhenii i zadachakh partii" [On the political situation and tasks of the party] [1917], 355.

21. Karl Radek, "The Paths of the Russian Revolution" [1922], 62.

22. V. I. Lenin, *Shag vpered, dva shaga nazad (Krizis v nashei partii)* [One step forward, two steps back (The Crisis in our party)] [1904], in *PSS*, 8:254. Compare with the official English translation in *LCW*, 7:267: "the *petty-bourgeois mode of existence* (working in isolation or in very small groups, etc.)."

23. V. I. Lenin, "O 'levom' rebiachestve i o melkoburzhuaznosti" ["Left-wing" childishness and the petit-bourgeois mentality], serialized in *Pravda*, 9–11 May 1918, in *PSS*, 36:296. Compare with the English translation in *LCW*, 27:336: "Clearly in a small-peasant country, the petty-bourgeois element predominates and it must predominate, for the great majority of those working the land are small commodity producers."

24. E. H. Carr, "The Russian Revolution and the Peasant," 87–88.

25. Ibid., 88n4.

26. Donald W. Treadgold, "Was Stolypin in Favor of Kulaks?" 6; the emphasis is Treadgold's. He quotes from a letter written by Stolypin to Nicholas II, as quoted in M. N. Pokrovskij, *A Brief History of Russia*, 2 vols. (London: Martin Lawrence, 1933), 2:291, and from M. P. [Marija Petrovna] Bok, *Vospominanija o moem otse P. A. Stolypine* [Memories of my father, P. A. Stolypin] (New York: Chekhov Publishers, 1953), 204.

27. George Tokmakoff, "Stolypin's Agrarian Reform: An Appraisal," 137.

28. Leonid I. Strakhovsky, "The Statesmanship of Peter Stolypin: A Reappraisal," 361, quoting *Stenograficheskii otchet gosudarstvennogo soveta za 1910 g.* [Stenographic report of the state council for 1910] (St. Petersburg, 1911), 1136–45.

29. Ibid., 361–62.

30. Wolfe, "Lenin, Stolypin, and the Russian Village," 46.

31. Judith Pallot, *Land Reform in Russia, 1906–1917: Peasant Responses to Stolypin's Project of Rural Transformation*, 9.

32. Lenin, "Agrarian Programme of Social-Democracy," 424.

33. To describe the *mir* as "semi-feudal" does not, however, imply that the Russian empire under tsarism somehow existed outside the long reach of global capitalism. Following Jairus Banaji, it is helpful to distinguish between the mode of production understood as the labour process and the mode of production understood as the regime of accumulation. That is, even if the mode of labour in the countryside of the Russian empire retained precapitalist relations and structures, the commune was inserted into a national and world economy whose mode of production was capitalist, driven by the imperious needs of capital accumulation. See Jairus Banaji, *Theory and History: Essays on Modes of Production and Exploitation*, 45–102.

34. Lenin, "O 'levom' rebiachestve i o melkoburzhuaznosti" ["Left-wing" childishness and the petit-bourgeois mentality], in *PSS*, 36:296.

35. Tokmakoff, "Stolypin's Agrarian Reform," 129.

36. Ibid., 130.

37. S. M. Dubrovsky, "*Stolypinskaia reforma.*" *Kapitalizatsiia sel'skogo khoziaistva v XX veke* [The Stolypin reform: Capitalization of agriculture in the twentieth century], 13, 127. This section is also quoted, with a slightly different translation, in Leonid I. Strakhovsky, "The Statesmanship of Peter Stolypin: A Reappraisal," 362.

38. S. M. Dubrovsky, "*Stolypinskaia reforma.*" *Kapitalizatsiia sel'skogo khoziaistva v XX veke* [The Stolypin reform: Capitalization of agriculture in the twentieth century], 13, 127, quoted in Strakhovsky, "The Statesmanship of Peter Stolypin," 362. The translation here is my own.

39. Strakhovsky, "The Statesmanship of Peter Stolypin," 362, quoting Nicolas Savickij, "P. A. Stolypine," *Le Monde Slave* 12 (1933): 363–64.

40. David Mitrany, *Marx Against the Peasant: A Study in Social Dogmatism*, 226n7.

41. Krausz, *Reconstructing Lenin*, 98.

42. V. I. Lenin, "The Fourth Conference of the R.S.D.L.P.," *Proletarii*, 19 November 1907, in *LCW*, 13:142.

43. Lenin, "Agrarian Programme of Social-Democracy," 243.

44. Ibid. I have modified the standard English translation by translating "*zamedlennoe*" as "sluggish."

45. Lenin, "Agrarian Programme of Social-Democracy," 239.

46. Eric Foner, *Reconstruction: America's Unfinished Revolution, 1863-1877*, 71.

47. Quoted in ibid., 70.
48. Du Bois, *Black Reconstruction: An Essay toward a History of the Part Which Black Folk Played in the Attempt to Reconstruct Democracy in America, 1860-1880*, 206.
49. Quoted in ibid., 198.
50. Treadgold, "Was Stolypin in Favor of Kulaks?" 11. See also Pallot, *Land Reform in Russia, 1906–1917*, 10.
51. Alec Nove, *Studies in Economics and Russia*, 43.
52. Victor Serge, *Year One of the Russian Revolution*, 359.
53. Ibid., 360; Lev Kritsman develops this concept in chapter 5 of his book, *Geroicheskii period velikoi russkoi revoliutsii (Opyt analiza t. n. "voennogo kommunizma")* [The Heroic period of the great Russian revolution (An Attempt to analyze so-called "war communism")], 100–17. The forward and the introduction of Kritsman's book have been translated into English; see Kritsman, "Foreword." *Geroicheskii period velikoi russkoi revoliutsii* [The Heroic period of the great Russian revolution]; Kritsman, "Introduction." *Geroicheskii period velikoi russkoi revoliutsii* [The Heroic period of the great Russian revolution]. Kritsman, a prominent economist in the 1920s, by the 1930s, like so many others, was swept up in the Great Terror, and executed in 1938; see Kowalski, "Geroicheskii period russkoi revoliutsii" [The Heroic period of the Russian revolution].
54. Boris Souvarine, *Stalin: A Critical Survey of Bolshevism*, 274–76.
55. Krausz, *Reconstructing Lenin*, 321–22.
56. V. I. Lenin, "Speech in the Moscow Soviet," *Izvestiia VtsIK*, 24 April 1919, in *LCW*, 27:232.
57. Isaac Nachman Steinberg, *In the Workshop of the Revolution*, 254.
58. Ibid., 256.
59. Ibid., 260.
60. Ibid., 264.
61. Ibid., 264–65. By paupers, Steinberg is referring to what were called at the time the "poor peasants"—landless labourers for the most part—who for a few months were organized into committees as an attempt to create a base for the Bolsheviks in the countryside. The policy was not a success and was soon abandoned.
62. V. I. Lenin, "Speech to Propagandists on Their Way to the Provinces, January 23 (February 5) 1918," *Pravda*, 6 February 1918, in *LCW*, 26:514, 515.
63. Ibid., 514–15.
64. Krausz, *Reconstructing Lenin*, 368.
65. Nove, *Studies in Economics and Russia*, 59.
66. Roy A. Medvedev, *The October Revolution*, 123.

67. His Bolshevik career stretched from the 1905 Revolution until 1911, including being elected to the Bolshevik Central Committee in 1907. See Rondan, "Nikolai Aleksandrovich Rozhkov (1868–1927): Historian and Revolutionary," 4 and 310.
68. N. A. Rozhkov, "Pis'mo N. A. Rozhkova V. I. Leninu. Petrograd, 11 ianvaria" [Letter from N. A. Rozhkov to V. I. Lenin, Petrograd, 11 January 1919], 78.
69. Krausz, *Reconstructing Lenin*, 228.
70. The exact reference is to armed, punitive, military detachments used on the battlefield to "block" deserters, in this context, used to combat "speculation" (trade) in food.
71. Rozhkov, "Pis'mo N. A. Rozhkova V. I. Leninu [Letter from N. A. Rozhkov to V. I. Lenin]," 78.
72. Ibid., 78–79. Rozhkov is citing a difficult-to-translate proverb, which roughly signifies that, if the conditions exist, shady characters will emerge.
73. Leon Trotsky, "The Fundamental Questions of the Food and Agrarian Policy" [1920], 70.
74. Erik C. Landis, "The Fate of the Soviet Countryside—March 1920," 220.
75. Leon Trotsky, *My Life: An Attempt at an Autobiography* [1930], 464.
76. Landis, "The Fate of the Soviet Countryside—March 1920," 231–32.
77. Alec Nove, *An Economic History of the U.S.S.R.*, 61.
78. Leonard Schapiro, *The Origin of the Communist Autocracy: Political Opposition in the Soviet State, First Phase, 1917–1922*, 214.
79. Nove, *Economic History of the U.S.S.R.*, 62, citing Kritsman, "Geroicheskii period Russkoi revoliutsii" [The Heroic period of the Russian revolution], *Vestnik kommunisticheskoi akademii* [Bulletin of the communist academy] 19 (1924).
80. Rozhkov, "Pis'mo N. A. Rozhkova V. I. Leninu [Letter from N. A. Rozhkov to V. I. Lenin]," 78.
81. Moshe Lewin, "Who Was the Soviet Kulak?" 189, 191.
82. Cited in Treadgold, "Was Stolypin in Favor of Kulaks?" 11.
83. V. I. Lenin, "Report on Combating the Famine" [Newspaper report, *Pravda* and *Izvestiia VTsIK*, 5 June 1918], in *LCW*, 27:436.
84. Lenin, "Reply to a Peasant's Question" [Newspaper article, *Pravda*, 14 February 1919], in *LCW*, 36:502.
85. Lenin, "Telegram to Yevgenia Bosch – August 9, 1918" [first published 1924], *LCW*, 36:489.
86. Lenin, "Session of the Petrograd Soviet" [Speech, *Severnaia kommuna*, 14 March 1919], in *LCW*, 29:25.
87. Carr, "Russian Revolution and the Peasant," 81.
88. Ibid., 85.

89. Leon Trotsky, *Stalin: An Appraisal of the Man and His Influence*, ed. and trans. Alan Woods, 690; cf. Leon Trotsky, *Stalin: An Appraisal of the Man and His Influence*, ed. and trans. Charles Malamuth, 405–6.

90. Trotsky, *Stalin*, ed. Woods, 584; cf. Trotsky, *Stalin*, ed. Malamuth, 408.

91. Stanisław Swianiewicz, *Forced Labour and Economic Development: An Enquiry into the Experience of Soviet Industrialization*, 118, quoting Boris Brutzkus, *Der Fünfjahresplan und seine Erfüllung* [The Five-year Plan and its Fulfillment] (Leipzig: Deutsche wissenschaftliche Buchhandlung, 1932), 47–49.

92. Trotsky, *Stalin*, ed. Woods, 581; Trotsky, *Stalin*, ed. Malamuth, 408.

93. Souvarine, *Stalin*, 551.

94. Wolfe, "Lenin, Stolypin, and the Russian Village," 53.

Chapter 6: Poland and Georgia—The Export of Revolution

1. Leon Trotsky, "Declaration of the Bolshevik-Leninist Delegation at the Conference of Left Socialist and Communist Organizations" [1933], 40. The First Congress, held in 1919, while important historically because it was the founding meeting of this new workers' international, is in quite a different category from the three that followed. The latter were large affairs, drawing hundreds of delegates from parties all around the world— some of these parties with large memberships and considerable influence in their countries. The first, convened in siege conditions in Moscow in March, brought together only fifty-one delegates from working-class organizations that were, for the most part, "still small and inexperienced." See John Riddell, *Founding the Communist International—Proceedings and Documents of the First Congress: March 1919*, 1.

2. John Riddell, ed., *To the Masses: Proceedings of the Third Congress of the Communist International, 1921*, 90n29.

3. Orlando Figes, *A People's Tragedy: The Russian Revolution, 1891–1924*, 698.

4. Ibid., 698–99.

5. Ibid., 699.

6. Ibid., 700–703.

7. Lenin, "Politicheskii otchet TSK(b) na IKH vserossiiskoi konferentsii RKP(b) i zakliuchitel'noe slovo po itogam obsuzhdeniia otcheta" [Political report of the Central Committee of the RCP(b) at the ninth all-Russian Conference of the RCP(b) and the final word on the results of the discussion of the report]. [Shorthand report, 22 September 1920]. See also Lenin, "Politicheskii otchet TSK RKP(b) na IKH Vserossiiskoi konferentsii RKP(b) i zakliuchitel'noe slovo po itogam obsuzhdeniia otcheta

[Political report of the Central Committee of the RCP(b) at the ninth all-Russian Conference of the RCP(b) and the final word on the results of the discussion of the report]," 373; See also Lenin, "Political Report of the Central Committee [1920], in *The Unknown Lenin: From the Secret Archive*, ed. Pipes, 97. A second English-language translation of Lenin's speech is available, in a collection edited by Al Richardson: Lenin, "Political Report of the Central Committee of the Russian Communist Party (Bolshevik) to the Ninth Conference of the RCP(B)" [1920], in *In Defence of the Russian Revolution: A Selection of Bolshevik Writings, 1917–1923*. Throughout, I principally rely on the more readily accessible Pipes translation, but in this case, I have provided my own. Pipes uses the term "great power" to describe Poland. The Russian original will not sustain the notion that Lenin was calling Poland a "great power," a term exclusively reserved for the economic and military powers of the day (such as Britain, France, and the United States). No one would reasonably place a newly sovereign nation such as Poland into that category.

8. Lenin, "Political Report of the Central Committee," in *Unknown Lenin*, ed. Pipes, 98.

9. Ibid. The first square-bracketed insert is from the Pipes edition. The second is my own addition.

10. Tamás Krausz, *Reconstructing Lenin: An Intellectual Biography*, 296.

11. Lenin, "Political Report of the Central Committee," in *Unknown Lenin*, ed. Pipes, 99.

12. Rosa Luxemburg, "What Does the Spartacus League Want?" [1918], 356–57.

13. P. Iu. Savel'ev and S. V. Tiutiukin, "Iulii Osipovich Martov (1873–1923): The Man and the Politician," 79.

14. Kirsteen Davina Croll, "Soviet-Polish Relations, 1919–1921," 19–20.

15. Leon Trotsky, *My Life: An Attempt at an Autobiography*, 457.

16. Krausz, *Reconstructing Lenin*, 295.

17. Pierre Broué, *Trotsky*, 269.

18. Proceedings of the Second Congress are available in John Riddell, ed., *Workers of the World and Oppressed Peoples, Unite! Proceedings and Documents of the Second Congress, 1920*.

19. Riddell, *Workers of the World and Oppressed Peoples*, 1:135–39.

20. Victor Serge, *Memoirs of a Revolutionary*, 125.

21. Ibid., 125–26.

22. Lenin, "Political Report of the Central Committee," in *Unknown Lenin*, ed. Pipes, 98–99.

23. Serge, *Memoirs of a Revolutionary*, 126.

24. Werner T. Angress, *Stillborn Revolution: The Communist Bid for Power in Germany, 1921–1923*, 67.

25. Serge, *Memoirs of a Revolutionary*, 126.

26. Ibid., 127.

27. Adam Zamoyski, *Warsaw 1920: Lenin's Failed Conquest of Europe*, 69.

28. Serge, *Memoirs of a Revolutionary*, 111.

29. Edgar Vincent D'Abernon, *The Eighteenth Decisive Battle of the World: Warsaw, 1920*, 107–8.

30. Richard H. Rowland, "Geographical Patterns of the Jewish Population in the Pale of Settlement of Late Nineteenth Century Russia," 207.

31. Grover C. Furr III, "New Light on Old Stories About Marshal Tukhachevskii," 297n11.

32. Ibid., 297. Grover Furr III is quoting from a conversation recorded by Pierre Fervacque (the nom de plume of Remy Roure) in *Le chef de l'Armée rouge* (Paris: Fasquelle, 1928).

33. Orlando Figes, "The Red Army and Mass Mobilization During the Russian Civil War, 1918–1920," 195–96. Trotsky was born Lev Davydovitch Bronstein. See Trotsky, *My Life*, 3n1.

34. Zamoyski, *Warsaw 1920*, 129.

35. V. I. Lenin, "Report on Red Army Pogroms, with Lenin's Reaction, 17–18 October 1920," 117.

36. Isaac Babel, "The Red Cavalry Stories" [1926], 279.

37. William Henry Chamberlin, *The Russian Revolution, 1917–1921*, 2:309.

38. Trotsky, *My Life*, 458–59.

39. Lenin, "Political Report of the Central Committee," in *Unknown Lenin*, ed. Pipes," 106.

40. Zamoyski, *Warsaw 1920*, 111 and 129.

41. Leon Trotsky, *Stalin: An Appraisal of the Man and His Influence*, ed. and trans. Alan Woods, 464; Leon Trotsky, *Stalin: An Appraisal of the Man and His Influence*, ed. and trans. Charles Malamuth, 327.

42. Trotsky, *Stalin*, ed. Woods, 466; Trotsky, *Stalin*, ed. Malamuth, 328–29.

43. Broué, *Trotsky*, 269.

44. Chamberlin, *Russian Revolution*, 2:306, 310.

45. Ibid., 2:306.

46. Broué, *Trotsky*, 269.

47. Krausz, *Reconstructing Lenin*, 303, quoting Karl Radek, "Vystuplenie K. Radeka na IKH konferentsii RKP (b) o polozhenii v Pol'she" [Speech by K. Radek at the Ninth conference of the RCP(b) about the situation in Poland] [1920], in *Komintern i ideia mirovoi revoliutsii* [The Comintern and the idea

of world revolution], ed. Y. S. Drabkin, 200–205 (Moscow: Nauka, 1998), 202, 204.

48. Serge, *Memoirs of a Revolutionary*, 126.

49. Radek, "Vystuplenie K. Radeka" [Speech by K. Radek], 203–4.

50. Krausz, *Reconstructing Lenin*, 303, quoting Lenin, in Drabkin, ed., *Komintern i ideia mirovoi revoliutsii* [The Comintern and the idea of world revolution], 208.

51. Trotsky, *Stalin*, ed. Woods, 471; Trotsky, *Stalin*, ed. Malamuth, 332, quoting from S. E. Rabinovich, *Istoriia grazhdanskoi voiny: Chebnoe posobie dlia voennykh shkol RKKA* [History of the civil war: A Manual for military schools of the Red Army] (Moscow Party Publishing House, 1933).

52. Trotsky, *Stalin*, ed. Woods, 471; cf. Trotsky, *Stalin*, ed. Malamuth, 332.

53. Trotsky, *Stalin*, ed. Woods, 464–65; Trotsky, *Stalin*, ed. Malamuth, 327–28.

54. Trotsky, *Stalin*, ed. Woods, 383; Trotsky, *Stalin*, ed. Malamuth, 298.

55. Thomas M. Twiss, *Trotsky and the Problem of Soviet Bureaucracy*, 67, 68, quoting Lenin.

56. V. I. Lenin, "Letter to the Congress: The Question of Nationalities or 'Autonomisation' and The Question of Nationalities or 'Autonomisation' (Continued)," part of Lenin's "Testament" [1922], *Kommunist*, 1956, in *LCW*, 36:605–11.

57. Edvard Radzinsky, *Stalin*, 25.

58. Eric Lee, *The Experiment: Georgia's Forgotten Revolution, 1918–1921*, 138.

59. Philip Mendes, *Jews and the Left: The Rise and Fall of a Political Alliance*, 131.

60. Ibid., 7. W. E. B. Du Bois would insist that the experience of Radical Reconstruction in certain of the former confederate states, in the years after the US civil war, should be added to this list. See W. E. B. Du Bois, *Black Reconstruction: An Essay Toward a History of the Part Which Black Folk Played in the Attempt to Reconstruct Democracy in America, 1860–1880*. Both Radical Reconstruction and the Gurian Republic are rarely mentioned in discussions of self-rule by the oppressed.

61. Lee, *Experiment*, 12, 14, 9.

62. Ibid., 146.

63. Ibid., 38. Table 1, in the conclusion to this book, gives a slightly different figure for the Mensheviks (roughly 570,000), but the wide gap is still evident.

64. Boris Souvarine, *Stalin: A Critical Survey of Bolshevism*, 300.

65. Lee, *Experiment*, 218.

66. Ibid., 226.

67. Ibid., 227–28, quoting Donald Rayfield, *Edge of Empires: A History of Georgia* (London: Reaktion Books, 2012), 342.

68. Jeremy Smith, "The Georgian Affair of 1922: Policy Failure, Personality Clash or Power Struggle?" 524.

69. Leon Trotsky, *Between Red and White: A Study of Some Fundamental Questions of Revolution with Particular Reference to Georgia*, 10.

70. Brian Pearce, "'Export of Revolution,' 1917–1924," 106.

71. Trotsky, *My Life*, 482–83; see V. I. Lenin, "To L.D. Trotsky," dictated by phone, 1923, in *LCW*, 45:607.

72. Stephen Jones, "The Establishment of Soviet Power in Transcaucasia: The Case of Georgia, 1921–1928," 616.

73. Mikhail Tukhachevsky, "General Toukhatchevsky's Narrative," 166.

74. Ibid., 167.

75. Ibid., 167–68.

76. Stasi is an acronym for the notorious security and intelligence service of the former Stalinist state in East Germany.

77. Leon Trotsky, "Speech at a General Party Membership Meeting of the Moscow Organization, July 1921," 8.

78. Karl Radek, "Session of the *Zentrale* with the Representative of the Executive Committee for Germany Friday, January 28, 1921," 285.

79. D'Abernon, *Eighteenth Decisive Battle of the World*, 117.

80. Ibid., 118.

81. Ian D. Thatcher, "Trotskii, Lenin and the Bolsheviks, August 1914–February 1917," 114.

82. V. I. Lenin, "The Break-up of the 'August' Bloc," *Put' pravdy*, 15 March 1914, in *LCW*, 20:160.

83. Robert Service, *Trotsky: A Biography*, 129, quoting Leon Trotsky, "Trotsky to N.S. Chkheidze, 1 April 1913," Nicolaevsky Collection, Stanford University: Hoover Institute Archive, box 656, folder 5, 1–2.

84. Leon Trotsky, *Nashe slovo*, 1916, no. 87, 1, quoted in Thatcher, "Trotskii, Lenin and the Bolsheviks," 106.

85. Leon Trotsky, *Our Political Tasks*, 121–28.

86. V. I. Lenin, *Shag vpered, dva shaga nazad* [One step forward, two steps back], in *PSS*, 8:370.

Chapter 7: Germany and Hungary—The United Front

1. Ian Birchall, "Grappling with the United Front," 199.

2. David Morgan, *The Socialist Left and the German Revolution: A History of the German Independent Social Democratic Party, 1917–1922*, 398–99, quoting Arkadi Maslow, *Die Internationale* (KPD), 1 June 1921, 254.

3. Pierre Broué, *The German Revolution, 1917–1923*, 501.

4. John Riddell, ed., *To the Masses: Proceedings of the Third Congress of the Communist International, 1921*, 20.
5. Ibid.
6. Broué, *German Revolution*, 506.
7. Werner T. Angress, *Stillborn Revolution: The Communist Bid for Power in Germany, 1921–1923*, 217n55.
8. Broué, *German Revolution*, 507–15.
9. John Riddell, introduction to *To the Masses*, 6–7.
10. Broué, *German Revolution*, 875.
11. Paul Levi, "Our Path: Against Putschism" [1921].
12. Ian Birchall, "Review of Jean-François Fayet's Karl Radek (1885–1939)," 266.
13. Riddell, *To the Masses*, 1090–96.
14. Ibid., 1079–86.
15. Ibid., 1088–90.
16. See Paul Kellogg and John Riddell, *Luxemburg, Lenin, Levi: Rethinking Revolutionary History* [2/3]; and Paul Kellogg, "Lost in Translation: Explaining the Tragedy of Germany's 1921 March Action."
17. Broué, *German Revolution*, 469.
18. Riddell, *To the Masses*, 1061n1.
19. Ibid., 1062.
20. Ibid., 15.
21. David Fernbach, introduction to Paul Levi, *In the Steps of Rosa Luxemburg: Selected Writings of Paul Levi*, 5–6.
22. Riddell, *To the Masses*, 1080.
23. Ibid., 501.
24. Broué, *German Revolution*, 471.
25. Ibid., 471–72.
26. Riddell, *To the Masses*, 1064.
27. Ibid.
28. Ibid., 1087.
29. Ibid., 571–83.
30. Ibid., 1090–97.
31. Ibid., 305–45.
32. Ibid., 204n42.
33. Ben Lewis, "The Four-Hour Speech and the Significance of Halle," 22n38.
34. Fernbach, introduction to Levi, *In the Steps of Rosa Luxemburg*, 10.
35. Ben Lewis, ed., *Zinoviev and Martov: Head to Head in Halle*.
36. Lewis, "Four-Hour Speech and the Significance of Halle," 31.
37. Riddell, *To the Masses*, 276n3.
38. Paul Levi, "The Lessons of the Hungarian Revolution," 71.

39. Rosa Luxemburg, "What Does the Spartacus League Want?" 356–57.

40. Ferenc Tibor Zsuppán, "The Early Activities of the Hungarian Communist Party, 1918–19," 320.

41. Béla Menczer, "Béla Kun and the Hungarian Revolution of 1919," 304–5.

42. Levi, "Lessons of the Hungarian Revolution," 76, quoting Karl Radek, "Document 3: Karl Radek, 'The Lessons of the Hungarian Revolution,'" in *International Communism in the Era of Lenin: A Documentary History*, ed. Helmut Gruber (Greenwich, Conn: Fawcett Publications, 1967), 160. Originally published in *Die Internationale* II, no. 21 (25 February 1920).

43. Ibid., 77.

44. Chris Harman, *The Lost Revolution: Germany, 1918 to 1923*, 211.

45. Fernbach, introduction to Levi's *In the Steps of Rosa Luxemburg*, 17.

46. Broué, *German Revolution*, 516.

47. Angress, *Stillborn Revolution*, 92.

48. Broué, *German Revolution*, 468–72.

49. Ibid., 449–58, 875–88.

50. Kellogg and Riddell, *Luxemburg, Lenin, Levi*; Kellogg, "Lost in Translation."

51. Harman, *Lost Revolution*, 219.

52. Morgan, *Socialist Left and the German Revolution*, 45.

53. Ibid., 391.

54. Harman, *Lost Revolution*, 269, 279.

55. Ian Birchall, "Grappling with the United Front," 195.

56. Duncan Hallas, *The Comintern*, 164.

57. Leon Trotsky, "International Pre-conference of the Left Opposition Presents Thesis," quoted in ibid., 8.

58. Hallas, *Comintern*, 8–9.

59. Duncan Hallas, "On Building a Socialist Alternative, Part II," 5.

60. Hallas, *Comintern*, 164.

61. Hallas, "On Building a Socialist Alternative," 164.

62. Ian Birchall, *Tony Cliff: A Marxist for His Time*, 400–401.

63. Tony Cliff, *The Bolsheviks and World Revolution*, 110.

64. Ibid., 111.

65. Tony Cliff, *The Sword of Revolution, 1917–1923*, 132.

66. Ibid., 217.

67. Lenin, "Politicheskii otchet TSK" ["Political report of the Central Committee"], 374.

68. Zamoyski, *Warsaw 1920*, 68; see also V. I. Lenin, "Telegram to Stalin, 23 July 1920," 90.

69. Mikhail Tukhachevsky, "Revolution from Without" [1920].

70. Isaac Deutscher, *The Prophet Armed: Trotsky, 1879–1921*, 1:473.

71. Leon Trotsky, "Opening and Closing Speeches in the Discussion on Military Doctrine," 306.

72. Tony Cliff, *Revolution Besieged*, 36.

73. Birchall, "Grappling with the United Front," 199.

74. John Riddell, ed., *Toward the United Front: Proceedings of the Fourth Congress of the Communist International, 1922*, 6.

75. Karl Marx, "Theses on Feuerbach" [1845] (original version), 4.

76. Birchall, "Grappling with the United Front," 197.

Chapter 8: Trotsky on Stalinism—The Surplus and the Machine

1. Charles Malamuth, "Editor's Note," in Leon Trotsky, *Stalin: An Appraisal of the Man and His Influence*, ed. and trans. Charles Malamuth, ix.

2. Rob Sewell, "Background to Trotsky's *Stalin*," xxxi.

3. Quoted in ibid., xix.

4. Alan Woods, "Editor's Note," in Leon Trotsky, *Stalin: An Appraisal of the Man and His Influence*, ed. Alan Woods, xxxviii.

5. Ibid.

6. For the two occurrences, see Trotsky, *Stalin*, ed. Malamuth, 239, 340.

7. Woods, "Editor's Note," xxxviii.

8. Nathalie Babel, preface to *The Complete Works of Isaac Babel*, 24. In fact, it was preceded by an analysis of Stalin's rise to power written by the Russian-born American journalist Isaac Don Levine, also titled *Stalin* and published in 1931.

9. Michel Surya, *Georges Bataille: An Intellectual Biography*, 161. Born Boris Lifschitz, Souvarine was still an infant when his family moved to Paris in 1897.

10. Hella Mandt, "The Classical Understanding: Tyranny and Despotism," 65.

11. Trotsky, *Stalin*, ed. Woods, 674.

12. Jean Louis Panné, *Boris Souvarine, le premier desenchanté du communisme*, 131–49.

13. Surya, *Georges Bataille*, 159.

14. Boris Souvarine, "Postscript: The Counter-Revolution," 674.

15. Joseph Stalin, "The Right Deviation in the C.P.S.U.(B.): Speech Delivered at the Plenum of the Central Committee and Central Control Commission of the C.P.S.U.(B.) in April 1929. (Verbatim Report)," 55.

16. "Industrialisation and the Grain Problem" was one of many long speeches that Stalin delivered during a nine-day plenum of the Communist Party. Taking up more than thirty typeset pages in the twelfth volume of his

collected works, the speech picks up the heretofore ridiculed ideas of Preobrazhensky (outlined in chapter 2) and adopts them in their entirety. See Joseph Stalin, "Industrialisation and the Grain Problem: Speech Delivered on July 9, 1928." The emotion with which Stalin challenges the label of feudalist exploitation, as he adopts Preobrazhensky's policies and the need for a "tribute" from the peasantry, will pique the curiosity of any avid researcher.

17. Boris Souvarine, *Stalin: A Critical Survey of Bolshevism*, 564–65.
18. While calling itself a party, the SWP of Trotsky's time was actually more a political current, with two thousand members across the United States in 1935. Constance Ashton Myers, *The Prophet's Army: Trotskyists in America, 1928–1941*, 113.
19. Trotsky, James, and Curtiss, "The Discussions in Coyoacán."
20. C. L. R. James, "Russia—A Fascist State."
21. Dunayevskaya was born Raya Shpigel in what is today Ukraine, changing to Rae Spiegel upon emigrating to the United States.
22. "Obituary: Raya Dunayevskaya."
23. Raya Dunayevskaya, "The Union of Soviet Socialist Republics Is a Capitalist Society."
24. Trotsky, *Stalin*, ed. Malamuth, 410.
25. Trotsky, *Stalin*, ed. Woods, 594–95.
26. Alan Woods, bridging passage in Trotsky, *Stalin*, ed. Woods, 718.
27. Alan Woods, "Editor's Afterword: Trotsky's *Stalin*—a Marxist Masterpiece," 695.
28. Trotsky, *Stalin*, ed. Woods, 690; cf. Trotsky, *Stalin*, ed. Malamuth, 405–6.
29. Trotsky, *Stalin*, ed. Woods, 690; Trotsky, *Stalin*, ed. Malamuth, 406.
30. Trotsky, *Stalin*, ed. Woods, 717; Trotsky, *Stalin*, ed. Malamuth, 408.
31. Trotsky, *Stalin*, ed. Woods, 718.
32. Ibid.
33. Souvarine, *Stalin*, 564. Thanks to Abigail Bakan for suggesting looking for parallels in Souvarine with Trotsky's notes on surplus product.
34. Souvarine, "Postscript," 674.
35. Trotsky, *Stalin*, ed. Woods, 6; Trotsky, *Stalin*, ed. Malamuth, xv.
36. Trotsky, *Stalin*, ed. Woods, 43; Trotsky, *Stalin*, ed. Malamuth, 30. The translation by Woods does not include the bracketed gloss "[political machine]."
37. Trotsky, *Stalin*, ed. Woods, 61; Trotsky, *Stalin*, ed. Malamuth, 45.
38. Trotsky, *Stalin*, ed. Woods, 68; Trotsky, *Stalin*, ed. Malamuth, 51.
39. Trotsky, *Stalin*, ed. Woods, 184; Trotsky, *Stalin*, ed. Malamuth, 143.
40. Trotsky, *Stalin*, ed. Woods, 82; Trotsky, *Stalin*, ed. Malamuth, 61.

41. Trotsky, *Stalin*, ed. Woods, 83; Trotsky, *Stalin*, ed. Malamuth, 62.

42. Leon Trotsky, *Our Political Tasks*.

43. Trotsky, *Stalin*, ed. Woods, 83; Trotsky, *Stalin*, ed. Malamuth, 62.

44. Trotsky, *Stalin*, ed. Woods, 675.

45. Ibid., 673.

46. Ibid.

47. Souvarine, *Stalin*, 129–30. G. V. Plekhanov was labelled "father of Russian Marxism" by many, including by his biographer Samuel Baron. An ally of Lenin in the early years of *Iskra*, he divided from him definitively in 1914 when Plekhanov came out as an "ardent proponent of the Allied fight against the Central Powers." See Samuel H. Baron, *Plekhanov: The Father of Russian Marxism*, 323.

48. Trotsky, *Stalin*, ed. Woods, 175–76; Trotsky, *Stalin*, ed. Malamuth, 136–37.

49. Souvarine, *Stalin*, 64.

50. Quoted in ibid; cf Trotsky, *Our Political Tasks*, 117.

Chapter 9: A Movement's Dirty Linen

1. Leon Trotsky, *My Life: An Attempt at an Autobiography*, 142.

2. Ante Ciliga, *The Russian Enigma*, 274.

3. Leon Trotsky, *Stalin: An Appraisal of the Man and His Influence*, ed. Alan Woods, 105–6, 115; Leon Trotsky, *Stalin: An Appraisal of the Man and His Influence*, ed. Charles Malamuth, 88.

4. Boris Souvarine, *Stalin: A Critical Survey of Bolshevism*, 88.

5. Ibid. There are clear parallels here to the substitutionist "theory of the offensive" developed by Nikolai Bukharin and Mikhail Tukhachevsky, a theory that led to the catastrophic 1920 invasion of Poland examined in chapter 6 and the equally catastrophic 1921 "March Action" in Germany, examined in chapter 7.

6. Ibid., 89.

7. Quoted in ibid., 90.

8. Ibid., 90.

9. Ibid.

10. Ibid., 74, quoting Filipp Makharadze, *Sketch of the Divergences within the Party* (Tiflis: State Georgian Press, 1927).

11. Trotsky, *Stalin*, ed. Woods, 95; Trotsky, *Stalin*, ed. Malamuth, 72.

12. Isaac Don Levine, *Stalin*, 70.

13. Bertram D. Wolfe, *Three Who Made a Revolution: A Biographical History of Lenin, Trotsky, and Stalin*, 393. The conversion to US dollars is based on Samuel H. Williamson, "Seven Ways to Compute the Relative Value

of a U.S. Dollar Amount—1774 to Present," and Leonard Schapiro, *The Communist Party of the Soviet Union*, 20n1.

14. Souvarine, *Stalin*, 94.
15. Robert Service, *The Strengths of Contradiction*, 185.
16. Schapiro, *Communist Party of the Soviet Union*, 119.
17. Nikolai Nikolaevich Popov, *Outline History of the Communist Party of the Soviet Union*, 1:247.
18. Ibid., 1:249.
19. Jane Barnes Casey, *I, Krupskaya: My Life with Lenin*, 270.
20. Robert Chadwell Williams, *The Other Bolsheviks: Lenin and His Critics, 1904–1914*, 166; Trotsky, *Stalin*, ed. Woods, 174; Trotsky, *Stalin*, ed. Malamuth, 135.
21. Popov, *Outline History of the Communist Party of the Soviet Union*, 1:269.
22. James D. White, *Lenin: The Practice and Theory of Revolution*, 96.
23. Abraham Ascher, ed., *The Mensheviks in the Russian Revolution*, 23.
24. V. I. Lenin, "The Sixth (Prague) All-Russia Conference of the R.S.D.L.P." [1912], in *LCW*, 17:451–86.
25. Ibid., 17:483.
26. Williams, *Other Bolsheviks*, 167–68, quoting V. I. Lenin, "*Pis'mo advokatu zh. Diuko de la Ai* [Letter to Attorney M. Ducos de La Haille]" [10 June 1912], in *Leninskii sbornik* [Lenin miscellany] (Moscow: Publishing House of Political Literature, 1975), 38:62–65.
27. Trotsky, *Stalin*, ed. Woods, 133; Trotsky, *Stalin*, ed. Malamuth, 103.
28. Trotsky, *Stalin*, ed. Woods, 132; Trotsky, *Stalin*, ed. Malamuth, 101.
29. Iulii Martov, "Spasiteli ili uprazdniteli? (Kto i kak razrushal RSDRP)" [Saviours or destroyers? (Who destroyed the RSDRP and how)] [1911]; available in an abridged English translation by Iulii Martov, "Saviours or Destroyers?"
30. Iulii Martov, "Saviours or Destroyers?" [1911]. 71.
31. Ibid., 73.
32. Quoted in P. Iu. Savel'ev and S. V. Tiutiukin, "Iulii Osipovich Martov (1873–1923): The Man and the Politician," 36.
33. V. I. Lenin, "The Bourgeois Intelligentsia's Methods of Struggle Against the Workers" [1914], in *LCW*, 20:477.
34. Quoted in Israel Getzler, *Martov: A Political Biography of a Russian Social Democrat*, 134.
35. Lenin, "Bourgeois Intelligentsia's Methods of Struggle Against the Workers," 476.
36. R. C. Elwood, "Scoundrel or Saviour? Solzhenitsyn's View of Roman Malinovskii," 164–65.

37. Savel'ev and Tiutiukin, "Iulii Osipovich Martov (1873–1923): The Man and the Politician," 36.

38. Souvarine, *Stalin*, 124.

39. Trotsky, *Stalin*, ed. Woods, 142; Trotsky, *Stalin*, ed. Malamuth, 110.

40. Trotsky, *Stalin*, ed. Woods, 141; Trotsky, *Stalin*, ed. Malamuth, 109.

41. Trotsky, *My Life*, 218–19.

42. Trotsky, *Stalin*, ed. Woods, 125; Trotsky, *Stalin*, ed. Malamuth, 96.

43. Souvarine, *Stalin*, 92.

44. Ibid., 125.

45. Ibid., 126.

46. Ibid., 105.

47. Schapiro, *Communist Party of the Soviet Union*, 138.

48. Thanks to my friend Charnie Guettel for pointing out the underemphasized importance of the political volunteer.

49. Souvarine, *Stalin*, 106.

50. Ibid.

51. Ibid., 107.

52. J. L. H. Keep, *The Rise of Social Democracy in Russia*, 288.

53. Martov, "Spasiteli ili uprazdniteli?" [Saviours or destroyers?], 3, quoted in Keep, *Rise of Social Democracy in Russia*, 290.

54. Souvarine, *Stalin*, 107.

55. Iulii Martov, *Die Geschichte der Russischen Socialdemokratie* [History of Russian Social Democracy] (Berlin: Dietz, 1926), 268, quoted in Ruth Fischer, *Stalin and German Communism*, 22.

56. Fischer, *Stalin and German Communism*, 22.

57. Martov, *Geschichte*, 268, quoted in Fischer, *Stalin and German Communism*, 22.

58. Karl Marx and Frederick Engels, *The German Ideology* [1846], 52–53.

59. Karl Marx, "Theses on Feuerbach" (original version), 5, 3.

60. Abigail B. Bakan, "Marx and 'Politics of Difference'? Exploitation, Alienation and Oppression." 9.

61. Paul Kellogg, "Ruthless Criticism of All That Exists."

62. V. I. Lenin, "Backward Europe and Advanced Asia," *Pravda*, 23 April 1913, in *LCW*, 19:99–100.

63. Leon Trotsky, *1905* [1907]; Leon Trotsky, "Results and Prospects" [1906]; Leon Trotsky, "The Permanent Revolution" [1930].

64. Edward W. Said, *Orientalism*.

65. Trotsky, *Stalin*, ed. Woods, 7; Trotsky, *Stalin*, ed. Malamuth, 1.

66. Trotsky, *Stalin*, ed. Woods, 179; Trotsky, *Stalin*, ed. Malamuth, 140.

67. Trotsky, *Stalin*, ed. Woods, 8; Trotsky, *Stalin*, ed. Malamuth, 2.

68. Trotsky, *Stalin*, ed. Woods, 10; Trotsky, *Stalin*, ed. Malamuth, 3.

69. Souvarine, *Stalin*, 115, 203, 487.

70. Isaac Deutscher, *Stalin: A Political Biography*, 368.

71. Trotsky, *1905*, 8, 336.

72. Tamás Krausz, *Reconstructing Lenin: An Intellectual Biography*, 103.

73. See Leon Trotsky, *The History of the Russian Revolution* [1932], 1:3–4, 6, 7, 98, 411, 466.

74. V. I. Lenin, "Two Tactics of Social-Democracy" [1905], in *LCW*, 9:48.

75. V. I. Lenin, "The Agrarian Programme of Social-Democracy," in *LCW*, 13:277.

76. Wolfe, *Three Who Made a Revolution*, 404.

77. V. I. Lenin, "What the 'Friends of the People' Are and How they Fight the Social-Democrats" [1894], in *LCW*, 1:235.

78. V. I. Lenin, "The Tasks of the Russian Social-Democrats" [1897], in *LCW*, 2:336.

79. V. I. Lenin, "The Heritage We Renounce" [1897], in *LCW*, 2:516; "The Workers' Party and the Peasantry," *Iskra*, January 1901, in *LCW*, 4:423.

80. V. I. Lenin, "Review of Home Affairs," *Zaria*, December 1901, in *LCW*, 5:278.

81. V. I. Lenin, *What Is to Be Done? Burning Questions of Our Movement* [1902], in *LCW*, 5:373.

82. V. I. Lenin, "Draft Programme of the Russian Social-Democratic Labour Party," *Iskra*, February 1902, in *LCW*, 6:27; "Material for Working Out the R.S.D.L.P. Programme" [1902], in *LCW*, 41:46–47.

83. Lenin, "Two Tactics of Social-Democracy," 54.

84. Ibid., 59.

85. V. I. Lenin, "'Oneness of the Tsar and the People, And of the People and the Tsar,'" *Proletarii*, 29 August 1905, in *LCW*, 9:192.

86. V. I. Lenin, "Pervye itogi politicheskoi gruppirovki" [The First results of the political alignment], *Proletarii*, 31 October 1905, in *PSS*, 12:10. Compare with the English-language translation, "our autocracy's Asiatic savagery," in *LCW*, 9:399.

87. V. I. Lenin, "Mezhdu dvukh bitv" [Between two battles], *Proletarii*, 25 November 1905, in *PSS*, 12:57. Compare with the English-language translation, "unmitigated Asiatic backwardness," in *LCW*, 9:464.

88. V. I. Lenin, "A Revolution of the 1789 or 1848 Type?" [1905], in *LCW*, 8:258.

89. V. I. Lenin, "Report on the Question of the Participation of the Social-Democrats in a Provisional Revolutionary Government" [1905], in *LCW*, 8:393.

90. V. I. Lenin, "The Socialist Party and Non-Party Revolutionism," *Novaia zhizn'*, November 1905, in *LCW*, 10:76.

91. V. I. Lenin, "The Dissolution of the Duma and the Tasks of the Proletariat" [1906], in *LCW*, 11:113.

92. V. I. Lenin, "Pered burei" [Before the storm], *Proletarii*, 21 August 1906, in *PSS*, 13:332. The English translation inserts the word "tyranny" after Asiatic, but that word is not in the original (see *LCW*, 11:136).

93. V. I. Lenin, "Before the Storm," *Proletarii*, 21 August 1906, in *LCW*, 11:139.

94. V. I. Lenin, "An Attempt at a Classification of the Political Parties of Russia," *Proletarii*, 30 September 1906, in *LCW*, 11:229.

95. Lenin, "Agrarian Programme of Social-Democracy," 278, 329; Lenin, "The Lessons of the Revolution," *Rabochaia gazeta*, 30 October 1910, in *LCW*, 16:304.

96. Lenin, "Agrarian Programme of Social-Democracy," 325.

97. V. I. Lenin, "The Agrarian Question in Russia Towards the Close of the Nineteenth Century" [1908], in *LCW*, 15:139.

98. V. I. Lenin, "Stolypin and the Revolution," *Sotsial-demokrat*, 18 October 1911, in *LCW*, 17:249–50.

99. V. I. Lenin, "Speech Delivered in the Name of the R.S.D.L.P. at the Funeral of Paul and Laura Lafargue," *Sotsial-demokrat*, 8 December 1911, in *LCW*, 17:304–5.

100. V. I. Lenin, "The Development of Revolutionary Strikes and Street Demonstrations," *Sotsial-Democrat*, 12 January 1913, in *LCW*, 18:476.

101. V. I. Lenin, "An Increasing Discrepancy: Notes of a Publicist," *Prosveshchenie*, 22 February 1913, in *LCW*, 18:563.

102. V. I. Lenin, "Notes of a Publicist," *Sotsial-demokrat*, 15 June 1913, in *LCW*, 19:230.

103. V. I. Lenin, "Russian Government and Russian Reforms," *Pravda truda*, 26 September 1913, in *LCW*, 19:393.

104. V. I. Lenin, "Critical Remarks on the National Question," *Prosveshchenie*, December 1913, in *LCW*, 20:51.

105. Lenin, "Bourgeois Intelligentsia's Methods of Struggle Against the Workers," 465.

106. V. I. Lenin, "The Right of Nations to Self-Determination," *Prosveshchenie*, June 1914, in *LCW*, 20:419.

107. Cynthia Ozick, introduction to Isaac Babel, *The Complete Works of Isaac Babel*, 16.

108. Nathalie Babel, preface to Isaac Babel, *The Complete Works of Isaac Babel*, 19.

109. Ibid., 27–28.

110. Ibid., 28.

111. Ibid., 25.

Chapter 10: Lenin—Beyond Reverence

1. Paul Le Blanc, "Paul Le Blanc on Tamás Krausz's *Reconstructing Lenin: Sorting Through Lenin's Legacy.*"
2. Paul Buhle, "Lenin for Today."
3. Ibid.
4. Tamás Krausz, *Reconstructing Lenin: An Intellectual Biography*, 15, 19.
5. Ibid., 357.
6. Ibid., 12.
7. Ibid., 47, 50, 68, 70, 74.
8. Martin Empson, "Pick of the Year"; Le Blanc, "Paul Le Blanc on Tamás Krausz's *Reconstructing Lenin.*"
9. Georgii Nazarovich Golkov, *Vladimir Il'ich Lenin: Biograficheskaia khronika, 1870–1924* [Vladimir Il'ich Lenin: Biographical timeline, 1870–1924]. See https://leninism.su/biograficheskie-xroniki-lenina.html.
10. Ibid.
11. Krausz, *Reconstructing Lenin*, 79.
12. Ibid., 107.
13. Ibid., 67.
14. Ibid., 355.
15. V. I. Lenin, "The Third International and Its Place in History," *The Communist International*, 1919, in *LCW*, 29:310.
16. Krausz, *Reconstructing Lenin*, 100.
17. Rosa Luxemburg, "The Mass Strike, the Political Party and the Trade Unions."
18. Leon Trotsky, *1905*.
19. Luxemburg, "Mass Strike," 179.
20. Ibid., 173.
21. Ibid., 175–78.
22. Ibid., 178.
23. Ibid., 179.
24. Trotsky, *1905*, xiii.
25. Ibid., 251.
26. Pierre Broué, *Le parti bolchévique: Histoire du P.C. de l'U.R.S.S*, 72.
27. Ibid., 73–74.
28. Ibid., 72.
29. Israel Getzler, *Martov: A Political Biography of a Russian Social Democrat*, 104–5.
30. Broué, *Le parti bolchévique*, 73.
31. Leon Trotsky, *My Life: An Attempt at an Autobiography*, 176.

32. V. I. Lenin, "Our Tasks and the Soviet of Workers' Deputies," *Novaia zhizn'*, November 1905, first published in 1940, in *LCW*, 10:21.

33. Ibid.

34. Ibid., 19.

35. Trotsky, *My Life*, 176.

36. James D. White, *Lenin: The Practice and Theory of Revolution*, 74.

37. Broué, *Le parti bolchévique*, 73.

38. Boris Souvarine, *Stalin: A Critical Survey of Bolshevism*, 79–80.

39. V. I. Lenin, "Lessons of the Moscow Uprising," *Proletarii*, 29 August 1906, in *LCW*, 11:171.

40. V. I. Lenin, "The Lessons of the Revolution," *Rabochaia gazeta*, 30 October 1910, in *LCW*, 16:296–304.

41. Author's calculations based on textual analysis of *LCW*, vol. 8.

42. Leon Trotsky, *Stalin: An Appraisal of the Man and His Influence*, ed. Woods, 115; Trotsky, *Stalin: An Appraisal of the Man and His Influence*, ed. Malamuth, 88. Ellipses in original.

43. Trotsky, *Stalin*, ed. Woods, 99; Trotsky, *Stalin*, ed. Malamuth, 75.

44. V. I. Lenin, "Lessons of the Moscow Uprising," *Proletarii*, 29 August 1906, in *LCW*, 11:171.

45. V. I. Lenin, "Lecture on the 1905 Revolution," 9 January 1917, *Pravda*, 22 January 1925, in *LCW*, 23:248.

46. Broué, *Le parti bolchévique*, 73, quoting Lenin as cited in Hugo Anweiler, *Der Rätebewegung in Russland, 1905–1921* [The Council Movement in Russia, 1905–1921] (Leyde: Brill, 1960), 103.

47. V. I. Lenin, *What Is to Be Done? Burning Questions of Our Movement.*

48. Krausz, *Reconstructing Lenin*, 31.

49. China Miéville, *October: The Story of the Russian Revolution*, 8; see also 305–6.

50. Tariq Ali, *The Dilemmas of Lenin: Terrorism, War, Empire, Love, Revolution*, 72.

51. Miéville, *October*, 305. Tariq Ali says that his own "attempts to read Chernyshevsky at the ages of seventeen, thirty-two and seventy-two were miserable failures. The last time I managed to read over a hundred or so pages and could grasp his appeal, which lay in the truths he recounted and elements of utopia he included, rather than the book's effectiveness as fiction." See Ali, *Dilemmas of Lenin*, 258n8.

52. Ali explains the book's lack of appeal to a contemporary audience, citing Vera Zasulich, who said that the author was "hampered by censorship" and forced to "write in allusions and hieroglphys." Only those immersed in his

milieu and context could decipher the book. Others, said Zasulich, would "find him dull and empty." Quoted in Ali, *Dilemmas of Lenin*, 258–59n8.

53. Nathan Haskell Dole and S. S. Skidelsky, preface to Tchernuishevsky [Chernyshevsky], *A Vital Question; or, What Is to Be Done?* iii.

54. Richard Peace, "Nihilism," 126.

55. Michael R. Katz and William G. Wagner, "Introduction: Chernyshevsky, *What Is to Be Done?* and the Russian Intelligentsia."

56. Ivan Sergeyevich Turgenev, *Fathers and Sons*, 213.

57. Nikolay Chernyshevsky, *What Is to Be Done?* 281.

58. Ibid., 280–82.

59. Ibid., 288.

60. Katz and Wagner, "Introduction," 17.

61. Chris Matthew Sciabarra, *Ayn Rand: The Russian Radical*, 27.

62. Editor's annotation in Nikolai Tchernuishevsky [Chernyshevsky], *A Vital Question; or, What Is to Be Done?* 233n. Dmitry Karakozov was executed in September 1866 for his attempt on the life of Alexander II. His was the first in a series of attempted assassinations, one of which finally succeeded (in March 1881).

63. Lenin, *What Is to Be Done? Burning Questions of Our Movement*.

64. V. I. Lenin, "Narodniks on N.K. Mikhailovsky," *Put' pravdy*, 22 February 1914, in *LCW*, 20:118.

65. V. I. Lenin, "'The Peasant Reform' and the Proletarian-Peasant Revolution," *Sotsial-demokrat*, 19 March 1911, in *LCW*, 17:123.

66. Ibid.

67. V. I. Lenin, "Draft for a Speech on the Agrarian Question in the Second State Duma" [1907], in *LCW*, 12:292. First published in 1925.

68. Buhle, "Lenin for Today," referencing Georg Lukács, *Lenin: A Study on the Unity of His Thought*.

69. Krausz, *Reconstructing Lenin*, 10.

70. Martin Jay, *Marxism and Totality: The Adventures of a Concept from Lukács to Habermas*, 120, quoting Lukács, *Lenin*, 9.

71. Ibid., 10.

72. Karl Radek, "Lenin" [1923], 80.

73. Leon Trotsky, "Lenin Is Dead" [1924], 210. The English language translation of Trotsky's autobiography includes an even more startling example of reverence: "I realized only too well what Lenin meant to the revolution, to history, and to me. He was my master." A more accurate translation might be "Lenin was my teacher." Either choice, however, has a reverential "feel." See Leon Trotsky, *My Life: An Attempt at an Autobiography*, 394;

Leon Trotsky, *Moia zhizn': Opyt avtobiografii* [*My life: An attempt at an autobiography*], 2:123.

74. Bertram D. Wolfe, introduction to Trotsky, *Lenin: Notes for a Biography*, 7.

75. Jay, *Marxism and Totality*, 120–21, quoting Lukács, *Lenin*, 66.

76. The idea of a relationship between a contemporary left-wing tendency to inflate the role of individual socialists and the hegemonic framework of liberal individualism was first suggested to me by Abigail Bakan.

77. Leon Trotsky, *The History of the Russian Revolution*, 1:329.

78. Ibid., 329–30.

79. Ibid., 330.

80. Krausz, *Reconstructing Lenin*, 357.

81. Ibid., 154–55.

82. Trotsky, *My Life*, 249–50.

83. Getzler, *Martov*, 144.

84. Brian Pearce, "Lenin and Trotsky on Pacifism and Defeatism," 32–33.

85. Ibid., 33.

86. Ibid., 34.

87. Ibid., 33.

88. Ibid., 34.

89. Pierre Broué, *Trotsky*, 155.

90. White, *Lenin*, 139–40.

91. Anonymous, "Memoirs of a Bolshevik-Leninist," 77.

92. Pearce, "Lenin and Trotsky on Pacifism and Defeatism," 30, quoting V. I. Lenin, "To Inessa Armand" [25 December 1916], in *LCW*, 35:268.

93. "*Reconstructing Lenin: An Intellectual Biography*, by Tamás Krausz," https://monthlyreview.org/product/reconstructing_lenin/.

Chapter 11: Intellectuals and the Working Class

1. Alexander Potresov, "Lenin, Versuch Einer Charakterisierung" [Lenin: An Attempt at a Characterization] [1927], 412.

2. Tamás Krausz, *Reconstructing Lenin: An Intellectual Biography*, 115.

3. V. I. Lenin, "What Is to Be Done? Burning Questions of Our Movement," in *LCW*, 5:375–76.

4. Ibid., 383–84.

5. Iulii Martov, *Krasnoe znamia v Rossii: Ocherk istorii russkogo rabochego dvizheniia* [Red banner in Russia: An essay on the history of the Russian labour movement] [1900].

6. Savel'ev and Tiutiukin, "Iulii Osipovich Martov (1873–1923): The Man and the Politician," 15.

7. V. I. Lenin, "A Retrograde Trend in Russian Social-Democracy" [1899], in *LCW*, 4:258. First published in 1924.

8. Krausz, *Reconstructing Lenin*, 121.

9. Ibid., 253.

10. V. I. Lenin, *One Step Forward, Two Steps Back*, in *LCW*, 7:367; V. I. Lenin, *Shag vpered, dva shaga nazad* [One step forward, two steps back], in *PSS*, 8:387.

11. V. I. Lenin, *Shag vpered, dva shaga nazad* [One step forward, two steps back], in *PSS*, 8:333. Here, more than elsewhere in the book, you will find my own translations from the Russian-language fifth edition of Lenin's *Collected Works*, rather than the more accessible English-language translation of the fourth edition. I was taken aback, upon collecting all his writings on intellectuals into one place, by the extent of invective and insult employed. I wanted to be sure that this was not being exaggerated by the manner in which these excerpts had been translated. I did find a few occasions where liberties were taken. For the "Onward!" quotation, the fourth edition translators offer "endless, tedious word-chopping of your intellectuals," which is colourful but uses a bit too much poetic licence (*LCW*, 7:345n1). Later, the translators randomly use the modifiers "contemptible little" rather than "petty" before the words "government official" (*LCW*, 11:461), but such modifiers are completely absent from the original. These choices, while reflecting a certain shared enthusiasm for Lenin's attack on intellectuals as a group, are distracting and misleading. However, on the whole, I concluded that the fourth edition translation is an accurate reflection of the Russian original.

12. Lenin, *One Step Forward, Two Steps Back*, 385.

13. Lenin, *Shag vpered, dva shaga nazad* [One step forward, two steps back], 309, 311–12, 314.

14. Ibid., 333.

15. Lenin, *One Step Forward, Two Steps Back*, 355, 361, 384.

16. Ibid., 389.

17. Lenin, *Shag vpered, dva shaga nazad* [One step forward, two steps back], 381.

18. Lenin, *One Step Forward, Two Steps Back*, 364.

19. Ibid., 355.

20. Ibid., 396.

21. Lenin, *Shag vpered, dva shaga nazad* [One step forward, two steps back], 390.

22. Ibid., 370.

23. V. I. Lenin, "Chego my dobivaemsia? (k partii)" [What we are working for (to the party)] [1904], in *PSS*, 9:8. First published in 1923.

24. V. I. Lenin, "Plekhanov i Vasil'ev" [Plekhanov and Vasilyev], *Proletarii*, 7 January 1907, in *PSS*, 14:238.

25. V. I. Lenin, "Vybornaia kampaniia sotsial-demokratii v Peterburge" [The Social-democratic election campaign in St. Petersburg], *Prostiye rechi*, 21 January 1907, in *PSS*, 14:295.

26. V. I. Lenin, "Vybory po rabochei kurii v Peterburge" [The Elections in the worker curia in St. Petersburg], *Prostye rechi*, 30 January 1907, in *PSS*, 14:345.

27. Ibid., 347.

28. V. I. Lenin, "Bor'ba S. D. i S. R. na vborakh v rabochei kurii v S.-Peterburge" [The Struggle between SDs and SRs in the Elections in the Worker Curia in St. Petersburg], *Prostye rechi*, 30 January 1907, in *PSS*, 14:352.

29. V. I. Lenin, "Preface to the Russian Translation of Karl Marx's *Letters to Dr. Kugelmann*" [1907], in *LCW*, 12:107.

30. Ibid., 111.

31. V. I. Lenin, "The Second Duma and the Second Revolutionary Wave," *Proletarii*, 11 February 1907, in *LCW*, 12:115.

32. Ibid.

33. V. I. Lenin, "The Election Results in St. Petersburg," *Proletarii*, 11 February 1907, in *LCW*, 12:121.

34. V. I. Lenin, "The Menshevik Tactical Platform," *Questions of Tactics*, April 1907, in *LCW*, 12:261.

35. V. I. Lenin, "Angry Embarrassment: The Question of the Labour Congress," *Questions of Tactics*, April 1907, in *LCW*, 12:328.

36. Ibid.

37. Ibid., 330.

38. Ibid.

39. Ibid.

40. V. I. Lenin, "The Fifth Congress of the Russian Social-Democratic Labour Party" [1907], in *LCW*, 12:449.

41. V. I. Lenin, "The Attitude Towards Bourgeois Parties" [1907], in *LCW*, 12:508.

42. V. I. Lenin, "Notes of a Publicist," *Voice of Life*, 22 August 1907, in *LCW*, 13:73.

43. V. I. Lenin, "Revolution and Counter-Revolution," *Proletarii*, 20 October 1907, in *LCW*, 13:115.

44. Ibid., 120.

45. V. I. Lenin, "The Agrarian Programme of Social-Democracy," in *LCW*, 13:265.

46. Ibid., 426.

47. Peter Hudis and Kevin B. Anderson, "Editors' Note," in Rosa Luxemburg, *The Rosa Luxemburg Reader*, 248.

48. Rosa Luxemburg, "Organizational Questions of the Russian Social Democracy" [1904], 253–54.

49. V. I. Lenin, "One Step Forward, Two Steps Back—Reply by N. Lenin to Rosa Luxemburg" [1904], in *LCW*, 7:477 and 480.

50. See, in particular, Lars T. Lih, *Lenin Rediscovered: What Is to Be Done? in Context*.

51. Theodore Dan, *The Origins of Bolshevism* [1946], 24.

52. Thanks to Abigail Bakan for suggesting this point.

53. Israel Getzler, *Martov: A Political Biography of a Russian Social Democrat*, 1–2.

54. Orlando Figes, "'Down with the Jew Kerensky!' Judeophobia, Xenophobia and Popular Anti-Semitism in the 1917 Revolution," 10–11.

55. Abigail Bakan calls antisemitism an "unclear and imperfect term." She argues that "historic anti-Semitism, as anti-Judaism, was dissimilar from modern anti-Semitism, as anti-Jewish racism; the former allowed for the possibility of conversion, while the latter was considered a feature of biological assignment associated with 'Jewish blood.' Jews have historically been the victims of both anti-Judaism and anti-Jewish racism, which tend to be termed, confusingly and without differentiation, 'anti-Semitism.'" See Abigail B. Bakan, "Race, Class, and Colonialism: Reconsidering the 'Jewish Question,'" 255.

56. Marc Ferro, *October 1917: A Social History of the Russian Revolution*, 238.

57. Raphael R. Abramovitch, *In tsvey revolutsyes, di geshikhte fun a dor* [In two revolutions, the history of a generation], 2:85. Thanks to Kay Schweigmann-Greve for this reference, and for providing an English language translation of the relevant portion. The two-volume study of the Russian Revolution from which this comes was written by Raphael Abramovitch and published in Yiddish in 1944. It has yet to be translated into English. Kay also introduced me to the importance of Isaac Steinberg's role in and writing about the revolution.

58. Richard Hofstadter, *Anti-intellectualism in American Life*, 4, quoting Arthur Schlesinger, Jr., "The Highbrow in Politics," *Partisan Review* 20 (March–April 1953): 162–65.

59. V. I. Lenin, "What Is to Be Done? Burning Questions of Our Movement," in *LCW*, 5:423.

60. V. I. Lenin, "The Convening of the Third Party Congress," *Vpered*, 28 February 1905, in *LCW*, 8:179.

61. Mikhail Baitalsky, *Notebooks for the Grandchildren: Recollections of a Trotskyist Who Survived the Stalin Terror*, 15–16.

62. Vadim Z. Rogovin, *1937: Stalin's Year of Terror*, 158–59, quoting Y. Larin, *Evrei i antisemitizm v SSSR* [The Jews and antisemitism in the USSR] (Moscow-Leningrad: Gosizdat, 1929), 241–42.

63. Ibid., 154–55.

64. Leon Trotsky, "Thermidor and Anti-Semitism" [1937], *The New International*, May 1941, 92. Compare with the translation in Rogovin, *1937: Stalin's Year of Terror*, 157.

65. Trotsky, "Thermidor and Anti-Semitism," 93. Compare with the translation in Rogovin, *1937: Stalin's Year of Terror*, 160.

66. Suzanne Rosenberg, *A Soviet Odyssey*, 111.

67. Nadezhda A. Joffe, *Back in Time: My Life, My Fate, My Epoch—The Memoirs of Nadezhda A. Joffe*, 222.

68. Philip Mendes, *Jews and the Left: The Rise and Fall of a Political Alliance*, 131.

69. Leonard Schapiro, "The Rôle of the Jews in the Russian Revolutionary Movement," 156.

70. Ibid., 160.

71. Richard H. Rowland, "Geographical Patterns of the Jewish Population in the Pale of Settlement of Late Nineteenth Century Russia," 207.

72. Abraham Ascher, ed., *The Mensheviks in the Russian Revolution*, 12.

73. Schapiro, "Rôle of the Jews in the Russian Revolutionary Movement," 165.

74. Rowland, "Geographical Patterns of the Jewish Population in the Pale of Settlement of Late Nineteenth Century Russia," 207.

75. Isaac Deutscher, *Stalin: A Political Biography*, 91.

76. Joseph Stalin, "The London Congress of the Russian Social-Democratic Labour Party (Notes of a Delegate)" [1907], 52–53.

77. Deutscher, *Stalin*, 91.

78. Robert C. Tucker, *Stalin as Revolutionary, 1879–1929: A Study in History and Personality*, 140.

79. Jeffrey Brooks, *Thank You, Comrade Stalin! Soviet Public Culture from Revolution to Cold War*, 143.

80. V. I. Lenin, "To P. B. Axelrod—February 27, 1901," in *LCW*, 35:58.

81. Leon Trotsky, "The Latest Falsification of the Stalinists" [1939], 266.

82. V. I. Lenin, "The Judas Trotsky's Blush of Shame" [1911], in *LCW*, 17:45, corrected against the original Russian; V. I. Lenin, "O kraske styda u iudushki Trotskogo" [About little Judas Trotsky's blush of shame] [*Pravda*, no. 21, 21 January 1932], in *PSS*, 20:96.

83. Trotsky, "Latest Falsification of the Stalinists," 267.

84. Robert Service, *Trotsky: A Biography*, 409.

85. Adam Bruno Ulam, *The Bolsheviks: The Intellectual and Political History of the Triumph of Communism in Russia: With a New Preface*, 283.

86. V. I. Lenin, "What the 'Friends of the People' Are" [1894], in *LCW*, 1:291.

87. V. I. Lenin, "Casual Notes," *Zaria*, April 1901, in *LCW*, 4:406.

88. V. I. Lenin, "Fighting the Famine-Stricken," *Iskra*, October 1901, in *LCW*, 5:237–38.

89. V. I. Lenin, "The Victory of the Cadets and the Tasks of the Workers Party," April 1906, in *LCW*, 10:215.

90. V. I. Lenin, "Yet Another Anti-Democratic Campaign," *Nevskaia zvezda*, 2 and 9 September 1912, in *LCW*, 18:316.

91. V. I. Lenin, "Review of Home Affairs," *Zaria*, December 1901, in *LCW*, 5:258.

92. V. I. Lenin, "Political Struggle and Political Chicanery," *Iskra*, 15 October 1902, in *LCW*, 6:252.

93. V. I. Lenin, "Banality Triumphant," *Nashe ekho*, 3 April 1907, in *LCW*, 12:342.

94. V. I. Lenin, "A Police-Patriotic Demonstration Made to Order," *Proletarii*, 12 March 1908, in *LCW*, 13:481.

95. V. I. Lenin, "Notes of a Publicist: On Ascending a High Mountain" [unfinished, unpublished article, February 1922]. First published in *Pravda*, 16 April 1924, in *LCW*, 33:205.

96. Trotsky, "Latest Falsification of the Stalinists," 266.

97. I. P. Foote, "M. E. Saltykov-Shchedrin: The Golovlyov Family," 56.

98. David Aberbach, "Hebrew Literature and Jewish Nationalism in the Tsarist Empire, 1881–1917," 146.

99. Benjamin Nathans, *Beyond the Pale: The Jewish Encounter with Late Imperial Russia*, 129.

100. Shmuel Ettinger, "The Modern Period," 884.

101. N. P. Kolikov, "Ukazatel' imen" [Index of names], 590.

Conclusion: Ends and Means

1. V. I. Lenin, "'Left-Wing' Childishness," serialized in *Pravda*, 9–11 May 1918, in *LCW*, 27:340.

2. Petrograd Committee of the RSDLP (Bolshevik), "The Lost Document" [1917], 111.

3. Isaac Steinberg, *In the Workshop of the Revolution*, 78.

4. Ibid., 79–80.

5. Ibid., 81–82.

6. Andrej Kalpašnikov, *A Prisoner of Trotsky's*, 137.

7. John Spargo, *"The Greatest Failure in All History": A Critical Examination of the Actual Workings of Bolshevism in Russia*, 143.

8. Iurii Vladimirovich Goťe, *Time of Troubles: The Diary of Iurii Vladimirovich Goťe*, 98.

9. China Miéville, *October: The Story of the Russian Revolution*, 316.

10. Elias Heifetz, *The Slaughter of the Jews in the Ukraine in 1919*.

11. Ibid., 180–81.

12. Ibid., 85.

13. Ibid., 89.

14. Ibid., 85.

15. Orlando Figes, *A People's Tragedy: The Russian Revolution, 1891–1924*, 525.

16. Rosa Luxemburg, "What Does the Spartacus League Want?" 352, quoted in Steinberg, *In the Workshop of the Revolution*, 268–69. Steinberg's translation is slightly different than the source here cited.

17. Iulii Martov, "Doloi smertnuiu kazn'!" [Down with the death penalty!] [July 1918], 375. For an alternate translation, see https://www.marxists.org/archive/martov/1918/07/death-penalty.htm.

18. Ibid., 379.

19. Leon Trotsky, *Lenin: Notes for a Biography* [1924], 122.

20. Steinberg, *In the Workshop of the Revolution*, 145. Trotsky's account includes a sarcastic put-down of Steinberg: "I do not know what queer wind blew him toward the revolution and into the Council of People's Commissars." See Trotsky, *Lenin*, 123. This sarcasm is unwarranted. The Left Social-Revolutionaries, of which Steinberg was a leading member, had a mass hearing among the peasantry, its main support, according to Steinberg, lying "in the villages." It would soon become clear, with the results from the elections to the Constituent Assembly, that Bolshevik support in those villages was risible. But, as Steinberg points out, the Left SR was also a significant force in the cities: "Large masses of workers (in Petrograd alone no less than 45,000 workers were members of the Left Social-Revolutionary Party) and soldiers and sailors also supported the party." See Steinberg, *In the Workshop of the Revolution*, 49.

21. Quoted in George Leggett, *The Cheka: Lenin's Political Police: The All-Russian Extraordinary Commission for Combating Counter-Revolution and Sabotage, December 1917 to February 1922*, 114, quoting *Severnaia kommuna* [Northern commune], Petrograd, No. 109, 19 September 1918, 2.

22. V. I. Lenin, "To G.F. Fyodorov" [August 1918], in *LCW*, 35:349.

23. V. I. Lenin, "Telegram to Yevgenia Bosch—August 9, 1918," in *LCW*, 36:489.

24. V. I. Lenin, "To G. Y. Zinoviev" [June 2018], in *LCW*, 36:336.

25. V. I. Lenin, "A Militant Agreement for the Uprising," *Vpered*, 21 February 1905, in *LCW*, 8:163.

26. V. I. Lenin, "Lessons of the Moscow Uprising," *Proletarii*, 29 August 1906, in *LCW*, 11:177.

27. Nicolas Werth, "A State Against Its People: Violence, Repression, and Terror in the Soviet Union," 27, quoting L. M. Spirin, *Klassy i partii v grazhdanskoi voine v Rossii* [Classes and parties in the civil war in Russia] (Moscow: Thought Publishers, 1968), 180.

28. The letter was "signed by the President Committee of the Russian Communist Party, the President of the Nolinsk Extraordinary Staff for Struggle Against Counter-revolution, the Secretary of the Staff, the Nolinsk Military Commissar and Member of the Staff." See Werth, "A State Against Its People," 28, quoting L. M. Spirin, *Klassy i partii v grazhdanskoi voine v Rossii* [Classes and parties in the civil war in Russia], 180.

29. Bulletin of the Cheka, "Why Are You Soft?" [September 1918], 27–28; see also William Henry Chamberlin, *The Russian Revolution, 1917–1921*, 2:70–71.

30. Miéville, *October*, 312.

31. Steinberg, *In the Workshop of the Revolution*, 152.

32. Ibid., 153–54.

33. Ibid., 156.

34. Tony Cliff, *Revolution Besieged*, 15.

35. Steinberg, *In the Workshop of the Revolution*, 230–31.

36. Richard Pipes, *The Russian Revolution*, 526.

37. Leggett, *Cheka*, 4–5.

38. Ibid., 15.

39. Pipes, *Russian Revolution*, 526. Richard Pipes's scholarship on the Russian Revolution is part of the standard literature, and his writings are cited throughout this book. This requires some commentary. Pipes's name has become symbolic with right-wing anti-communism, a reputation justly earned. In the 1970s, Pipes was an influential member of the notorious Team B, hired by then CIA director (and later president) George H. W. Bush. The work of the Team B section in which Pipes participated played a role in laying the foundation for the Reagan-era arms buildup, a policy whose intention was to destabilize the Soviet Union, and which largely succeeded. See Anne Hessing Cahn, "Team B: The Trillion-Dollar Experiment." But should Pipes's political actions disqualify his scholarship? The book that made Pipes's reputation was his first, *The Formation of the Soviet Union: Communism and Nationalism, 1917–1923*. Jeremy Smith, in *The Bolsheviks and the National Question, 1917–23*, an authoritative parallel study, calls Pipes's book "the most influential treatment" of the national question in the Soviet Union, a treatment that draws very negative conclusions (x). For Pipes, writes Smith, "nothing positive can be found

in the Bolsheviks' approach to the national question." Smith sets out to "challenge many of Pipes' assumptions and conclusions." However, he states unequivocally: "I do not challenge the accuracy of Pipes' account, which is based on the most thorough research given the materials available at the time" (xi). It is in the same spirit that I use Pipes's research into the 1917–18 anti-Bolshevik strike movements.

40. Pipes, *Russian Revolution*, 526–27.

41. Ibid., 527–28.

42. Alexander Rabinowitch, "The October Revolution," 89.

43. Miéville, *October*, 294.

44. John Gooding, *Socialism in Russia: Lenin and His Legacy, 1890–1991*, 58.

45. Pipes, *Russian Revolution*, 529.

46. Alexander Rabinowitch, *The Bolsheviks Come to Power: The Revolution of 1917 in Petrograd*, 306, 308.

47. Leggett, *Cheka*, 15.

48. Sovnarkom, "Meeting of the Council of People's Commissars, December 7, 1917," 6.

49. Leggett, *Cheka*, 16, quoting from the Sovnarkom meeting minutes, available in ed. G. A. Belov et al., *Iz istorii vserossiiskoi chrezvychainoi komissii 1917-1921 gg.: Sbornik dokumentov* [From the history of the all-Russian emergency commission of 1917-1921: Collection of documents] (Moscow: State Publishing House of Political Literature, 1958), 72.

50. Ibid., 17.

51. Pipes, *Russian Revolution*, 529.

52. Werth, "State Against Its People," 62.

53. Sovnarkom, "Meeting of the Council of People's Commissars," 7.

54. "Establishment of the Extraordinary Commission to Fight Counter-Revolution," 26.

55. Laura Engelstein, *Moscow, 1905: Working-Class Organization and Political Conflict*, 6.

56. Victor Serge, *Memoirs of a Revolutionary* [1951], 94.

57. Victor Serge, *Year One of the Russian Revolution* [1930], 82–107.

58. Ibid., 103–4.

59. Ibid., 104, quoting Lev Kritsman, *Geroicheskii period velikoi russkoi revoliutsii* [The Heroic period of the great Russian revolution], 23. Serge is paraphrasing Kritsman, but the phrases emphasized in Serge are also emphasized in Kritsman: "The technical intelligentsia plays a *double* role in capitalist production, not only as *the organizer of production*, but also as *the organizer of exploitation.*"

60. Serge, *Year One of the Russian Revolution*, 93.

61. Roger Pethybridge, *The Spread of the Russian Revolution: Essays on 1917*, 17.

62. Ibid., 20.

63. Leon Trotsky, *The History of the Russian Revolution*, 2:231.

64. Steinberg, *In the Workshop of the Revolution*, 16–39.

65. Leggett, *Cheka*, 4–5.

66. P. Iu. Savel'ev and S. V. Tiutiukin, "Iulii Osipovich Martov (1873–1923): The Man and the Politician," 66.

67. Pethybridge, *Spread of the Russian Revolution*, 52.

68. Steve A. Smith, "Petrograd in 1917: The View from Below," 76.

69. Grégoire Aronson, "Ouvriers russes contre le bolchévisme," 202.

70. Oliver Henry Radkey, *Russia Goes to the Polls: The Election to the All-Russian Constituent Assembly, 1917*, 138.

71. Ibid., 160.

72. Rosa Luxemburg, "The Russian Revolution" [1918], 300.

73. Raphael R. Abramovitch, *The Soviet Revolution, 1917–1939*, 127–28.

74. Spargo, *Greatest Failure in All History*, 142, quoting Inna Ratinikov, *How the Russian Peasants Fought for a Constituent Assembly*, 30 May 1918, in John Spargo, *Bolshevism* (New York: Millibuch & Co., 1919), 331–84.

75. Chamberlin, *Russian Revolution*, 1:369.

76. Adam Bruno Ulam, *The Bolsheviks: The Intellectual and Political History of the Triumph of Communism in Russia: With a New Preface*, 396.

77. Israel Getzler, *Kronstadt, 1917–1921: The Fate of a Soviet Democracy*, 181, quoting L. S. Malchevsky (ed.), *Vserossiiskoe uchreditel'noe sobranie* [The all-Russian constituent assembly] (Moscow: Gos. izd-vo, 1930), 33–34.

78. William G. Rosenberg, "Russian Labor and Bolshevik Power: Social Dimensions of Protest in Petrograd after October," 117.

79. Ibid., 118.

80. Vladimir Brovkin, "Politics, Not Economics Was the Key," 245.

81. Ibid., 248.

82. Ibid., 250.

83. See Jonathan Aves, *Workers Against Lenin: Labour Protest and the Bolshevik Dictatorship*; Samuel Farber, *Before Stalinism: The Rise and Fall of Soviet Democracy*; Israel Getzler, *Kronstadt, 1917–1921*; Simon Pirani, *The Russian Revolution in Retreat, 1920–24: Soviet Workers and the New Communist Elite*.

84. Figes, *A People's Tragedy*, 716.

85. Aves, *Workers Against Lenin*, 107.

86. Ibid., 111–12.

87. Getzler, *Kronstadt, 1917–1921*, 258, quoting L. Martov, "Kronshtadt," *Sotsialisticheskii vestnik*, no. 5, 5 April 1921.

88. Ibid.

89. Leon Trotsky, *Their Morals and Ours: The Marxist View of Morality*, 37.

90. Luxemburg, "The Russian Revolution," 305.

91. Rosa Luxemburg, "What Does the Spartacus League Want?" [1918], 352.

Bibliography

Aberbach, David. "Hebrew Literature and Jewish Nationalism in the Tsarist Empire, 1881–1917." In *The Emergence of Modern Jewish Politics: Bundism and Zionism in Eastern Europe*, edited by Zvi Gitelman, 132–50. Pittsburgh: University of Pittsburgh Press, 2003.

Abramovitch, Raphael R. *In tsvey reyolutsyes, di geshikhṭe fun a dor* [In two revolutions, the history of a generation]. 2 vols. New York: The Workmen's Circle (Der Arbeter-Ring), 1944. Repr. Amherst, MA: National Yiddish Book Center, Steven Spielberg Digital Yiddish Library No. 00869. http://archive.org/details/nybc200869.

———. *The Soviet Revolution, 1917–1939*. Translated by Vera Broido-Cohn. London: George Allen and Unwin, 1962.

Abramovitsch [Abramovitch], Raphael, Vassily Suchomlin, and Irakli Tsereteli. *Der Terror gegen die sozialistischen Parteien in Russland und Georgien* [The Terror against socialist Parties in Russia and Georgia]. Berlin: JHW Dietz Nachfolger, 1925.

Ali, Tariq. *The Dilemmas of Lenin: Terrorism, War, Empire, Love, Revolution.* London: Verso Books, 2017.

Allen, Michael E. *The Gulag Study*. 5th ed. Washington, DC: Joint Commission Support Directorate, Defense Prisoner of War/Missing Personnel Office, 2005.

Andrew, Edward. "Class in Itself and Class Against Capital: Karl Marx and His Classifiers." *Canadian Journal of Political Science / Revue canadienne de science politique* 16, no. 3 (1983): 577–84.

Angress, Werner T. *Stillborn Revolution: The Communist Bid for Power in Germany, 1921–1923*. Princeton, NJ: Princeton University Press, 1963.

Anonymous. "Mémoires d'un bolchevik-léniniste." In *Renaissance du bolchévisme en U.R.S.S: Mémoires d'un bolchévik-léniniste*, edited by Pierre Frank, 29–168. Paris: François Maspéro, 1970.

———. "Memoirs of a Bolshevik-Leninist." In Saunders, *Samizdat*, 51–188.

Antonov-Ovseyenko, Anton. *The Time of Stalin: Portrait of a Tyranny*. New York: Harper and Row, 1981.

Applebaum, Anne. *Gulag: A History*. New York: Random House, 2003.

———. *Iron Curtain: The Crushing of Eastern Europe 1944–56*. Toronto: McClelland and Stewart, 2012.

Aronson, Grégoire. "Ouvriers russes contre le bolchévisme." *Le contrat social* 10, no. 4 (1966): 201–11.

Ascher, Abraham, ed. *The Mensheviks in the Russian Revolution*. Documents translated by Paul Stevenson. London: Thames and Hudson, 1976.

Associated Press. "Moscow Denies Famine Deaths." *New York Evening Post*, 30 March 1933.

Aves, Jonathan. *Workers Against Lenin: Labour Protest and the Bolshevik Dictatorship*. London: I. B. Tauris, 1996.

Axelrod, Pavel Borisovich. "Ob'edinenie rossiiskoi sotsial-demokratii i ee zadachi" [The Unification of Russian social democracy and its tasks]. *Iskra*, no. 55 (15 December 1903) and *Iskra*, no. 57 (15 January 1904).

Babel, Isaac. *The Complete Works of Isaac Babel*. Edited by Nathalie Babel. Translated by Peter Constantine. New York: Norton, 2005.

———. "The Red Cavalry Stories" [1926]. In *Complete Works of Isaac Babel*, 197–334.

Babel, Nathalie. "Preface." In Babel, *Complete Works of Isaac Babel*, 19–28.

Baitalsky, Mikhail. *Notebooks for the Grandchildren: Recollections of a Trotskyist Who Survived the Stalin Terror*. Translated by Marilyn Vogt-Downey. Atlantic Highlands, NJ: Humanities Press, 1995.

Bakan, Abigail B. "Marx and 'Politics of Difference'? Exploitation, Alienation and Oppression." *Against the Current* (July–August 2018): 8–9.

———. "Race, Class, and Colonialism: Reconsidering the 'Jewish Question.'" In *Theorizing Anti-racism: Linkages in Marxism and Critical Race Theories*, edited by Abigail B. Bakan and Enakshi Dua, 252–79. Toronto: University of Toronto Press, 2014.

———. "Review of *Capitalism and Unfree Labour: Anomaly or Necessity?* by Robert Miles." *Science and Society* 55, no. 2 (1991): 235–36.

Balmforth, Tom. "Vorkuta: Gulag Is Gone, but a Virtual Prison Has Taken Its Place." *RadioFreeEurope/RadioLiberty*, 4 March 2013. http://www.rferl.org/content/stalin-gulag-vorkuta/24918538.html.

Banaji, Jairus. *Theory and History: Essays on Modes of Production and Exploitation*. Historical Materialism Book Series 25. Leiden: Brill, 2010.

Barenberg, Alan. "From Prison Camp to Mining Town: The Gulag and Its Legacy in Vorkuta, 1938–1965." PhD diss., Department of History, University of Chicago, 2007.

———. *Gulag Town, Company Town: Forced Labor and Its Legacy in Vorkuta*. New Haven, CT: Yale University Press, 2014.

Baron, Samuel H. *Plekhanov: The Father of Russian Marxism*. Stanford, CA: Stanford University Press, 1963.

Berger, Joseph. *Shipwreck of a Generation: The Memoirs of Joseph Berger*. London: Harvill, 1971.

Birchall, Ian. "Grappling with the United Front." *International Socialism* 135 (Summer 2012): 195–205.

———. "Review of Jean-François Fayet's Karl Radek (1885–1939)." *Historical Materialism* 14, no. 3 (2006): 259–74.

———. *Tony Cliff: A Marxist for His Time*. London: Bookmarks, 2011.

Bojko, Diana, Wanda Chudzik, Vasyl Danylenko, Karbarz-Wilińska, Serhiy Kokin, Petro Kulakovsky, Robert Kuśnierz, Serhiy Lanovenko, Marcin Majewski, and Yuriy Shapoval, eds. *Holodomor: The Great Famine in Ukraine 1932-1933*. Poland and Ukraine in the 1930's-1940's. Unknown Documents from the Archives of the Secret Services. Warsaw: Institute of National Remembrance, Commission of the Prosecution of Crimes against the Polish Nation, 2009.

Broido, Vera. *Daughter of Revolution: A Russian Girlhood Remembered*. London: Constable, 1998.

———. *Lenin and the Mensheviks: The Persecution of Socialists under Bolshevism*. Boulder: Westview Press, 1987.

Brooks, Jeffrey. *Thank You, Comrade Stalin! Soviet Public Culture from Revolution to Cold War*. Princeton, NJ: Princeton University Press, 2000.

Broué, Pierre. *Communistes contre Staline: Massacre d'une génération*. Paris: Fayard, 2003.

———. *The German Revolution, 1917–1923*. Edited by Ian Birchall and Brian Pearce. Translated by John Archer. Historical Materialism Book Series 5. Leiden: Brill, 2005.

———. *Le Parti bolchévique: Histoire du P.C. de l'U.R.S.S.* Paris: Éditions de Minuit, 1963.

———. *Révolution en Allemagne: 1917–1923*. Paris: Éditions de Minuit, 1971.

———. *Trotsky*. Paris: Fayard, 1988.

Brovkin, Vladimir. "Politics, Not Economics Was the Key." *Slavic Review* 44, no. 2 (1985): 244–50.

Buca, Edward. *Vorkuta*. London: Constable and Robinson, 1976.

Buhle, Paul. "Lenin for Today." *Counterpunch*, 10 April 2015. http://www.counterpunch.org/2015/04/10/lenin-for-today/.

Bulletin of the Cheka. "Why Are You Soft?" [September 1918]. In "Communism Outside the United States—Section B: The U.S.S.R.," part 1 of *The Communist Conspiracy: Strategy and Tactics of World Communism*, by Committee on Un-American Activities, U.S. House of Representatives, 27–28. Washington, DC: Government Printing Office, 1956.

Burawoy, Michael. "Reflections on the Class Consciousness of Hungarian Steelworkers." *Politics & Society* 17, no. 1 (1989): 1–34.

Cahn, Anne Hessing. "Team B: The Trillion-Dollar Experiment." *Bulletin of the Atomic Scientists* 49, no. 3 (1993): 23–31.

Carr, Edward Hallett. "The Russian Revolution and the Peasant." In *Proceedings of the British Academy, 1963*, 69–94. London: Oxford University Press, 1964.

Casey, Jane Barnes. *I, Krupskaya: My Life with Lenin*. Boston: Houghton Mifflin, 1974.

Chamberlin, William Henry. *The Russian Revolution, 1917–1921*. 2 vols. New York: Grosset and Dunlap, 1965. First published 1935 by Macmillan (New York).

Chernov, Georgii Aleksandrovich. *Iz istorii otkritiia pechorskogo ugol'nogo basseina* [From the history of the discovery of the Pechora coal basin]. 2nd ed. Syktyvkar: Komi knizhnoe izd-vo, 1989.

Chernyshevsky, Nikolay. *What Is to Be Done?* Translated by Michael R. Katz. Ithaca: Cornell University Press, 1989. First published 1863 in Russian.

Chumakova, Aleksandra. "Memoirs of Aleksandra Chumakova." In Saunders, *Samizdat*, 189–205.

CIA. *The World Factbook 1987*. Washington, DC: Central Intelligence Agency, 1987. http://www.geographic.org/wfb1987/.

———. *The World Factbook 1989*. Washington, DC: Central Intelligence Agency, 1989. https://www.theodora.com/wfb1989/.

———. *The World Factbook 1990*. Washington, DC: Central Intelligence Agency, 1990. https://www.theodora.com/wfb/1990/index.html.

———. *The World Factbook 1991*. Washington, DC: Central Intelligence Agency, 1991. https://www.theodora.com/wfb/1991/index.html.

Cienciala, Anna M., Natalia S. Lebedeva, and Wojciech Materski, eds. *Katyn: A Crime Without Punishment*. Documents translated by Marian Schwartz, Anna M. Cienciala, and Maia A. Kipp. New Haven: Yale University Press, 2008.

Ciliga, Ante. *Dix ans au pays du mensonge déconcertant*. Paris: Éditions Champ Libre, 1977. First published 1938 by Éditions Gallimard (Paris).

———. *The Russian Enigma*. Translated by Fernand G. Fernier, Anne Cliff, Hugo Dewar, and Margaret Dewar. London: Ink Links, 1979. First published 1938 in French by Éditions Gallimard (Paris)

———. "Verkhneural'snii politizoliator" [Verkne-Uralsk political isolator]. *Sovremennye zapiski* [Modern notes] 66–67 (1938): 351–84.

Cliff, Tony. *Revolution Besieged*. Vol. 3 of *Lenin*. London: Pluto Press, 1978.

———. *The Bolsheviks and World Revolution*. Vol. 4 of *Lenin*. London: Pluto Press, 1979.

———. "The Revolutionary Party and the Class, or Trotsky on Substitutionism." *International Socialism*, 1, no. 2 (Autumn 1960): 14–16.

———. *The Sword of Revolution, 1917–1923.* Vol. 2 of *Trotsky.* London: Bookmarks, 1990.

———. "Trotsky on Substitutionism." In *Party and Class,* by Tony Cliff, Duncan Hallas, Chris Harman, and Leon Trotsky, 26–46. London: Pluto Press, 1973.

Cohen, Stephen F. *Bukharin and the Bolshevik Revolution: A Political Biography, 1888–1938.* New York: Random House, 1971.

———. "Introduction" to Antonov-Ovseyenko, *The Time of Stalin: Portrait of a Tyranny.* New York: Harper and Row, 1981.

Colley, Margaret Siriol. *Gareth Jones: A Manchukuo Incident.* Newark: N. L. Colley, 2001.

Commission internationale contre le régime concentrationnaire. *Livre blanc: Sur les camps de concentration soviétiques.* Paris: Le Pavois, 1951.

Conquest, Robert. *Kolyma: The Arctic Death Camps.* New York: Viking Press, 1978.

———. *The Great Terror: Stalin's Purge of the Thirties.* Toronto: Macmillan, 1968.

Croll, Kirsteen Davina. "Soviet-Polish Relations, 1919–1921." PhD diss., University of Glasgow, 2009.

D'Abernon, Edgar Vincent. *The Eighteenth Decisive Battle of the World: Warsaw, 1920.* London: Hodder and Stoughton, 1931.

Dan, Theodore. *The Origins of Bolshevism.* Edited and translated by Joel Carmichael. New York: Schocken Books, 1970. First published 1946 in Russian.

De Ste. Croix, G. E. M. *The Class Struggle in the Ancient Greek World: From the Archaic Age to the Arab Conquests.* Ithaca, NY: Cornell University Press, 1981.

Deutscher, Isaac. *Stalin: A Political Biography.* London: Oxford University Press, 1949.

———. *The Prophet Armed: Trotsky, 1879–1921.* Vol. 1 of *The Prophet: Trotsky, 1879–1940.* London: Oxford University Press, 1954.

Dobbs, Michael. "Miners Strike Is 'Warning' in Ukraine." *Washington Post,* 1 November 1989.

———. "Soviet Miners Vote to End 1-Day Strike." *Washington Post,* 27 October 1989.

Dobrovol'skii, Dmitrii, and Liudmila Peppel'. "Revoliutsiia, vosstanie, perevorot: Semantika i pragmatika" [Revolution, uprising, overturn: Semantics and pragmatics]. *Scando-Slavica* 58, no. 1 (2012): 77–100.

Dole, Nathan Haskell, and S. S. Skidelsky. "Preface." In Tchernuishevsky [Chernyshevsky], *A Vital Question; or, What Is to Be Done?* iii–ix.

Drabkin, Y. S., ed. *Komintern i ideia mirovoi revoliutsii* [The Comintern and the idea of world revolution]. Comintern Documents, 1920. Reprint, Moscow: Nauka, 1998.

Dronin, Nikolai M., and Edward G. Bellinger. *Climate Dependence and Food Problems in Russia, 1900–1990: The Interaction of Climate and Agricultural Policy and Their Effect on Food Problems*. Budapest: Central European University Press, 2005.

Du Bois, W. E. B. *Black Reconstruction: An Essay Toward a History of the Part Which Black Folk Played in the Attempt to Reconstruct Democracy in America, 1860–1880*. New York: Harcourt, Brace, 1935.

Dubrovsky, S. *Stolypinskaia reforma: Kapitalizatsiia sel'skogo khoziaistva v XX veke* [The Stolypin reform: Capitalization of agriculture in the twentieth century]. Leningrad: Priboi, 1925.

Dunayevskaya, Raya. "The Union of Soviet Socialist Republics Is a Capitalist Society." *Internal Discussion Bulletin*, Workers' Party, March 1941. https://www. marxists.org/archive/dunayevskaya/works/1941/ussr-capitalist.htm#f9.

Duranty, Walter. "Russians Hungry, But Not Starving." *New York Times*, 31 March 1933.

The Economist (US). "Northern Lights-Out: Russia." 6 March 1993.

Elwood, R. C. "Scoundrel or Saviour?: Solzhenitsyn's View of Roman Malinovskii." *Canadian Slavonic Papers* 19, no. 2 (1977): 161–66.

Empson, Martin. "Pick of the Year." *Socialist Review* 408 (December 2015). http:// socialistreview.org.uk/408/pick-year.

Engelstein, Laura. *Moscow, 1905: Working-Class Organization and Political Conflict*. Stanford, CA: Stanford University Press, 1982.

Ermacora, Matteo. "Rural Society." *International Encyclopedia of the First World War*, 6 January 2017. http://encyclopedia.1914-1918-online.net/article/rural_ society.

"Establishment of the Extraordinary Commission to Fight Counter-revolution." *Pravda*, 1917. In "Communism Outside the United States—Section B: The U.S.S.R.," part 1 of *The Communist Conspiracy: Strategy and Tactics of World Communism*, by Committee on Un-American Activities, U.S. House of Representatives, 26. Washington, DC: Government Printing Office, 1956.

Ettinger, S. "The Modern Period." In *A History of the Jewish People*, edited by H. H. Ben-Sasson, 727–1096. Cambridge, MA: Harvard University Press, 1976.

Fagan, Gus. "Introduction." In *Selected Writings on Opposition in the USSR, 1923–30*, by Khristian Georgievich Rakovskiĭ, edited by Gus Fagan, 7–64. London: Allison and Busby, 1980.

Falkus, Malcolm E. *The Industrialisation of Russia, 1700–1914*. London: Macmillan Press, 1972.

FAOSTAT. "Crops and Livestock Products, Wheat, Import Quantity, Export Quantity." Food and Agriculture Organization of the United Nations, 12 May 2016. http://faostat.fao.org/faostat/en/#data/TP.

Farber, Samuel. *Before Stalinism: The Rise and Fall of Soviet Democracy*. London: Verso, 1990.

"Fashistskii perevorot v Germanii: ('Bol'shevik-Leninets' No. 2 [12]. 1933)" [The Fascist coup in Germany: ("Bolshevik-Leninist" No. 2 [12]. 1933)]. *Ab Imperio* no. 4 (2017): 195–229.

Fein, Esther B. "Soviet Miners Strike in Defiance of Ban." *New York Times*, 26 October 1989.

Fernbach, David. "Introduction." In *In the Steps of Rosa Luxemburg: Selected Writings of Paul Levi*, 1–32.

Ferro, Marc. *October 1917: A Social History of the Russian Revolution.* Translated by Norman Stone. Boston: Routledge and Kegan Paul, 1980.

Figes, Orlando. *A People's Tragedy: The Russian Revolution, 1891–1924.* New York: Penguin, 1998.

———. "'Down with the Jew Kerensky!' Judeophobia, Xenophobia and Popular Anti-Semitism in the 1917 Revolution." *Jewish Quarterly* 45, no. 2 (1998): 5–11.

———. "The Red Army and Mass Mobilization During the Russian Civil War, 1918–1920." *Past and Present* (November 1990): 168–211.

Filtzer, Donald. "From Mobilized to Free Labour: De-Stalinization and the Changing Legal Status of Workers." In *The Dilemmas of De-Stalinization*, edited by Polly Jones, 168–84. London: Routledge, 2006.

———. *Soviet Workers and Late Stalinism: Labour and the Restoration of the Stalinist System after World War II.* Cambridge: Cambridge University Press, 2002.

Fischer, Benjamin B. "The Katyn Controversy: Stalin's Killing Field." Central Intelligence Agency, Studies in Intelligence: Historical Perspectives, 1999–2000. https://www.cia.gov/static/5a3e46e77b3c417a15bcf927e7b049cc/Stalins-Killing-Field.pdf.

Fischer, Ruth. *Stalin and German Communism.* Cambridge, MA: Harvard University Press, 1948.

Fitzpatrick, Sheila. "*War and Society* in Soviet Context: Soviet Labor Before, During, and After World War II." *International Labor and Working-Class History* 35 (1989): 37–52.

Fokin, Alexander. "Tetradi verkhneural'skogo politicheskogo izoliatora: Predstavlenie istochnika i razmyshleniia o ego znachenii [The Notebooks of the Verkhne-Uralsk political isolator: Introduction of a source and reflections on its significance]." *Ab Imperio*, no. 4 (2017): 177–94.

Foner, Eric. *Reconstruction: America's Unfinished Revolution, 1863–1877.* The New American Nation Series. New York: Harper & Row, 1989.

Foote, I. P. "M. E. Saltykov-Shchedrin: The Golovlyov Family." *Forum for Modern Language Studies* 4, no. 1 (1968): 53–63.

Forward. "History." *Forward.* Accessed 7 May 2019. https://forward.com/about-us/history/.

Frank, Pierre, ed. *Renaissance du bolchévisme en U.R.S.S: Mémoires d'un bolchévik-léniniste*. Paris: François Maspéro, 1970.

Friedgut, Theodore, and Lewis Siegelbaum. "Perestroika from Below: The Soviet Miners' Strike and Its Aftermath." *New Left Review* I/181 (May–June 1990): 5–32.

Furr, Grover C., III. "New Light on Old Stories About Marshal Tukhachevskii." *Russian History / Histoire russe* 13, nos. 2–3 (1986): 293–308.

Gamache, Ray. *Gareth Jones: Eyewitness to the Holodomor*. Cardiff: Welsh Academic Press, 2016.

Gaucher, Roland. *Opposition in the U.S.S.R., 1917–1967*. New York: Funk and Wagnalls, 1969.

GC–ISO. *The Comintern Debate on Workers' Unity: NYC Book Launch for John Riddell's "To the Masses."* YouTube. New York, 19 May 2016. https://www.youtube.com/watch?v=yUtUl_IZHbs.

Georgakas, Dan. "October Song." In *Abandon Automobile: Detroit City Poetry 2001*, edited by Melba Joyce Boyd and M. L. Liebler, 132. Detroit: Wayne State University Press, 2001.

Gerland, Brigitte. "500,000 Live in Huts Beneath Arctic Snow, Glad of Free Speech." *Globe and Mail*, 8 February 1954.

———. "Rare Eyewitness Report of Soviet Labor Camp Given by 'Graduate.'" *Christian Science Monitor*, 3 May 1954.

———. "Student Intellectuals and Religionists Form Backbone of Resistance in Soviet Slave Camps." *Globe and Mail*, 9 February 1954.

———. "Vorkuta (1950–53): Oppositional Currents and the Mine Strikes." In Saunders, *Samizdat*, 217–34.

Getty, J. Arch, Gábor T. Rittersporn, and Viktor N. Zemskov. "Victims of the Soviet Penal System in the Pre-war Years: A First Approach on the Basis of Archival Evidence." *American Historical Review* 98, no. 4 (1993): 1017–49.

Getzler, Israel. *Kronstadt, 1917–1921: The Fate of a Soviet Democracy*. Cambridge: Cambridge University Press, 1983.

———. *Martov: A Political Biography of a Russian Social Democrat*. Cambridge: Cambridge University Press, 1967.

Globe and Mail. "250,000 Slaves Strike in Red Camp." *Globe and Mail*, 6 February 1954.

Gooding, John. *Socialism in Russia: Lenin and His Legacy, 1890–1991*. New York: Palgrave, 2001.

Golkov, Georgii Nazarovich, ed. *Vladimir Il'ich Lenin: Biograficheskaia khronika, 1870–1924* [Vladimir Il'ich Lenin: biographical timeline, 1870–1924]. 12 vols. Moscow: Institute Marxism-Leninism, 1970–82. https://leninism.su/biograficheskie-xroniki-lenina.html

Gorky, Maxim. "On the Russian Peasantry." In *The Russian Peasant, 1920 and 1984*, edited by R. E. F. Smith, 15–32. London: Routledge, 1977.

Goťe, Iurii Vladimirovich. *Time of Troubles: The Diary of Iurii Vladimirovich Goťe.* Edited, translated, and introduced by Terence Emmons. Princeton, NJ: Princeton University Press, 1988.

Gramsci, Antonio. "The Modern Prince." In *Selections from the Prison Notebooks*, edited by Quintin Hoare and Geoffrey Nowell-Smith, 123–205. New York: International, 1971.

Gray, John. "Three Yeltsin Supporters Killed Outside Russian Parliament." *Globe and Mail*, 21 August 1991.

Greeman, Richard. "The Death of Communism and the New World Order." *Left History* 1, no. 1 (1993): 56–66.

Haimson, Leopold H. *Russia's Revolutionary Experience, 1905-1917: Two Essays.* New York: Columbia University Press, 2005.

———. *The Making of Three Russian Revolutionaries: Voices from the Menshevik Past.* New York: Cambridge University Press, 1987.

Hallas, Duncan. "On Building a Socialist Alternative, Part II." *Socialist Worker* [Toronto] (December 1987): 5.

———. *The Comintern.* London: Bookmarks, 1985.

Harman, Chris. *The Lost Revolution: Germany, 1918 to 1923.* London: Bookmarks, 1982.

Haynes, Michael. *Russia: Class and Power, 1917–2000.* London: Bookmarks, 2002.

Haynes, Michael, and Rumy Husan. *A Century of State Murder? Death and Policy in Twentieth-Century Russia.* London: Pluto Press, 2003.

Hegel, Georg Wilhelm Friedrich. "Preface." In *Philosophy of Right*. Translated by S. W. Dyde. London: G. Bell, 1896. https://www.marxists.org/reference/archive/hegel/works/pr/philosophy-of-right.pdf.

Heifetz, Elias. *The Slaughter of the Jews in the Ukraine in 1919.* New York: Thomas Seltzer, 1921.

Hofstadter, Richard. *Anti-intellectualism in American Life.* New York: Knopf, 1963.

Hudis, Peter, and Kevin B. Anderson. "Editors' Note." In Rosa Luxemburg, *The Rosa Luxemburg Reader*, edited by Peter Hudis and Kevin B. Anderson, 248. New York: Monthly Review Press, 2004.

Institute of National Remembrance. "Decision to Commence Investigation into Katyn Massacre." Press release, 30 November 2004. http://www.ipn.gov.pl/en/news/77,dok.html.

James, C. L. R. "Russia—A Fascist State." *New International* 7, no. 3 (1941): 54–58.

———. *The Black Jacobins: Toussaint L'Ouverture and the San Domingo Revolution.* New York: Vintage Books, 1963. First published 1938 by Secker and Warburg (London).

Jay, Martin. *Marxism and Totality: The Adventures of a Concept from Lukács to Habermas.* Berkeley: University of California Press, 1984.

Joffe, Maria. *Odna noch': Povest' o pravde* [One long night: A Tale of truth]. Sakharov Center, 1978. https://www.sakharov-center.ru/asfcd/auth/?t=book&num=674.

———. *One Long Night: A Tale of Truth.* Translated by Vera Dixon. London: New Park Publications, 1978.

Joffe, Nadezhda A. *Back in Time: My Life, My Fate, My Epoch—The Memoirs of Nadezhda A. Joffe.* Translated by Frederick S. Choate. Oak Park, Michigan: Mehring Books, 1995.

———. *Vremia nazad: Moia zhizn', moia sud'ba, moia epokha* [Back in time: My life, my fate, my epoch]. Sakharov Center, 1995. https://www.sakharov-center.ru/asfcd/auth/?t=book&num=991.

Jones, Gareth. "Fate of Thrifty in U.S.S.R." *Times-Union,* 14 January 1935.

———. "Russia—Land of Starvation." *Syracuse Journal,* 12 January 1935.

———. "Soviet Collective Farm Move Caused Famine in Russia, Says Gareth Jones." *Syracuse American,* 11 June 1933.

Jones, Stephen. "The Establishment of Soviet Power in Transcaucasia: The Case of Georgia, 1921–1928." *Soviet Studies* 40, no. 4 (1988): 616–39.

Kagarlitsky, Boris. "USSR—A Voice of the Socialist Opposition." *Socialist Worker* [London] (7 October 1989): 8.

Kalpašnikov, Andrej. *A Prisoner of Trotsky's.* New York: Doubleday and Page, 1920.

Katz, Michael R., and William G. Wagner. "Introduction: Chernyshevsky, *What Is to Be Done?* and the Russian Intelligentsia." In *What Is to Be Done?* by Nikolai Chernyshevsky, 1–36. Translated by Michael R. Katz. Ithaca: Cornell University Press, 1989.

Keep, J. L. H. *The Rise of Social Democracy in Russia.* Oxford: Clarendon Press, 1963.

Kellogg, Paul. "Coalition Building, Capitalism and War: Review Article of John Riddell, *To the Masses: Proceedings of the Third Congress of the Communist International, 1921.*" *Socialist Studies / Études socialistes* 12, no. 1 (2017): 169–80.

———. "Grappling with Our History: The March Action, the Russo-Polish War, and the United Front." *Socialist Studies / Études socialistes* 9, no. 1 (2013): 176–91.

———. "Leninism: It's Not What You Think." *Socialist Studies / Études socialistes* 5, no. 2 (2009): 41–63.

———. "Lost in Translation: Explaining the Tragedy of Germany's 1921 March Action." Presentation, We Are Many, Chicago, 28 June 2012. http://wearemany.org/a/2012/06/lost-in-translation-explaining-tragedy-of-germanys-1921-march-action.

———. "Ruthless Criticism of All That Exists." *Against the Current* (May–June 2018): 19–20.

———. "The Only Hope of the Revolution Is the Crowd: The Limits of Žižek's Leninism." *International Journal of Žižek Studies* 2, no. 2 (2008). http://zizekstudies.org/index.php/IJZS/article/viewFile/82/79.

Kellogg, Paul, and John Riddell. *Luxemburg, Lenin, Levi: Rethinking Revolutionary History* [2/3]. YouTube. Toronto, 14 December 2013. https://www.youtube.com/watch?v=nXDjm_lC4Ow.

Knickerbocker, H. R. "Famine Grips Russia, Millions Dying, Idle on Rise, Says Briton." *New York Evening Post*, 29 March 1933.

Kolikov, N. P. "Ukazatel' imen" [Index of names]. In *Polnoe sobranie sochinenii tom 6* [The complete collected works, vol. 6], by V. I. Lenin, 558–99. 5th ed. Moscow: Publishing House of Political Literature, 1963.

Kolle, Herdis. "The Russian Post-Emancipation Household: Two Villages in the Moscow Area." Master's thesis, University of Bergen, 1995. https://bora.uib.no/handle/1956/1203.

Kostiuk, Hryhory. "The Accursed Years from Lukianivka Prison to the Tragedy at Vorkuta (1935–40)." *Critique: Journal of Socialist Theory* 27, no. 1 (1999): 159–80.

Kowalski, Ronald I. "Geroicheskii period russkoi revoliutsii" [The Heroic period of the Russian revolution]. *Revolutionary Russia* 2, no. 2 (1989): 5–8.

Kramer, Mark. "The Early Post-Stalin Succession Struggle and Upheavals in East-Central Europe: Internal-External Linkages in Soviet Policy Making (Part 1)." *Journal of Cold War Studies* 1, no. 1 (1999): 3–55.

Krausz, Tamás. *Reconstructing Lenin: An Intellectual Biography.* Translated by Bálint Bethlenfalvy and Mario Fenyo. New York: Monthly Review Press, 2015.

Kritsman, Lev. "Foreword." *Geroicheskii period velikoi russkoi revoliutsii* [The Heroic period of the great Russian revolution]. Translated by Ronald I. Kowalski. *Revolutionary Russia* 2, no. 2 (1989): 9–10.

———. *Geroicheskii period velikoi russkoi revoliutsii (Opyt analiza t. n. "voennogo kommunizma")* [The Heroic period of the great Russian revolution] (An Attempt to analyze so-called "war communism")]. Moscow: Gosudarstvennoe izdatel'stvo [State publishing house], 1926.

———. "Introduction. *Geroicheskii period velikoi russkoi revoliutsii* [The Heroic period of the great Russian revolution]. Translated by Ronald I. Kowalski. *Revolutionary Russia* 2, no. 2 (1989): 11–17.

Landis, Erik C. "The Fate of the Soviet Countryside—March 1920." In *Was Revolution Inevitable? Turning Points of the Russian Revolution*, edited by Tony Brenton. New York: Oxford University Press, 2017.

Le Blanc, Paul. *October Song.* Chicago: Haymarket Books, 2017.

———. "Paul Le Blanc on Tamás Krausz's *Reconstructing Lenin*: Sorting Through Lenin's Legacy." *Links: International Journal of Socialist Renewal* (20 March 2015). http://links.org.au/node/4330.

Lee, Eric. *The Experiment: Georgia's Forgotten Revolution, 1918–1921*. London: Zed Books, 2017.

Leggett, George. *The Cheka: Lenin's Political Police: The All-Russian Extraordinary Commission for Combating Counter-Revolution and Sabotage, December 1917 to February 1922*. Oxford: Clarendon Press, 1981.

Lenin, Vladimir Il'ich. *Lenin: Collected Works (LCW)*. 45 vols. Translation of the fourth, enlarged Russian edition. Moscow: Progress Publishers, 1960–70.

———. "Political Report of the Central Committee of the Russian Communist Party (Bolshevik) to the Ninth Conference of the RCP(B) [Shorthand report, 22 September 1920]." In Richardson, *In Defence of the Russian Revolution*, 134–58.

———. "Political Report of the Central Committee RKP(b) to the Ninth All-Russian Conference of the Communist Party, 20 September 1920." In Pipes, *The Unknown Lenin: From the Secret Archive*, 95–115.

———. "Politicheskii otchet TSK RKP(b) na IKH vserossiiskoi konferentsii RKP(b) i zakliuchitel'noe slovo po itogam obsuzhdeniia otcheta" [Political report of the central committee of the RCP(B) at the ninth all-Russian Conference of the RCP(B) and the final word on the results of the discussion of the report]. [Shorthand report, 22 September 1920.] In *Neizvestnye dokumenty 1891–1922* [Unknown documents, 1891–1922], 370–94. Moscow: ROSSPEN (Russian State Archive of Social and Political History), 2000.

———. *Polnoe sobranie sochinenii (PSS)* [The complete collected works]. 5th ed. 55 vols. Moscow: Publishing House of Political Literature, 1960–75.

———. "Report on Red Army Pogroms, with Lenin's Reaction, 17–18 October 1920." In Pipes, *Unknown Lenin*, 116–18.

———. "A Retrograde Trend in Russian Social-Democracy" [1899]. First Published in 1924. In *LCW*, 4:255–85. Moscow: Progress Publishers, 1960.

———. "The Right of Nations to Self-Determination." *Prosveshchenie* Nos. 4, 5 and 6 (June 1914). In *LCW*, 20:393–454. Moscow: Progress Publishers, 1964.

———. "Telegram to Stalin, 23 July 1920." In Pipes, *Unknown Lenin*, 93.

Levi, Paul. *In the Steps of Rosa Luxemburg: Selected Writings of Paul Levi*. Edited and translated by David Fernbach. Historical Materialism Book Series 31. Leiden: Brill, 2011.

———. "The Lessons of the Hungarian Revolution" [1920]. In *In the Steps of Rosa Luxemburg*, 70–78.

———. "Our Path: Against Putschism" [1921]. In *In the Steps of Rosa Luxemburg*, 119–65.

Levine, Isaac Don. *Stalin*. New York: Cosmopolitan Book Corporation, 1931.

Lewin, M. "Who Was the Soviet Kulak?" *Soviet Studies* 18, no. 2 (1966): 189–212.

Lewis, Ben. "The Four-Hour Speech and the Significance of Halle." In Lewis, *Zinoviev and Martov*, 7–38.

———, ed. *Zinoviev and Martov: Head to Head in Halle.* Translated by Ben Lewis and Lars T. Lih. London: November Publications, 2011.

Liebman, Marcel. *Leninism Under Lenin.* Translated by Brian Pearce. London: Merlin Press, 1975.

———. *The Russian Revolution: The Origins, Phases and Meaning of the Bolshevik Victory.* Translated by Arnold J. Pomerans. New York: Jonathan Cape, 1970.

Lih, Lars T. *Lenin Rediscovered: What Is to Be Done? in Context.* Historical Materialism Book Series 9. Leiden: Brill, 2006.

Lipper, Elinor. *Eleven Years in Soviet Prison Camps.* Chicago: Regnery, 1951.

Lorkovic, Tatjana. "Microform Collection: The All-Union Population Census, [1937 and] 1939." Yale University Library, Slavic and East European Collection, 2009.

Lovestone, Jay. "The Meaning of the Soviet Purges." In *The "American Exceptionalism" of Jay Lovestone and His Comrades, 1929–1940: Dissident Marxism in the United States,* edited by Paul Le Blanc and Tim Davenport, Historical Materialism Book Series 83, 297–306. Leiden: Brill, 2015.

Lukács, Georg. *Lenin: A Study on the Unity of His Thought.* Translated by Nicholas Jacobs. London: New Left Books, 1970. First published 1924 in German by Verlag der Arbeiterbuchhandlung (Vienna).

Luxemburg, Rosa. "Introduction to Political Economy" [1910]. In *Economic Writings 1,* vol. 1 of *The Complete Works of Rosa Luxemburg,* edited by Peter Hudis, translated by David Fernbach, Joseph Fracchia, and George Shriver, 89–300. London: Verso Books, 2013.

———. "The Mass Strike, the Political Party and the Trade Unions" [1906]. Translated by Patrick Lavan. In *The Rosa Luxemburg Reader,* 168–99.

———. "Organizational Questions of the Russian Social Democracy" [1904]. Translated by Richard Taylor. In *The Rosa Luxemburg Reader,* 248–65.

———. *The Rosa Luxemburg Reader.* Edited by Peter Hudis and Kevin B. Anderson. New York: Monthly Review Press, 2004.

———. "The Russian Revolution" [1918]. Translated by Bertram D. Wolfe. In *The Rosa Luxemburg Reader,* 281–310. First published 1922 in German.

———. "What Does the Spartacus League Want?" [1918]. Translated by Martin Nicolaus. In *The Rosa Luxemburg Reader,* 349–57.

Malenkov, G. M. "Comrade Stalin—Leader of Progressive Mankind." In *"Pravda Articles," On the Occasion of the 70th Birthday of Joseph Vissarionovich Stalin, December 21, 1949.* Moscow: Foreign Languages Publishing House, 1950. https://www.marxists.org/archive/malenkov/1949/12/21.htm.

Mandel, David. "The Independent Miners' Union: Three Interviews." *Socialist Alternatives* 1, no. 2 (1992): 141–61.

———. *Perestroika and the Soviet People: Rebirth of the Labour Movement.* Montréal: Black Rose Books, 1991.

———. "The Rebirth of the Soviet Labour Movement: The Coalminers' Strike of July 1989." In *Perestroika and the Soviet People*, 51–78.

———. "Strike Wave of March–April 1991." In *Perestroika and the Soviet People*, 155–207.

Mandel, Ernest. *Beyond Perestroika: The Future of Gorbachev's USSR*. Translated by Gus Fagan. London: Verso, 1991.

Mandt, Hella. "The Classical Understanding: Tyranny and Despotism." In *Totalitarianism and Political Religions*, vol. 3 of *Concepts for the Comparison of Dictatorships: Theory and History of Interpretations*, edited by Hans Maier, translated by Jodi Bruhn, 25–100. New York: Routledge, 2007.

Martov, Iulii Osipovich. "Deklaratsiia fraktsii men'shevikov-internatsionalistov i evreiskoi sotsialisticheskoi rabochei partii poalei-tsion, zachitannaia Iu. O. Martovym [Declaration of the Menshevik-Internationalist and Jewish Socialist Labour Party (Paole-Tsion) fractions, read out by Iu. O. Martov]." *Izvestiia*, no. 207 (26 October 1917).

———. "Doloi smertnuiu kazn'!" [Down with the death penalty!] [July 1918]. In *Izbrannoe* [Selected works], 373–83.

———. *Izbrannoe* [Selected works]. Edited by S. V. Tyutyukin, O. V. Volobuev, and I. Kh. Urilov. Moscow, 2000.

———. *Krasnoe znamia v Rossii: Ocherk istorii russkogo rabochego dvizheniia* [Red banner in Russia: An Essay on the history of the Russian labour movement, 1900]. Geneva: Revolutionary Organization "Social-Democrat."

———. "Mirovoi bol'shevizm" [World Bolshevism]. In *Izbrannoe* [Selected works], 393–432.

———. *Mirovoi bol'shevizm* [World Bolshevism]. Edited by Fedor Dan. Berlin: Spark, 1923.

———. "O politicheskom polozhenii i zadachakh partii" [On the political situation and tasks of the party] [1917]. In *Izbrannoe* [Selected Works], 349–60.

———. "Saviours or Destroyers?" [1911]. In *The Mensheviks in the Russian Revolution*, edited by Abraham Ascher, translated by Paul Stevenson, 70–73. London: Thames and Hudson, 1976.

———. "Spasiteli ili uprazdniteli? (kto i kak razrushal RSDRP)" [Saviours or destroyers? (Who destroyed the RSDRP and how)] [1911]. In *Izbrannoe* [Selected works], 260–321.

Marx, Karl. "Die Sog. Ursprüngliche Akkumulation" [The So-called Primary Accumulation] [1867]. In *Das Kapital. Band I—Kritik Der Politischen Ökonomie* [Capital. Volume I—A critique of political economy], edited by Friedrich Engels. In *Karl Marx Friedrich Engels Gesamtausgabe (MEGA)*, II-10:641–94. Berlin: Dietz Verlag, 1991.

————. *The Poverty of Philosophy* [1847]. In *Marx and Engels Collected Works (MECW)*, 6:105–212. London: Lawrence and Wishart, 1976.

————. "Provisional Rules of the Association" [1864]. In *MECW*, 20:14–16. London: Lawrence and Wishart, 1985.

————. "The So-Called Primitive Accumulation" [1867]. In *Capital. Volume I—A Critique of Political Economy*, edited by Friedrich Engels, translated by Samuel Moore and Edward Aveling, 704–64. *MECW*, 35. London: Lawrence and Wishart, 1996.

————. "Theses on Feuerbach" [1845]. Original version. In *MECW*, 5:3–5. London: Lawrence and Wishart, 1976.

————. "Theses on Feuerbach" [1845]. Edited by Engels. In *MECW*, 5:6–8. London: Lawrence and Wishart, 1976.

Marx, Karl, and Frederick Engels. *The German Ideology* [1846]. Translated by Clemens Dutt, W. Lough, and C. P. Magill. In *MECW*, 5:19–539. London: Lawrence and Wishart, 1976.

M. B. [Ivan Mitrofanovich Khoroshev] "Trotskisty na Vorkute" [Trotskyists at Vorkuta]. *Socialist Courier* 41 (October 1961): 201–4.

————. "Trotskyists at Vorkuta (An Eyewitness Report)." In Saunders, *Samizdat*, 206–16.

McCauley, Martin. *Stalin and Stalinism*. Revised 3rd ed. New York: Routledge, 2013.

McLuhan, Marshall. *The Medium Is the Message*. New York: Bantam Books, 1967.

Medvedev, Roy A. *Let History Judge: The Origins and Consequences of Stalinism*. New York: Vintage Books, 1973.

————. *The October Revolution*. Translated by George Saunders. New York: Columbia University Press, 1979.

Menczer, Béla. "Béla Kun and the Hungarian Revolution of 1919." *History Today* 19, no. 5 (1969): 299–309.

Mendes, Philip. *Jews and the Left: The Rise and Fall of a Political Alliance*. New York: Palgrave Macmillan, 2014.

Miéville, China. *October: The Story of the Russian Revolution*. London: Verso Books, 2017.

Miles, Robert. *Capitalism and Unfree Labour: Anomaly or Necessity*. New York: Taylor and Francis, 1987.

Mitrany, David. *Marx Against the Peasant: A Study in Social Dogmatism*. Chapel Hill: University of North Carolina Press, 1951.

Morgan, David W. *The Socialist Left and the German Revolution: A History of the German Independent Social Democratic Party, 1917–1922*. Ithaca, NY: Cornell University Press, 1975.

Morris, Rosalind C. "Ursprüngliche Akkumulation: The Secret of an Originary Mistranslation." *Boundary 2* 43, no. 3 (2016): 29–77.

Muggeridge, Malcolm. "The Soviet's War on the Peasants." *Fortnightly Review* [London] (May 1933): 558–64.

Mukerjee, Madhusree. *Churchill's Secret War: The British Empire and the Ravaging of India During World War II.* New York: Basic Books, 2010.

Myers, Constance Ashton. *The Prophet's Army: Trotskyists in America, 1928–1941.* Westport, CT: Greenwood Press, 1977.

Nathans, Benjamin. *Beyond the Pale: The Jewish Encounter with Late Imperial Russia.* Berkeley: University of California Press, 2004.

Negretov, P. I. "How Vorkuta Began." *Soviet Studies* 29, no. 4 (1977): 565–75.

Nemakov, N. I. *Kommunisticheskaya partiya—organizator massovogo kolkhoznogo dvizheniya (1929–1932 gg.)* [Communist Party—organizer of the mass collective farm movement (1929–1932)]. Moscow: Publishing house of Moscow University, 1966.

Nil'skii, Mikhail [Ivan Mitrofanovich Khoroshev]. *Vorkuta.* Samizdat edition, 1986, 74–75.

———. "Vorkutinskaia tragediia" [The Vorkuta tragedy]. *Kontinent* 18 (1978): 279–308.

Nove, Alec. *An Economic History of the U.S.S.R.* London: Penguin Books, 1969.

———. "Introduction." In *The New Economics,* by Evgeny Preobrazhensky. Translated by Brian Pearce. Oxford: Clarendon Press, 1965.

———. *Studies in Economics and Russia.* Houndmills, Dasingstoke: Macmillan, 1990.

"Obituary: Raya Dunayevskaya." *Capital and Class* 11, no. 2 (1987): 190.

Oxford English Dictionary. 2016. "Anvil, N." *OED Online.* Oxford University Press. http://www.oed.com.

Ozick, Cynthia. "Introduction." In *Complete Works of Isaac Babel,* 13–17.

Pallot, Judith. *Land Reform in Russia, 1906–1917: Peasant Responses to Stolypin's Project of Rural Transformation.* Oxford: Clarendon Press, 1999.

Pal'veleva, Lilia. "Arestantskie slova" [Convict terms.] *Radio Svoboda [Radio Liberty],* 22 May 2014. https://www.svoboda.org/a/25393602.html.

Panin, Dimitri. *The Notebooks of Sologdin.* Translated by John Moore. New York: Hutchinson, 1976.

Panné, Jean Louis. *Boris Souvarine, le premier desenchanté du communisme.* París: Robert Laffont, 1993.

Peace, Richard. "Nihilism." In *A History of Russian Thought,* edited by William Leatherbarrow and Derek Offord, 116–40. Cambridge: Cambridge University Press, 2010.

Pearce, Brian. "'Export of Revolution,' 1917–1924." *Labour Review* 3, no. 4 (1958): 104–8, 117–19.

———. "Lenin and Trotsky on Pacifism and Defeatism." *Labour Review* 6, no. 1 (1961): 29–38.

Pethybridge, Roger. *The Social Prelude to Stalinism.* London: Macmillan, 1974.

———. *The Spread of the Russian Revolution: Essays on 1917.* London: Macmillan Press, 1972.

Petrograd Committee of the RSDLP (Bolshevik). "The Lost Document" [1917]. In *The Stalin School of Falsification*, by Leon Trotsky, translated by Max Shachtman. New York: Pioneer, 1937.

Petrov, Igor'. "Nastoiashchee imia respondenta #440" [The real name of respondent #440]. 22 April 2017. https://labas.livejournal.com/1165734.html.

Pipes, Richard. *The Formation of the Soviet Union: Communism and Nationalism, 1917–1923.* Revised ed. Cambridge, MA: Harvard University Press, 1968. First published 1954.

———. *Russia Under the Bolshevik Regime.* New York: Knopf Doubleday, 2011.

———. *The Russian Revolution.* New York: Vintage Books, 1990.

———, ed. *The Unknown Lenin: From the Secret Archive.* Basic translation of Russian documents by Catherine A. Fitzpatrick. New Haven: Yale University Press, 1996.

Pirani, Simon. *The Russian Revolution in Retreat, 1920–24: Soviet Workers and the New Communist Elite.* London: Routledge, 2008.

Popov, Nikolai Nikolaevich. *Outline History of the Communist Party of the Soviet Union.* Edited by A. Fineberg. 2 vols. New York: International, 1934.

Potresov, Alexander. "Lenin: Versuch Einer Charakterisierung" [Lenin: An Attempt at a Characterization]. *Die Gesellschaft: Internationale Revue für Sozialismus und Politik* 4, no. 2 (1927): 405–18.

Preobrazhensky, Evgeny. *The New Economics.* Translated by Brian Pearce. First English ed. Oxford: Clarendon Press, 1965. First published 1926 in Russian.

Prigorovski, Mikhail Mikhailovich, ed. *The Coal Resources of the USSR.* Moscow: Chief Editorial Office of the Mining-Fuel and Geological Prospecting Literature, 1937.

Rabinowitch, Alexander. *The Bolsheviks Come to Power: The Revolution of 1917 in Petrograd.* New York: W. W. Norton, 1978.

———. "The October Revolution." In *Critical Companion to the Russian Revolution, 1914–1921*, edited by Edward Acton, Vladimir Iu. Cherniaev, and William G. Rosenberg. Bloomington: Indiana University Press, 1997.

Radek, Karl. "Lenin" [1923]. In Richardson, *In Defence of the Russian Revolution,* 76–81.

———. "The Paths of the Russian Revolution" [1922]. In Richardson, *In Defence of the Russian Revolution,* 35–75.

———. "Session of the *Zentrale* with the Representative of the Executive Committee for Germany Friday, January 28, 1921." In *The Comintern: Historical Highlights,*

Essays, Recollections, Documents, edited by Milorad M. Drachkovitch and Branko Lazitch, 285–93. Stanford: Hoover Institution on War, Revolution, and Peace, Stanford University, 1966.

———. "Vystuplenie K. Radeka na IKH konferentsii RKP (b) o polozhenii v Pol'she" [Speech by K. Radek at the Ninth conference of the RCP(b) about the situation in Poland] [1920]. In *Komintern i ideia mirovoi revoliutsii* [The Comintern and the idea of world revolution], edited by Y. S. Drabkin, 200–205. Moscow: Nauka, 1998.

Radkey, Oliver Henry. *Russia Goes to the Polls: The Election to the All-Russian Constituent Assembly, 1917*. Ithaca: Cornell University Press, 1989.

Radzinsky, Edvard. *Stalin*. Toronto: Doubleday, 1996.

Rand, Ayn. *Atlas Shrugged*. New York: Dutton, 1957.

———. *The Fountainhead*. New York: New American Library, 1943.

"Reconstructing Lenin: An Intellectual Biography, by Tamás Krausz." *Monthly Review*, 2021. https://monthlyreview.org/product/reconstructing_lenin/.

Rees, John. "Gorbachev Defied as Miners Strike Again." *Socialist Worker* [London] (11 November 1989): 5.

Reiman, Michal. *The Birth of Stalinism: The USSR on the Eve of the "Second Revolution."* Translated by George Saunders. Bloomington: Indiana University Press, 1987.

Remnick, David. *Lenin's Tomb: The Last Days of the Soviet Empire*. New York: Vintage Books, 1994.

———. "Striking Soviet Miners Push Radical Demand for Political Change." *Washington Post*, 26 March 1991.

Richardson, Al, ed. *In Defence of the Russian Revolution: A Selection of Bolshevik Writings, 1917–1923*. Translated by Brian Pearce. London: Porcupine Press, 1995.

Riddell, John. *Founding the Communist International—Proceedings and Documents of the First Congress: March 1919*. New York: Pathfinder Press, 1987.

———. "Introduction." In Riddell, *To the Masses*, 1–52.

———. "Introduction." In *Founding the Communist International: Proceedings and Documents of the First Congress, March 1919*, edited by John Riddell, 3:1–27. The Communist International in Lenin's Time series. New York: Pathfinder Press, 1987.

———, ed. *To the Masses: Proceedings of the Third Congress of the Communist International, 1921*. Historical Materialism Book Series 91. Leiden: Brill, 2015.

———, ed. *Toward the United Front: Proceedings of the Fourth Congress of the Communist International, 1922*. Historical Materialism Book Series 34. Leiden: Brill, 2012.

———, ed. *Workers of the World and Oppressed Peoples, Unite! Proceedings and Documents of the Second Congress, 1920.* 2 vols. The Communist International in Lenin's Time series. New York: Pathfinder, 1991.

Rogovin, Vadim Z. *1937: Stalin's Year of Terror.* Translated by Frederick S. Choate. Oak Park, MI: Mehring Books, 1998.

———. *Stalin's Terror of 1937–1938: Political Genocide in the USSR.* Translated by Frederick S. Choate. Oak Park, MI: Mehring Books, 2009. First published 1997 in Russian.

Rondan, John. "Nikolai Aleksandrovich Rozhkov (1868–1927): Historian and Revolutionary." PhD Diss., University of Wollongong, 1996.

Rosefielde, Steven. *Red Holocaust.* New York: Routledge, 2009.

Rosenberg, Suzanne. *A Soviet Odyssey.* Toronto: Oxford University Press, 1988.

Rosenberg, William G. "Russian Labor and Bolshevik Power: Social Dimensions of Protest in Petrograd after October." In *The Workers' Revolution in Russia, 1917: The View from Below,* edited by Daniel H. Kaiser, 98–131. Cambridge: Cambridge University Press, 1987.

Rossi, Jacques. *The Gulag Handbook: An Encyclopedia Dictionary of Soviet Penitentiary Institutions and Terms Related to the Forced Labor Camps.* New York: Paragon House, 1989.

Rowland, Richard H. "Geographical Patterns of the Jewish Population in the Pale of Settlement of Late Nineteenth Century Russia." *Jewish Social Studies* 48, no. 3–4 (1986): 207–34.

Rozhkov, N. A. "Pis'mo N. A. Rozhkova V. I. Leninu. Petrograd, 11 ianvaria" [Letter from N. A. Rozhkov to V. I. Lenin. Petrograd, 11 January] [1919]. In *Men'sheviki v bol'shevistskoi Rossii. 1918–1924. Men'sheviki v 1919-1920 gg* [Mensheviks in Bolshevik Russia. 1918–1924. The Mensheviks in 1919–1920], edited by Z. Galili and A. Nenarokov. Moscow: ROSSPEN (Russian State Archive of Social and Political History), 2000, 78–79.

Rummel, R. J. *Lethal Politics: Soviet Genocides and Mass Murders Since 1917.* New Brunswick, NJ: Transaction, 1996.

Said, Edward W. *Orientalism.* New York: Vintage Books, 1979.

Saunders, George. "Introduction: Currents in the Soviet Opposition Movement." Foreword and introduction to Saunders, *Samizdat,* 7–44.

———, ed. *Samizdat: Voices of the Soviet Opposition.* New York: Monad Press, 1974.

Savel'ev, P. Iu., and S. V. Tiutiukin. "Iulii Osipovich Martov (1873–1923): The Man and the Politician." *Russian Studies in History* 45, no. 1 (2006): 6–92.

Savickij, Nicolas. "P. A. Stolypine." *Le Monde Slave* 12 (1933): 360–83.

Schapiro, Leonard. *The Communist Party of the Soviet Union.* 2nd ed. New York: Random House, 1971.

———. *The Origin of the Communist Autocracy: Political Opposition in the Soviet State, First Phase, 1917–1922*. London: Macmillan, 1977.

———. "The Rôle of the Jews in the Russian Revolutionary Movement." *The Slavonic and East European Review* 40, no. 94 (1961): 148–67.

Schmemann, Serge. "Strike by Soviet Miners Spreads in Rising Challenge to Kremlin." *New York Times*, 28 March 1991.

———. "Yeltsin Has an Offer for Striking Miners." *New York Times,* 1 May 1991.

Schodolski, Vincent J., and Thom Shanker. "Soviet Coal Miners Stage Big 1-Day Strike." *Chicago Tribune*, 12 July 1990.

Scholmer, Joseph. *Vorkuta*. Translated by Robert Kee. London: Weidenfeld and Nicolson, 1954.

Schwarz, Solomon M. *Labor in the Soviet Union*. New York: Praeger, 1952.

Sciabarra, Chris Matthew. *Ayn Rand: The Russian Radical*. University Park: Pennsylvania State University Press, 2013.

Serbyn, Roman. "The First Man-Made Famine in Soviet Ukraine: 1921–1923." *Ukrainian Weekly,* 6 November 1988.

Serge, Victor. "A Letter and Some Notes." *The New International* 5, no. 2 (1939): 53–54.

———. *Memoirs of a Revolutionary* [1951]. Translated by Peter Sedgwick. First uncut and annotated English ed. New York: New York Review Books, 2012.

———. *Year One of the Russian Revolution*. Translated by Peter Sedgwick. London: Allen Lane and the Penguin Press, 1972. First published 1930 in French.

Service, Robert. *Stalin: A Biography*. Cambridge, MA: Harvard University Press, 2004.

———. *The Strengths of Contradiction*. Vol. 1 of *Lenin: A Political Life*. Bloomington: Indiana University Press, 1985.

———. *Trotsky: A Biography*. Cambridge, MA: Harvard University Press, 2009.

Sewell, Rob. "Background to Trotsky's *Stalin*." In *Stalin: An Appraisal of the Man and His Influence,* by Leon Trotsky, xix–xxxiv. Edited and translated by Alan Woods. London: Wellred Books, 2016.

Shalamov, Varlam. "Major Pugachov's Last Battle." In *Kolyma Tales*, 241–56. Translated by John Glad. London: Penguin Classic, 1994.

Shumuk, Danylo. *Life Sentence: Memoirs of a Ukrainian Political Prisoner*. Edited by Ivan Jaworsky. Translated by Ivan Jaworsky and Halya Kowalska. Edmonton: Canadian Institute of Ukrainian Studies, University of Alberta, 1984.

Smith, Jeremy. *The Bolsheviks and the National Question, 1917–23*. London: Macmillan, 1999.

———. "The Georgian Affair of 1922: Policy Failure, Personality Clash or Power Struggle?" *Europe-Asia Studies* 50, no. 3 (1998): 519–44.

Smith, Steve A. "Petrograd in 1917: The View from Below." In *The Workers' Revolution in Russia, 1917: The View from Below*, edited by Daniel H. Kaiser, 59–80. Cambridge: Cambridge University Press, 1987.

Sneider, Daniel. "Yeltsin's Deal with Strikers Tests Pact with Gorbachev." *Christian Science Monitor*, 3 May 1991.

Socialist Project. *Book Launch: Toward the United Front* [1/3]. YouTube. OISE, Toronto, 2013. https://www.youtube.com/watch?v=VL_qK8_mxL8.

———. *Luxemburg, Lenin, Levi: Rethinking Revolutionary History*. 3 videos. YouTube. Beit Zatoun, Toronto, 2013. https://www.youtube.com/watch?v=WULnMo7-ICg.

SocResVideo. *John Riddell—United Fronts in the 20th and 21st Centuries*. YouTube. London, 2013. https://www.youtube.com/watch?v=J8RIWmZ_8Aw.

Solomon, Michel. *Magadan*. Toronto: Chateau Books, 1971.

Solzhenitsyn, Aleksandr I. *In The First Circle*. Translated by Harry T. Willetts. First uncensored edition. New York: HarperCollins, 2009.

———. *The First Circle*. Translated by Thomas P. Whitney. New York: Harper and Row, 1968.

———. *The Gulag Archipelago*. Vol. 1. Translated by Thomas P. Whitney. New York: Harper and Row, 1973.

———. *The Gulag Archipelago*. Vol 2. Translated by Thomas P. Whitney. New York: Harper and Row, 1975.

———. *The Gulag Archipelago*. Vol. 3. Translated by H. T. Willets. New York: Harper and Row, 1978.

Souvarine, Boris. "Postscript: The Counter-Revolution." In Souvarine, *Stalin*, 597–676.

———. *Stalin: A Critical Survey of Bolshevism*. Translated by C. L. R. James. New York: Longman, Green, 1939. First published 1935 in French.

Sovnarkom. "Meeting of the Council of People's Commissars, December 7, 1917." In *Revelations from the Russian Archives: Documents in English Translation*, edited by Diane Koenker and Ronald D. Bachman, 6–7. Washington, DC: Library of Congress, 1997.

Spargo, John. *"The Greatest Failure in All History": A Critical Examination of the Actual Workings of Bolshevism in Russia*. New York: Harper and Brothers, 1920.

Stalin, Joseph. "Dizzy with Success: Concerning Questions of the Collective-Farm Movement" [1930]. In Stalin, *Works*, 12:197–205.

———. "Industrialisation and the Grain Problem: Speech Delivered on July 9, 1928." In Stalin, *Works*, 11:165–96.

———. "The London Congress of the Russian Social-Democratic Labour Party (Notes of a Delegate)" [1907]. In Stalin, *Works*, 2:47–80.

———. "The Right Deviation in the C.P.S.U.(B.): Speech Delivered at the Plenum of the Central Committee and Central Control Commission of the C.P.S.U.(B.) in April 1929. (Verbatim Report)." In Stalin, *Works*, 12:1–113.

———. *Works*. 13 vols. Edited and translated by the Marx-Engels-Lenin Institute of the Central Committee, Communist Party of the Soviet Union (Bolshevik). Moscow: Foreign Languages Publishing House, 1946–54.

Steinberg, Isaac Nachman. *In the Workshop of the Revolution*. New York: Rinehart, 1953.

Strakhovsky, Leonid I. "The Statesmanship of Peter Stolypin: A Reappraisal." *The Slavonic and East European Review* 37, no. 89 (1959): 348–70.

Sukhanov, Nikolai Nikolaevich. *The Russian Revolution, 1917: A Personal Record*. Edited and translated by Joel Carmichael. Princeton, NJ: Princeton University Press, 1964. Abridged version of 7-volume 1922 edition.

———. *Zapiski o revoliutsii* [Notes on the revolution]. 7 vol. Berlin, St. Petersburg, and Moscow: Z. I. Grzhebin, 1923.

Surya, Michel. *Georges Bataille: An Intellectual Biography*. London: Verso, 2002.

Swain, Geoffrey. *The Origins of the Russian Civil War*. New York: Longman Group Limited, 1996.

Swianiewicz, Stanisław. *Forced Labour and Economic Development: An Enquiry into the Experience of Soviet Industrialization*. London: Oxford University Press, 1965.

———. *In the Shadow of Katyn: Stalin's Terror*. Translated by Witold Swianiewicz. Pender Island, BC: Borealis, 2002.

———. *Lenin jako ekonomista* [Lenin as an economist] [1930]. Reprint, Poznan: Wydawnictwo Głosy, 1983.

———. *Polityka gospodarcza Niemiec Hitlerowskich* [The economic policy of Hitler's Germany]. Warszawa: Polityka, 1938.

Taghabon, Kevin. *Book Launch—To the Masses: Proceedings of the 3rd Congress of the Communist International* (1 of 6). YouTube. York University, Toronto, 2016. https://www.youtube.com/watch?v=on1iy3__m4U.

Tashtemkhanova, R. M. *Nemetskaia shkola sredneazievedeniia i kazakhstaniki: Uchebnoe posobie dlia studentov istoricheskikh fakul'tetov* [The German school of Central Asian and Kazakh studies: A Manual for history students]. Pavlodar, Kazakhstan: Pavlodar State University, 2005. https://refdb.ru/look/1588051-pall.html.

Tauger, Mark B. "The 1932 Harvest and the Famine of 1933." *Slavic Review* 50, no. 1 (1991): 70–89.

Tchernuishevsky [Chernyshevsky], Nikolai G. *A Vital Question; or, What Is to Be Done?* Translated by Nathan Haskell Dole and S. S. Skidelsky. New York: Thomas Y. Crowell and Co., 1886. First published 1863 in Russian.

Teplitzky, Jonathan, dir. *Churchill*. London: Embankment Films, 2017.

Thatcher, Ian D. "The St Petersburg/Petrograd Mezhraionka, 1913–1917: The Rise and Fall of a Russian Social Democratic Workers' Party Unity Faction." *The Slavonic and East European Review* 87, no. 2 (2009): 284–321.

———. "Trotskii, Lenin and the Bolsheviks, August 1914–February 1917." *Slavonic and East European Review* 72, no. 1 (1994): 72–114.

Thompson, E. P. *The Making of the English Working Class*. London: Penguin Books, 1963.

The Times of London. "Marshal Tito's Land Policy." 9 August 1949.

Tokmakoff, George. "Stolypin's Agrarian Reform: An Appraisal." *Russian Review* 30, no. 2 (1971): 124–38.

Tottle, Douglas. *Fraud, Famine and Fascism: The Ukrainian Genocide Myth from Hitler to Harvard*. Toronto: Progress Books, 1987.

Treadgold, Donald W. "Was Stolypin in Favor of Kulaks?" *American Slavic and East European Review* 14, no. 1 (1955): 1–14.

Trotsky, Leon. *1905*. Translated by Anya Bostock. New York: Vintage Books, 1971. First published 1907 in Russian.

———. *Between Red and White: A Study of Some Fundamental Questions of Revolution with Particular Reference to Georgia*. London: Communist Party of Great Britain, 1922.

———. "Declaration of the Bolshevik-Leninist Delegation at the Conference of Left Socialist and Communist Organizations" [1933]. In *Writings of Leon Trotsky [1933–34]*, edited by George Breitman and Bev Scott, 37–44. New York: Pathfinder Press, 1975.

———. "The Fundamental Questions of the Food and Agrarian Policy" [1920]. In *The New Course*, translated by Max Shachtman, 69–70. Ann Arbor: University of Michigan Press, 1965.

———. *The History of the Russian Revolution*. 3 vols. Translated by Max Eastman. New York: Simon and Schuster, 1937. First published 1932 by University of Michigan Press (Ann Arbor).

———. "Opening and Closing Speeches in the Discussion on Military Doctrine Held by the Military Science Society Attached to the Military Academy of the Workers' and Peasants' Red Army, November 1, 1921." In *How the Revolution Armed: The Military Writings and Speeches of Leon Trotsky*. Translated and annotated by Brian Pearce, 5:299–311. London: New Park, 1981.

———. "The Latest Falsification of the Stalinists" [1939]. In *Writings of Leon Trotsky [1932–33]*, edited by Naomi Allen and George Breitman, 266–68. New York: Pathfinder Press, 1972.

———. "Lenin Is Dead" [1924]. In *Lenin: Notes for a Biography*, 209–11.

———. *Lenin: Notes for a Biography* [1924]. Translated and annotated by Tamara Deutscher. New York: Capricorn Books, 1971.

———. *Moia zhizn': Opyt avtobiografii* [My life: An Attempt at an autobiography]. 2 vols. Berlin: Energiadruck, 1930.

———. *My Life: An Attempt at an Autobiography* [1930]. New York: Pathfinder Press, 1970.

———. *Nashi politicheskie zadachi (takticheskie i organizatsionnye voprosy)* [Our political tasks (tactical and organizational questions)]. Geneva: Rossiiskoi Sotsialdemokraticheskoi Rabochii Partii, 1904.

———. *Our Political Tasks*. London: New Park, 1979. First published 1904 in Russian.

———. "The Permanent Revolution" [1930]. In *The Permanent Revolution and Results and Prospects*, edited by Helen Gilbert, translated by John G. Wright and Brian Pearce, 137–315. Seattle: Red Letter Press, 2010.

———. "Results and Prospects" [1906]. In *The Permanent Revolution and Results and Prospects*, edited by Helen Gilbert, translated by John G. Wright and Brian Pearce, 33–136. Seattle: Red Letter Press, 2010.

———. *The Revolution Betrayed* [1937]. New York: Pathfinder Press, 1973.

———. "Speech at a General Party Membership Meeting of the Moscow Organization, July 1921." In *The First Five Years of the Communist International*, translated by John G. Wright, 2:1–43. New York: Monad Press, 1972.

———. *Stalin: An Appraisal of the Man and His Influence*. Edited and translated by Charles Malamuth. New York: Grosset and Dunlap, 1941.

———. *Stalin: An Appraisal of the Man and His Influence*. Edited and translated by Alan Woods. London: Wellred Books, 2016.

———. "Stalinism and Bolshevism: Concerning the Historical and Theoretical Roots of the Fourth International" [1937]. In *Writings of Leon Trotsky [1936–37]*, edited by Naomi Allen and George Breitman, 416–31. New York: Pathfinder Press, 1978.

———. *Their Morals and Ours: The Marxist View of Morality*. Sydney: Resistance Books, 2000.

———. "Thermidor and Anti-Semitism" [1937]. *The New International* 72, May (1941): 91–94.

———. "To the Bulgarian Comrades, October 4, 1930." In *Writings of Leon Trotsky [1930–31]*, edited by George Breitman and Sarah Lovell, 44–46. New York: Pathfinder Press, 1973.

Trotsky, Leon, C. L. R. James, and Charles Curtiss. "The Discussions in Coyoacán." In *Leon Trotsky on Black Nationalism and Self-Determination*, edited by George Breitman, 33–70. 1939. New York: Pathfinder Press, 1978.

Tucker, Robert C. *Stalin as Revolutionary, 1879–1929: A Study in History and Personality*. New York: W. W. Norton, 1973.

Tukhachevsky, Mikhail. "General Toukhatchevsky's Narrative." In *The Eighteenth Decisive Battle of the World: Warsaw, 1920*, by Edgar Vincent D'Abernon. London: Hodder and Stoughton, 1931. First published 1920.

———. "Revolution from Without" [1920]. *New Left Review* I/55 (May–June 1969): 91–97.

Turgenev, Ivan Sergeyevich. *Fathers and Sons*. Translated by Rosemary Edmonds. Baltimore: Penguin Books, 1965. First published 1862 by Grachev and Co. (Moscow).

Twiss, Thomas M. *Trotsky and the Problem of Soviet Bureaucracy*. Historical Materialism Book Series 67. Leiden: Brill, 2014.

Ukrainian National Association. "30 U.N. Member-States Sign Joint Declaration on Great Famine." *Ukrainian Weekly*, 16 November 2003. http://www.ukrweekly.com/uwwp/pdf-archive/.

Ulam, Adam Bruno. *The Bolsheviks: The Intellectual and Political History of the Triumph of Communism in Russia: With a New Preface*. Boston: Harvard University Press, 2009.

United Nations. "GDP, at Constant 2005 Prices—National Currency." National Accounts Main Aggregates Database. New York: United Nations Statistics Division, December 2016. http://unstats.un.org/.

———. "Population." National Accounts Main Aggregates Database. New York: United Nations Statistics Division, December 2016. http://unstats.un.org/.

Viola, Lynne. *The Unknown Gulag: The Lost World of Stalin's Special Settlements*. New York: Oxford University Press, 2007.

Viola, Lynne, V. P. Danilov, N. A. Ivnitskii, and Denis Kozlov, eds. *The War Against the Peasantry, 1927–1930*. Vol. 1 of *The Tragedy of the Soviet Countryside*. New Haven: Yale University Press, 2005.

Volkogonov, Dmitri. *Stalin: Triumph and Tragedy*. New York: Grove Weidenfeld, 1991.

Weekly People. "The World News in Brief." 8 April 1933, 1.

Werth, Nicolas. "A State Against Its People: Violence, Repression, and Terror in the Soviet Union." In *The Black Book of Communism: Crimes, Terror, Repression*, by Stéphane Courtois, Nicolas Werth, Jean Louis Panné, Andrzej Paczkowski, Karel Bartošek, and Jean-Louis Margolin, 33–268. Edited by Mark Kramer. Translated by Jonathan Murphy and Mark Kramer. Cambridge, MA: Harvard University Press, 1999. First published 1997 in French.

White, James D. *Lenin: The Practice and Theory of Revolution*. New York: Palgrave, 2001.

Williams, Robert Chadwell. *The Other Bolsheviks: Lenin and His Critics, 1904–1914*. Bloomington: Indiana University Press, 1986.

Williamson, Samuel H. "Seven Ways to Compute the Relative Value of a U.S. Dollar Amount—1774 to Present." *MeasuringWorth*, 2018. https://www.measuringworth.com/uscompare/.

Wolfe, Bertram D. "Introduction." In Trotsky, *Lenin: Notes for a Biography*, 7–24.

———. "Lenin, Stolypin, and the Russian Village." *Russian Review* 6, no. 2 (1947): 44–54.

———. *Three Who Made a Revolution: A Biographical History of Lenin, Trotsky, and Stalin*. New York: Cooper Square Press, 2001. First published 1948.

Woods, Alan. "Editor's Afterword: Trotsky's *Stalin*—a Marxist Masterpiece." In Trotsky, *Stalin*, 691–98.

Zamoyski, Adam. *Warsaw 1920: Lenin's Failed Conquest of Europe*. London: William Collins, 2008.

Žižek, Slavoj. "Afterword: Lenin's Choice." In *Revolution at the Gates: Žižek on Lenin—The 1917 Writings*, by V. I. Lenin, 165–338. 2nd ed. London: Verso, 2002.

Zsuppán, Ferenc Tibor. "The Early Activities of the Hungarian Communist Party, 1918–19." *Slavonic and East European Review* 43, no. 101 (1965): 314–34.

Index

bolshevism, 105, 109–10; Lukács's defence of, 244

Bonaparte, Napoleon, 151, 163, 199

"Bread, peace, and land!" 13, 87

Brezhnev, Leonid, xix

Brickworks (prison and execution site), xxiv, 40, 42, 45, 59

Broido, Eva, 17, 44, 263, 307n52

Broido, Vera, 44

Broué, Pierre, 34, 37, 43, 145, 152, 153, 161, 168, 169, 178, 179, 180, 181, 234–36, 247; on the evolution of Lenin's thinking about the 1905 revolution, 238; works by: *Révolution en Allemagne: 1917–1923* [*The German Revolution, 1917–1923*], 178

Brovkin, Vladimir, 293

Brusilov, A. A., 145

Buca, Edward, xxv, 57, 63–64, 65, 66, 69–71, 72, 74; massacre at his labour camp, 70–71; works by: *Vorkuta*, 317n59

Buhle, Paul, 229, 242

Bukharin, Nikolai, 21, 22, 34, 43, 55, 169, 174, 184, 196, 221, 238, 339n5

Burawoy, Michael, 78

Butyrka prison (Moscow), 7, 11, Byelorussia. *See* Belarus

capitalism, 55, 74, 90, 107, 117, 118, 120, 126, 127, 165, 174, 181, 199, 201, 220, 223, 260; and agrarian capitalism, 115, 123; and anti-capitalism, 164, 258, 298; and state capitalism, 62, 197, 271; in the Americas, 56–57

capitalist farming, 122–23, 127

Carr, E. H., "The Russian Revolution and the Peasant," 329

Caucasus, 156, 158, 205, 211–12, 233, 234

Central Committee of the RSDLP (Unified), 287–88

Chamberlin, William, 99, 150, 152, 291

Cheka Weekly (or *Bulletin of the Cheka*), 278

Chekas (or GPU, NKVD, KGB), 51, 148, 158, 273, 275, 276, 278–79, 311n15, 315n10; abuses by, 279; and Kronstadt uprising, 97–98; and strikebreaking, 283–95; formation of, 97–98, 285; mandate of, 284

Chernov, Georgii Aleksandrovich, 57, 59

Chernov, Viktor, 292

Chernyshevsky, Nikolay, 190, 230, 238–42, 243, 244, 345n51; works by: *What Is to Be Done?*, 238–42

Chicago Tribune, 81

Chumakova, Aleksandra, xxv, 36

Churchill, Winston, 67, 309n88

Ciliga, Ante, 26, 40–41; works by: *La vérité en prison* [*Pravda in Prison* (*Truth in Prison*)], 41; *Le Bolchevik militant* [*The Militant Bolshevik*], 41; *The Russian Enigma*, 313n57; *Dix ans au pays du mensonge déconcertant*, 313n57

Civil War (US), 127–28

civil wars, 14, 15, 22, 25, 74, 93, 97, 129, 130, 148, 157, 278. *See also* Russian Civil War

class: class consciousness, xxvii, 82, 83, 95, 108; "class in itself," 89–90; "class for itself," 89–91, 91; class self-awareness, 95; class, formation of a new, xxii, 11, 75, 93, 107, 109, 110, 121, 136, 137, 189, 201, 271, 272, 279, 287, 29; class, objective approach, 90; class, subjective approach, 90; "corporal-academic," 50; intellectuals, 45, 50, 78, 139, 152, 190, 216, 249–99; intelligentsia, 120, 130, 159, 250, 251–52, 256–58, 268, 280, 285; manual labour and "manual labourers," 257, 258, 284–85; mental labour and

over dispersal of, 292; purpose of, 288

Constitutional Democrats (Kadets), 111–12, 290

Cossacks, 4, 210, 282; as antisemites, 150

Council of People's Commissars (Sovnarkom), 111, 272, 276, 283, 353n20

Cromwell, Oliver, 165, 298

D'Abernon, Edgar, 148, 162

Dallin, David, 263

Dan, Theodor [Fedor], 256–57, 263, 265, 280; on the Russian word "intelligentsia" 256–57

"Declaration of the 46" (October 1943), 34

death of Stalin (1953), x, xiii, 30, 66–67, 77, 159, 261, 318n73

death penalty, 12, 23, 46, 275–76

deportations, xi, 26, 37, 138, 196, 249, 277

Derev'ianko, General, 71

de Ste. Croix, G. E. M., 90

Deutscher, Isaac, 185, 222, 264

discourse: anti-intellectualism, 190, 249–58, 269, 299; antisemitism, 149, 156, 259–62, 264–66, 268, 350n55; Asiatic, 221, 222, 223–25; European, 105, 163, 165, 220, 222, 224, 225; Orientalism / Orientalist, 219–25, 264, 269

Donbass, 35, 79; strike by coal miners (1989) in the, 81

Donetsk, 79–80, 81

Dostoyevsky, Fyodor, 268

Dranovsky, Lyova (Comrade Granovsky), 31–32

Du Bois, W. E. B., xv, 128, 333n60

Dubrovsky, S. M., 125

Dunayevskaya, Raya, 189, 197, 226, 338n21; on 1939 Stalin–Hitler pact, 197

Duranty, Walter, 18

Dybenko, Pavel (People's Commissar of Naval Affairs), 272–73, 292

Dzerzhinsky, Felix (head of the Cheka), 148, 155, 160, 283

East Berlin workers' uprising (1953), 67, 68, 72

Eastern Europe, 67, 121, 161

economy: coal, 29, 30, 40, 54–60, 65, 71, 73, 79, 80; coal miners / coal mining, xiv, xv, 29–30, 32, 52, 54, 57–60, 65, 77, 78, 80, 81, 82, 83, 87, 91; famine, 5, 14, 16–17, 18, 27, 53, 132, 195, 227; famine denial, 17–18, 20–25; means of production, 54, 89, 106, 110, 137, 138, 199, 200, 202; trade balance in USSR and former USSR, 87; net exports, wheat, USSR and former USSR, 88; output per capita, USSR and former USSR, 85, 86

economic policy: artificial famine, 137; enclosures, 24, 25, 54; forced collectivization, 16, 20, 21, 22, 25, 53, 54, 56, 130, 137, 196, 227; forced labour, ix, x, xi, xv–xviii, xxvi, 3, 16, 24, 30, 44, 49, 51–54, 56, 57–58, 59, 60–75, 91, 195; "forty acres and a mule," 127, 128; *glasnost* (openness), 77, 78, 81, 85, 91; Holodomor, 17, 25; New Economic Policy (NEP), 133–34, 199; *perestroika* (restructuring), 77–78, 81, 85; *perestroika* from below, 78–82; preliminary socialist accumulation, 55; primary accumulation (*ursprüngliche Akkumulation*), 54–55, 73, 315n25; *prodrazvestka* (requisitioning), 129; requisitioning, 7, 14, 20, 21, 23–24,

French Revolution, 107, 111, 163, 164, 165, 253
Friedgut, Theodore, 78

Garanin, Stepan Nikolaivich, 39–40, 312n52
General Jewish Labour Bund, 93, 156, 263
Geological Service of the USSR, 58
Georgakas, Dan, "October Song," 5
Georgia, 55, 155–60; attempted coup by Bolsheviks (1919) in, 157; Bolshevik rule over, 155; Central Committee of the Communist Party of, 155, 160; lack of antisemitism in, 156; massacres in, 158–59; Menshevik base in, 156; retaliation against rebels in, 158–59. See also invasion of Georgia by Russia and Tiflis
Georgians, 66, 158, 160, 264; Georgian Communists, 155; Georgian independence, 159; Georgian Mensheviks, 55, 155–57; Georgian Socialists, 158
Gerland, Brigitte, xxv, 61–62, 66, 68, 69, 71
German army, 12, 110, 276
German Communist Party (KPD), 144, 165, 167, 168, 170, 171, 173–74, 175, 178–79, 180, 182, 184, 186; expulsion of Paul Levi from, 170, 175, 178–79; manifesto of, 275, 297–98
Germany, East and West, 67–68
Getzler, Israel, 105, 235, 246, 292, 294
Gevorkian, Sokrat, 38
glasnost (openness), 77, 78, 81, 85, 91. See also perestroika
Glukhovka textile mill, 36
Gogol, Nikolai, 268
Golovlyov, Porfirii "Little Judas" (character), 267–69
Gorbachev, Mikhail, 77–78, 79, 81, 83, 84–85

Gorky, Maxim, xxix, 9,
grain, 10, 13, 14–15, 21–24, 53, 116; requisitioning (forcible seizure) of, 7, 14, 20, 21, 23–24, 56, 132–34, 139, 196, 293, 294. See also wheat
Gramsci, Antonio, 110, 163
Graves, Major General William, 274
Great Britain, 7, 18, 24, 54, 148; enclosure movement in, 24–25, 54
Great Depression, USA (1930s), 86
Great Famine, Ukraine (1932–33), 16, 17, 20, 21, 24, 25, 227; UN resolution (2003), 25
Great Recession (2008), 86
Great Russian chauvinism, 145, 147, 155, 159, 160
Great Terror (1937–38), xxiv, 26–28, 32, 43, 52, 139, 227, 261, 296; number of victims during, 27
Great War (1914–18), xix, xxv, 9, 50, 93, 114, 117, 125, 137, 149, 179, 218, 220, 246, 296
Greeman, Richard, 85
Grimm, Robert, 246, 248
Grossbauern ("big peasants"), 127–28
Group of Democratic Centralism (or Decists), 38, 62
Gubernia Executive Committee (in Penza), 136
Gulag Archipelago, x, xv. See also Solzhenitsyn
Gulag system, ix–xi, 49, 51, 74; as described by Solzhenitsyn ix–x; number of forced labourers in, xi, xvi; origins of, 49; women prisoners in, xxv
Gurian Republic (1902–06), 156–57, 158, 333n60; crushed uprising in, 158; Bolsheviks and Mensheviks in, 157–58

Haimson, Leopold, 8, 95

world market, 115

World War I. *See* Great War

World War II, xi, 54, 199, 221, 222, 274

Yagoda, Genrikh, 37

Yeltsin, Boris, 83–85

Zaria (*Dawn*), 249, 250

Zemlya i Volya (Land and Freedom),
    130

Zetkin, Clara, 170–71, 175, 180, 186–87,
    213–14, 215, 248; and Paul Levi,
    169, 171, 173, 174, 178, 179, 187;
    influence of, 179, 180, 186; works
    by: "Resolution by Clara Zetkin on
    March Action," 170

Zhelezniakov, Anatolii, 292

Zhitomir (Ukraine) 150

Zimmerwald anti-war conference
    (1915), 245–47; as turning point
    in constructing a New Left,
    247–48; Lenin and "revolutionary
    defeatism" at, 246–47

Zinoviev, Grigory, 174–75, 184, 187, 246,
    294, 310; and Lev Kamenev, 26, 34,
    35, 38, 46, 209; 1918 speech by, 277;
    1920 speech by, 176